Winterthur Portfolio 9

Winterthur Portfolio 9

Edited by Ian M. G. Quimby

Published for

The Henry Francis du Pont Winterthur Museum

by the University Press of Virginia

Charlottesville

Statement of Editorial Policy

The objective of The Henry Francis du Pont
Winterthur Museum in publishing *Winterthur
Portfolio* is to make available to the serious student an
authoritative reference for the investigation and
documentation of early American culture.

The publication will present articles about many
aspects of American life. Included will be studies that
will extend current information about objects used
in America in the seventeenth, eighteenth, and
nineteenth centuries; or about the makers, the
manufacture, the distribution, the use, and the settings
of such objects. Scholarly articles contributing to
the knowledge of America's social, cultural, political,
military, and religious heritage, as well as those
offering new approaches or interpretations concerning
research and conservation of art objects, are
welcome.

Ian M. G. Quimby, *Editor*
Polly Anne Earl, *Assistant Editor*

Contents

The Battle of the Sideboards

Kenneth Ames

FOR SOME TIME now, cautious historians of furniture have been trying to deemphasize the importance of the furniture shown at the great exhibitions of the nineteenth century. Peter Floud, for instance, has argued that the availability of catalogs from these events and the distinctive nature of the furniture illustrated in them have led many to equate exhibition furniture with the average furniture of the day.[1] Floud quite correctly points out that the picture given by the exhibitions is a false one and that reliance upon the ubiquitous catalogs leads to erroneous conclusions about the nature of nineteenth-century furniture. All this is not to say that exhibition furniture is not important, but rather that it must be interpreted with care. As most students of the period agree, exhibition pieces were shown primarily for their novelty or inventiveness, and it is exactly in these qualities that their importance lies. As Elizabeth Aslin noted, "these exhibitions were in effect the taste-makers of the second half of the nineteenth century."[2] The great pieces of furniture shown at the exhibitions embodied the ideals of the age. They should be understood as signposts, charting and directing the course of furniture evolution.

The second half of the nineteenth century saw a rash of international exhibitions following the success of the Crystal Palace exhibition in London in 1851. These exhibitions sponsored and, indeed, promoted an intense international rivalry in all fields of endeavor. At each, great pieces of furniture competed with one another for acclaim. Names, reputations, and, in the end, aesthetic empires were at stake.

While exhibitions continued throughout the rest of the century and still occur today, the twenty-five years from 1851 to 1876 were the most significant for furniture. During this period the competition was most intense. These years saw France's position as the font of furniture inspiration first affirmed, then challenged, and ultimately denied as England, for a brief time, assumed that role. The story of the French eclipse is told in the furniture of the exhibitions.

There can be no doubt that the international exhibitions of the nineteenth century were seen as competitions. Sources of the period stress again and again the competitive nature of these events. They were repeatedly described as "great competitive examinations,"[3] "great and universal competitive exhibitions," and "trials for supremacy." One writer stated that "rivalry, without hostility, is a definition at once concise and significant of the principle of all international exhibitions."[4] In 1876 Walter Smith found this same attitude enshrined in the Century Vase, made by the Gorham Manufacturing

[1] Peter Floud, "Furniture," in *The Early Victorian Period, 1830–1860*, ed. Ralph Edwards and L. G. G. Ramsey (London: The Connoisseur, 1958), pp. 36–37.

[2] Elizabeth Aslin, *Nineteenth Century English Furniture* (New York: Thomas Yoseloff, 1962), p. 36.

[3] Walter Smith, "Industrial Art," in *The Masterpieces of the Centennial International Exhibition 1876*, 3 vols. (Philadelphia: Gebbie & Barrie, 1876), 2: 46.

[4] Art Journal, *The Illustrated Catalog of the Universal Exhibition* (London: Virtue & Co., 1867), pp. xi, xii, 3.

Company to celebrate the United States of America's first one hundred years as a nation. The culmination of the vase's lavish and expansive design was a figure of "America holding aloft the olive branch of peace and the wreath of honor, summoning Europe, Asia, and Africa to join with her in the friendly rivalry with which she enters on the second century of her existence."[5]

A few years earlier, the *Art Journal*'s editors had written in the same vein about the Universal Exhibition of 1867 in Paris, making it clear that a sense of rivalry existed in all aspects of the fair.[6] Indeed, one could say that no facet of any of these events was free from the competitive spirit. The major buildings at each successive exhibition vied with their predecessors in daring and scale. Although economic and political factors sometimes intervened, each successive fair generally tried to surpass the others in the extent of its grounds and in the acreage covered by exhibition buildings. For example, Americans fondly noted that the Centennial buildings offered about seventy-five acres of exhibition space, making that exhibition the largest to that date.[7]

Tabulations were kept on the number of visitors, for here too there was rivalry. The Crystal Palace had witnessed almost 6,040,000, but nearly 9,800,000 people passed through the gates in Fairmount Park. The numbers of exhibitors were also a tallying point, and these too mounted with each exhibition. London, in 1851, had hosted about 14,000 exhibitors. By 1867 the Paris Universal Exhibition saw that number swell to over 42,000. And even though the broad expanse of the Atlantic Ocean added many miles to Europeans' travel, Philadelphia saw over 30,000 exhibitors in 1876.[8] In these international exhibitions, then, nations vied with each other to stage increasingly grand and impressive shows.

This spirit of competition was rampant in the furniture courts; for furniture, like so many arts of the nineteenth century, was undergoing the pains of adjusting to social and technological changes then taking place. Increased numbers of middle-class patrons had replaced aristocrats as the con-

sumers of furniture, furniture now inexpensively made by recently invented power machinery. Styles from the past were widely imitated, and homes were fitted with furniture called Grecian, Gothic, Elizabethan, Renaissance, Louis XIV, or Romanesque. But while the middle class basked in its new-found opulence, critics were busy attacking the trends they saw. Some were disappointed in an age of which they had expected so much novelty and excitement. From our modern viewpoint, we can see that the nineteenth century put its distinctive mark on everything it touched, but critics of the day saw only copying, and the copying of degenerate styles at that.

Ralph Wornum's response to the furniture he saw in London's Crystal Palace in 1851 is in many ways typical of the criticism of his time. "There is nothing new in the exhibition in ornamental design: not a scheme, not a detail that has not been treated over and over again in ages that are gone."[9] And a later commentator on that same event declared "*copying* was the law of the whole community of producers—copying undisguised and self-complacent, which without aiming at any mental effort of its own, was content to reproduce (probably for the thousandth time) works that expressed the thoughts of other men." Critics said that hand power had replaced the nobler quality of mind power. Some, too, pointed out the glaring disparity between the imaginative exhibition buildings of the time and their unimaginative contents. One even went so far as to say "it would be but scant justice to the exhibition building of 1851 to affirm that in itself it embodied more true originality of both conception and execution, than it contained beneath the spacious covering of its wide-spread roofs"[10] (Fig. 1).

At the Crystal Palace in 1851, a lavishly carved sideboard by Henri Fourdinois of Paris was the most widely admired article of furniture (Fig. 2). This grand piece was in the Renaissance revival style, a French contribution to the nineteenth century that relied heavily on the conceptions of Renaissance and Mannerist designers such as Androuet Du Cerceau, Jean Goujon, Hugues Sambin, Vredeman de Vries, and a host of others. In the eclectic manner typical of the nineteenth century, a variety

[5] Smith, "Industrial Art," p. 56.

[6] Art Journal, *Illustrated Catalog*, pp. ix–xii.

[7] J. S. Ingram, *The Centennial Exposition Described and Illustrated* (Philadelphia: Hubbard Bros., 1876), p. 115.

[8] James D. McCabe, *The Illustrated History of the Centennial Exhibition* (Philadelphia: National Publishing Co., 1876), pp. 885–90.

[9] Ralph Nicholson Wornum, "The Exhibition As a Lesson in Taste," in Art Journal, *The Industry of All Nations* (London: George Virtue, 1851), p. v***.

[10] Art Journal, *Illustrated Catalog*, p. 39.

FIG. 1. Crystal Palace, exterior view. From cover of the "World's Fair Polka," a popular musical composition published in New York in 1851 to commemorate the great exhibition held in London that year. (Photo, Winterthur.)

of details from the seventeenth and eighteenth centuries and other sources were added to sixteenth-century motifs. The Renaissance revival style was not limited to furniture but was found as well in contemporary architectural examples such as Etienne-Hippolyte Godde and Jean-Baptiste Cicéron Lesueur's extension of the Hôtel de Ville in Paris of 1837–49 and Louis-Tullius-Joachim Visconti and Hector-Martin Lefuel's new Louvre of 1852–57. It also appeared in the notable pattern books of an architect such as César Daly and in the international mansard craze, which ultimately left its mark on most parts of the westernized world. Both architecture and furniture in this style shared a highly sculptural quality and an emphasis on pediments, often broken and ornamented with elaborate cartouches. The Renaissance revival style in both architecture and furniture became widely popular after 1840 and remained in vogue into the 1870s.

The Fourdinois sideboard won praise even from English commentators. They admitted that it was, indeed, magnificent. The editors of the *Art Journal* rhapsodized: "Undoubtedly one of the most superb specimens of cabinet-work to be seen in the Exhi-

bition. . . . Whether we consider the elaborate richness of the design, or its skillful execution, we must award it the highest merit. . . . The style of the Renaissance has certainly never been more successfully carried out in an article of furniture." And Ralph Wornum wrote: "This great French sideboard is in every respect one of the noblest works in the exhibition and its decorations are completely typical of the relations of the uses of the object. The entire food of man, both meat and drink, and the means and localities by and from which it is procured, are all charmingly expressed, and disposed in exquisite ornamental symmetry."[11]

That this important piece should be a sideboard was significant since the sideboard was still a relatively new piece of furniture, largely the creation of the rapid social changes of the eighteenth century. The basic concept of the sideboard, of course, goes back to the cupboards, credenzas, dressers, and buffets of the medieval and Renaissance periods. The direct ancestor of the modern sideboard seems to have appeared in a design for a sideboard table flanked by two urns on pedestals created by Robert

[11] Art Journal, *Industry of All Nations*, p. 285; Wornum, "The Exhibition As a Lesson in Taste," p. xii***.

FIG. 2. Henri Fourdinois, sideboard. From Art Journal, *The Industry of All Nations* (London: George Virtue, 1851), p. 285. (Photo, Winterthur.)

and James Adam for Osterley Park in 1767. Shortly afterwards in the work of Thomas Shearer, the pedestals migrated from the sides of the table to underneath it, creating the familiar late eighteenth- and early nineteenth-century form (Fig. 3). The French apparently followed English incentive, as they had with the dining table, and naturalized the sideboard. In the first half of the nineteenth century, it gradually grew, filling in below and expanding above until it reached the majestic proportions of the Fourdinois example.

Fourdinois's sideboard was by no means the only one exhibited in London. By the middle of the century, the sideboard had become the prime exhibition piece. The cabinetmaker who wished to earn a reputation for himself, who wished to impress customers and rivals with his design and manufacturing skills, made a point of displaying his most lavish sideboard. As one English writer put it, the sideboard was the "*pièce de résistance.*"[12]

No other single piece of furniture rose to such unprecedented heights in the nineteenth century. No piece better described the society and its interests, its beliefs, its obsessions. The Fourdinois sideboard, like so many others, for all intents and purposes, ceased being furniture in any traditional sense of the word and became instead an exercise in invention and carving performed with a sharp eye on the market. In 1857 Richard Redgrave accurately described the situation when he wrote: "Each manufacturer is striving his utmost to attain notice and reward . . . by an endeavour to catch the consumers by startling novelty or meretricious decoration, leading, in most cases, to an extreme redundancy of ornament. The goods are like the gilded cakes in the booths at our country fairs, no longer for use, but to attract customers."[13]

The scale of the Fourdinois sideboard was so massive and its detail so lavish that the finished

[12] J. Beavington Atkinson, "The Furniture of the Universal Exhibition," in Art Journal, *Illustrated Catalog*, p. 202.

[13] *Report on the Present State of Design As Applied to Manufactures* (London, 1857), as quoted in Floud, "Furniture," p. 36.

FIG. 3. Sideboard, England, ca. 1800. Mahogany; H. 37″, W. 84″, D. 28½″. (Victoria and Albert Museum, London.)

work lay far beyond the financial means of all but the most wealthy. Even had the price been low, few homes had dining rooms immense enough to contain the piece. At this point, a new element entered the realm of furniture patronage. The governments of various nations, continuing and amplifying a practice dating back to regional and national trade fairs earlier in the century, assumed the role of patron and purchased outstanding exhibition pieces. The best example of this activity is seen in the series of purchases made by the British government for the museum in South Kensington, now known as the Victoria and Albert Museum. Certain pieces were purchased for their didactic value and instead of vanishing from sight into the privacy of individual homes, the pieces were placed on essentially permanent display. Government involvement perpetuated a reciprocal pattern in which furniture designers produced furniture suitable only for museums. Museums complied by purchasing these oversized and overelaborate pieces and placing them on display.

Although varied in proportion and detail, most sideboards exhibited in 1851 were conceptually like that by Fourdinois; a rectangular base, either open or enclosed, supported huge panels or mirrors and shelves, all surrounded by an elaborate framework. Renaissance details were accompanied by richly carved attributes of food and plenty. Intended to impart iconographic significance to the piece, the carving included allegorical figures, swags of fruit and vegetables, and representations of dead game (Fig. 4). These ornaments were often so profuse that the sideboard nearly failed to bring to mind its supposed function and resembled instead the massive carved wooden altarpieces that may have served as remote prototypes. In a way, the sideboard had become an altarpiece for the dining room, where the nineteenth century worshipped what Lewis Mumford called "the goods life."[14]

[14] Mumford, *Technics and Civilization* (New York: Harcourt, Brace & Co., 1934), p. 105.

FIG. 4. Detail of Fourdinois sideboard showing painted panel and stag. From Art Journal, *The Industry of All Nations* (London: George Virtue, 1851), p. 285. (Photo, Winterthur.)

FIG. 5. Howard and Son, sideboard. From Art Journal, *The Industry of All Nations* (London: George Virtue, 1851), p. 79. (Photo, Winterthur.)

While English designers had produced a number of sideboards for exhibition at the Crystal Palace, compared to the example by Fourdinois, all were decidedly less impressive. Most were of the low horizontal sort, dating conceptually from the later years of the Regency. Among the many shown were examples by the following firms. Howard and Son of London showed a sideboard in what today is often called the naturalistic style because of the profusion of meticulously carved floral details (Fig. 5). The back and front of this piece were inlaid with plate glass. T. W. Caldecott, London, contributed a sideboard of old English oak in the Renaissance style, replete with a rich game *ferronnerie* (Fig. 6). Johnstone and Jeanes, also of London, displayed a sideboard of mahogany in a style described as "Italian of the best period" (Fig. 7). A figure of the young Bacchus was placed at each end, and carved grapes and vines abounded. Cookes and Sons of Warwick presented the now well-known Kenilworth Sideboard, carved with scenes representing episodes from Sir Walter Scott's romance of that name (Fig. 8). Lastly, Gillow of London exhibited a piece "of bold design and spirited execution" (Fig. 9). Two great eagles supported a slab

backed by elaborate rococo scrolls and foliage capped with a pineapple. The *Art Journal's* editors praised it for showing "a freedom from too great slavishness of idea, a determination to get rid of the trammels of conventional styles." To modern eyes this piece seems to have gone too far in casting off conventional styles, for it is often used to represent the decline of design in Victorian England. Certainly, in few pieces have function and ornament been less successfully wedded.[15]

The most impressive example of English craftsmanship was by the prominent London firm of Jackson and Graham (Fig. 10). The firm was one of the most publicized furniture houses of the day and worked primarily in the French style. The Jackson and Graham piece emphasizes the importance of French authority, for although made in Britain, it was designed by the French artist Eugène Prignot, employed by the firm after 1849. Thus paradoxically, the best English example in 1851 was the most French. This evidence of cultural colonialism was not lost on English critics.

[15] Art Journal, *Industry of All Nations*, pp. 16, 79, 118, 123.

Fig. 6. T. W. Caldecott, sideboard. From Art Journal, *The Industry of All Nations* (London: George Virtue, 1851), p. 118. (Photo, Winterthur.)

Fig. 7. Johnstone and Jeanes, sideboard. From Art Journal, *The Industry of All Nations* (London: George Virtue, 1851), p. 16. (Photo, Winterthur.)

FIG. 8. Cookes and Sons, sideboard. From Art Journal, *The Industry of All Nations* (London: George Virtue, 1851), p. 123. (Photo, Winterthur.)

FIG. 9. Gillow, sideboard. From Art Journal, *The Industry of All Nations* (London: George Virtue, 1851), p. 203. (Photo, Winterthur.)

Fig. 10. Jackson and Graham, sideboard. From Art Journal, *The Industry of All Nations* (London: George Virtue, 1851), p. 186. (Photo, Winterthur.)

The Fourdinois sideboard had proclaimed unequivocally France's foremost position in the art of furniture, much to the chagrin of the English. As a result, the note of rivalry that was apparent in 1851 intensified in later exhibitions. The catalogs of subsequent exhibitions read increasingly like descriptions of contests. The exhibitions were seen as bloodless battlefields on which the great houses of various nations sallied forth to overcome their rivals. Even the language used to describe contestants and their entries took on a tournament quality: "Once again Messrs. Trollope and Gillow, fully armed, enter the lists determined on victory."[16]

French success in 1851 sparked two different responses in English furniture makers. On the one hand, there were imitators who accepted French supremacy in design but sought to outdo the French in their own style. On the other hand, there

[16] Atkinson, "Furniture of the Universal Exhibition," p. 202.

Fig. 14. James Lamb, sideboard. From Art Journal, *Illustrated Catalog of the International Exhibition 1862* (London and New York: James S. Virtue, 1862), p. 145. (Photo, University of Pennsylvania Library.)

Fig. 15. Clement George and Son, sideboard. From Art Journal, *Illustrated Catalog of the International Exhibition 1862* (London and New York: James S. Virtue, 1862), p. 276. (Photo, University of Pennsylvania Library.)

FIG. 16. Jackson and Graham, sideboard. From Art Journal, *Illustrated Catalog of the International Exhibition 1862* (London and New York: James S. Virtue, 1862), p. 34. (Photo, University of Pennsylvania Library.)

FIG. 17. Wright and Mansfield, cabinet. London, 1867. Mahogany, decorated with satinwood veneers and Wedgwood plaques; H. 140″, W. 93″, D. 27″. (Victoria and Albert Museum, London.)

FIG. 18. Holland and Sons, sideboard, designed by Bruce J. Talbert. From Art Journal, *The Illustrated Catalog of the Universal Exhibition of 1867* (London and New York: Virtue & Co., 1867), p. 60. (Photo, Winterthur.)

Aslin notes that the firm sought " 'to avoid production or copy of any foreign period and to illustrate English art in every respect.' "[17]

A more useful piece for our purposes was a sideboard designed by Bruce J. Talbert and made by Holland and Sons (Fig. 18). Talbert was just compiling his *Gothic Forms Applied to Furniture, Metal Work and Decoration for Domestic Purposes* and was a major exponent of the Gothic-inspired art furniture then coming into vogue in England.

[17] Aslin, *Nineteenth Century English Furniture,* p. 88.

A few pieces in this style had already been exhibited in 1862, most notably those by William Burges and Norman Shaw. Historically, the reformed Gothic style of the Talbert sideboard proved more important than that of the Wright and Mansfield cabinet, but both were significant for their rejection of the Renaissance revival style. And while both were still historicizing, they were by no means French.

Although English examples of French influence were still being exhibited, for example the side-

FIG. 19. Trollope and Sons, sideboard. From Art Journal, *The Illustrated Catalog of the Universal Exhibition of 1867* (London and New York: Virtue & Co., 1867), p. 181. (Photo, Winterthur.)

board by Trollope and Sons of London (Fig. 19), hostility toward French design had become far more outspoken. This is especially apparent in the comments written by J. Beavington Atkinson for the *Art Journal*'s catalog of the exhibition. He began by suggesting that "French furniture is not so much superior to, as different from, the English," but as he progressed his tone became more strident and his caution diminished. He accused French furniture of being "expressly designed for ostentation in grand palaces of the times of the Louis." To

him, French taste was degenerate. It was denounced for "exaggeration, excess and affectation." The Renaissance style was singled out for special abuse. It was "a style of proverbial corruption," and Atkinson went on to claim that "French cabinetmakers limit themselves all but exclusively to those corrupt and fantastic forms of the Renaissance which pandered to the vices of a profligate court, and became degenerate in the decay of a dynasty."[18]

[18] Atkinson, "Furniture of the Universal Exhibition," pp. 196, 197, 210.

FIG. 20. Henri Fourdinois, cabinet. From Art Journal, *The Illustrated Catalog of the Universal Exhibition of 1867* (London and New York: Virtue & Co., 1867), p. 34. (Photo, Winterthur.)

Some of these outbursts can be traced to legitimate aesthetic outrage, but the majority, one suspects, were a reflection of Britain's humiliation at finding herself the most politically powerful nation on earth yet still a cultural colony of France. These words served as a warning of impending aesthetic independence.

The French themselves, instead of rejecting the Renaissance, delved even more deeply into it. In 1862 and 1867 Henri Fourdinois exhibited cabinets that were strong historicizing essays in the French Renaissance style (Figs. 20, 21), in a way even more Renaissance than the originals upon which they were modeled. The French also worked in the

FIG. 21. Henri Fourdinois, cabinet. Paris, 1867. Ebony, inlaid with box- and pearwoods; H. 98″, W. 61″, D. 20½″. (Victoria and Albert Museum, London.)

FIG. 22. Sideboard from the Spanish court. From *Gems of the Centennial Exhibition . . . at the Philadelphia International Exhibition of 1876* (New York: D. Appleton & Co., 1877), p. 123. (Photo, Winterthur.)

FIG. 23. Sideboard from the German court. From *Gems of the Centennial Exhibition . . . at the Philadelphia International Exhibition of 1876* (New York: D. Appleton & Co., 1877), p. 127. (Photo, Winterthur.)

Louis XVI and neo-grec styles, but neither of these represented a significantly different aesthetic.

The turning point in the battle of the sideboards seems to have been the Philadelphia Centennial. Of French furniture at the Centennial, little was notable, for it presented nothing new. The French style could still be seen in the productions of nations under her cultural thralldom, and examples from Spain and Germany showed that French authority was still strong in those countries (Figs. 22, 23). The English exhibit, on the other hand, was largely free of French accent. One writer found it

superior to that of any other country, an encomium to which the British had been building since 1851. An examination of catalogs from the Centennial shows that British production again fell into two broad categories. One style, best exemplified by the firm of Wright and Mansfield (Fig. 24), was eighteenth-century neoclassicism; the other was the more prevalent reformed Gothic or art furniture style, represented by firms like Collinson and Lock, Cooper and Holt (Fig. 25), Cox and Son, and Shoolbred and Company.

Perhaps the best way to judge the success of Eng-

FIG. 24. Wright and Mansfield, sideboard. From Walter Smith, "Industrial Art," in *The Masterpieces of the Centennial International Exhibition,* 3 vols. (Philadelphia: Gebbie & Barrie, 1876), 2:288. (Photo, Winterthur.)

lish productions is to examine the American exhibits at the exposition. Since the early nineteenth century and the time of the émigré cabinetmaker, Charles Honoré Lannuier, American taste had generally followed the fashions of France. Now at the Centennial a number of American works were shown that relied on Britain for their inspiration. Those still relying on France, like the sideboards by Allen and Brother of Philadelphia (Fig. 26) and George A. Schastey of New York (Fig. 27), were impressive enough, but were clearly the creations of a dying style. Far more important and exciting were the English-influenced pieces. Among others to be noted were a sideboard by Ellin and Kitson of New York (Fig. 28) and another by an unidentified

Cincinnati producer, probably the Mitchell and Rammelsberg Furniture Company (Fig. 29).

The Philadelphia Centennial and the Paris exhibition of 1878 (which was largely a repeat performance of 1876) were really the last two international exhibitions to witness intense competition in furniture. After the 1870s, the nature of the furniture trade seems to have changed. Grand and imposing pieces of furniture became less common and the furniture exhibited conformed more closely to that for normal domestic consumption. Manufacturers may have grown weary of more than two decades of contests but, whatever the reason, they gradually lost interest in international exhibitions. A number of periodicals devoted to furniture

FIG. 25. Cooper and Holt, sideboard. From *Gems of the Centennial Exhibition . . . at the Philadelphia International Exhibition of 1876* (New York: D. Appleton & Co., 1877), p. 94. (Photo, Winterthur.)

Fig. 26. Allen and Brother, sideboard. From Walter Smith, "Industrial Art," in *The Masterpieces of the Centennial International Exhibition,* 3 vols. (Philadelphia: Gebbie & Barrie, 1876), 2:13. (Photo, Winterthur.)

FIG. 27. George A. Schastey, sideboard. From *Gems of the Centennial Exhibition . . . at the Philadelphia International Exhibition of 1876* (New York: D. Appleton & Co., 1877), p. 140. (Photo, Winterthur.)

Fig. 28. Ellin and Kitson, sideboard. From *Gems of the Centennial Exhibition . . . at the Philadelphia International Exhibition of 1876* (New York: D. Appleton & Co., 1877), p. 136. (Photo, Winterthur.)

Fig. 29. Unidentified Cincinnati cabinetmaker (probably the Mitchell and Rammelsberg Furniture Company), sideboard. From *Gems of the Centennial Exhibition . . . at the Philadelphia International Exhibition of 1876* (New York: D. Appleton & Co., 1877), p. 141. (Photo, Winterthur.)

emerged in the 1870s and 1880s and provided a vehicle for new designs and information about various aspects of the trade so that exhibitions no longer performed that function. Furniture continued to be shown at exhibitions and occasional pieces still impressed audiences, but the great days were over.

In the end, it would be immoderate to claim that these twenty-five years of international competi-

tion, these bouts of sublimated warfare, were the sole motivating factors in the creation of England's essentially nationalistic reform style and the termination of France's undisputed hegemony in the field of furniture. Nonetheless, the importance of these exhibitions is greater than usually acknowledged. Without them, there is no doubt that the history of furniture in the nineteenth century would have been far different.

Of Muslins and Merveilleuses

Excerpts from the Letters of Josephine du Pont and Margaret Manigault

Betty-Bright P. Low

THE EIGHTEENTH and nineteenth centuries met in the middle of a decade of undress. In women's fashions it was the era of the "merveilleuse," characterized by marvelous daring and by slight fabric artfully utilized. The sizable gauze veil that constituted the whole of Mme. Hamelin's attire on her celebrated promenade through the Tuileries garden and Mme. Jérôme Bonaparte's muslin and lace wedding gown, which one Baltimorean declared would fit easily into a gentleman's pocket, won for those two ladies[1] a niche in the annals of style.

By 1795 the social structure of Paris, traditional fountainhead of fashion, had been demolished by the Revolution and the ensuing Terror. Only the illusion of its leadership remained as a stimulus to national creativity. French stylists rose to the challenge. That they turned to British innovation as a point of departure was justified by the fact that Rose Bertin,[2] former dressmaker to Marie Antoinette and her court, had moved her atelier to London, thereby injecting a French influence into the English fashion scene. In any case, the simple chemise, which closely resembled the traditional undergarment of that name, was introduced by the British and then adapted by French couturiers to the new age of undress. The long sleeves set in by British dressmakers were shortened or removed, leaving the arms bared. The neckline, which like the waist was controlled by a drawstring, was lowered and the waist raised. Temporarily the skirt was hiked to reveal at least the calf, ornamentation was minimal, and the careful draping of the chemise was considered the secret of both its decency and its success. Thus France added its special cachet to an English creation and thereby produced the dress that with minor modifications would be basic fashion until around 1810. Made of India muslin, silk, fine cambric, dimity, percale, or tulle, the chemise was so universally adopted in Paris that women of the French capital were variously called Dianas, nymphs, goddesses, white shadows, or, by critics of the new style, Phrynes, hetaerae, or other maliciously unflattering names.

Louis-Sébastien Mercier, who, with Pierre-An-

[1] Fortunée Lormier-Lagrave Hamelin, wife of a banker and army contractor, was a Creole beauty of the Bonaparte clique known for her dancing, her rages, and her rose perfume. She never completed her promenade in the Tuileries because of the crowds massed to observe. Her outing inspired similar incidents, notably on May 28, 1799, when two women newly arrived from the provinces walked entirely décolletées through the Allée des Orangers. Henry Lachouque, *Bonaparte et la Cour Consulaire* (Paris: Bloud & Gay, 1958), p. 33; F. V. A. Aulard, *Paris Pendant la Réaction Thermidorienne et sous le Directoire,* 5 vols. (Paris: L. Cerf, 1898–1902), 5: 538. Elizabeth Patterson (1785–1879), a Baltimore beauty, married Jérôme Bonaparte, younger brother of Napoleon, on December 24, 1803. Later, when the emperor refused to recognize the marriage, Jérôme wed the Princess of Württemberg and became King of Westphalia.

[2] Rose Bertin (1747–1813) fled Paris in 1792, lived for a time among the French royal refugees at Coblenz, then emigrated to England where, despite financial difficulties, her talents as a couturière were widely acclaimed. After her return to France in 1795, her ties to the ancien régime limited her to a secondary position among her colleagues. Emile Langlade, *Rose Bertin,* adapted from French by Angelo S. Rappoport (London: J. Long, 1913).

toine Leboux de La Mésangère,[3] was an outstanding chronicler of the fashion and customs of 1800, related the new style to the liberation of the spirit that followed the Revolution. To jettison restrictive undergarments was to manifest physically the new civic and social freedom. Mercier looked upon the period as a necessary historical purgative. Other commentators have since variously attributed the extremism of the late 1790s to the influence of the French painter Jacques-Louis David, to a national détente at all levels, to the excitement emanating from the archaeological discoveries of classical antiquity in Italy, and to the effort to recapture the glories of Greece and Rome in a new era of classicism.

The Revolution had submerged everything—traditions, morals, language, throne, altar, fashions and manners; but the specific lightness of the people swam on top of carelessness, of romancing, of pertinency, that never-dying spirit, grumbling and laughing, precious foundation of the national character, reappeared on the morrow of the storm more alert, more vivacious, more indomitable than ever. As nothing remained of the past, and as it was impossible to improvise in a day[,] society with its harmonies, its usages, its garments entirely unedited, they borrowed the whole from ancient history and nations which have disappeared.[4]

These "modern Greeks" with their diaphanous chemises did not appear only in France. The amorphous styles quickly floated to the United States where a concurrent search for national identity was under way. In his recent *Charleston in the Age of the Pinckneys*, George C. Rogers remarked that "in the 1790's, there was more of an emphasis on fashion than intellect, a striving for form rather than

substance."[5] But fashion and form found in America were considerably more substantial than their French counterparts. Whereas in Paris a lady's wardrobe of 1800, excluding wrap but including jewelry and shoes, ideally weighed but eight ounces,[6] even in the most cosmopolitan East Coast cities of the United States more conservative attitudes drastically modified French styles.

The story of the adaptation of Athenian robes and their accoutrements in this country is suggested in various journals and memoirs of turn-of-the-century figures. It is vividly depicted in the letters of Gabrielle Josephine de La Fite de Pelleport du Pont and Margaret Izard Manigault.[7] From the excerpts of their correspondence presented here, threads of fashion can be followed from Paris to Charleston and New York. The dialogue of two perceptive ladies moving in elevated circles in different cities brings trends into focus and places the dress of 1800 in its proper life-style context.

Josephine du Pont (1770–1837; Fig. 1) was an offspring of the ancien régime. Her father, the Marquis de Pelleport, had been in the service of the comte d'Artois, youngest brother of Louis XVI. In her early years she moved with ease in the Versailles milieu, where her training in the social graces of the day replaced formal education. She had briefly considered entering a convent just before meeting Victor du Pont (1767–1827). Victor, spirited elder son of the physiocrat Pierre Samuel du Pont de Nemours (1739–1817), aspired to a career in the foreign service of his country. Twice, in 1787 and in 1791, he had visited the United States in the entourage of French diplomats, and on both occasions he formed friendships in addition to those derived

---

[3] Louis-Sébastien Mercier (1740–1814), French author and playwright, chronicled pre-Revolutionary Paris, then in 1798 produced the six volumes of *Le Nouveau Paris* (Paris: Fuchs, C. Pougens & C.-F. Cramer, 1798). Pierre Antoine Leboux de La Mésangère (1761–1831) authored *Costumes Parisiennes de la Fin du 18ᵉ Siècle et du Commencement du 19ᶜ*, begun in June 1797 and continued until 1821. Its twenty volumes, with colored engravings of fashion prints, were published in Paris, at the office of the *Journal des Dames et des Modes*, the fashion publication edited by La Mésangère from December 1800 until 1831. Similarly, a collection of fifty-two colored engravings devoted to styles of the late eighteenth and early nineteenth centuries was issued by La Mésangère as *Modes et Manières du Jour à Paris* (n.d.). One hundred fifteen caricatures entitled *Bon Genre* and first issued in the early years of the nineteenth century were later, in 1827, published in Paris with commentary by La Mésangère as *Observations sur les Modes et les Usages de Paris*.

[4] Octave Uzanne, *The Frenchwoman of the Century* (London: John C. Nimmo, 1886), p. 16.

[5] George C. Rogers, Jr., *Charleston in the Age of the Pinckneys* (Norman: University of Oklahoma Press, 1969), p. 109.

[6] [Max von Boehn], *Modes & Manners of the Nineteenth Century*, trans. M. Edwardes, 3 vols. (London: J. M. Dent, 1909), 1:102.

[7] The letters of both women are in the collections of the Eleutherian Mills Historical Library, Greenville, Del. (hereafter EMHL). After the Civil War Margaret Manigault's letters were returned by the du Pont family to her son, Charles I. Manigault, in exchange for the letters of Josephine du Pont. The du Pont letters were subsequently inherited by Colonel H. A. du Pont and in turn by his son Henry Francis du Pont, whose collection of family letters is now at EMHL. The Manigault letters were later acquired by a member of the du Pont family who presented them to the library so that the entire correspondence would be preserved in a single depository.

FIG. 1. Attributed to Louis Léopold Boilly, *Gabrielle Josephine du Pont* (Mrs. Victor du Pont). France, ca. 1798. Oil on wood; Oval 12½″, W. 10″. (Hagley Museum.)

from his father's connections with high-ranking American political figures.

But the Terror interrupted Victor du Pont's progress in the diplomatic service. Indeed the status of the entire du Pont family was precarious in 1793. Du Pont de Nemours was liable to be held accountable for his past services to the French crown, and Irénée du Pont, Victor's younger brother, was in jeopardy for printing material with political overtones. Victor himself had not fulfilled his military obligations to the government, and he was serving in the militia at Ferrières at the time Josephine de Pelleport entered his life. Compounding the dangers surrounding the couple's brief courtship, Josephine insisted on being married by a Catholic priest even though denial of secular authority over marriages was then considered treasonable. In March 1794 at Bois-des-Fossés, the du Pont home, the Curé of Bransles agreed to conduct the wedding ceremony, which was performed in such haste and secrecy that the bride had no time to call

her sister, "who was watching a game of backgammon down-stairs," as a witness. The civil ceremony took place several weeks later.[8]

When Victor received an appointment later that year as secretary of legation to Pierre Auguste Adet, French minister to the United States, Josephine du Pont showed no reluctance about leaving France and devoting herself to helping her husband as he advanced in his chosen diplomatic career. Less than three months after their arrival in the United States, he was named French consul in Charleston. The du Ponts began their life there in September 1795.

Charleston was thriving and the cotton trade was booming. The society of America's principal Southern port was still in flux. The mercantile community consisted not only of bankers and import-export merchants but also of retailers, artisans, and planters seeking the diversions of the city. It was a cosmopolitan community in the largest sense, and enterprising newcomers were readily accepted. French refugees who crowded in after the 1790s uprisings on the island of Santo Domingo were welcomed, and they enriched the local scene with their talents and high spirits. When Josephine and Victor du Pont arrived, Francophile enthusiasm had been dampened by Edmond Charles Genêt's machinations before his recall[9] and by political squabbling in the local French community. Victor du Pont's natural gifts for diplomacy helped him represent his government creditably within the factions at work among his compatriots and within the American community as well. The refusal of President Adams to recognize his appointment as consul general replacing Philippe Joseph Létombe in May 1798 ended his diplomatic career, but it did not erase the respect in which he was held by Charlestonians such as the Gabriel Manigaults.

That respect was enhanced by du Pont's consistent efforts to defend American shipping interests before the French government during the year 1798, following his return to France. In 1799 when

[8] B. G. du Pont, *Lives of Victor and Josephine du Pont* (privately published, 1930), p. 69.

[9] Genêt (1763–1834), French minister plenipotentiary to the United States, initially received considerable encouragement in his scheme to outfit privateers in Charleston and to use American ports as bases for preying on British shipping. This plan together with his intentions to recapture West Indian islands for France, wrest Florida from Spain, and incite revolution in Canada led President Washington to demand his recall in 1794.

the entire du Pont family emigrated to America, Victor du Pont and his father, Pierre Samuel du Pont de Nemours, established a commission firm in New York,[10] and such prominent names as Barclay, Hamilton, Livingston, Watts, Church, LeRoy, and Bayard figured among those who welcomed the newcomers.

At least five of these families had ties with the Manigaults, through Alice Izard, née De Lancey,[11] Margaret Manigault's mother. Her marriage to Ralph Izard, distinguished South Carolina planter and statesman, had bridged the society of New York and Charleston. A further cosmopolitan dimension was added to the life of the Izard family when they left their extensive plantation holdings to live abroad for an extended period. Thus the eldest daughter, Margaret Izard Manigault (1768–1824; Fig. 2), spent ten years in France and was educated there. She acquired an unusual appreciation for French culture and achieved an enviable proficiency in the language before she returned to the United States to marry Gabriel Manigault (1758–1809) in May 1785.

The Manigault name was as deeply implanted in South Carolina's history as that of Izard. Three generations before, the first Manigault in this country had arrived as a Huguenot refugee, settled in Charleston, and then acquired land to the west. Gabriel Manigault inherited a number of plantations, both rice and cotton, including The Oaks, which stood next to the famous Izard estate The Elms on Goose Creek. Like other descendants of early landowners, he preferred the activity of the city to country life. He occupied himself with the management of his investments, his estates, and their produce. His avocation was architecture. Consequently, he designed and built a home for his young wife on the southeast corner of Meeting and George streets,[12] in Charleston. Sojourns at The Oaks or other plantations and at Sullivan's Island

FIG. 2. Gilbert Stuart, *Margaret Manigault* (Mrs. Gabriel Manigault). New York, 1794. Oil on canvas; Oval 28″, W. 23″. (Albright Knox Art Gallery: Photo, Eleutherian Mills–Hagley Foundation.)

[10] Du Pont de Nemours, Père et Fils & Cie., parent firm of E. I. du Pont de Nemours & Co.

[11] Mrs. John Watts and Mrs. Thomas Barclay were sisters of Alice de Lancey Izard. Mesdames Church, Hamilton, and Livingston were distantly connected.

[12] The Manigault residence on Meeting Street was demolished in the 1930s to make room for a gas station. Fortunately an example of Gabriel Manigault's architectural talent has been preserved in Charleston, where the house he designed and built for his brother, Joseph Manigault, is open to the public.

routinely punctuated the Manigaults' year, as did Race Week in February, with its attendant balls, theater parties, and social gatherings.

Margaret Manigault's family ties and her position of established wealth in Charleston society assured wider horizons for her than many women of her day could hope for. Yet her principal concern was her husband and home. She had four living children and was expecting another at the time Victor and Josephine du Pont arrived in South Carolina.

Josephine du Pont's first child, Amelia Elizabeth, was born in January 1795, just four months after she came to Charleston. In such circumstances, a non-English-speaking woman in a strange new environment far from family needed a confidante. To a close friend she wrote: "This place offers no resources for making close friends. One must be resigned to preparing endless as well as ruinously expensive, toilettes in order to partake of their sumptuous teas, or else stay absolutely alone. My husband is almost always overwhelmed by business matters and dinner invitations, which I refuse in order not to have to reciprocate, which is infinitely more costly when there are women. You see how sorely I need a sister or a friend at my side."[13]

Margaret Manigault stepped easily into the role of friend and social guide. She had much to offer in this new association: reassurance in a new community, experience in handling the needs of an infant, encouragement to display musical talents, readiness to share opinions of French reading matter, support in the choice of fashions, and the bond of French as a common language. Margaret Manigault represented to her new French friend "the model of domestic felicity, of kind virtues, of good social order."[14]

What then did Josephine du Pont bring to the nascent friendship? Perhaps she recalled associations of carefree childhood days and memories of France. Certainly she radiated an image of good humor in the midst of routine, adaptability in the face of change, and loyalty to established values in social interchange. In a diary of 1796, Margaret Manigault described her: "She has seen a great deal of the world. . . . She has the agreeable vivacity of her own country tempered by the solid virtues of ours. . . . In addition to all this a very handsome face, a sweet, interesting countenance, and manners which after all that has already been said may be supposed to be perfect."[15]

The contrasts between the two women only added interest to their friendship. Margaret Manigault was Protestant; Josephine du Pont was Catholic. Margaret was well-traveled; Josephine's voyages were just beginning. Margaret was securely established in Charleston and her life governed by routine. Josephine, having left her native land for the first time, was seeking roots in a new society. Margaret Manigault felt the dichotomy of English and French influences; Josephine du Pont was French to the core.

Yet what they shared was far stronger than such

differences: intelligence, graciousness, love of music, reading, understanding of the French language and temperament. Even more important, their values were similar: husband, children, and home, followed by a lively interest in people. They placed equal emphasis on the social amenities, which they felt should be pursued with studied reserve. To make a strong impression in society was very important, but personal privacy should be cherished at all costs.

The excerpts from the du Pont-Manigault letters presented here deal in large part with the social problem of how to cultivate the art of being uncommon but never outlandish, of being remarked as a person worthy of emulation, both in conduct and appearance. Such a goal demanded that the two women keep abreast of the latest styles from abroad, but that they convert the extreme to the acceptable in the context of their immediate surroundings. And for women, in the setting of post-Revolutionary American society, dress was a major element in forming the image presented to the world.

To depend solely upon draping the soft, ethereal chemise with its narrow skirt in order to protect decency would surely jar American circles oriented to English decorum, even more than it affected the French themselves. The tunic overdress mentioned by Margaret Manigault[16] was one of several answers to the problem, an answer that in principle had the additional merit of echoing antiquity. In practice, undergarments were not ordinarily discarded. They are not mentioned in the du Pont-Manigault letters of the 1800 period, but commentaries on fashion at that time frequently refer to flesh-colored pantaloons or matching underskirts. Long corsets with stays laced in back were also commonly used in America.

Outer layers provided additional covering to the chemises of 1800. Most often a scarf served this purpose. The small, fichu-type neckerchief that had long been popular was still useful for morning wear, but later in the day it gave way to a larger scarf. Scarves, or shawls, for evening wear were elaborately trimmed. Sometimes the border was a reprise of the chemise edging on three sides (Fig. 3). In other cases, fine lace, embroidery, or fringe rimmed the center square. The material varied considerably from veiling and muslins to velvets and

[13] Translation from Josephine du Pont to Mme. Auriol Rumilly, Jan. 25, 1796, The Henry Francis du Pont Collection of Winterthur Manuscripts (hereafter WMSS), Group 3, Series D (hereafter 3/D), EMHL.

[14] Josephine du Pont to Margaret Manigault, Jan. 27, 1800, WMSS 3/D, EMHL.

[15] Diaries of Margaret Manigault, Accession 502 (hereafter Acc. 502), EMHL. The diaries, in three volumes, were transcribed and edited by Joseph Patrick Monigle, "The Diaries of Mrs. Gabriel Manigault, 1793–1809" (M.A. thesis, University of Delaware, 1959), p. 48.

[16] Margaret Manigault to Josephine du Pont, June 27, 1800, Acc. 502, EMHL.

FIG. 3. Silk-embroidered muslin dress and scarf, ca. 1800. Drawstring neck and waist; hem edging in double rows of French knots forming interlocking rings between double rows of satin-stitch cording; surmounted by a row of open wreaths in satin-stitch foliage motif. Square scarf repeats edging on three sides and at each end of fourth, leaving plain-hemmed center area for easy draping at neck. Dress and scarf modeled by Mrs. John J. Danko. Side chair, probably New York City, 1820–30. Mahogany with gilded animal forelegs and applied brass bosses on cresting rail and skirt, upholstered in plain-woven taffeta; H. 33¼″, W. 18¹⁵⁄₁₆″, D. 19¾″. (Dress and scarf, Hagley Museum; chair, Winterthur 71.134: Photo, Winterthur.)

satins. Always these outer garments were designed more for adornment than as a safeguard against the elements. "In one year eighteen ladies caught fire and eighteen thousand caught cold"[17] lamented an anonymous commentator, echoing physicians' records of the day.

The ladies themselves remarked on the drawbacks of such flimsy coverings. For example, Georgette Ducrest, in her memoirs, amusingly noted the intense discomfort of two Parisian merveilleuses who visited the Montanvert glacier field in ephemeral outfits. "We climbed the mountains in an extremely thick fog, which uncurled the feathers on their hats and made them look rather like brooms. Their sheer robes, half-opened over the chest, made them freeze; and their very thin-soled, light-colored slippers could scarcely lead them back to the inn."[18]

Common solutions to the problem of warmth before the era of central heating were the mantelet, the spencer, or the redingote. The du Pont-Manigault letters trace the eclipse of the first. The mantelet, a short shoulder cape, fell from grace as the shawl became more popular (Fig. 13). It was not immediately discarded from the wardrobe, rather it was altered: additional rows of edging were applied to lengthen it and render it transitional.[19] As fine cashmeres entered the fashion picture, it disappeared completely, and the shawl became all-important.

The spencer (Fig. 11), a short jacket with or without tails, with long or short sleeves, enjoyed popularity among the fashionables of the decade, and beyond. In 1799 it was sufficiently new in America to elicit Margaret Manigault's particular notice when worn by Mme. de Pestre in Charleston.[20] Inspired by British styles, the spencer had been introduced in France around 1795 by a small group of Frenchwomen who sought to imitate masculine fashions. But modifications quickly made it un-

[17] Elisabeth McClellan, *Historic Dress in America, 1607–1870*, 2 vols. (New York: Benjamin Blom, 1969), 2:26.

[18] Translation from Georgette Ducrest, *Mémoires sur l'Impératrice Joséphine, ses Contemporains, la Cour de Navarre et de la Malmaison*, 3 vols. (Brussels: Veuve de Mat, 1828), 1:172.

[19] Josephine du Pont to Margaret Manigault, Apr. 26, 1800, WMSS 3/D; Margaret Manigault to Josephine du Pont, June 27, 1800, Acc. 502, EMHL.

[20] Margaret Manigault to Josephine du Pont, Dec. 22, 1799, Acc. 502, EMHL.

deniably feminine when rendered in fabrics that ranged from velvets tipped or lined with fur to silks and laces.

The full-length redingote (Fig. 14) was important in several ways. Indeed its versatile coatlike pattern made it second only to the chemise in general use. Styled in wadded fabric, a fashion treatment again emanating from Britain, it warmed the goddesses emerging from a winter presentation at the Paris Opera. Made of a lighter-weight material, it served as a comfortable dressing gown at home by the fireside. As adapted by Josephine du Pont, fashioning her pastel pink-dyed Philadelphia dimity dress with fullness at the back and with the front coatline delineated vertically by white ribbons, this style provided variety in a wardrobe principally composed of chemises. Or made of gray taffeta and edged with white fur, it became a stunning evening gown.[21]

Two other outer garments for winter figure in the du Pont–Manigault letters. The witzchoura, a full-sleeved mantle, usually fur-lined, originated in western Europe and was in vogue in England before it was imported to the scene of French galas. The mameluke,[22] a full-backed cloak, derived its name from the flowing garment worn by the legendary Mameluke warriors of Egypt, who were defeated by Napoleon in the campaign of 1798. It was adapted from Eastern styles in Europe prior to its appearance in Charleston.

The "white shadows," both French and American, could hardly be universally content with lack of color beneath their cloaks. A very plain white dress is unbecoming unless its wearer is beautiful, and a Madame Récamier is rare. Therefore, by 1798 the whiteness that stood out so frothily against black-dominated men's wear was modified to include pastels and figured sheers. Josephine du Pont's first hesitant mention of the new color amaranth[23] coincided with the earliest references to pinkish purple as a high-fashion hue in France.

The basic chemise dress was further individualized by means of decorative trim. By late 1800 the

popularity of embroidered borders, crewel bands, lace, cording, and ribbons was challenged by metallic edgings, feathers, fringes, and painted borders. The prevailing fondness for Greek and Etruscan embroidery was extended to include floral and foliage motifs such as the iris worked in silk on Josephine du Pont's fine muslin chemise (Figs. 4, 5).

New York and Charleston merchants had great difficulty maintaining a stock of handsome garnitures, so great was the demand. Fine laces were ever

Fig. 4. Silk-embroidered muslin dress belonging to Josephine du Pont, ca. 1800. Drawstring neck; empire waist banded with satin-stitch leaves outlined in French knots and connected by vines of knots between overstitch border; elbow-length sleeves gathered at the shoulder, with rolled tuck at mid-sleeve, edged with waist design; satin-stitch iris motif forming front panel from mid-waist and bordering lower skirt above a repetition of the waist edging set over a plain hem. Dress modeled by Mrs. John J. Danko. Pier table, stamped by Charles-Honoré Lannuier, New York City, 1805–10. Mahogany with marble top, brass moldings and gallery; H. 36½", W. 37", D. 14 3⁄16". Armchair with square back, New York City, ca. 1800. Mahogany upholstered with late-eighteenth-century French silk satin; H. 35", W. 21½", D. 18½". From a set of two armchairs and ten side chairs owned originally by Victor du Pont. (Dress, Hagley Museum; pier table and armchair, Winterthur 61.1693 and 57.835.1: Photo, Winterthur.)

[21] Josephine du Pont to Margaret Manigault, Dec. 10, 1798, Nov. 3, Dec. 20, 1800, WMSS 3/D, EMHL.

[22] Josephine du Pont to Margaret Manigault, Dec. 10, 1798, WMSS 3/D; Margaret Manigault to Josephine du Pont, June 27, 1800, Acc. 502, EMHL.

[23] Josephine du Pont to Margaret Manigault, Nov. 3, 1800, WMSS 3/D, EMHL.

FIG. 5. Back view of silk-embroidered muslin dress belonging to Josephine du Pont, showing eight-piece waist pattern and 2½-foot train bordered by iris motif extending from front of dress. (Photo, Winterthur.)

in short supply, as Margaret Manigault discovered when she needed black Valenciennes. After a fruitless search in New York shops, Josephine du Pont indicated that type of lace was becoming rare even in France where the taste currently favored malines and English lace.[24] Point de Bruxelles was among the most elegant and expensive laces, and its use was invariably remarked in both New York and Charleston.[25] The news of a ship arriving with a

fresh supply of "fantasies" was greeted with as much enthusiasm as a twentieth-century end-of-the-season sale. Josephine du Pont enjoyed a special advantage because of her first-hand knowledge of the boutiques and her personal contacts in Paris and because Victor du Pont, with his commission business, could occasionally be persuaded to reserve shipping space for a carton of fashions.

A corner of that carton was frequently set aside for a new hat of the latest Paris confection. In the turn-of-the-century wardrobe, hats became the principal means of expressing individuality. Wide brims were going out of style, but biggins, caps, and morning bonnets remained, to be worn at home along with the newer bandeaux (decorative headbands). Variety was seemingly infinite, with fantasy bonnets, casques (helmets), and turbans the favored shapes for social occasions. The textures and ornaments combined in the construction of these chapeaux ranged as widely as the designs. Velvets, satins, silks, crepes, organdies, straws, furs, tulles, or any combination thereof were surmounted with feathers and plumes of varying lengths and types. Peacock, ostrich, egret, and cock were all favored feathers used singly or in combination. During the last two years of the eighteenth century, a turban decorated with "esprit," a type of feather bouquet, was the epitome of style (Fig. 14). The choice of plumes and the angle of their placement was considered by some connoisseurs of fashion to be the key to judging the character of the wearer.[26]

Or, in lieu of plumage, the language of flowers spoke from milady's chapeau, where gillyflowers, poppies, or roses perched as chic accents. In 1800 buckles and metallic decorations became the vogue, along with embroidery. Short face veils were soon a popular addition to the helmet or turban base. Longer lace or tulle veils never ceased to enjoy wide use, especially for evening. The classic purity of

[24] Josephine du Pont to Margaret Manigault, July 10, 1800, WMSS 3/D, EMHL. There was relatively little demand for black lace during the half century preceding the Restoration. The entire French lace industry was in a state of economic depression during the last decade of the eighteenth century. Max von Boehn, *Modes & Manners, Ornaments* (London: J. M. Dent & Sons, 1929), pp. 27–28.

[25] Josephine du Pont to Margaret Manigault, July 10, Dec. 20, 1800, WMSS 3/D, EMHL. Laces first took their names from their place of manufacture, but by 1800 the terms were generic. Valenciennes, worked by bobbins and later machines, was characterized by its regular mesh square or diamond-shaped foundation, or trellis. Malines, or Mechlin, was distinguished by its clear pattern outline, which gave

the effect of embroidery. English, or point d'Angleterre, was a misnomer for Flemish lace, often the finest point de Bruxelles. Outstanding for its fineness of thread and intricacy of design, point de Bruxelles was a soft pillow lace, with connecting links supplied by needle and with the border of the foundation used in the pattern. Louise Ade Boger and H. Batterson Boger, eds. and comps., *The Dictionary of Antiques and the Decorative Arts: A Book of Reference for Glass, Furniture, Ceramics, Silver, Periods, Styles, Technical Terms, etc.* (New York: Charles Scribner's Sons, 1957).

[26] Edmond Lefèvre, *Le Commerce et l'Industrie de la Plume pour Parure.* (Paris: published by the author, 1914), p. 18.

black and white millinery so popular in 1798 Paris was quickly colored by a vogue for jonquil, poppy, nacarat,[27] lilac, and green. Blue was much less frequently used, but not ignored, judging from Margaret Manigault's black satin head-hugger trimmed in steel-colored metal with blue and white plumes.[28]

The coiffures beneath such extraordinary head-dresses changed almost as rapidly as millinery styles. In 1798 Josephine du Pont had renounced powdered wigs and was wearing a blond creation. She remarked on the Titus (cropped) hairstyles in Paris, for men and women. In 1800 Margaret Manigault confirmed that powdered wigs were passé in Charleston, that the same short wigs being worn in New York were the style in Carolina, and that her own had been obtained from Philadelphia. But her efforts to purchase a little blond circlet recommended by her friend were in vain. As her agent, Josephine du Pont made repeated visits to the coiffeur in New York, only to be told at last that the hair intended for the circlet had been burned in the oven by mistake. Local efforts to copy European styles were extensive; in the case of Josephine du Pont's wigs, the coiffeur ruined six before he succeeded in copying one well. A well-executed hairpiece sold profitably, if the twelve-dollar price for a wig is any criterion. But the wig business was not very stable because of shifting styles and scarcity of materials. In the late spring and summer of 1800 Josephine du Pont was exposing her own hair much of the time, as well as using her blond wig. Her hair, cut short, was washed daily. Such simple coiffures as she adopted enabled her to boast that her toilette took but twenty minutes,[29] a tribute to her, even in the age of undress.

Twenty minutes allowed very little time for cosmetics and accessories. The du Pont-Manigault letters suggest that these two ladies at least favored a natural look. Remarks on the excess of rouge used by the Bingham ladies of Philadelphia support this impression and are confirmed elsewhere in writings on this period.[30] Rejection of powdered wigs further underlines the moderate utilization of paint and powder in American society in 1800.

Jewels of the day were onyx, topaz, diamonds, and pearls, often used with cameos. They are infrequently mentioned in the letters. Exceptions are the vogue of long necklaces and diamond pendant earrings admired by Josephine du Pont at the Paris Opera, her description of Angelica Church's diamond buckle and crescent pin as an important part of her toilette at Mrs. Stoughton's loo party, and Margaret Manigault's note of a small gold ornament required to fasten a fichu, and her request for earrings from Paris.[31] Specific accessories are also ordinarily fleeting subjects in the correspondence: the gift of a fan, the wearing of flat, thin-soled slippers, veils, ribbons, bands, full-length gloves. But Margaret Manigault's purchase of French silk stockings proved such an ordeal that the procurement and shipment cover a three-month period in the letters.[32]

Knitted silk sleeves with taffeta stripes were accessory novelties in 1800 in New York when Josephine du Pont received some in her fashion shipment from Paris.[33] Colorful supplements to the high gathered sleeve of the chemise, they varied in length. They served as a decorative band attached under the edge of the sleeve or were sometimes sewn onto the cuff of a long sleeve to be used as a wristlet. When the sleevelets arrived in New York, the news was promptly transmitted to Charleston, so that Margaret Manigault could be a pacesetter there. Soon afterwards, a newspaper announcement of a quantity shipment to New York signaled the more general popularity and availability of the accessory.

---

[27] Geranium red color, cited as "une couleur directoriale" in Louis Madeleine Ripault, *Une Journée de Paris* (Paris: Johanneau, 1797), p. 176.

[28] Margaret Manigault to Josephine du Pont, Nov. 25, 1800, Acc. 502, EMHL.

[29] Josephine du Pont to Margaret Manigault, July 30, 1798, WMSS 3/D; Margaret Manigault to Josephine du Pont, June 27, 1800, Acc. 502; Josephine du Pont to Margaret Manigault, Dec. 20, May 6, July 10, 1800, WMSS 3/D, EMHL.

[30] Josephine du Pont to Margaret Manigault, May 18, 1800, WMSS 3/D, EMHL. The rouging of the Bingham ladies was also noticed by contemporaries such as Mrs. John Adams, Mrs. William Stephens Smith, and Mrs. Benjamin Stoddert. Gilbert Vail remarks, "In contrast to the opulence and glitter of the Colonial era, the years 1789–1800 saw a diminishing in the extensive use of cosmetics. For a time it was considered not chic to paint, powder and patch to the extent it had formerly been practised." *A History of Cosmetics in America* (New York: The Toilet Goods Association, 1947), p. 79.

[31] Josephine du Pont to Margaret Manigault, Dec. 10, 1798; Dec. 20, 1800, WMSS 3/D, Margaret Manigault to Josephine du Pont, Dec. 24, Aug. 17, 1800, Acc. 502, EMHL.

[32] Margaret Manigault to Josephine du Pont and Josephine du Pont to Margaret Manigault, Feb. 24 to May 24, 1800, Acc. 502 and WMSS 3/D, EMHL.

[33] Josephine du Pont to Margaret Manigault, Sept. 10, 1800, WMSS 3/D, EMHL.

New fashion was communicated by sample, by letter, and also by picture. Magazines of the period displayed the styles coming from France and England. American belles avidly sought pages from *Journal des Modes, Costumes Parisiens,* or *Gallery of Fashion*[34] by means of which they could either guide their modistes or invent. If possible they subscribed to one or more of the journals but, without a friend abroad who could supervise mailing, it was safer to obtain copies of single pages as the opportunity presented itself. It was not uncommon for prints from the fashion pages to inspire clever hands to dye, remake, and disguise last year's dresses. Both Margaret Manigault and Josephine du Pont were adept at this art.

Fortunate indeed was the lady who, before a picture itself reached America, received a sufficiently detailed description of the latest feature attire at a ball or the theater to reproduce a facsimile. Equally fortunate was the lady who had help in executing the immense quantity of handwork required for an elegant ensemble. Both Margaret Manigault and Josephine du Pont enjoyed the latter advantage, although the letters indicate they each possessed a high degree of competence as needlewomen. Their skill is hardly surprising, since the art of needlework was an essential part of a lady's education.

Despite such skill, the printed picture or the minute written description did not always suffice in reproducing the latest style. Patterns of organdy, muslin, or paper were sometimes enclosed in letters to supplement the instructions. Unfortunately those mentioned in the du Pont-Manigault letters have not survived. Margaret Manigault employed still another device, the fashion doll of pre-Revolutionary days, to portray a British style for her friend; she dressed a wax doll *à la mode du jour* as a gift for Amelia du Pont and as a pattern for her mother.[35]

Hints of the future market for mail-order ready-to-wear apparel are scattered through the letters. About nine years earlier, finished garments for women had first been offered for sale in Paris chez Mme. Teillard.[36] Mme. Teillard became Citizeness Lisfrand, and her 1794 trade catalogue for her

Maison Egalité, Paris (Figs. 6, 7), announced nine basic styles, among them the newly popular chemise, with prices for completed dresses in a choice of fabrics. Following the dress and undergarment selections were instructions for supplying measurements, arranging payment, and estimating mailing charges. Tagged threads indicating bust and waist dimensions, side length from underarm to hip, length and thickness of arm, and the wearer's height were required with an order for apparel. By July 1800 the ordering process was already somewhat simplified. Josephine du Pont advised Margaret Manigault that a paper blouse pattern and a thread the measure of the dress length would suffice to obtain a finished gown from one of the best and most expensive Paris couturiers.[37] Subsequent letters reveal that such an order was eventually placed.

In the meantime, Margaret Manigault enriched her wardrobe by at least one ready-made gown from London. Much earlier in the year she had enthused over her "crape Nelson hat with ostrich feathers and gold esprit"[38] of English importation. Her dual fashion orientation was an accepted practice. Francophile though she was, Margaret Manigault had strong ties with England. She lived with the reality of anti-French sentiments of the day, but was ever careful to shield a highly valued friendship from shifting political currents. The rivalry of London and Paris was realistically and lightheartedly acknowledged by both women in their descriptions of new acquaintances who showed patriotic leanings and in their fashion dialogue. Generally, their letters are partial to Parisian influences because of the combination of Margaret Manigault's sympathy for the French and Josephine du Pont's staunch loyalty to her native land.

The good-humored fashion competition in which they engaged transcended the question of British innovation versus French flair. In actuality the challenge to be among the most fashionable cosmopolitans in Charleston and New York easily overrode any question of style origins. The mechanics of procurement demanded cooperation, and the translation of European fashion into the immediate American social scene demanded ingenuity. The rarified circles in which the two women moved in their respective cities attest to their success.

[34] The *Journal des Modes* (1799–1806) and *Costumes Parisiens* (1797–1821) were published in Paris, while *Gallery of Fashion* (1794–1802) was issued from London to depict fashion there.

[35] Margaret Manigault to Josephine du Pont, Dec. 24, 1800, Acc. 502, EMHL.

[36] [Von Boehn], *Modes & Manners of the Nineteenth Century,* 1:98.

[37] Josephine du Pont to Margaret Manigault, July 10, 1800, WMSS 3/D, EMHL.

[38] Margaret Manigault to Josephine du Pont, Nov. 24, Feb. 24, 1800, Acc. 502, EMHL.

To dress as well as possible with the means at hand was more than mere challenge. It was an obligation felt keenly by Josephine du Pont, who subtly criticized her sisters-in-law for their reluctance to spend time on their appearance, and by Margaret Manigault, who more openly judged American women in general as being lax in their attention to appearance.[39] The meticulously planned toilette was as important a part of social life as was the ritual of receiving and returning visits, or the card games for evening entertainments. Indeed, ritual appeared to play a significant role in the life-style of the upper classes in New York and Charleston alike. Servants, hospitality, and affluence characterized the planter's easy pace in Carolina, but rules governed his drawing room. North and South in the United States a gentleman needed a formal and independent introduction to the husband before he could accept an invitation from the wife. A gentleman's acquaintance with a family did not necessarily mean that wives would exchange visits. And greeting a lady while a gentleman was in dusty travel attire labeled him as rude.[40] Such observations suggest the beginnings of rigidity in American etiquette, just as qualifying remarks in the letters concerning Creole background and an individual's ability to grace a social gathering imply a degree of snobbery on the part of the writers.[41]

The dominance of fashion and social form in the du Pont-Manigault correspondence is exaggerated by the editing, which omits most political, family, and business references. That decision was dictated by the judgment that Josephine du Pont's and Margaret Manigault's fashion comments are a valuable addition to the literature on American lifestyles in this period. To enhance readability, punctuation has been modernized and abbreviated names, other than du Pont or Manigault, are usually given in full. Every attempt has been made in the translations to honor the spritely style of the original letters. Josephine du Pont's penchant for diminutives remains; so does Margaret Manigault's

quick, but vivid, method of disposing of one subject after another. It would be unfortunate for the letters to lose the color of the prearranged code system Margaret and Josephine used for members of the Charleston French community (Cicada, Wasp, Bee, Butterfly, and so on). Josephine du Pont slightly modified the customary code in assigning appellations to ladies of the Church family in New York.[42] Usually some lapse in such references has aided in identifications.

It would be unlikely for two people to correspond so extensively without surrendering to gossip. Josephine du Pont and Margaret Manigault, highly intelligent, spirited young women moving within the carefully delineated spheres prescribed for them in the society of 1800, relied on exchanges of news to challenge and alleviate boredom. The gossip in their correspondence derives some value from its revelation of the manners of the day. Angelica Church shocked New York society by receiving while reclining in her bedroom; Mme. de Caradeux imitated her "days"; Mme. de Pestre played the coquette and won wagers at the Jockey Club races in Charleston; the young Blakes, newlyweds, went alone from their wedding to an almost unfurnished house.[43] All such anecdotal remarks give perspective to the social life of the American aristocracy at the turn of the century.

The correspondence of Margaret Manigault and Josephine du Pont covered a period of twenty-eight years, from 1796, shortly after Josephine came to Charleston, to 1824, when Margaret died. A fitting tribute to their lasting friendship is the survival of 553 of the letters they exchanged. The letters printed here that focus on the world of fashion in 1800 are but the tip of an iceberg. Later, preoccupation with dress disappeared from the du Pont-Manigault correspondence. At the turn of the century, greater social success lay ahead for Josephine du Pont, to be followed by the humiliating experi-

---

[39] Josephine du Pont to Margaret Manigault, Feb. 22, Sept. 10, 1800, WMSS 3/D; Margaret Manigault to Josephine du Pont, Apr. 13, 1800, Acc. 502, EMHL.

[40] Margaret Manigault to Josephine du Pont, Aug. 17, 1800, Acc. 502, Josephine du Pont to Margaret Manigault, Apr. 18, Sept. 10, 1800, WMSS 3/D, EMHL.

[41] Josephine du Pont to Margaret Manigault, May 18, Sept. 10, Oct. 23, 1800; Margaret Manigault to Josephine du Pont, Nov. 24, 1800.

[42] The du Pont family name in this period was frequently written Du Pont. *La Cigalle,* or Cicada, may be identified as Mme. Labatut; the Bee or B., as Judge Bee; the Wasp, *la Guêpe,* the buzzing or stinging animal and the chameleon as Mme. de Pestre; the *Chercheur des Oranges* ("seeker of oranges") or *Papillon* ("butterfly") as Mr. George Izard. Instead of entomological designations, Josephine du Pont chose le Déclin ("the decline") for Angelica Schuyler Church and *Belle et bonne* ("lovely and kind") for her daughter Catharine.

[43] Josephine du Pont to Margaret Manigault, May 18, 1800, WMSS 3/D; Margaret Manigault to Josephine du Pont, Feb. 24, Feb. 8, 1800, Acc. 502, EMHL.

MAISON ÉGALITÉ,

GALERIE DU COTÉ DE LA RUE DE LA LOI,

AU PAVILLON D'OR, n° 41;

Magasin de Vêtemens pour les Citoyennes et Enfans, dans tous les genres imaginables, tant pour parure, que demi parure, le négligé et pour bal.

La C.ne. LISFRAND, jadis TEILLARD, Auteur des Robes de Fantaisie;

A l'honneur de prévenir les Citoyennes qui ont la bonté de lui donner leur confiance, pour les objets nouveaux qu'elle a de faits pour le Printems & l'Eté, en toutes sortes d'étoffes, comme Pékin rayé; Républicaines sans envers, façonnées, veloutées; Pékini rayé; Florence; Gragramme; Chinoises; Raz de soie; Sicilienne; Sicilienne toute Soie: Taffetas d'Italie, rayé, chiné & uni; Sirsakas rayé; Mousselines rayées, unies et peintes à Jouy; Linon uni et broché; Nankin; Naukinette; Toiles peintes; Gaze forte rayée; Crêpe, Mousselinette rayée, &c.

La Citoyenne LISFRAND, jadis TEILLARD, fait exécuter toutes sortes de Bonnets & Chapeaux élégans, et des Bonnets à la républicaine (ce bonnet est d'une forme délicieuse, et d'autant plus commode qu'il sied à ravir, coëffé ou sans l'être) depuis 18 jusqu'à 120 liv. Elle fait aussi la commission en tout genre, comme Dentelles, Bijoux, Fleurs, Plumes, Rouges, Gants, Odeurs, Bas, Souliers, & généralement tout ce qui concerne la parure des Citoyennes. Elle fait aussi la partie des Meubles.

REDINGOTES A LA RÉPUBLICAINE.

Ce vêtement dégage le col, donne une grande finesse à la taille, le devant est partie chemise & draperie, avec une ceinture à la Flore, retombante: elle ferme par des gances pardevant; elle est d'une superbe tournure.

En Pékin et velouté.	110
Pékini doublé.	100
Républicaine sans envers	105
Gragrame et Chinoise	84
Sirsakas	72
Raz de soie.	88
Mousseline garnie.	100
Linon.	90
Mousselinette.	90
Nankinette.	72
Sicilienne soie.	78
Gaze forte.	100
Taffetas.	90

ROBES RONDES A LA CARMAGNOLE.

Celle-ci enveloppe entiérement, forme à volonté le Doliment Arménien, et réunit le vêtement rond: sa tournure est extraordinaire & parfaite.

En Pékin velouté.	130
Pékini doublé.	125
Républicaine sans envers.	130
Gragrame et Chinoise.	90
Nankin.	90
Mousseline.	90
Linon.	100
Toile peinte.	75
Nankinette et Raz de soie	78
Taffetas.	128

ROBES CHEMISES A LA FANFAN.

Elle prend du haut du col, couvre la poitrine, enveloppe entiérement, & donne à la taille beaucoup de grace; le derrière de la taille se ferme par des nœuds de rubans, à volonté, une ceinture à la modeste la ferme sur le devant, avec trois boutons d'acier. Elle est d'un beau simple.

En Pékin.	135
Pékini doublé.	120
Républicaine sans envers.	130
Gragrame.	90
Taffetas d'Italie.	120
Nankin.	90
Mousseline unie ou rayée.	90
Linon.	100
Toile peinte.	78
Mousselinette rayée.	100
Sicilienne de soie.	85
Nankinette.	78
Crêpe.	90

CARACOS ET JUPES A LA ZÉLICA.

Bon pour la campagne & monter à cheval; cette coupe dessine la taille avec beaucoup d'élégance, & donne une tournure svelte. Il sied à ravir.

En Nankin.	85
Gragrame.	90
Raz de soie.	95
Nankinette.	80
Toile peinte.	78
Sicilienne.	75
Sirsakas.	80

ROBES ET JUPES A LA GRECQUE.

Pour parure & demi-parure: elle fait robe & jupe habillée & caraco à la Vénus. Elle est d'une tournure admirable.

En Pékin et velouté.	160
Républicaine sans envers.	150
Taffetas uni rayé ou chiné.	145
Raz de soie.	125
Nankin et Sirsakas.	120
Gragrame.	125
Linon uni ou broché.	130
Nankinette rayée.	110
Sicilienne toute de soie.	102

FIG. 6. Trade catalog of Maison Egalité, a women's and children's clothing store owned by Citizeness Lisfrand (Paris: Delaguette, ca. 1794). Broadside; H. 10½", W. 9¼". (Eleutherian Mills Historical Library.)

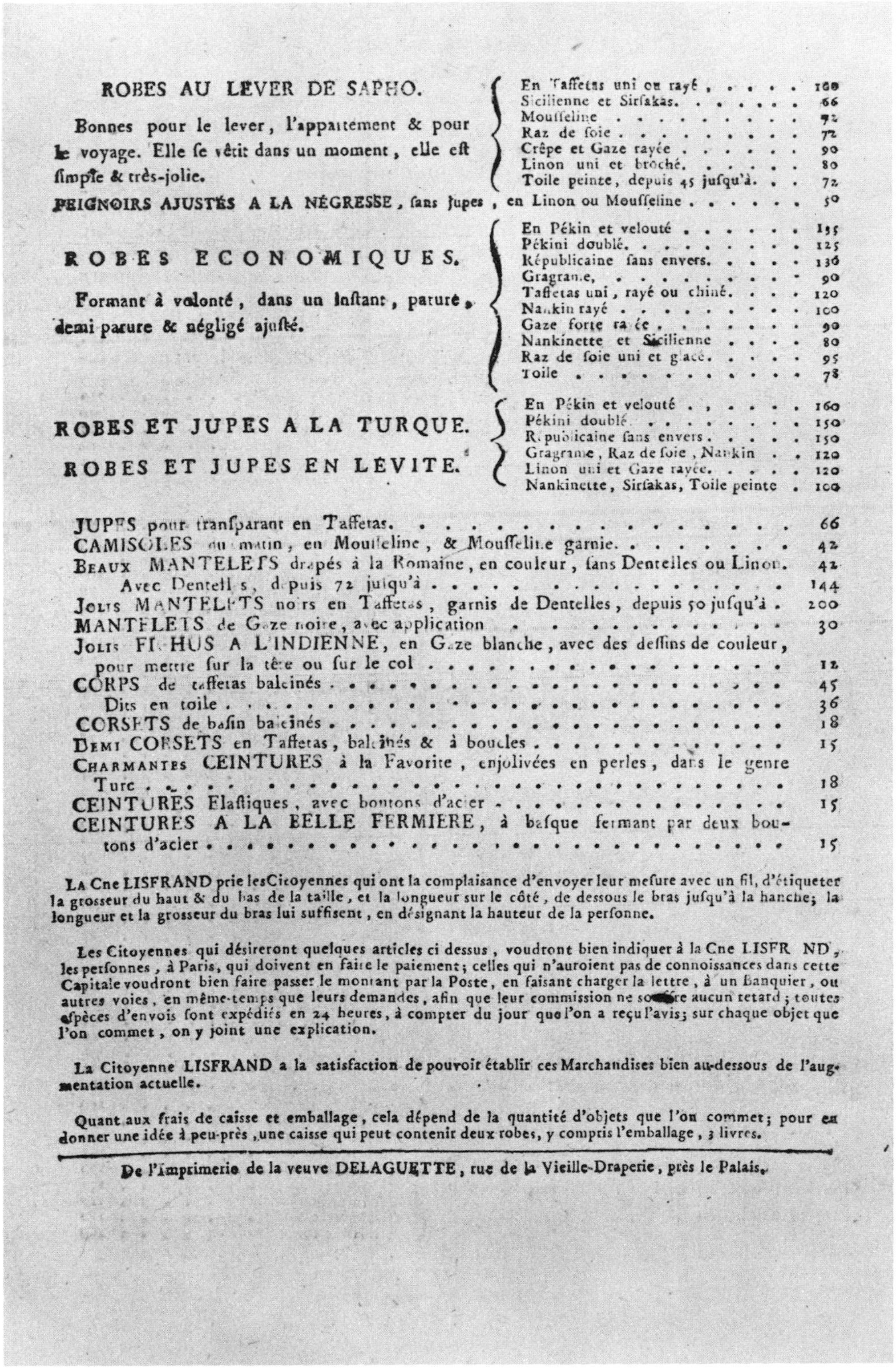

ROBES AU LEVER DE SAPHO.

Bonnes pour le lever, l'appartement & pour le voyage. Elle se vêtit dans un moment, elle est simple & très-jolie.

PEIGNOIRS AJUSTÉS A LA NÉGRESSE, sans jupes,

En Taffetas uni ou rayé , ...	160
Sicilienne et Sirsakas.	66
Mousseline	72
Raz de soie	72
Crêpe et Gaze rayée	90
Linon uni et broché.	80
Toile peinte, depuis 45 jusqu'à. . .	72
en Linon ou Mousseline	50

ROBES ECONOMIQUES.

Formant à volonté, dans un instant, parure, demi parure & négligé ajusté.

En Pékin et velouté	135
Pékini doublé.	125
Républicaine sans envers.	136
Gragrame, ...	90
Taffetas uni, rayé ou chiné. . .	120
Nankin rayé	100
Gaze forte rayée	90
Nankinette et Sicilienne	80
Raz de soie uni et glacé.	95
Toile	78

ROBES ET JUPES A LA TURQUE.
ROBES ET JUPES EN LÉVITE.

En Pékin et velouté . , . . .	160
Pékini doublé	150
Républicaine sans envers	150
Gragrame , Raz de soie , Nankin . .	120
Linon uni et Gaze rayée. . . .	120
Nankinette, Sirsakas, Toile peinte .	100

JUPES pour transparant en Taffetas.	66
CAMISOLES du matin, en Mousseline, & Mousseline garnie.	42
BEAUX MANTELETS drapés à la Romaine, en couleur, sans Dentelles ou Linon.	42
Avec Dentelles, depuis 72 jusqu'à	144
JOLIS MANTELETS noirs en Taffetas, garnis de Dentelles, depuis 50 jusqu'à .	200
MANTELETS de Gaze noire, avec application	30
JOLIS FICHUS A L'INDIENNE, en Gaze blanche, avec des dessins de couleur, pour mettre sur la tête ou sur le col	12
CORPS de taffetas balcinés	45
Dits en toile	36
CORSETS de basin balcinés	18
DEMI CORSETS en Taffetas, balcinés & à boucles	15
CHARMANTES CEINTURES à la Favorite, enjolivées en perles, dans le genre Turc	18
CEINTURES Elastiques, avec boutons d'acier	15
CEINTURES A LA BELLE FERMIERE, à basque fermant par deux boutons d'acier	15

La Cne LISFRAND prie les Citoyennes qui ont la complaisance d'envoyer leur mesure avec un fil, d'étiqueter la grosseur du haut & du bas de la taille, et la longueur sur le côté, de dessous le bras jusqu'à la hanche; la longueur et la grosseur du bras lui suffisent, en désignant la hauteur de la personne.

Les Citoyennes qui désireront quelques articles ci dessus, voudront bien indiquer à la Cne LISFRAND, les personnes, à Paris, qui doivent en faire le paiement; celles qui n'auroient pas de connoissances dans cette Capitale voudront bien faire passer le montant par la Poste, en faisant charger la lettre, à un Banquier, ou autres voies, en même-temps que leurs demandes, afin que leur commission ne souffre aucun retard; toutes espèces d'envois sont expédiés en 24 heures, à compter du jour que l'on a reçu l'avis; sur chaque objet que l'on commet, on y joint une explication.

La Citoyenne LISFRAND a la satisfaction de pouvoir établir ces Marchandises bien au-dessous de l'augmentation actuelle.

Quant aux frais de caisse et emballage, cela dépend de la quantité d'objets que l'on commet; pour en donner une idée à peu-près, une caisse qui peut contenir deux robes, y compris l'emballage, 3 livres.

De l'Imprimerie de la veuve DELAGUETTE, rue de la Vieille-Draperie, près le Palais.

FIG. 7. Verso, trade catalog of Maison Egalité. (Eleutherian Mills Historical Library.)

ence of her husband's business failure,[44] a subsequent period of uncertainty, then almost three years of frontier life in the small settlement of Angelica, New York. Finally, in 1809, she came to live in Delaware beside the Brandywine Creek, where Victor headed a woolen factory and was later elected to the Delaware legislature.

For Margaret Manigault, too, the future meant change. Trips from Charleston to New York heralded an eventual transplantation north. The Manigaults moved to Philadelphia in 1807 and acquired the estate of Clifton on the road to Bristol,

Pennsylvania. The death of Gabriel Manigault in 1809 was the most severe of several blows, as childhood diseases and consumption diminished the family to three surviving children.[45] Such shifts from shadow to substance lay in the future, however. Until 1805 the concern was fashion and form. The discourse of Margaret Manigault and Josephine du Pont thus coincided happily with the decade of undress. Its story is one of fashion in its formative stages, of individual creativity and taste. At that time the fabric of contemporary style was slight indeed, but its artful utilization by two perceptive ladies establishes a flattering portrait of two merveilleuses in America.

[44] Victor du Pont supplied provisions for the French forces in Santo Domingo, only to have the French government refuse payment in 1803. Also, Napoleon failed to recognize as legitimate debts the money advanced to his brother by Victor du Pont's firm. Lack of profit from several voyages on top of the overwhelming expenses incurred by advances to the French government meant the failure of Victor du Pont de Nemours & Co. of New York in August 1805.

[45] Edward Manigault died in 1808; Emma in 1815; Caroline in 1817; Charlotte in 1819; and Elizabeth Manigault Morris with her ten-year-old son Lewis perished in a hurricane at Sullivan's Island in September 1822. Of a total of twelve children, only Henry and Charles Manigault and Harriet Manigault Wilcocks survived their mother.

The Correspondence

Mrs. Victor du Pont to Mrs. Gabriel Manigault
(in French)
Bordeaux   30 July 1798

Finally, my kind friend,[46] separated by an immense sea and deprived perhaps forever of the happiness of seeing you again,[47] I at least glimpse the possibility of a chat with you and sending this letter safely and promptly.

Mrs. Pin[c]kney, who will deliver it,[48] will tell you how well fate served in bringing about our meeting here, how happy I was to find her, and what pleasure I had speaking of you, your dear family, of that lovely Carolina. But first I owe you some details concerning our crossing. You may have learned from a ship, which we met in the river nearing Bordeaux and which was bound for Philadelphia, that it took us 26 days. The winds from the Grand Banks on were constantly favorable; we met only a Jersey corsair which, thanks to our lucky star and the eloquence of our captain, respected our diplomatic status. Two days later we entered the river. Almost in port, an ignorant river pilot threw our ship onto a sand bar. We would be marooned there yet had it not been for the energy, the ability of the crew and help from a frigate moored nearby. On that occasion I acquired a rather good reputation for courage by taking the situation calmly and refusing to flee with almost all the women, whom fear piled into the lifeboats. I decided in advance that I and my poor little children would be very unhappy in such a melee, and I maintained a serene exterior to the end, although the ship was absolutely on its side and Mr. Du Pont had left it to go by dory to ask the frigate captain for a lifeboat to transport us there. . . . But it is time to leave for the second time that Noah's ark, where we were 103 passengers, among whom were

about 30 women and 23 children, not counting 17 dogs, 1 goat, 2 sheep, 5 parrots, 3 canaries, 7 squirrels. Who but the French would think of traveling thus accompanied! . . . If I see a "spectacle," it seems I only partially enjoy it without you. In the shops, your absence is perhaps felt even more keenly because I remember those sweet moments of friendship, of conversation as we did our errands. When I meet these pretty merveilleuses—I feel a renewed need to judge them with you, to know what you would think of the present fashion. As for me, I think it is not altogether that simple and noble kind of dress we like. At least there is enough elegance, prettiness, becoming styles. When I look at myself with my blond wig, my hat or my bonnet, which adorns the back of my head more than the front, my black crepe shawl trimmed with [rows of ? . . .] cloak lace sewn edge to edge, my flat shoes, my robe hiked at the side—I am not absolutely displeased with the effect. . . .

Mrs. Victor du Pont to Mrs. Gabriel Manigault
(in French)
Paris   25 August 1798

. . . In the same house [as the rest of the du Pont family] we occupy a rather nice, small four-room apartment, which we more or less had to commandeer.[49] I am comfortable and independent. We meet together for meals. Our plans and projects for the future are, and can only be, uncertain. Those of the family are equally in suspense. My husband feels the disfavor of the government towards his father.[50] Nevertheless his [own] conduct and his administration have been praised. . . . In the meantime, we breathe the air of this country with pleasure enough, and we are getting back somewhat into the mainstream. I must admit my dear friend, Paris is most fascinating, and everything that is style, spectacle, promenade is truly enchanting. Oh, how I miss you at every turn. I would be somewhat ashamed to [write] so enthusiastically about this Paris if the authority of Mme. [Pinckney] did not give me some confidence. She will speak of it more

---

[46] Both Margaret Manigault and Josephine du Pont frequently buried the salutation in the opening sentence of their letters.

[47] Josephine du Pont did not expect to see America again. After her husband's diplomatic appointment was revoked, the couple hoped to arrive in Paris soon enough to dissuade his family from their plans to emigrate.

[48] Mary (Stead) Pinckney was in Bordeaux to embark on her return trip to Charleston. Her husband, Charles Cotesworth Pinckney, a principal in the XYZ affair, had spent months trying to negotiate in Paris to ease tensions between America and France.

[49] There was an acute housing shortage in Paris. The du Ponts lived temporarily at the Hôtel d'Angivillers, rue de l'Oratoire.

[50] Victor du Pont's father, Pierre Samuel du Pont de Nemours (1739–1817), had been imprisoned at La Force following the coup d'état of September 4, 1797. He resigned from the Conseil des Anciens nine days later, withdrew from public affairs, and laid plans for the family's emigration.

FIG. 8. A. Lynch, etching of Parisian merveilleuses. Plate opposite page 32 from Octave Uzanne, *The Frenchwoman of the Century* (London: John C. Nimmo, 1886). (Photo, Winterthur.)

favorably than you might have expected. Assuredly I believe that there are some extraordinary and rather shocking occurrences [Fig. 8]. But those details do not strike anyone who does not seek them. The public places offer nothing indecent, strange costumes are outmoded, and in general women's fashions are very pretty. The men have exactly the same appearance as our American "*merveilleux*" and Mr. Du Pont discovered he was like everyone else with his short Titus haircut. The women have them too, and this fashion is extremely convenient, especially when we have a wig for the sake of variety. The Grecian hairdos, which Mme. P[inckney] likes so much, are absolutely out of style. White hats are very much in vogue, and rather like the one I sent you, except that they are smaller. Little fantasy bonnets, which I like immensely, are being worn, but I would not know how to describe them to you since there are no two alike. They are tied under the chin and are very becoming.

I have already seen Tivoli, the Elysée, Bagatelle. Some shows. All brilliant indeed. The first two are charming gardens, perfectly illuminated, where there are concerts, balls, fireworks displays. I finally saw Mme. Tallien,[51] who did not seem as deliciously pretty as we had been led to believe. Nor did her toilette have anything very remarkable about it. In addition, there are a Mme. de Noailles,[52] a Mme. Récamier, and two others,[53] who receive the plaudits. I think no matter what is said that there is still very good company in Paris. Mme. de Staël has a rather nice salon. . . .[54] I have rediscovered some society here, but the great misfortune is that everything costs so much money. As we have so little, we have decided very sagely to take care of our harvests in the country,[55] where we shall stay until winter. . . . Madame Adet[56] who used to

be so cool made a great effort to welcome me. You would never believe it, but they have a great desire to go back to America. Apropos, good Pétry is here.[57] Mr. Du Pont has seen him. I believe he would prefer to be in Charleston. . . . A few days ago we had a very interesting visit from Mme. de La Fayette[58] and her daughter. They lunched with my mother-in-law and they, too, would like very much to be in your country, as would so many others. For despite all the brilliant and tranquil exterior there is still a residue of fomentation and the Jacobins again threaten, but [here a large portion of the MS is torn, as Mrs. du Pont continues, and on the verso discusses availability, style and cost of furniture]. . . . There is the loveliest mirror I have ever seen [see Fig. 9], one which goes forward and backwards at will, decorated in white marble and in gilded brass, at a cost of ten louis.[59] A small [veneer?] secretary, the handsomest commodes, a chiffonier costs from fifteen to twenty [louis]. Charming mahogany chairs with green leather for two [louis] apiece. So you will still have a good many things for your two hundred guineas.[60] Don't forget that I am ready to serve you in anything you wish to request, and I look forward to doing so. . . .

Mrs. Victor du Pont to Mrs. Gabriel Manigault (in French)

Paris   10 Dec. 1798

. . . Just recently I went to two balls, usually peopled by the most brilliant and the best. We fell badly. They were sparsely attended, and the women danced less well and were less elegant than I expected. I was consoled at the opening of the Opera. There the women were perfectly and very richly

[51] Thérésa Cabarrús Tallien (1773–1835), known as "Notre-Dame de Thermidor," was an influential social figure during the Directory and the early Bonaparte years.

[52] Perhaps Mme. de Noailles, née de Laborde.

[53] Perhaps Mesdames Longe and Hamelin.

[54] The manuscript is torn. Josephine du Pont notes that her father-in-law intends to take her with him to the famed de Staël salon.

[55] At the du Pont property, Bois-des-Fossés, in the Loiret.

[56] Mme. Pierre Auguste Adet, wife of the former French minister to the United States, under whom Victor du Pont served as first secretary of legation in 1795.

[57] Jean Baptiste Pétry, consul for Philadelphia until President Adams revoked his exequatur in 1798, had previously lived in Charleston.

[58] Marie Adrienne Françoise de Noailles, Marquise de La Fayette, was less than a year removed from imprisonment at Olmütz, where one of her husband's companions in detention had been Jean Xavier Bureaux de Pusy, son-in-law of Mme. Pierre Samuel du Pont de Nemours.

[59] Probably this is "The 'Psyche,' a pier glass swinging loosely in a standing frame, the idea of which had only been possible since technique had discovered how to cut sheets of glass of sufficient size for it." [Von Boehn], *Modes & Manners of the Nineteenth Century*, 1:72; The value of the louis d'or was about twenty francs, or $4.80.

[60] A guinea was approximately $5.00.

Fig. 9. Merveilleuse leaning on a cheval glass. Pencil sketch, probably by one of the daughters of E. I. du Pont after a fashion plate ca. 1800. H. 8", W. 5". (Eleutherian Mills Historical Library.)

trimmed *vitchouras.* Bonnets are likewise Turkish,[61] a velvet base surrounded by organdy or fur. *Titus* hairdos, or crops, are coming into vogue. Little blond wigs, which invariably take ten years off the age of the wearer, are the most popular, but no longer those with corkscrew curls. The dresses are made in different ways, but most generally they are still "chemises." The women who do not leave their arms bare resort to silk sleeves held in place by very small fichus [bands]. Rounded figures are required; the women eat heavily to fatten themselves. You can imagine how attractive one must be to stand a dress without a single bit of lace around it, although one can keep from looking indecent by the way it is made.

I beg you, on my recommendation, make a dress with a wide redingote back cut in front like Mme. Pinck[ney's]. But instead of its being open and overlapped, it must be closed, with very few folds in front so that it clings like a redingote. Then sew four rows of white satin baby ribbon from [the midpoint? MS torn] of the waist to the bottom in the middle of the front and [MS torn] distance apart so as to make it appear that the dress is open and held together only by bobbins [MS torn]. . . . If you have too much trouble executing the redingote shape, you can make a chemise-type dress with long sleeves. At present I am having some fine dimity, which I brought back from Philadelphia, dyed a pale pink, and I intend making the above arrangement with white and pink bobbins and a little fringe around it. Remaking almost all my dresses without great expenditures, I find myself just about as well dressed as others. You think, I wager, of the lack of a carriage, which is indeed sad. But the two women with whom I go out have cabriolets. And on occasions when one must appear to perfection, very good carriages can be found to rent. Nothing is more ordinary than being three in a cabriolet. It is wide enough not to be too crowded, and one of our husbands takes us. I was going to mention my teas. In spite of my small lodging, I sometimes gather 7 or 8 for *brelan* [card game similar to poker], and then I make tea. It is as pleasant and more varied than such an undertaking can be in America because having several different groups of acquaintances, I can assort them in various ways. . . .

attired, generally in lovely muslins with a great abundance of necklaces and pendant earrings of diamonds, cameos, or black stones surrounded by large fine pearls. [They wore] velvet hats, many poppy-colored, draped in white satin with superb white feathers as long as we were wearing them in America but curved and falling from the hat like weeping willows. They are also wearing some of those peacock feathers that are so common where you are. The most beautiful cost up to [MS torn]. . . . [Dresses were] superb, solid pastel muslin, with the lining wider than the ones Mme. Pinckney brought you. To drape one well is truly an art. Coming out of the theater, the women who are so lightly clad find nice little wadded redingotes at the door. The most elegant are Turkish-style, fur-

[61] Turkish- and Egyptian-style influences rivaled neoclassical trends as Bonaparte's campaigns drew attention to the eastern Mediterranean.

Mrs. Manigault to Mrs. du Pont
(in English)
Sullivan's Island   24 July 1798[62]

. . . The wide ocean now separates us, and we perhaps may never meet. . . . Even should fate join us once more, it is much pleasanter to grow old together, and to slide insensibly from the enjoyments and pleasures of youth into those of a different season than to be mortified by the alteration which even a few years' absence will make visible. These reflections are rather gloomy, and I reproach myself for imparting them. I must tell you by way of excuse that it has been raining hard, and blowing all the morning, and you must recollect that Sullivan's Island is not very enlivening upon these occasions. You will perhaps wonder at my being here. It was not that I found our house in Charleston too warm, but my little Emma[63] was cutting teeth, and was exceedingly indisposed, and Dr. Baron[64] advised change of air. . . . I am in Mr. J[oseph] M[anigault]'s house, we had lent ours to my brother Harry;[65] he, his wife and his little child propose staying as long as I do. We are very good neighbours, very sociable, and agreeable, I assure you. We dine and sup together every day and like each other much. I hear nothing of the animals upon our list. . . . The Papillon[66] is now endeavoring to amuse itself with another flower, fair, delicate and soft, as the other was dark, strong, and not soft. Were you to hear his raptures! His encomiums on the delicate nose of his new charmer; he who thought a nose of very little consequence. You don't know this novelty. I never saw her, but they say she is really beautiful. She strums a little upon a spinet. In speaking of her accomplishments, he magnifies that paltry instrument to a piano. Ainsi du reste, I suppose. . . . I am in some hopes of your meeting my friend [Mme. Pinckney] at Bordeaux. It will be a great comfort to her to meet you before she departs, and by her, you may safely write. You know that the money, which was sent to Paris to buy furniture, was put into her hands, when she arrived there. I have very lately heard from her that she never employed it (unless perhaps a small part of it to buy a few books for me, but of which I am not certain). It was at one time placed in the hands of a banker. As we now have no inclination for furniture, Mr. M[anigault] wishes that wherever the money may be, your companion could manage so as to get possession of it, and hold it as his own, considering his right to it as founded on his having left equal to that in Mr. M.'s hands here. Mr. M. will do the same on his part. . . . I need explain this no farther; the prudential motive which occasions it, must easily be perceived. . . .[67] You will see some [people] of your acquaintance. Perhaps a very great friend of yours, of gothic mien,[68] may come, and ask me for commands. If so, I shall pen an epistle on purpose for him. . . . My sister[69] passed a week with me since I came here. Mrs. Blake, two Mrs. Wrights, Miss Middletons and we have had the celebrated Claudia.[70] We likewise have a fine

---

[62] During the summer months there was an exodus from Charleston because of yellow fever epidemics. As did other wealthy Charlestonians, Gabriel and Margaret Manigault owned a home on Sullivan's Island. The du Ponts visited them there in 1796. Manigault diaries, vol. 1, Acc. 502, EMHL. These excerpts are arranged as they were received and answered by Mrs. du Pont, and not in chronological order.

[63] Emma Manigault (1797–1815).

[64] Alexander Baron, of 124 Queen Street, was described by La Rochefoucauld-Liancourt as "a Scotchman, and physician of great celebrity in Charleston, where, it is asserted, he makes thirteen thousand dollars a year." François de La Rochefoucauld-Liancourt, *Travels Through the United States of North America . . . in the years 1795, 1796, and 1797*, 4 vols. (London: R. Phillips, 1800), 2:435.

[65] Henry Izard (1771–1826) brother of Margaret Manigault, was the first of the family to become acquainted with Victor du Pont, who mentioned Henry in the journal of his 1791 trip to the United States in the retinue of the Comte de Moustier. WMSS 3/D, EMHL. Henry Izard's wife was Emma Middleton.

[66] Probably George Izard (1776–1828), Margaret Mani-

gault's brother, whose attraction to the musically talented Ninette Peïre (see note 79) had distressing consequences in 1802, when the lady's brother challenged him to a duel. George Izard survived his wounds, married the widow Shippen, and became governor of the Arkansas Territory.

[67] These were the years of the quasi-war, when Franco-American relations were strained almost to the breaking point. In case war actually erupted, du Pont funds left in Charleston would serve to cancel out Manigault funds in du Pont hands in France. Thus funds of both families would be secure.

[68] Louis Augustin Guillaume Bosc d'Antic (1759–1828), French naturalist, was formerly vice-consul of France in Wilmington, N.C., and lived for a time in Charleston. He is also referred to as "the uncouth friend" and "the Ostrogoth" in the letters.

[69] Anne Izard Deas (1779–1862), sister of Margaret Manigault.

[70] Of these prominent South Carolina planter family names, both the Blakes and the Middletons were related to Margaret Manigault. Claudia Smith later became the second

little curricle [wheeled chaise usually drawn by two horses] belonging to Mr. Nisbett.[71] There is a little billiard room to which the gentlemen resort in the morning. Sometimes after having met in the afternoon to drink wine, they establish a whist. I know somebody [Victor du Pont] who would like the life they lead here very well, particularly as guns, and segars are not excluded and as oysters are very fine, and in great abundance. I wish that somebody had a good house, and a horse and chair &c &c here. But alas! . . . Let me know how your piano does and whether you find any improvement had been made in music during your absence. I have seen nothing new since those variations of Dussek.[72] Let me know when you hear a finer voice than Mlle. Remoussin's,[73] and a more agreeable performer. I am told that they give very much into the genre bouffon in France now. Is it true? . . .

Mrs. du Pont to Mrs. Manigault
(in French)
Paris,   18 April 1799

. . . You will undoubtedly be surprised to learn that part of our family will have crossed the ocean without our being part of that avant-garde. . . .[74] We have decided not to leave until October, when we hope all the political differences will be entirely "settled" and will make for harmony between our two nations.

I have great need of your example and your courage to be completely resigned to an increase in family at this time;[75] my children are so young, our position so unstable in the foreseeable future that such an event necessarily complicates our plans and makes them difficult for me. . . . Yet I will vow to

you, my friend, the pleasure it gives me just to think of being closer to you, of adopting as my native land a happy and peaceful country, of raising my children there sheltered from the vices and corruptions here, of rebuilding there an independent fortune, and finally of being well received. . . . I cannot conceal from you that it would be perhaps very painful to me if they did not give Mr. Du Pont all the credit due him for the chivalrous devotion with which he has constantly defended the American cause since his return [to France] and the efforts he has expended to be useful to individuals as well. . . .[76] I have received from you only one letter written from Sullivan['s Island], brought by Cairoche[77] and which he kept for two months before delivering it because it was in some trunks that were held up. I cannot believe you have not written more often. . . . This latest conformity of our situations pleases me and encourages me in the new task that awaits me. . . .[78] I intend to raise the babe entirely in the American manner and teach him to eat biscuit as soon as he arrives in the world. . . . On the subject of fashion, I am sending you some issues from my collection [possibly *Bon Genre* caricatures], which is far from the attractiveness and truth of your Gallery of Fashion but which, though somewhat in the vein of caricatures, may give you some slight idea of the trends of the moment . . . I am also sending a fan which, entirely unworthy of its brilliant destiny will perhaps recall me to your mind in the midst of some tumultuous assembly. . . . I am still not at all consoled over your not having a piece of furniture. They excel in this line [see Fig. 10]. The Greek beds are truly delightful and almost all the shapes of chairs and furniture are new. . . .

---

wife of Henry Izard. The Mrs. Wrights were probably of the family of Chief Justice Robert Wright of South Carolina.

[71] Perhaps Sir John Nesbit of Dean Hall, a South Carolina horseman, who was very popular among the ladies.

[72] Jean Louis Dussek (1761–1812), Czech pianist and composer, was acclaimed in turn-of-the-century Paris.

[73] Perhaps the daughter of Daniel Remoussin, 29 Blausain Street. *Charleston Directory*, 1801.

[74] Mme. du Pont de Nemours, her son-in-law Bureaux de Pusy, and her granddaughter Sara sailed from Rotterdam on May 10, 1799. Despite their ship's being detained for six weeks by the English, they arrived in New York well ahead of the rest of the family.

[75] On June 1, Josephine du Pont gave birth to a son, Samuel François du Pont, who lived but five days.

[76] During the year Victor du Pont spent in France before emigrating in 1799, much of his time was occupied in defending the cause of captured American ship captains and seamen and securing their release.

[77] Etienne Cairoche, agent of the French consulate in Charleston, was left in charge when Victor du Pont departed for Philadelphia in 1797.

[78] Mrs. Manigault was pregnant when she wrote in July 1798.

FIG. 10. A. Lynch, etching of Parisian ladies at home. Plate opposite page 68 from Octave Uzanne, *The French-woman of the Century* (London: John C. Nimmo, 1886). (Photo, Winterthur.)

Mrs. Manigault to Mrs. du Pont
(in English)
Charleston 15 April 1799

If this letter ever reaches you, my dear friend, it will be through the good offices of Miss Ninette Peïre.[79] She offered yesterday to enclose it to a relation of hers at Hambourg. About a fortnight ago, Mr. Morphy[80] did the same to his brother at Cadiz. . . . I every day lament the impracticability of keeping up a regular intercourse. . . . Do you know that Mrs. Pinckney has recd. letters repeatedly from her friends in France? The only two I have recd. from you were that by Mrs. P. & one written immediately after your arrival at Paris. . . . Charleston has been, & is much more particularly dull than usual. Yet they play at le grand Mufti [high fashion] & la Musique. A propos of the last—I have got my harp in order, & amuse myself with it—but I have no strings except those which are on it, & they will not last long. I have taken up another old occupation too. I have worked several gowns au tambour—that is, a border in color'd worsteds,[81] & I like the employment much. How [does?] your little Piano succeed? I still have mine but look [to buy?] one of our friend Bradford's grandissimos.[82] He had a collection of them taken at Sea about 2 months ago, with Harps, & strings, & music. And I lost a fine pacotille [parcel of goods] in the same way. When shall we see the end of all these troubles? When shall we shake hands, & make friends again? Have you seen the Ostrogoth? I am reading *L'Etude de la Nature* of Bernardin de St. Pierre,[83] & Mrs. P. & I are going this week to visit the jardin de la République.[84] My garden improves. I expect

one of these days to receive a precious cargo from the uncouth friend, & I really believe he was sincere. Our modes change almost as rapidly here as they do with you. The English fashions are—No, I must not tell you what they are. . . .

Mrs. Manigault to Mrs. du Pont
(in English)
Charleston 11 May 1799

It is from Mrs. Pinckney's house that I write to you, my ever dear, & amiable Friend. She is not well, & I am nursing her. . . . It appears to me that there is nothing in the new world worth writing about. Yet, I would fain tell you something of those you know. Mme. de Pes[tre],[85] Mrs. Mor[phy] & Mlle. Nin[ette Peïre], are all gone to Mr. de Pes—'s house in the country. He bought a place about 8 miles from Town, to which you may go either by land or water, with a house of 4 rooms, 2 cabinets, & a Piazza with several &c very pleasantly situated for about £150. I wish you had such a one, & such a house in town, & such a little carriage. . . . I must tell you about your sweet neighbour, Mrs. Legare.[86] She bought old Lefevre's[87] carriage, thinking, I suppose, that when one had that, it was the easiest thing in the world to borrow a pair of horses, a coachman now, — then from ones neighbours. She sent her compliments & asked for mine, one morning. She had them, & after driving her about sometime, they returned, with her comp[limen]ts again, & "she would be very very much obliged to me if I would lend them to her now, & then, morning, or

[79] Ninette Peïre, of a wealthy Santo Domingo emigrant family, lived with her sister, Mrs. Diego Morphy. Her mother, remarried, and four step-brothers were also in Charleston. Louis Manigault, "Family History," 3 vols. (Original copy in the Charleston Museum, Charleston, S.C.) Photoprint in Acc. 149, EMHL, 1:232–46.

[80] Don Diego Morphy, Spanish consul in Charleston, was godfather to the Victor du Ponts' son, Charles Irénée.

[81] This embroidery consists of looped stitches similar to chain stitch worked with a fine hook on a frame.

[82] Thomas Bradford's music store was at 76 Church Street. *Charleston Directory*, 1801.

[83] Jacques Henri Bernardin de St. Pierre, the French novelist, was related to Josephine du Pont by his marriage to her niece, Charlotte Désirée de La Fite de Pelleport.

[84] "At some distance from the road [to Charleston] lies a garden, where a French botanist, who is paid by the French government, raises the trees of the country from the seed as well as layers, and sends them to Mr. Thouin at Paris. . . .

This garden answers extremely well the views of Mr. Thouin, to domesticate in France the greatest possible number of the productions of all countries, for which purpose he has formed nurseries in the French dominions, under different degrees of latitude, to accustom exotic plants to the French climate by insensible degrees." La Rochefoucauld-Liancourt, *Travels Through the United States*, 2:434–35.

[85] Mme. de Pestre, described by Mrs. du Pont as "my most mortal enemy," was disliked by Mrs. Manigault as well, and labeled La Guêpe. Her husband was active in the Charleston Jockey Club. Josephine du Pont to Margaret Manigault, Apr. 26, 1800, WMSS 3/D, EMHL.

[86] Probably Mrs. Thomas Legaré, 50 Tradd Street. *Charleston Directory*, 1801.

[87] Perhaps Stephen Lefevre, merchant, 171 Meeting Street. The elderly Mr. Lefevre, respected friend and correspondent of Victor du Pont, is not fully identified. His letters deal especially with French-American-Spanish affairs. WMSS 3/A, EMHL.

an evening." I thought of the figs . . .[88] I won't tell you what else I did. . . .

How goes on Music? I have been buying a collection of very excellent music this morning—6 volumes bound. With what pleasure should I play it over with you. I am grown very fond of my Tambour work, in color'd worsted. So if you have any new patterns I will work them. . . . We all talk of you very often. Do they wear Mamelouc cloaks, & Egyptian head dresses with you? Our fashions make momies of us. I wish I could send you a leaf of the Gallery of Fashion. It looks like a Kamochatka girl who is going to be married. And some of our gentlemen (Mr. J[oseph] M[anigault] & B[ee])[89] pore over it with delight, and pronounce it charming.

Mrs. Manigault to Mrs. du Pont
(in English)
Charleston   22 Dec. 1799

[Thank] you for your kind, & amiable letter by your mother, & for . . . the beautiful fan, & for the curious, & entertaining, & astonishing, & very acceptable Costumes Parisiens. They have amused my company & afforded me several hints. We think one of the gentlemen very like Mr. Du Pont. . . . I think with very great pleasure of your return to America. It will be satisfactory to inhabit the same Continent, to live under the same Government. But you seem to have very little idea of this our state. And I cannot help lamenting that. In point of climate I think there is little choice. They have the Yellow Fever in all the large Cities to the Northward. Here we had it last year, but still confined to Strangers.[90] And we have the resource of Sullivan's Island. . . . I was interrupted by that Brother [George Izard] who at this moment engrosses all our attention—He is appointed Aide de Camp to Genl. [Alexander] Hamilton, & is exceed-

ingly well pleased to have so pleasant a station as that of Elizabeth Town 15 miles from New York. . . . As for our French Society . . . La Cigalle[91] is very domestic & very happy as far as we know. I have not seen her since she gave birth to a little boy. She & her husband live in a small comfortable house in Tradd Street. He is extremely industrious, & a very good husband. Takes lodgers, boarders, scholars. Teaches drawing, & music, & French. Plays at the Theatre, at the Concert, with the Military Band. Does every thing, & is esteemed. . . . La Guêpe—Nobody ever sees. Except on horse back with a red Spencer. Janry 1 1800 It is to you that I dedicate my first leisure moments in this new Century. May it bring to you ease, tranquility, health, plenty, & every good that ever blessed the happiest among the most favored mortals! . . .

You recollect Mr. Daniel Bl[ake] who was engaged to be married to Miss Middleton.[92] He is lately returned—just as he went. All the Mid—s went into the Country to pass the Christmas holydays as is very much the custom here. Miss Mid— alone insisted upon staying in Town, actually did stay by herself in their house. One would think she had had a presentiment of what was to happen. On Christmas day as she was sitting writing to her Mother—without being announced even by the arrival of a vessel, (for he came to Town in a boat, & left his vessel over the Bar) who should appear but Mr. Bl— and there will soon be a wedding certainly. . . .

You have brought out a fine collection of new music I dare say—and books—What is there de nouveau, et de joli? Have you read a novel of Mme. de Genlis called "Rash vows" or "The dangers of Enthusiasm"?[93] It is an interesting thing. How I should have liked to give you a few commissions! And I know, my friend, that you would have been kind enough to take pleasure in executing them. It was very mortifying, after having destined a small sum to ones fancies, & little enjoyments, to have it returned untouched.

[88] Charleston fig trees were proclaimed by Mrs. du Pont to produce the most delicious fruit in America. The specific incident referred to here is not known.

[89] Joseph Manigault (1763–1843) was the only brother of Gabriel Manigault. Judge Thomas Bee, former lieutenant governor of South Carolina, was closely connected with the development of the College of Charleston. He and Joseph Manigault served together as trustees. The college, chartered in 1785, held its first commencement in 1794. Harriott Horry [Rutledge] Ravenel, *Charleston, the Place and the People, by Mrs. St. Julien Ravenel* (New York: Macmillan, 1907), p. 348.

[90] Foreign residents of Charleston and newcomers.

[91] Mme. Labatut, wife of Peter Labatut (or Labattut), drawing master, 37 Blausain Street. *Charleston Directory,* 1802.

[92] The Blakes were among the leading South Carolina planter families, as were the Middletons.

[93] Stéphanie Félicité Ducrest de St. Aubain, Comtesse de Genlis, afterwards Marquise de Sillery (1746–1830), popular and prolific French novelist, published *Les Voeux Téméraires, ou l'Enthousiasme* in 1799. *Rash Vows,* the English translation, appeared the same year.

A certain Ostrogoth of botanizing memory promised without any provocation, to send me books, & plants, whenever any opportunity offer'd. But he would not trust you I suppose. . . .

Mr. Bee has the prospect of making the College a respectable seminary. He has two clergymen from England, one of whom promises to be an acquisition to society. He himself, Mr. Bee, excepting that he is twice as large, is in every respect just as you left him. . . .

Mrs. du Pont to Mrs. Manigault
(in French)
New York   27 Jan. 1800

What good fortune led you, my dear friend, to charge your brother with the charming letter he was kind enough to deliver to me while you thought us still at the mercy of the waves, or not even yet put to sea, or detained in England! How kind it was of you, and what pleasure you gave us! . . . You are well and no disruptive event seems to have troubled the serenity, the happiness and the union you so enjoyed when I left you. May you long remain the picture and the model of domestic felicity, of kind virtues, of good social order, and may I once again see and emulate [you] . . . I believe I explained the reason that forced us to divide [for the voyage]. . . . We found [our friends][94] well and settled in a rather pretty country place they had just acquired, situated at Berghen Point on the arm of the sea that separates the island of New York from the continent and faces Staten Island. We have christened it Good Stay. The crossing by sea takes ¾ hours when the wind is good, 3 hours when it is contrary. The history of this little establishment is rather curious: two Frenchmen (formerly men of quality, now woodcutters, carpenters, boatmen, but still good company on occasion) created it almost with their bare hands, planted the garden in excellent fruit trees, finished the house &c &c. One is the brother of Mde. de Maulde, my mother-in-law's friend. . . .[95] They began by ceding a lodging and ended by selling. [Our family] immediately decided to enlarge this house by two small

wings so as to make it habitable in the summer for our four families. Mr. de Puzy[96] is directing the project and promises it will be ready in three months. They are all there, except for our staying here. We need country mice and city mice, and we will be the latter in our small colony. . . . So for our part we are very happy to have our small town house where we will keep a stopping-off place for those going and coming from Good Stay. But since there is no perfect joy we are as contraried as we were when we arrived in Charleston by the impossibility of finding a house vacant. In the meantime we are in a rather bad pension where our friends debarked[97] and where I fear we will be obliged to spend yet another two weeks. At the present time there is available only some houses that the fever ravaged; we have been led to believe that by February 1st we will easily find something. . . . *Les Costhumes Parisiens* [see Fig. 11] pleased you? I thought it would. Unfortunately I have the latest issues only as they are <u>modified</u> for my own use. I doubt, even though they may be nothing less than extreme, to be able to make much use of them here. From the little I have seen, the women are rather poorly got up, and I find as much difference between their appearance and what I left in Charleston as there is between Paris and here.

If you were here we would try to incite a small revolution in this sphere, but alone there is no way. Prejudice against French fashion would be too heavy against me. In my discouragement were the season not so far along I would have sent you a box containing, among other things, a "very smart" nacarat velvet hat with white gillyflowers. It will not be appreciated here, I assure you, for the women seem perfectly happy with their antique white-powdered floating chignons, their immense hats, &c. &c., which are dated by at least 10 years. You ask me for news of the Ostrogoth. I saw him four times in all, twice as the spoiled child of the Directory and two others as persecuted by the Jacobins; "it is a fact," but the most curious part of

[94] The advance party of the du Pont family, Mme. du Pont de Nemours, her son-in-law Jean Xavier Bureaux de Pusy (1750–1806), and his small daughter.

[95] This Frenchman was probably Charles Henri Lambert Marie Preudhomme de Borre (1755–1816). The other is unknown.

[96] Bureaux de Pusy was trained as an engineer in the course of his military education. During his residence at Goodstay he was asked to serve as consultant on the fortifications for the city of New York.

[97] Victor du Pont's account book indicates that his family boarded in New York with a Mrs. Shakerly. Longwood Manuscripts (hereafter LMSS) 2/B, EMHL; *Longworth's City Almanac* for 1800 lists a J. H. Shackerly, merchant, 76 Maiden Lane and 15 Liberty Street, the address to which several du Pont letters were directed.

(284)

FIG. 11. *Coeffure en Fichu. Spencer de Velours* ("Scarf headdress and velvet spencer.") Plate 284 from *Costume Parisien*, ed. Pierre Antoine Leboux de La Mésangère (Paris, 1800). Colored etching; H. 6½", W. 4". (Eleutherian Mills Historical Library.)

his story pertains to a trip prompted by his friend La Reveillière in order to influence the elections. He collected (while botanizing I suppose) a petite 16- or 17-year-old Languedoc girl of burnished visage who speaks a Gascon patois that even he does not understand. He wrapped her up like his other insects in the diligence that was leaving the next day for Paris, where he married her upon arrival.[98]

[98] Louis-Marie de Lareveillière-Lépeaux (1753–1824) was in the waning days of his power in the Directory. Departmental assemblies in France were selecting electors in the weeks prior to the meeting of the electoral assembly on April 11. Bosc d'Antic married, on April 9, 1799, his cousin Suzanne Bosc.

He saw us afterwards, without opening his mouth concerning this fine novel. . . .

You cannot regret any more than I that I could not receive your shopping list. With what pleasure I would have chosen some of those lovely pieces of Greek-inspired furniture.[99] I am equally sorry not to have given in to the temptation of bringing some for us, but the danger of seizure on leaving a French port would really have been too great. I held out only for my faithful piano, which has enjoyed a certain success in my little circle and which I brought here safe and sound, but with precious little new music. As for new books, Mr. D. P. has a few. I think some of them are very unusual ones worthy of an armoire built especially to contain them; it will fortunately not have to be very large. The rest are English translations of those insignificant novels which, like bad wines, cannot stand the sea voyage. We do, however, have a consignment of Mr. de Liancourt's work. . . .[100]

[99] "The language, the table, the furniture, all was become the prey of the fashion. . . . Did she dress in Greek style? at once the furniture must be Greek. Did she assume the Turkish turban and tunic? immediately the sofas and carpets of Turkey displayed their dazzling colors. Did she dress herself in the Egyptian manner? mummies must make their appearances, sphinxes, clocks in monolith, and her reception-room was furnished on the instant like an Arab tent. The favorite piece of furniture was the bed, which was ordinarily of citron or of mahogany, boat-shaped, with ornaments of pure gold, finely chased; cashmeres and Indian muslins, bordered with lace, were used for curtains; the pillows were covered with Brussels point; the counterpanes were of bordered satin." Uzanne, *The Frenchwoman of the Century*, p. 75. Neither Mrs. du Pont nor Mrs. Manigault evinced literal adherence to such French styles of the Consulate period. Rather, availability, practicality, and the ever-present English influences dictated a more eclectic approach to fashions and furnishings.

[100] L'Imprimerie de du Pont, the printing establishment operated by E. I. du Pont prior to the family's emigration, published the Duc de La Rochefoucauld-Liancourt's *Voyage dans les Etats-Unis d'Amérique fait en 1795, 1796, et 1797* in 1799. Disposition of a consignment of fifty sets is recorded by Victor du Pont in his record of accounts in 1800. Of these, eight sets were "sent to Paine in Charleston." LMSS 2/B, EMHL.

Mrs. Manigault to Mrs. du Pont
(in English)
Charleston   8 Feb. 1800

. . . I saw last night M. Fournier & M. Vandoeuvre[101]—They both appeared delighted to hear of your safe arrival—They are comfortably settled, & live together in a small house which they hire. . . . You have certainly had the advantage of seeing Mme. La Heuse,[102] who has told you every interesting particular about herself, rendered still more interesting by her agreeable person, & manner. . . . Mme. de Pestre gives a great ball tonight. I dont know how she means to people it. None of those that I know are going—not even B[ee], who seemed a little hurt at being left out of the question. . . . To shew you how well the reputation of the buzzing animal is established, she used to wear a wig (for I can find no figurative expression) but got tired of it, & carried it to Miss Van Rhyn[103] to sell. I saw the dirty little horror there, & asked who in the world could have sent such a fright to her. "Why," said she, "it was —— & she might have spared herself the trouble. For who would wear any thing after her?" Very well observed of the old dutch woman, was it not? I believe there is now but one voice upon the subject. Mme. Labatut keeps very much at home. She is a good Wife, & a good Mother I believe; for she never goes out. . . . And in every respect, we are I think just as you left us. Excepting, & I had almost forgot to mention it, that my drawing room is now disfigured by a grand Piano, whose delicious tone makes us forget its deformity.[104] It is without exception the sweetest, & most powerful instrument I ever heard. My sister's is a mere Chaudron [tinny, old piano] to it. Dont you tell that. But ask my Brother about it. Such a Piano! And a Bass like an Organ. Oh that you could try it! . . . Have not you yourself vested some of your pocket money in fans, ribbons, feathers &c? Where is your house? Who lives in it with you? Who are you intimate with? How do you pass your Evenings? (Remember all the reflections that we made upon the score of too great a seclusion.) You are in good hospitable hands among the Le Roys and Bayards—Pray mention me to both the ladies of that name; They were very [nice] to me when I was in New York,[105] & their bonhommie, their unaffected hospitality, even their boisterous mirth, displaying the genuine goodness of their hearts, won mine. Pray tell them that I should have great pleasure in renewing my acquaintance with them. . . . Mr. D. Bl— was married about a week ago to Miss An— M—n, in the morning, & the new pair travelled off immediately solus cum sola to take possession of a house belonging to them, one room only of which was furnished— . . . We have made the acquisition of a new, & very pleasant member of society—Mrs. Henry Middleton.[106] She was in France, you know, while Mrs. Pinckney was there, & was as much pleased with it as the most partial could desire. She was delighted with the Costumes Parisiens, & says that they give a much more accurate notion of things than the Gallery of Fashion. I had given orders to have some famous sweet Potatoes packed up in a barril, in the hope of recalling poor little Charleston to your mind, & of impressing your dear little children with a favorable opinion of their native soil. . . .[107] There are some good actors here this [winter], & they perform the famous new piece Pizarro[108] to a charm.

---

[105] Herman Le Roy and William Bayard were partners in a leading New York mercantile firm. They handled du Pont mail and shipments in the period immediately following the family's arrival. The Manigaults were in New York from November 1793 through August 1794, according to Mrs. Manigault's diary. Vol. 1, Acc. 502, EMHL.

[106] Mrs. Henry Middleton, before her sojourn in France, held a musicale Wednesday evenings in her Charleston home. Rogers, *Charleston in the Age of the Pinckneys*, p. 112.

[107] Charles Irénée du Pont (1797–1869) was, like his older sister, born in Charleston.

[108] "*Pizarro*, a tragedy taken from the German Drama of Kotzbue and adapted to the English Stage by Richard Brinsley Sheridan," opened on January 24 and played for five days to enthusiastic audiences in Charleston. Mr. Chalmers played the title role; Mrs. Placide had the part of Elvira; Jones painted the scenery. Eola Willis, *The Charleston Stage in the XVIII Century* (Columbia, S.C.: The State Company, 1924), p. 456.

---

[101] John Vandoeuvre is listed in the 1801 *Charleston Directory* as residing at 6 Cumberland Street. Mr. Fournier is not identified.

[102] Mme. La Heuse of Trenton, N.J., not further identified.

[103] Miss A. E. Van Rhyn had a small shop in her home at 134 Broad Street. *Charleston Directory*, 1802.

[104] Grand pianos were then unusual in Charleston. Their bulky, rectangular form might well be considered anomalous to the elegance of an 1800 salon.

Mrs. Manigault to Mrs. du Pont
(in English)

Feb. 24 1800

... Mr. Du Pont has thought of us more than once, I dare say, if he recollected that this was the season of the Races.[109] The knowing ones were taken in as usual—Shark against the field! And Shark, poor Shark, was distanced. Colonel Hampton[110] won the purse every day, & very considerable bets beside. I think if you had been here, you would have been tempted to stake the little Chapeau Nacara, against a splendid Crape Nelson hat with ostrich feathers, & gold Esprit, of the very last importation.[111] I won & lost some gloves, & won a bouquet. I heard that a certain little personage in a little green carriage which she took care to place so that the inhabitant was accessible on all sides, was in the habit of betting jewels.[112] I know that last year she betted the handsomest white, & the handsomest black silk feather (which were known to cost 5 dollars a piece) against a cockade. & she always wins. The races were not very brilliant....

Mme. Buonaparte amused me very much.[113]

---

[109] Race Week in mid-February was the climax of the Charleston social season. While the finest thoroughbreds of the South competed in the racing, balls, suppers, teas, and theater parties abounded. Court adjourned, stores closed, and shopkeepers manned colorful booths at the course built in 1792 by the Jockey Club, where Gabriel Manigault was among the original members. The club secretary noted with justifiable pride that all arrangements were made "to insure good order and etiquette; refinement and high breeding characterized those who prefer lingering about the Grand Stand" as quoted in Robert West Howard, *The Horse in America* (Chicago: Follett Publishing Company, 1965), p. 112.

[110] Wade Hampton (1754–1835), also among the organizers of the Jockey Club, was a famed thoroughbred enthusiast. His backcountry fortune having been enhanced by the location of the state capital at Columbia, Hampton became one of the nation's wealthiest men. George C. Rogers, Jr., *Evolution of a Federalist* (Columbia: University of South Carolina Press, 1962), p. 370.

[111] The victory of Horatio, Lord Nelson, over the French at the Battle of the Nile in 1798 inspired such British fashions as the round, gilt "Nelson balls" so popular as trimmings for hats, spencers, and so on. Whether such trim or a military shape determined the Nelson designation for Margaret Manigault's crepe chapeau is unclear.

[112] Mme. de Pestre. Whereas gentlemen commonly bet money at the races, ladies more modestly wagered their newest fashion accessories. To bet jewels was both extravagant and sensational.

[113] The letter containing Josephine du Pont's comments concerning Joséphine Bonaparte is unfortunately missing from the collections.

What must she be now? Malines brodée will not now serve her purpose. Have you any good entertaining, observing, retailing correspondent in Paris? Certainly you could not leave the old world without providing yourself with that consolation. Did you not abonnée [subscribe] yourself for some amusing journal, for some accounts of the novelties, & curiosities? I should like of all things to be able to do so. .... Pray, do you ever venture out a shopping in New York? And if you do, will you undertake a little commission for me? Nothing more recherché than some french silk stockings. If there should be any good—such as would fit you—I should like one dozen. I missed an opportunity some months ago of providing myself, & now they are extravagantly high here. If you will be good enough to send the account to Mr. Edward Goold, Wall Street, he will pay it.

Were embroidered borders to gowns much the fashion when you left France? We are mighty fond of them here, and I am quite expert in finding out grecian patterns. Do you ever amuse yourself in that way? It is likewise the ton [prevailing fashion, vogue] to work very handsome borders for carpets, & to make the center of green cloth. I must have told you long ago, that Mr. M. had sold the house which he was building opposite to ours when you were here, & which my brother occupied during one year, to a Mr. Ogilvie.[114] His wife is a very charming woman. They are very rich, & just arrived from London, where they saw a great deal of company & lived in a very fashionable style. Their house is completely furnished, & in the most elegant manner. And she gives me particulars of all the pretty little inventions which have lately appeared. We are good neighbours—but I shall never meet with such a neighbour as I once had in an awkward odd-looking house which I never pass without a sigh. That house is now occupied by a Mme. de Beaugirard[115] if I heard the name right. She is of Mme. de Pestre's society; they, Mme. de la Rue (the pretty Melle. Nielle) & a Mme. de Ste. Marie,[116] give balls every week. They dance till 5

---

[114] Alexander Ogilvie lived with his family at 20 George Street. *Charleston Directory*, 1801.

[115] Mme. de Beaugirard succeeded the Victor du Ponts as occupant of the house at 50 Tradd Street. *Charleston Directory*, 1801.

[116] Mme. de la Rue was the daughter of the Santo Domingo planter, P. Niel[le]. Her husband, a Charleston merchant, lived on Meeting Street. *Charleston Directory*, 1801; Mme. de Ste. Marie has not been identified.

o'clock in the morning, until they are almost dead, & then boast how much they have amused themselves. There are many frenchmen of quality. . . . but in general we see very few french now. . . .

Mrs. du Pont to Mrs. Manigault
(in French)
New York   22 Feb. 1800

. . . Now to make my peace with you I am going to tell you a bit of what we are doing in this big city. After having languished nearly 6 weeks in a rather bad pension, we finally found a temporary respite in a "very gloomy house" situated in the very middle of Pearl Street, that is to say in the yellow fever district. Fortunately we have it only till the month of May, and we will leave then for a very nice house on Liberty Street,[117] near North River, which is in a healthy location, large, clean and comfortable. We are renting it for 280 £. There is no extra expenditure to be made, and we expect to be settled a little more decently than we were in Charleston. We will enjoy it very little this year, however, because we are going to spend the summer at Berghen Point, where they are building a small lodging for our use. That, my friend, is where if as your brother told us Mr. Manigault really intended to acquire something in the north, he should buy a small lot, give us his plans and let us build for you a pretty little house which Mr. de Puzy, as engineer, would lay out tastefully. You could always resell advantageously because this area is beginning to be better known. The only inconvenience is the boat trip to communicate with New York, but it would be slight for you who have no business there. Besides the vicinity of Staten Island, Elizabethtown especially, where there is a great deal of society, makes this location very agreeable. Land is much cheaper as are building costs. Everyone tells us the expense of adding on as we are doing would have cost double on Long Island. In any case, our family which lives in the country to avoid any kind of social obligation, etiquette &c and which is French to the core in this respect would have been miserable in a ceremonious neighbourhood. They wish to be true farmers. I don't know very well how we will fare there because we already have some social links with our future neighbours which will surely frighten them; my

sisters-in-law are extremely unsociable because they detest dressing up and they spoil their children dreadfully.[118] You are not forgetting I hope that you trained me rather well in this respect. In the family I pass for the "Elegante, the Merveilleuse," the "American" in sum. Mr. D. P. and I are thought to be entirely suited to staying in town. In any case with different tastes and habits we nonetheless form a group truly united in basic respects. . . . I was fortunate to bring with me an honest woman, far above what her background would indicate, who is strongly attached to me and to my children.[119] She is an excellent femme de chambre, excellent needlewoman, and competent to help with my toilette. In fact I can but praise her in all these respects. You mentioned embroidery in many of your letters; she is especially clever with crocheting. . . . I wanted to give you some social details but I do not have time. I was going to give you an account of two lovely balls at Mrs. Church's.[120] Do you know her? Certainly well by reputation, but have you ever seen her? And what do you think of her? I could not be more impressed with her ease of manner, her warm politeness, the fine training of her daughters,[121] and the excellent appearance of

---

[117] No. 91 Liberty Street, rented by the year, was home to the Victor du Ponts until 1803, when they took a house in Greenwich Street.

[118] Sophie Madeleine Dalmas du Pont (1775–1828), wife of Eleuthère Irénée du Pont, Victor's younger brother, and Françoise Julienne Ile-de-France Poivre Bureaux de Pusy (1770–1845), daughter of Mme. P. S. du Pont de Nemours by her first marriage to Pierre Poivre, were not fluent in English, a fact that further hindered their enjoyment of an active social life.

[119] "Fanny," whose full name did not appear on the passenger list of the *American Eagle* in 1799, came with the du Ponts to America. She remained in the employ of Josephine du Pont through 1800, when her fondness for Mr. du Pont dictated her dismissal. Mrs. du Pont noted that she soon acquired a post as housekeeper for a Frenchman, a merchant and bachelor. Josephine du Pont to Margaret Manigault, Jan. 25, 1801, WMSS 3/D, EMHL.

[120] Angelica Schuyler Church (Mrs. John Barker Church) was the most reputed hostess of New York at the turn of the century. Having returned to the city in 1797 after nine years in England where her husband's family and fortune were rooted, the daughter of General Philip Schuyler entertained frequently and lavishly at her home at 52 Broadway. Her special sympathy for the French had been reinforced by contact with émigrés in London and insured Josephine du Pont's warm reception in her circle of friends.

[121] One of the Church daughters, Catharine, became a close friend of Josephine du Pont and is referred to in the letters as "belle et bonne." The other Church daughter, Elizabeth, is mentioned in the Manigault diaries when she eloped with a Mr. Bunker in 1805. Vol. 3, Acc. 502, EMHL.

her home. As does Gl. Hamilton,[122] she overwhelms us with attention and kindness, which flatters us much. Except for that, I admit to you I do not find in the society of this area that varnish of manners so remarkable in Charleston. The women are not outstanding to look at and have absolutely no grace. And the men are gauche and not very polished. I agree that I should take longer before judging them, but I am speaking here only of the first impression. . . . You will notice by the date of this letter, my friend, that it stayed in my writing desk a long time because I lacked means of sending it. . . . I took care of your request and have just sent the stockings to Mr. Le Febvre, who is to sail from Philadelphia. . . . Thank you a thousand times for the potatoes. As you suspected, in spite of all they were spoiled, but the charming letter did arrive safely.

Mrs. Manigault to Mrs. du Pont
(in French)
Charleston   6 April 1800

. . . You would certainly do well, my good Friend, to send me an organdy pattern of some pretty little biggin,[123] if you have one. I am still wearing these round bonnets dating from the time of Queen Bertha. I had one sent from London—But it is the wrong kind—It is tight—stiff—"grézellé" [shrivelled]. Remember that woman who made us laugh so?

I leave you because today is Sunday and I must dress to go to my Mother's for dinner.[124]

Mrs. Manigault to Mrs. du Pont
(in English)
Charleston   13 April 1800

. . . Mr. M. is out of town. He is gone to pay a visit of Ceremony to his Plantations,[125] which is precisely the thing of all others which he detests. He cannot endure that sort of business, & finds neither credit nor profit by it. . . . It is too good of you to propose taking the trouble of superintending the building a house for us at Berghen Point. Being in your neighbourhood would make it a very desirable object, but the necessity of crossing the water would be an insuperable objection with us. I have made many enquiries about the place, & find every circumstance but one in its favor. That one, is an innumerable quantity of very large, & very venomous moschitoes. Perhaps this may be an exaggeration, & I shall not believe a word of it until I hear your report. . . . It gives me pleasure to know that you are une elegante, une merveilleuse, but I cannot perceive how those two qualifications should lead to your Conclusion—une Amériquaine enfin. It is my opinion that our ladies in general lose too much of their attention to appearance as soon as they have been married a few years & think only of their children. But I believe that is more the case here, than it is in N.Y. There they fall into another extreme. They hide their children away in their nurseries clothed in a stuff petticoat & callico frock, as soon as they come from their school & think only of themselves, & company. This I am sure must be repugnant to your principles. You are very fortunate to possess a woman who appears so well calculated not only to assist you in all the little ornaments of dress, but in the first education of your children. Such a person is invaluable in this country. I hope she is neither young nor handsome, & that she has made a vow of Celibacy. I have still my old woman, who is far from being perfect, but who has the merit of cleanliness, & some other essentials which make me tolerate her defects. You will find (How I exult in being able to say you will find) my Elizabeth almost a woman.[126] There is still a great deal to do—indeed almost every thing to do with her. She is wild, & childish, & this I encourage for several reasons the first of which is that by leading her to run about, & jump, & play they are very conducive to health. Her disposition is naturally very good, & her behavior to me affectionate, & remarkably attentive. Upon this foundation I hope to build. . . . Harry[127] is not improved in his

[122] Alexander Hamilton (1757–1804) was Angelica Church's brother-in-law, having married Elizabeth Schuyler in 1780.

[123] Originally a child's cap or nightcap, the biggin was adopted for morning wear.

[124] Alice de Lancey Izard lived in a house facing South Bay, at the end of Meeting Street in Charleston. Her husband Ralph had been an invalid since his stroke in 1797.

[125] Plantations were frequently managed by overseers while their owners lived in the city. The periodic visits that the owner made to check accounts, raise morale, and make decisions concerning management of the lands lasted from several days to several months.

[126] Elizabeth Manigault (1786–1822) was a young lady of fourteen. Seven years later she wed Lewis Morris, Jr., son of Colonel Morris of "Morrisania."

[127] Five years later Gabriel Henry Manigault (1788–1834) spent two years as a student at the Lycée Impérial in Paris, where he was graciously received by M. and Mme. du Pont de Nemours. He was a captain in the U.S. Army and then a South Carolina planter. In 1817 he married his cousin Anne Heyward by whom he had four children.

appearance. He is a rough, rude school boy. I hope that we shall by dint of patience, & perseverance chizzle away the angles; & irregularities, & that in course of time we shall produce from this block a polished statue. Charlotte & Harriet[128] are my pleasure, & my occupation. They are pretty looking little Twins, & read, & work with me all the morning. Master Charles[129] is Pet general—a nice, clean, pretty, smart, well behaved, honest, good little boy. I dread the time when he will be sent into the contagion of bad example. Emma is as sound as a Ball, fair, & rosy as a wax doll. . . . Poor little Anne[130] is the delicate fine lady of the family, she is thin & pale, because she is cutting teeth, I am now in the midst of the painful ceremony of weaning her. She takes it very well. It is well for you since I have got into this Chapter that the clock has struck two, & that I have not begun to dress, & that it is again Sunday, & that I dine at South Bay. All which produce an Adieu for the present. . . .

Mrs. du Pont to Mrs. Manigault
(in French)
New York   18 May 1800[131]

Imagine, my friend, I am furious at all officials imaginable, at Mr. D. P. very unjustly, but especially at that old Père le Febvre who takes it upon himself to leave Philadelphia precisely 24 hours before your stockings arrive. . . . I will send them to you by the very next ship. I hope you like them. They are somewhat lighter, but large and of fine silk. They cost 24 dollars wholesale. We have not yet drawn on Mr. Go[o]ld for that significant sum.

Do not hesitate when I can send you something. Although I find much less pleasure in shopping here than in Charleston, the purpose will lend

charm to the mission. In general I find the stores ill stocked and the merchants not very obliging, and everything as expensive as Charleston except the India muslins which are really very good bargains. . . . What elegant writing paper!![132] I had to be a consummate latinist to decipher the border. Take care in that regard, for I have been told that a very pious lady writing Mde. Hamilton without thinking sent her such a curious collection of sentences that they became the pleasure of the general for half a day. Speaking of that gl. I think you know that he is amiable, but very amiable and of a European turn. He speaks French extremely well. We are much indebted to him. He wrote Mr. Pickering[133] in the most flattering terms concerning Mr. D. P. and his father, and his kindness had preceded a very special letter of introduction to him which Gl. Pinckney was kind enough to send my father-in-law. I cannot tell you how touched we were by this mark of interest on his part. . . . I believe I told you that Mr. D. P. and his father were to spend two weeks in Philadelphia. They were highly pleased with their trip and the excellent welcome they received from the president, Mr. Pickering &c. Victor feels that Philadelphia is far more a capital than this town for its resources, entertainments, and that my Madame Ch[urch]'s elegance, and home fall short compared to dames Bingham Bearing and Co.[134] But that all the lovelies there wore such a large quantity of rouge that he could not recognize any of them. It is a bit late in the day for such a practice since almost none is worn in France now. . . .

All the details you relate on French society amused me I assure you, and the ball without people, and the wig, and the wagers. . . . All seemed worthy of the heroine. . . . I have not had the pleasure you seem to envy of seeing Mde. de la Heuse. She lives in Trenton. . . .

You ask how I spend my time. It is time to tell

[128] Charlotte (1792–1819) and Harriet (1793–1835) were but a year apart in age. The former never married. Harriet wed Samuel Wilcocks of Philadelphia in 1816 and had five children.

[129] Charles Izard Manigault (1795–1874) traveled extensively, then became a planter and revitalized the family fortune. Like his brother Henry, he married a daughter of Nathaniel Heyward of South Carolina. Elizabeth H. Manigault bore him seven children.

[130] Emma Manigault (1797–1815). Toddler Anne's health was indeed precarious. She died in midsummer.

[131] This letter, misdated, was actually written in April, according to internal evidence such as the status of the stocking shipment and remarks concerning the Charleston French community.

[132] Mrs. Manigault's letter of April 13 was written on heavy rag paper with an embossed border, which made edge scribbling difficult to decipher.

[133] At this time Timothy Pickering was still Secretary of State.

[134] Mrs. William Bingham and her daughters Anne (Mrs. Alexander Baring) and Maria Matilda Bingham de Tilly (later Mrs. Henry Baring) were social leaders in Philadelphia. Mrs. John Adams wrote in 1799 that rouging made the face of the latter "red as a brick hearth." Robert C. Alberts, *The Golden Voyage* (Boston: Houghton Mifflin Company, 1969), p. 378.

you. Surely I have already spoken of the Churches. There is where I have received the most thoughtfulness, the most affectionate welcome. Mlle. [Catharine Church] especially overwhelms me with notes, morning promenades, unpretentious dinners, loan of carriage, continual borrowings from my wardrobe &c &c. Nothing is warmer, despite my natural reserve. Next Mde. Stoug[h]ton,[135] an excellent lady who speaks French well and who every evening has a curious collection of Spaniards who play whist, loo and are sure to be found there. Next a Mrs. Sadler,[136] Irish lady who spent 3 years in France, loves everything French, even the Greek style which incidentally made her seem somewhat ridiculous on her return because her appearance does not lend itself naturally to it. But she is nonetheless a fine woman and her house perfectly arranged. She brought back some very pretty things from France, among others some superb mirrors. Apropos of which I cannot swallow the fact that in Mme. Ch.'s superb salon there is not a single inch of mirror. I intend to be frank and ask her why. On the other hand in her bedroom, in which she receives, there are two of the large mirrors that we coveted so at Mrs. Sauvage's[137] and that look extremely well there. But where was I—I forgot in the intimate circle a certain Mde. de Caradeux,[138] creole and devoted wife, well connected in American society. She possesses two very opposite reputations here. The French say horrible things about her and tell a multitude of rather compromising tales. Local people know only that she won laurels in Paris in high society, and she truly did acquire the grace of such an existence. As for the amiability on which one relies, I am very certain that were she to submit to the judgment of our kind Carolinians she would not fare so well. The welcome I received

from Mde. and Mlle. Ch[urch] determined hers. There is almost tenderness, but if I am not mistaken she does not like me very much. She receives on Tuesdays to ape Mde. Ch whose day is Thursday. It rather amuses me. She is a sister of a Mde. de Quercado with whom you are friendly. Among the French, we have yet another more interesting lady, Mde. Olive.[139] She is lovely looking, she has a charming family, a well appointed house. But she lives in the country, and that prevents my seeing her as often as I would like. One might perhaps accuse her of some slight affectation in doing the honors—in other words of being that French type who will never take the middle course between coquetry and duty that rather annoys the indifferent, especially in this country where, as I a hundred times admired in you, the women know so well how to accord the agreeable and the useful. But I am being a bit severe concerning that poor Mde. Olive whose greatest fault in my eyes is, I promise, that she resembles (in the face) Mde. [de] Pes[tre].

I will not mention the twenty-odd cards received and returned, which have no friendly consequences and which are very reminiscent of those visits I had such trouble making without you. . . . You suppose me to be friendly with Mde. Le Roy—a rather strange thing. She has not paid me a single visit. My husband has dined there and been received as an old friend. The women have remained out of the picture. Why? I do not know. I have not yet seen Mde. John Livingston[140] at all either, but that is because of illness. She has made excuses a number of times. Otherwise, many other old acquaintances of Mr. D. P. such as a Mde. Smith, a Mlle. Wate who they say was for a long time the beauty of New York. But enough. . . . I was forgetting, however, to tell you that I will be happy to see your aunt upon her return. I have already seen her several

---

[135] Mrs. Thomas Stoughton was the wife of the Spanish consul at New York. The Stoughtons lived at 36 Greenwich Street. *Longworth's New York City Almanac*, 1800.

[136] In 1800 Eliza Sadler (Mrs. Henry Sadler) resided at 18 Courtlandt. *Longworth's New York City Almanac*, 1800.

[137] Advertisements reveal that Madame Sauvage "merited confidence by her punctuality in filling orders left with her for working human hair up into rings, 'bracelates,' and lockets." Harriette Kershaw Leiding, *Charleston Historic and Romantic* (Philadelphia: J. B. Lippincott, 1931), p. 178.

[138] Mme. de Caradeux (née Le Doux) retained property in Puerto Rico after she came to New York and returned there in 1803. Caradeux descendants were living in Charleston, S.C., in 1881, according to a note in the papers of Mrs. Samuel Francis Du Pont. W9–40246, EMHL.

[139] Probably the wife of Nicholas Olive, merchant, 74 Broad. *New York City Directory*, 1795; Mme. Olive was hostess to Talleyrand and the La Tour du Pin Gouvernet family in New York in 1796. In her memoirs Mme. de La Tour du Pin notes: "We also became acquainted with a very interesting French merchant family, M. and Mme. Olive, who had eight charming children, of whom the oldest was less than ten years old. I went often to see them in the country where they had bought a pretty house in which to spend their summers." *Mémoires of Madame de La Tour du Pin*, ed. and trans. Felice Harcourt (New York: The McCall Publishing Co., 1971), p. 273.

[140] Perhaps Catharine Ridley Livingston (1751–1813), daughter of William and Susannah Livingston.

times with another of your mother's sisters,[141] and I have been sorely tempted to speak to her. But the ceremonial of introduction and my poor English have held me back. . . .

Mrs. du Pont to Mrs. Manigault
(in French)
New York   26 April 1800

. . . Finally, here are your stockings. At this moment we are in a state of confusion. It is a question of moving and piling furniture and trunks into the one room in our new house allotted to us up to the 15th. We are going to spend the interim in the country. [Goodstay] will truly be rather pretty when it is finished. But they are building, but they are planting, but they are topsy turvy now. And then there is a very noisy troop of children. And cases, trunks in all the hallways. The effect is comical, I swear to you. They have bought horses and the gentlemen labor together. Mr. Prudhomme de Borre, one of those two Frenchmen from whom they purchased [the place], remarked vividly to my sister Pusy whom he had surprised as she was soaping something: "Madame, we resemble Homeric heroes, we are driving our cattle and doing our wash!" There is the kind of spirit that animates Good Stay. We electrify each other. Victor is working every bit as hard as the rest, and I am trying not to seem too stupid, although they laugh at how freely they pardon me for putting on my gloves to go to the garden. I am thrilled at the idea of my new house. We are spending a great deal of money to get settled there [see Fig. 12],[142] but I feel I will never completely enjoy it until I have the happiness of welcoming you there as an intimate part of our family. . . .

Have you heard by chance of a very bitter disappointment for a multitude of ladies in this town,

and even for a certain French lady [Josephine du Pont herself] newly arrived from Paris who, anticipating a handsome ball at the home of the brilliant Mde. Ch., had prepared a really striking toilette certain to produce an effect. Well, it happened that a ship from London brought news of the death of the mother of the fat little Cincinnatus Cdr.[143] Burdened perhaps with a fortune of 60,000 £ sterling, she left them to him after having enjoyed them up to her 95th year. Yesterday was the date of that dear ball. Mde. and Mlle. de Veaublanc had come from Elizabeth town expressly for the occasion; Mde. Ch.'s entire family was in town. It was really very sad!!

Mde. John Rutledge[144] passed through (New York) again on her way back to New Port. . . . She spent three days with the Misses Pinckney[145] and her husband stayed at the home of le Déclin (note the designation) [Angelica Church]. They seem to have divulged all the Charleston gossip. Among other things, Mr. R. said that your fine father and you were very angry at the Chercheur d'oranges [George Izard] because he conducted himself very inconsiderately toward a French lady and then abandoned her. That tale at first seemed very ridiculous to me; your letter heightens my incredulity. Is it possible you would desire that marriage? . . .[146]

This letter was interrupted. I am finishing it now in the midst of the horrors of moving. I leave in two hours for the country. I am desolate. By mistake I packed two morning bonnet patterns. I will send them to you at the first opportunity. You are right. [MS torn—The ones?] we like so are no longer

---

[141] The four sisters of Alice de Lancey Izard were Ann de Lancey Cox (Mrs. John Cox), Elizabeth de Lancey, Susannah de Lancey Barclay (Mrs. Thomas Barclay), and Jane de Lancey Watts (Mrs. John Watts, Jr.). All were soon acquaintances of Josephine du Pont.

[142] Victor du Pont's expense book notes the April payment of $80 for rent of the house in Pearl Street and in September, $350 for rent through the coming year in their new quarters at 91 Liberty Street. In addition the move entailed April and May purchases of such items as "a dining mahogany table ($40.00); green edgeward plates and dishes at vendue ($5.75); a painted bed sted ($33.75); set of Wedgewood ware ($40.00); Side Board ($46.87); Secretary ($25.00); Bed and calico curtains ($15.00)." WMSS 3/B, EMHL.

[143] John Barker Church's mother died at her home in England. Church was a member of the Order of the Cincinnati by virtue of his service as commissary general to the French forces and as liaison officer between General Washington and Rochambeau. Lyman Horace Weeks, comp. and ed., *Prominent Families of New York* (New York: The Historical Co., 1897), p. 116.

[144] Mrs. John Rutledge, Jr., whose husband was, like his father before him, active in South Carolina federalist politics.

[145] Probably Maria and Harriott, daughters of Charles Cotesworth Pinckney.

[146] George Izard wrote some years later that pressure from her family induced Miss Peïre to plead with him for a sham engagement in order to calm tempers. Izard acceded, and related: "Our engagement was announced. Visits were exchanged between ladies of our respective families, and soon afterwards I was at New York." Acc. 149, EMHL. Whether the Manigaults knew the true story at the time this subject figured in the du Pont-Manigault letters is uncertain.

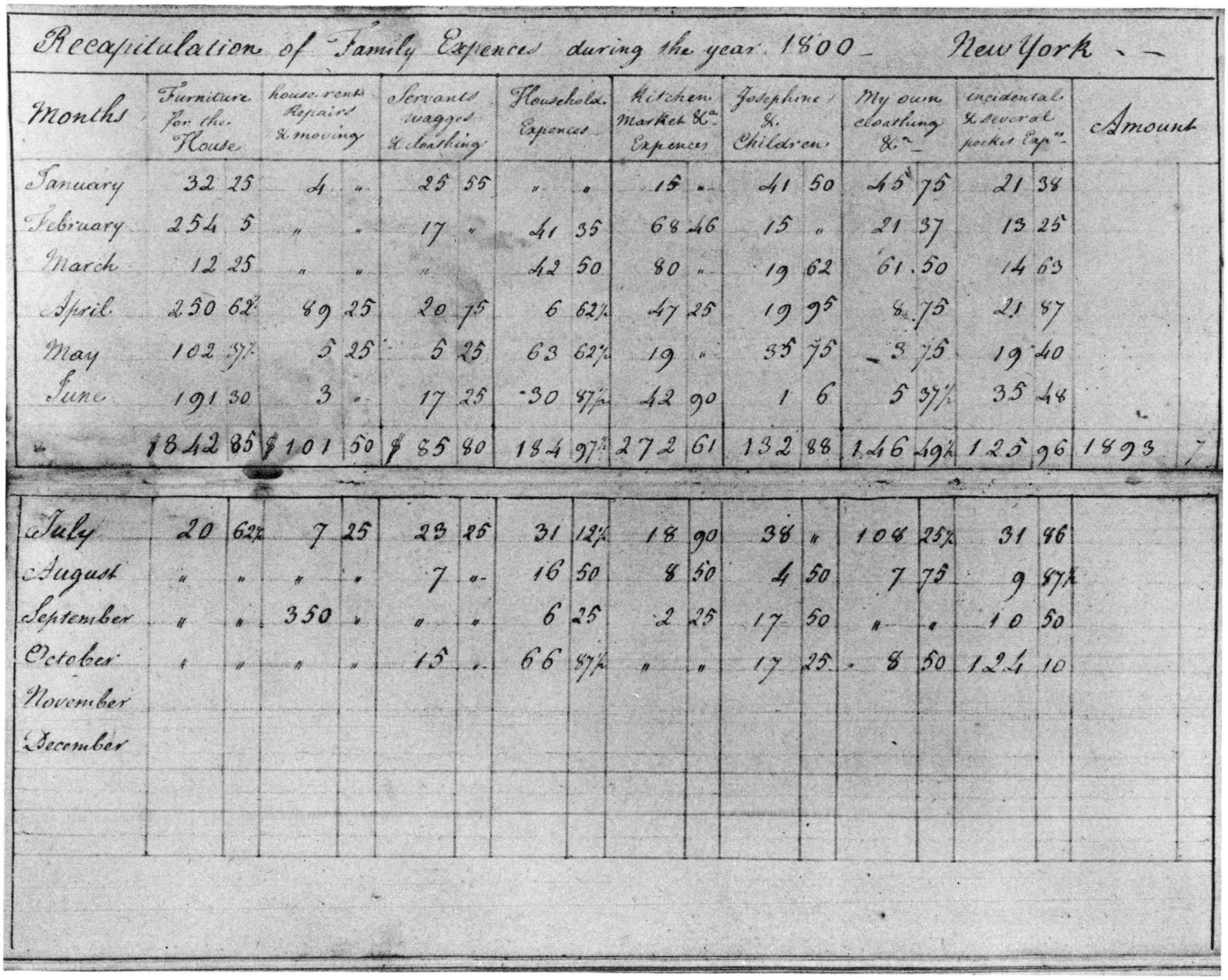

Months	Furniture for the House	House rents Repairs & moving	Servants wages & cloathing	Household Expences	Kitchen Market &c. Expences	Josephine & Children	My own cloathing &c.	Incidental & several pocket Exp.	Amount
January	32 25	4	25 55	"	15	41 50	45 75	21 34	
February	254 5		17	41 35	68 46	15	21 37	13 25	
March	12 25			42 50	80	19 62	61.50	14 63	
April	250 62	89 25	20 75	6 62½	47 25	19 95	8 75	21 87	
May	102 37	5 25	5 25	63 62½	19	35 75	3 75	19 40	
June	191 30	3	17 25	30 47½	42 90	1 6	5 37½	35 44	
	1842 85	101 50	85 80	184 97½	272 61	132 88	146 49½	125 96	1893 7
July	20 62	7 25	23 26	31 12½	18 90	38	104 25½	31 46	
August	"	"	7	16 50	8 50	4 50	7 75	9 47½	
September	"	3 50	"	6 25	2 25	17 50	"	10 50	
October	"	"	15	66 87½	"	17 25	8 50	124 10	
November									
December									

FIG. 12. Victor du Pont, account book, "Recapitulation of Family Expenses during the year 1800, New York." H. 7", W. 4½". (Longwood MSS. L2–304, Eleutherian Mills Historical Library.)

wearable. I hope you have also renounced mantelets. Take three and a half yards of black crape; sew on your lovely lace and pleat a tulle through the middle—around the neck only.[147] Leave the crape at its full width. That may frighten the ignorant somewhat, but no matter. One underlines drapes it, or else attaches it underlines discreetly with 2 pins in the front. Farewell, my friend, my house is turned upside down, my husband is grumbling and I am talking fashion. Apropos, please send me some pretty Greek designs if you have some. . . .

[147] The modified fichu, or the neck-ruffle shoulder piece described here, was a means of relieving the plainness of daytime dresses.

Mrs. Manigault to Mrs. du Pont
(in English)

24 April [1800]

. . . I am very much obliged to you for having so soon procured my stockings. They would come very opportunely now I assure you, & I was a little disappointed when old le F[ebvre] told me that he had them not. Is there any black lace in N. York? You know my passion for that article. It is become quite necessary to me from habit. If there should be any handsome at 2 or 3 dollars a yard I should be glad to have wherewithal to trim a cloak. There used to be in N.Y. a man by the name of Seaman who once had the greatest abundance of handsome black lace. But he is probably gone. . . .

Mrs. Manigault to Mrs. du Pont
(in English and French)
24 May 1800

Two of your letters have reached me my kind Friend, since I last wrote to you. Before I read them over, & answer them article by article, let me thank you for the stockings, which are very good, & for the dear little book. . . .

Your Victor adheres to his old opinions. He wrote long ago that "Les femmes de N.Y. n'etaient bonnes qu'a servir de femmes de Chambres à celles de P[aris]. Et je crois que ces dernières pensent bien comme lui."[148]

. . . What a brilliant set you have fallen into! But I should like to know why you fixed upon the appellation of Le Déclin. Is there any thing which indicates it? . . . "I very much like your Greek style superimposed on the Irish. That should be interesting." Somebody told me, if I recollect right, that glasses were out of fashion in England as ornaments for a Drawing room. I saw at N.Y. both Mme. Caradeux, & Mme. Olive. The first was at that time far from being une élégante; the latter was a very handsome woman whose husband, much older than herself, was said to be jealous. . . .

I am waiting impatiently for the Caps. I send you some patterns, all of which are of my own creation, & all of which I have worked, in shaded crewels, or silk. I have as many more at your service, for this kind of work amuses me prodigiously, & I always have some of it at hand. . . . I cannot imagine why Mrs. Le Roy should have been so distant. Perhaps she did not know that you are such a Proficient in English. She is a woman of very plain manners, but an excellent heart. . . .

I am impatient for the other books which Mr. Du P. mentions. Suzette a fait les délices de toute la famille—[149] . . . I thank you for the hint upon cloaks. What you indicated was already done with my Lace. However "la grande largeur" [the great width] appeared to me too warm for the summer. Are you still wearing wigs?

Mrs. du Pont to Mrs. Manigault
(in French)
Good Stay   6 May 1800

Mr. Du Pont is returning to Philadelphia for some days, my dear friend. I hope he will find a means of sending you this small package. I hope these [bonnet] patterns please you. They are simple and comfortable, especially when you use a small blond circlet. Tell me whether you are wearing wigs and whether you have abjured the antique powder. I will not be satisfied until I know. Mine have been the envy of all the women, and have made the fortune of a coiffeur who, after ruining a half dozen, managed to copy them rather well. He sells them for 12 dollars. But they are light, natural, charming, and above all very comfortable. I do not need but twenty minutes now for the most elaborate toilette. . . .

Mrs. Manigault to Mrs. du Pont
(in French)
Charleston   27 June 1800

. . . A thousand thanks for the bonnets. The batiste is enchanting. The crepe I have not yet made. And the organdy is very complicated. I will admit to you that I do not understand it at all. Nevertheless I have trimmed it the way you were kind enough and industrious enough to send it, and this evening I will expend the maximum effort of imagination and genius in an attempt to unravel the puzzle. I have made two in batiste. But I have used up almost all my valencienne. And if you have some that is pretty in your big city and about ____this____ width, I would greatly appreciate your buying some for me. As soon as any arrives here, women race for it. While I am writing about shopping requests, I will explain the black lace. I want some to trim [a] shawl (I dare not say Mantelet any more) to go out mornings [see Fig. 13]. That is, I want a good strong lace, and wide, about like that which you bought here shortly before your departure. And I would be willing to spend about two dollars. I will tell you that if you encourage me in the least I will dare ask M. D. P. to bring me some lovely [lace] from France.[150] But I will count on you to let me

---

[148] Translation: "New York women were only good enough to serve as chambermaids to Parisian ladies. And I think the latter fully agree with him."

[149] Possibly *La Dot de Suzette, ou histoire de Mme. de Senneterre, racontée par elle-même*, by J. Fiévée, was the book which "was the delight of the whole family."

[150] Victor du Pont was in doubt for some months about the advisability of a trip to France to solidify capital investment in Du Pont de Nemours, Père et Fils & Cie. and to solicit new business. He finally made the trip and kept a lively journal. *Journey to France and Spain 1801*, ed. Charles W. David (Ithaca, N.Y.: Cornell University Press, 1961).

FIG. 13. Pierre Antoine Leboux de La Mésangère, "Good-bye till this evening," Paris, ca. 1800. Plate opposite page 76 from [Max von Boehn], *Modes & Manners of the Nineteenth Century*, trans. M. Edwardes, vol. 1 (London: J. M. Dent & Co., 1909). (Eleutherian Mills Historical Library.)

know whether or not I should speak of shopping. I am still going to ask you for a *petit tour blond* [small blond circlet] like the ones you wear. I have seen them. You wish to know, my dear friend, whether I wear a wig? I have one, but I do not overwork it. It comes from Philadel— But the hair is too long in the back, &c. You know that I did not use much powder, even when you were here. I have not worn any for a century. We have bandeaus—Casque bonnets—Fichus, and I am loyal to them—Greek veils. We have Chemises à l'antique —tunics—redingotes—peignoirs—Houpelandes [see Fig. 14].[151] All that is old news, is it not?

[151] This succinct 1800 fashion list includes both tunics and overskirts (houppelandes), which effectively reduced the transparency of the gauzy chemise.

. . . Allow the small piece of furniture [probably a stool] which accompanies this letter to call me to your mind. My aunt was to deliver it to you, but it could not be found. Do not laugh at its simplicity —it is destined for the peaches of Good Stay.

My good aunt found you [to be] just as I had described. She expected to be enchanted, and was. Is not my little cousin pretty?[152]

All you tell me about le Déclin seems correct. It is precisely what I pictured from all I had heard. How fortunate Melle. Ch. is to have you! . . . I have not told you a hundred of all I wanted to write. But this letter will soon be followed by another. I read La R—e.[153] Some months ago I went very innocently to request this book at a bookshop. I paid for it and began to read it openly. That did not last long, as you may guess. I finished it, and took it back. Have you read les Voeux temeraires by Mme. de Genlis—and her Petits Emigrés?[154]

[152] This aunt was probably Mrs. John Watts, and the pretty cousin Mrs. John Livingston.

[153] Probably Marie Charles Joseph Pougens, *Julie ou la Religieuse de Nismes* (Paris: Du Pont, 1795/96). The social theme and the strong anticlerical tone in this tale of a woman chained and tormented for fifteen years in a convent would surely shock a conservative American Protestant lady of 1800.

[154] Mme. de Genlis published her novel *Petits Emigrés* in 1798, a year before *Les Voeux Téméraires*.

FIG. 14. Illustration from *Gallery of Fashion*, a fashion magazine, London, 1797. Page 101 from [Max von Boehn], *Modes & Manners of the Nineteenth Century*, trans. M. Edwardes, vol. 1 (London: J. M. Dent & Co., 1909). (Eleutherian Mills Historical Library.)

You do not say a word of that good Mrs. [Edward] Goold. Do you know she is the best woman in the world, and wonderfully intelligent? You have seen her son here. He had the presence of mind to send me a new book, recently arrived from London, which raised him several degrees in my opinion. . . .

Mrs. du Pont to Mrs. Manigault
(in French)
New York   10 July 1800

. . . I was taking the pen to write you this morning when a Carolina gentleman with letter in hand was announced. Quickly I went downstairs and I found . . . Mr. Fenwick[155] . . . I hope he at least departed happy with my syrup and fresh water, for you know that at this time it is intolerably hot and there is not a whisper of that excellent breeze that blows up so charitably from one end of Meeting Street to the other over the two handsomest piazzas of Charleston.[156] The beginning of next week we intend to take refuge in the country where the air is really excellent. . . . Did I tell you that all last winter I was adorned with that pretty embroidered turban [see Fig. 15]? Before I left Paris I had it arranged on a Greek crown of green velvet. . . . It won many compliments for me. What do you think of me for not thanking you for your pretty designs. They are charming. I am going to have the Greek one with the branch motif in it made. I am sending you some, including one from which I have a dress I like very much, for its Etruscan nature. As to what is seen here, nothing could be more sterile. I have not yet been tempted to imitate anyone, I promise you, and to solve my problems, I invent.

I am going to find the black and the white lace. You do not say how much yardage of valenciennes. No matter, if I find some that is pretty and inexpensive I will take some for myself too. . . . Think about it right away if you wish a box of fashions. I have made arrangements with one of my friends[157] who promised me that whenever I

FIG. 15. Illustration from a fashion magazine of 1800. Plate opposite page 33 from Julius M. Price, *Dame Fashion* (New York: Charles Scribner's Sons, 1913). (Photo, Eleutherian Mills–Hagley Foundation.)

wished she would select them at my marchande de modes, who is one of the best but rather expensive. I warn you that a certain "chapeau nacarat" cost me 2 louis, as did a bonnet with three feathers. I have already placed one order and I expect it in two months. If this first shipment is successful I will place another through Mr. D. P. [for] a ready-made dress. If you are tempted, send me a blouse pattern of paper and your length with a thread. I also have an excellent seamstress. We could request small taf[fe]tas [sleevelets] unlined and trimmed in

[155] Probably Edward Fenwick of Fenwick Hall, Tory sympathizer in the Revolution and another organizer of the fourth South Carolina Jockey Club; he was a distant cousin of Margaret Manigault, through the Izard line.

[156] Certainly the piazzas are those of the Ralph Izard home at the South Bay end of Meeting Street and the Manigault house further into the city on the same street.

[157] Mme. Auriol de Rumilly was Josephine du Pont's friend and fashion "agent" in Paris. Receipts and letter references to her shopping indicate she was helpful at least until 1807. WMSS 3/B and 3/D, EMHL.

the same color velvet. That would not be very expensive and would give us patterns. What do you think? We each have reputations to sustain and not much time to lose! I am told that you look better than ever. The same is not true of me. I am very much changed, and different from myself especially when I use my own hair, which happens very often since everyone uses wigs and since I wash my hair every day. It is black and short. I have had my teeth fixed. They are now all filed and consequently separated.[158] In all I really have another face, and one rarely gains by these little pleasantries when the thirty-year bell sounds. But no matter, you are very right to congratulate me on my friendship with Belle et bonne. Each day it grows. I really feel friendship and a deep interest in her. I am as worried as you at not seeing here any man worthy of her. . . . I would wish for her some amiable Carolinian. Ship me some if the occasion presents itself. . . . We spent last Tuesday at the home of le Déclin. She has been settled for fifteen days in a very pretty country house on the East River. Its location is charming, but boredom has I think somewhat reduced [appearances] in that lovely retreat. The husband spends almost all his time in town. The brothers run, and the three women are scarcely entertained. Belle et bonne came to spend the whole day with me yesterday. I gave her and Mde. de Caradeux a pretty little dinner. In the evening we met at Mde. Caradeux's where we found M. et Mde. Belossis[159] whom I believe I already mentioned to you. They are a very interesting family. They have a lovely house near Elizabeth Town. The husband is English, the wife German. They have charming children and are extremely rich. It is whispered that she is a German princess who married a lord. In any case she is a highly interesting woman. She speaks equally well in English, French, and Italian, not counting a little Latin, which she doesn't admit to, and her own tongue. She's an excellent musician, sings very well, plays the piano very well. . . . Elizabeth is marvelously peopled. Do you know the Rickets[160] family —old acquaintances of Mr. D. P. They seem to be very fine people. I saw them the other day at Mde. Church's and will gladly see them again at their home. We also have a Mr. and Mde. Cra[w]ford,[161] people of true merit whose acquaintance we have made. He closely resembles Mr. Rutledge your worthy governor[162] and is said to be very amiable. He is English but likes the French. . . .

15 July. I have just spent my morning, my friend, going from door to door to find the lace, and in vain the address of the merchant you indicated. No one has any and you will have to wait for an opportunity to get some from France. . . . As for the valencienne they didn't even know what I meant—it is Greek in New York. I will tell you it is becoming rare and very expensive in France where they now wear only superb embroidered malines or English. White veils of point de bruxelles cost 40 to 50 louis. . . . You must spend 10 to 12 louis for a black one but perhaps this folly can be replaced by another. They were throwing them entirely to one side on the shoulder. That was charming and draped perfectly. . . .

Mrs. Manigault to Mrs. du Pont
(in English)
Meeting Street   3 Aug. 1800

It is with great reluctance, my amiable Friend, that I now take up my pen. For I shall afflict your kind sympathizing heart, and renew my own grief. I have lost my little darling. . . . She was nineteen months old, and really a sweet Infant [Anne Manigault died July 27, 1800]. . . . Your last charming

[158] Mrs. du Pont's reasons for having her teeth filed are not specified. In his *Practical Observations on the Human Teeth* (London, 1783, p. 156), R. Woofendale states that teeth are filed to eliminate broken or jagged points, to impede development of cavities, to round tooth edges which are annoying to the tongue or cheek, or for ornamental purposes, as quoted in Samuel S. White, *A History of Dental and Oral Science in America* (Philadelphia, 1876), p. 105.

[159] Known in America as Belossis (with variant spellings), Lord Bolingbroke and his second wife lived at Liberty Hall until their return to England in 1806. Theodore Thayer, *As We Were: The Story of Old Elizabethtown* (Elizabeth, N.J.: Grassman Publishing Co., 1964), p. 164. In 1800 a George Richard Belasiz purchased 15½ acres of land in Elizabeth, N.J. Marilyn Ann Johnson, "Clockmakers and Cabinetmakers of Elizabethtown, New Jersey" (M.A. thesis, University of Delaware, 1963), p. 176.

[160] Probably Mr. and Mrs. James Ricketts of Elizabethtown, New Jersey. Edwin F. Hatfield, *History of Elizabeth, New Jersey* (New York: Carlton & Lanahan, 1868), p. 562. Paintings of a Mr. Ricketts done in 1807 appear in a list of the works of Thomas Sully. Edward Biddle and Mantle Fielding, *The Life and Works of Thomas Sully 1783–1872* (Philadelphia: Wickersham Press, 1921), p. 259.

[161] Mr. and Mrs. Cra[w]ford are not identified. Josephine du Pont stated in a note to her husband, March 24, 1800, that the Crawfords would be their neighbors on Liberty Street. WMSS 9-40222A, EMHL.

[162] South Carolina's Governor Edward Rutledge, who had died January 23, 1800.

letter of the 15th July revived my spirits at a moment when they stood in great need of such a cordial. You are gay, and happy and it appears to me that you have wherewithal to select a society which will satisfy you. You have a great resource among Strangers—Mr. & Mrs. Bellosis. Mr. & Mrs. Crawford. Mme. de Caradeux & above all Miss Church. And you have mentioned some others at different times w[ho] were not disagreeable. You cannot regret our poor City, my sweet friend though you will never cease to be regretted here. . . . [Mr. D. P.] has very obligingly asked us for commissions, & we shall with the freedom of old Friends accept his offer. Mine, I shall submit to you. In my next I will tell you all that I know of your Countrymen & women—which is not much. For we hardly see any but Messieurs Fournier, & Vandoeuvre, and the former with whom I have the most intercourse is very discreet.

. . . I thank you for the billet de Belle et bonne. It gives one an idea of her manner. Several of our gentlemen were well acquainted with her family. My Brother remembers her, & Mr. Deas[163] who was Secretary to Mr. Pinckney when he was Minister at the Court of Great Britain, saw a good deal of all that belonged to le Déclin. They were fortunate in possessing a young woman of good family, uncommonly charming, & accomplished. She was called by them Madelle. Félicité, & since married the Marquis de Chastel, in preference to accompanying them to America. . . .

You desire to have un aimable Carolinien shipped. That pink of perfection Mr. Burn is at this moment probably breathing the hot air of N.Y. He would not want a good word from your Victor. He, Mr. Burn, is on his way to Europe. He is to meet a friend of his, Mr. Wentworth, who was sufficiently pleased with a short visit he paid us last spring, to declare that he would return in the Winter. Mr. W. knew your friend [Miss Ch.] & had the misfortune to offend her at a ball at her own house, for which he was very much chagrined. . . .

Mrs. du Pont to Mrs. Manigault
(in French)
Berghen Point   10 September 1800

I apologize, my friend for not having immediately answered your last letter. Had any motive other than a sorrowful feeling held my pen it was

the fear of writing too strongly on the tender sympathy that made me share in your distress . . . I hope you have felt the need of distraction and that little preparations will have helped. If by a magic wand I could evoke in your bedroom a mahogany sofa trimmed with a handsome green material embroidered in brown and a draped Etruscan fringe in the most Greek manner it seems that I would see you resting there with greater ease. . . . You can imagine how impatiently I shall await news from you. Mr. D. P. returned ten days ago from his trip to Alexandria. . . . He pretends that area in many ways resembles dear Carolina and that even the clouds of turkey buzzards pleasantly called to his mind Charleston and its environs.[164] He met General [Charles Cotesworth] Pinckney who took him for a Virginian sailor because he was arriving from I know not where covered with dust and wearing an outlandish outfit. . . . He didn't dare greet Mde. P. since [his appearance] made him afraid of himself. En route he had met your wonderful Scot. He has been in New York expressly to give him dinner. He introduced him at the Churches but without any particular intention because [Mr. Burn] declares himself more than ever against all matrimonial ties. . . . I have not seen him. . . . [He] must be rather bored in New York where there is no one and where it is very hot. Very fortunately there has been no fever, but everyone had fled it in advance.

(Next week) . . . we are going to see Bethlehem, spend two days in Philadelphia and four or five in Wilmington with a very interesting French family which is most desirous of associating with us.[165] Some of them have already come to see us. They are rich, very gay and very amiable. Mr. Du Pont says the women are well brought up although Creole, are good musicians, love their husbands, and are raising their children in the American way. I really

---

[163] William Allen Deas, secretary to Thomas Pinckney when he was U.S. Minister to England, was Mrs. Manigault's brother-in-law. He married her younger sister, Anne.

[164] Flocks of turkey buzzards and their attendant odor dominated the Charleston markets throughout the nineteenth century. Of the buzzard, La Rochefoucauld-Liancourt wrote: "It is very common all over South Carolina, and, in some measure, worshipped by the inhabitants of the town." *Travels Through the United States,* 2:47.

[165] The Bauduys of Wilmington were indeed eager to be part of the du Pont endeavors. Alexandre Bauduy, Pierre Bauduy, and their sisters, Félicité Hamon (Mrs. William Hamon) and Selina Des Chapelles (Mrs. Alexandre Des Chapelles), formed the nucleus of a Wilmington group of French refugees from Santo Domingo uprisings. Having retained their holdings in the West Indies, the family was in a position to invest some capital. Pierre, or Peter, Bauduy (1769–1833) soon allied himself with E. I. du Pont's powdermaking venture, in what proved to be an ill-fated partnership fraught with misunderstandings.

need a little dissipation. Our house is so full of workers and still so poorly arranged that I have postponed going to Elizabeth town and even going out in our immediate neighborhood in order to avoid visits. I am reproached from all sides. You have no idea how shy they are here and how much they fear visitors. That contraries us and frequently embarasses us. Imagine, *Belle et bonne* came almost in spite of me. Although she is far from being demanding it desolates my sisters-in-law when they must make some expenditures on toilette and society. Except for that, our household is extremely happy and united. . . . I forgot to apologize to you for not having yet sent your circlet of hair. I had an argument over it with the maker who I believe profited from my absence in order to sell it. However he swore to me that he had not yet made it and that he had searched in vain for as much blond hair as I had specified in order to have a natural curl and a truly alluring effect. I have one made from Amelie's hair which is charming. Eventually I hope to get yours. I saw announced in a newspaper a case of wigs and knitted silk sleeves just arrived from France. If I were in New York I would surely be greatly tempted to make these two purchases for you. I no longer know how to dress with any other type sleeve, but I am afraid that this miserable case will make them very common. In Paris they were wearing gray, apricot combined with little taffeta strips of the same color. Nothing is prettier. Farewell my friend. I am going on horseback to accompany Mr. D. P. halfway to the New York road [see Fig. 16]. I made the same twenty-mile round trip several days ago. You see that enjoyment fed so imprudently in Charleston has in no way diminished. . . .

Mrs. Manigault to Mrs. du Pont
(in English and French)
Meeting Street   17 Aug. 1800
You have hardly yet received my last melancholy letter, in which I promised to write soon in a more sprightly style. . . . Here is your last, long, charming letter. I will answer it article by article. If anything can inspire cheerful, & pleasant ideas, that will. . . . I am sorry that my gentleman missed the pleasure of conversing with a charming french lady. It would have rejoiced him, & his account of the thing would have made a very pleasant table subject after one of our little suppers next winter. Mr. Fenwick was an old acquaintance of yours. He is not much of a lady's man. I have invited him sev-

FIG. 16. *Costume d'Amazône.* Plate 223 from *Costume Parisien,* ed. Pierre Antoine Leboux de La Mésangère (Paris, 1799). Colored etching; H. 10″, W. 6″. (Eleutherian Mills Historical Library.)

eral times to pass an evening here. But not having been formally visited by Mr. M. he declined. Cela n'est pas d'un homme qui a passé quelque tems en France.[166] You are now settled in the Country—& if the Moschitoes of whom most tragical tales are told, do not torment you, you certainly are enjoying many rural delights. Among others, a great fund of leisure hours, I hope. . . . When you first visited Charleston, you expected to find a poor little out-of-the-way Town, inhabited by a primitive set of people who had seen nothing, & knew nothing of the world. You found us rather better than you expected & saw every thing with an indulgent eye, magnifying what was tolerable, & excusing

[166] Translation: That is not at all like a man who has spent time in France.

what was not so. You carried away a too flattering impression. . . . I have much better authority than yours, & can take upon me to assert that if you are changée it is, if possible, en mieux. A person who was commissioned by me to take an accurate survey, sent in a very pleasing, & I make no doubt, a perfectly true relation. Indeed it could hardly be otherwise. Just returned from the Fountainhead of every thing that is fashionable, becoming, & beautifying. Besides you are happier, more settled, with more pleasing prospects, than when I had the pleasure of seeing you, more gay—& above all your health is good. . . .[167] I am going to make a shopping list which I will submit for your criticism and your correction. It could be longer and more extensive if I could consult you in person. But I do not wish in any way to risk tormenting, annoying and inconveniencing such an obliging friend. That being the case, around thirty Louis will be my spending limit. And I trust in you my dear friend for the disposition of this sum. If you think of some little articles . . . and if you think a pair of earrings might be added without inconvenience, that would please me very much. For since you left, I have not had any new ones. I would want them rather simple, and around 2 or 3 louis.

I have just received a shipment from England. It is the solid type this time. Dimity, Percale, Cotton batiste—do you know that merchandise? We wear only that. It is extremely handsome, fine light, white. And then linens. And above all, a Carpet. But what a Carpet! The background is handsome green material. And the border in tapestry, and it is I who will undertake that bit of handwork. The border is half a yard wide, and it is superb. Will you help me this winter?[168] I also received a little

table, a kind of Chiffoniere which ruins me and does not satisfy me at all. I wanted something entirely useful, for working—which contains all the little tools imaginable and which invites industry. And it is not that. In October I expect that Caisse d'importance. . . .[169]

You want to know what is happening here. We no longer see the Chameleon at all. Good Father Fou[rnier] who says almost nothing about his compatriots told me that people could no longer go to her home. She is too difficult, too unequal. Joseph [Manigault] who was enchanted with her little companion is disgusted. . . . I asked M. Fournier to give your message to the Cigale. Her husband, they say, has a fault connected with his infirmity [deafness]. He is suspicious, and that misfortune sometimes makes him unjust, and even brutal. Then he recognizes his mistake, throws himself on his knees and implores her pardon. We never see her. She lives a very secluded life. . . .

M. M. is doing the same thing as M. Du P. today (Sunday). He went to spend the day with his Brother at the Island. He took M. Bee, and invited Messieurs Fournier and Vandoeuvre along. I do not know what kept them from going. Charleston is a desert. Everyone is at the Island, where the comedy is played, where there is a billiard game &c &c. . . .

29th Aug. I have heard of M. Du Pont's travels. He has been seen in Alexandria accoutred like a true Virginian in Gingham coat & Sailor's pantaloons, & avoided the ladies. I dont know him by that description. But such as I remember him, & you always see him, pray remember me to. . . .

Mrs. du Pont to Mrs. Manigault
(in French)
Berghen Point   23 October 1800
. . . We returned a week ago from our little excursion. We visited Patterson, Bethlehem, Philadelphia, Wilmington. Victor, my little Charles and

---

[167] In reply, Josephine du Pont pointed out, "When I returned to France I wished before leaving once again, to enjoy in moderation whatever pleasant things I saw. For all things considered, I prefer to live in America for perhaps some ten years. You will easily understand then how, with these thoughts in mind and my prior knowledge of the country, my first steps here in New York were more assured. With all my heart I sought to present those who expected it, a French appearance which was sufficiently elegant to be remarked but which incorporated severe decency both in dress and comportment. This first won for me the acceptance of the Church family . . . and then others followed. . . ." Josephine du Pont to Margaret Manigault, Mar. 14, 1801, WMSS 3/D, EMHL.

[168] Margaret Manigault's new green cloth floor covering, already categorized in her letter of February 24 as the most stylish type in Charleston, was probably a "Scotch" or "ingrain" type. The pileless, doublecloth weavings were fre-

quently imported from England in the eighteenth century. Rodris Roth, *Floor Coverings in 18th-Century America* (Washington, D.C.: Smithsonian Press, 1967), p. 30. Although the double-woven carpeting was considered inferior in quality to the handsome pile products of the day, Margaret's plan to individualize her carpet by means of a handworked tapestry border would lend it distinction. To invite a friend's participation in such an ambitious project was not uncommon.

[169] Mrs. Manigault refers to her pregnancy. Her son Edward (1800–1808) was born in October.

I were in the chaise; my brother-in-law [Eleuthère Irénée du Pont] escorted us on horseback. The weather was frequently bad, yet we returned deeply satisfied with our pilgrimage. I had almost never traveled except by water in your beautiful country, and I found this sample sufficient to stimulate my curiosity. We are considering nothing less than a trip to Niagara in two or 3 years! Imagine that Mad. Colman (Nixon)[170] made the trip with her husband when she was six months pregnant. They had no accident, and they returned enchanted with the thing and the good accomodations they found. We spent a pleasant week in Wilmington at the home of Mr. Bauduy, whose very numerous family divided into four or five households represents in this country a unique gathering of amiable and harmonious French people. The women although creole merit all the praise I have heard concerning them. . . . There is in that society a Mad. Montgomery,[171] an Englishwoman raised in France who is said to be very amiable and who had been announced to me as being the woman who speaks the best French in the United States. Of course I was curious to judge the matter. She was absent but then she returned in time, the eve of my departure. And we met at a very elegant party they were giving for us that evening. She does indeed speak our language well and fluently and without accent. Also she seems Frenchified. Would you believe, my friend, all the praise I heard was not at all agreeable. It seemed to me that everyone who knew you only by name wanted to prove to me that one could easily meet a second Mrs. Manigault. And their Mad. Montgomery suffered from it in my judgment. I found her a handsome woman, but rather hard. I found that she had too far abandoned that base of natural reserve in the English and American character that is so becoming to all women. In a quarter of an hour I saw her speak to and attack 5 or 6 men with a singular volubility. With me she initiated conversation without pretext or introduction.

And to myself I made comparisons between her and you and between her and Miss Ch. And I remember very well that all in loving France and the French you knew not only how to preserve your character and native tint independent of foreign impulses, but also keep the superiority they give you in foreign society. I imagine it would be almost insulting to say of you "She is completely French" even taking it in the best sense. And I am convinced you would be of my opinion. As for Belle et Bonne, she can perhaps be reproached for a bit too much abandon in French society. But that stems from an excess of good will, and her natural candor sets limits. It has happened many times that I have had to defend American customs to her, and especially to le Déclin, who find there is no salvation outside of London and Paris. You know that she makes it a habit of receiving while lying down in her bedroom, which I cite to show how she flaunts this country's customs. Her daughter has not the slightest scruple about going out in the streets of N[ew] Y[ork], giving her arm to the first little Frenchman she meets, although she shows considerably more reserve towards the local man-in-the-street, whom she rather properly disdains. . . . Truly, I do not know how I could have written the least folly that could in any way weaken the excellent opinion I have sought to give you of her. . . . This house[172] is not yet finished. It is a very long replastering [job], which will never produce anything very pretty or regular inside. But it will give rather comfortable little lodgings and superb piazzas that will lend a very handsome appearance to the exterior of the house. Unfortunately the work is done by the day and consequently becomes very prolonged and very costly. . . . In about two weeks I will know whether or not Mr. D. P. will go to Europe. . . . [If he must], I will doubtless find support and consolation in our family. But what feeble compensations! Besides, our tastes are different, I like my independence, and I do not feel I have the courage to spend the winter here, where they will press me to stay although I am more necessary to them in town. . . .

The sum of £35 seems sufficient to cover what you wish. Beside each article I have added the approximate price and the total I got was £36. If I have the sad opportunity to send the list this winter I shall reread it carefully and will add some fan-

---

[170] Elizabeth Nixon Coleman was godmother to Amelia du Pont.

[171] Probably the wife of Robert Montgomery, Esq., of Wilmington and Philadelphia. The Montgomerys lived for some years in France before settling in Wilmington with their adopted daughter. The lure of the continent soon proved so strong that Mrs. Montgomery left her family, sailed for France, and "entered with spirit into the frivolities of Paris." Her daughter later sought to join her there, only to be rejected by that "cold, heartless woman." Elizabeth Montgomery, *Reminiscences of Wilmington* (Philadelphia: J. K. Collins, Jr., 1851), pp. 221–25.

[172] Goodstay. The remodeling of the house at Bergen Point yielded valuable experience and design information when E. I. du Pont was constructing his residence at Eleutherian Mills on the Brandywine in 1803.

tasies if they come to mind while cutting back on some other little things. Upon reflection I think I cannot scarcely entrust your list to any other than Mr. D. P. So you will have to be patient. . . .

. . . Be very careful to recover your health. . . . Thank you for the little bonnets. I admit that I consider myself fortunate not to need them and I say as in 21, *Content* [stand pat]. My two youngsters suffice. . . .

Mr. Burn after much indecision has left for London, it is said. . . . It is thought that he was tempted to go and judge the modern Greeks for himself. . . . You ask if I like percales? Very much. We are wearing them with very pretty little painted borders. The [carpet] tapes seem to me to be a sizable undertaking, but worthy of your courage. I envision it must be very pretty. If you find a way to send me a band of it, I will contribute with all my heart to the success of the enterprise. Fanny, my children's nurse of whom I think I have written in flattering terms embroidered a charming dress for me while I was away. It is a lovely Etruscan design worked in lilac silk on an India muslin. . . .

Incidentally, is it true that the de Pestres are seeking to sell their house and that they are to leave for Europe? . . . Is there any news of Mr. de la Chapelle?[173] Do you expect to see him again?

I hope that before answering such insignificant questions you will be good enough to write about your fine family and remember us very particularly to them. What of your new little sister-in-law?[174] Does she still play loo? And do you still play? . . . Tell us also of G[enera]l Pinckney and Mde. Are they still in Charleston? . . . Victor is still ashamed at not having had time to present his respects to the ladies except in pantaloons and white flannel coat. He really had no time to dress before their departure, which the g[enera]l told him was to occur at that very moment.

. . . [I would like] to know whether you have any pretty music that can be found in America, and some slightly unusual dress pattern that would be highly successful here where our belles drape themselves every which way. . . .[175]

Mrs. du Pont to Mrs. Manigault
(in French)
New York   30 Nov. 1800

. . . [Mr. D. P. will leave for France in about two weeks.] I will stay sadly where I am and my father-in-law will come to spend the winter with me. Irénée is to accompany his brother, but he will return by the same ship. The rest of the family will spend the winter in the country. This letter will be delivered to you by Cl. de Veaux[176] whom I do not know, but who has promised Victor to take charge of it and a little box made up from a larger one that came to me from Paris. It will provide you with a small sample. I am attaching a most informative extract from an English newspaper of 30 September that will completely reassure you concerning that amaranth color, which might perhaps seem vulgar. I believe it proper enough to make a morning dress for shopping, and I pray you to protect it enough to do it this honor. Tell me frankly whether you find it pretty? I am greatly pleased with the contents of that box which arrived in excellent condition. Buckles dominate. . . .

I am closer than ever to Belle et bonne. . . . Yesterday she sent me a charming gouache landscape very prettily framed on the back of which in her hand was an inscription in honor of our friendship. Every morning we have interminable consultations. I have made her . . . something of a coquette. She is uncertain in her tastes and has a high regard for mine. She has given Mr. D. P. a small list of commissions that will come to more than 200 g[our]des, not counting her mother's. If he wished to be very gallant, he could collect a full cargo of band boxes for our belles, but I am stubbornly opposed and claim that is an exclusive privilege for the three of

---

[173] Mr. de la Chapelle, not identified, may be the subject of La Rochefoucauld-Liancourt's comment, "I met in Charleston with a school-fellow of mine, Mr. de la Chapelle, a man of uncommon worth, and of the noblest and most generous mind. He has saved no more than fifteen hundred Louis d'or; and yet from his frugal mode of life he is able to do much good to others, by whom however his kindness is frequently abused." *Travels Through the United States,* 2:427–28.

[174] Charlotte Drayton Manigault married Joseph Manigault, brother of Gabriel and then a widower, on May 27, 1800.

[175] Here, for the first time since her return to America Josephine du Pont requests fashion advice from her Charleston friend.

[176] Colonel Andrea de Veaux, originally of Charleston, joined the British army during the Revolution. In 1797 he married Anna Maria Verplanck and settled at Red Hook, N.Y. He was active in the West Indies trade. *Ancestral Records and Portraits,* a compilation from the archives of Chapter I, The Colonial Dames of America (New York: by the editorial department of the Grafton Press, 1910), 2:503.

us only. . . . I am in a rather melancholic frame of mind, not very appropriate in society. And I believe in spite of the need for diversion, the promise I made to Mr. Du Pont and the little box, that I shall stay encased in my large draped redingote at my own fireside this winter. . . . In any case the idea is not very noble at present because there is not any ball, nor any concerts nor any big parties. Many households have illness or are in mourning. Mde. Church has not yet resumed her Thursdays. No one seems to want to begin, except Mde. Barclay,[177] whom I do not know, who has already given suppers. We fall back on the theater which is extremely boring. The men are engrossed in politics.[178] . . . What I like of your politics is that savoir vivre unites [opponents], not in their opinions but socially. Mde. Ch. brought us Colonel Burr[179] and seems to make a point of treating the chiefs of the party opposite to her own with the greatest distinction. I find such politics greatly to my liking. I have just reread your list of commissions. I will add two trims either of ribbon or something else, some gloves, bands. These little things are always prettiest in France. Silk sleeves assorted in your little taffetas. I hope all will be well made and will arrive safely.

Mrs. Manigault to Mrs. du Pont
(in English)
Charleston   24 Nov. 1800

At length, my dear Friend, my dismal forebodings & apprehensions have vanished . . . & I am the Mother of a fine, stout, healthy little boy. . . .[180]

The charming long letter containing an account of your pleasant little excursion arrived (by the Post, & not the Vessel you mention) a few days ago. You seem to give the preference very decidedly to Wilmington, of all the Towns you visited. However the society, or rather the family you describe, is very well calculated for that purpose. But what shall I say to the very flattering comparison you make? . . . What was Mrs. Montgomery's name before her marriage? In reading your account of the arrival which was to decide Mr. D. P.'s voyage, I was full of hope that the event would be known before the conclusion of your letter. We are exceedingly anxious about it. . . . How delightful it will be once more to have a free intercourse established between two Nations that we both love so well! In a good, large, convenient vessel a voyage to France would frighten me less than one to Rhode Island—and how much stronger, & more numerous the temptations! . . . I love the quiet, easy, & every way pleasant establishment which I now enjoy. You know it, therefore I will not lose time in enumerating all the various concomitant circumstances which compose it—and once deranged, how different would be the reorganization! Mr. M. often says "We are vegetating, our best days are passing away. Let us amuse ourselves while we may. Let us travel. Let us see what is so well worth seeing." . . . We shall see what all this will produce.[181]

So Mr. Burn has escaped. An Oracle (b) would have it that he ran away from a fair one here who was nothing less than coy, indeed who was ready to be his in any way. But I do not believe him so easily alarmed. The Jockey de P[estre][182] has offered his little territory for sale, & nobody will buy. The lady is said to be so altered as to be meconnoissable. She is never seen excepting in the morning courant les boutiques [touring the shops]. And Heaven knows why. For she has nothing to do with any of us. & the french society is altogether broken up. The ladies have all quarreled. Sometimes I hear of their little tracasseries [vexations], but indeed they are not worth detailing to you. Messieurs F[ournier] & V[andoeuvre] were very urgent with me the other day to commence an acquaintance with Mme. de la Rue (Niel). I was not much inclined to do so. But two days after their visit, this lady was seen parading the streets with a Be[a]u on each arm, & every favorable impression which F. & V. had made vanished. Madame Labat[t]ut lost her son a few months ago. She will lie in in February. Her husband continues to work like a horse & with all his

---

[177] Susannah de Lancey Barclay, wife of the British consul-general, Colonel Thomas Barclay.

[178] The presidential election was at hand, and discussion between Federalist and Republican factions was heated. Josephine du Pont assumed the future election of Charles C. Pinckney in her letters to Mrs. Manigault, who kept silent on political matters. Thomas Jefferson was elected.

[179] Aaron Burr (1756–1836), soon to be chosen Vice-President.

[180] Edward Manigault was the darling of his family until his death from measles in 1808.

[181] The Manigaults did travel north in 1801, after which trip they laid plans to move to Philadelphia.

[182] The full identification of the de Pestres is not established. The *Charleston Directory* of 1801 lists Horatio Depestre, planter, 3 Coming Street, whereas the 1802 directory gives his name as Hector.

exertions makes about 1200 dollars a year. That is very well, & he procures for her every comfort. I never see them. She stays very much at home they all say, & there are not wanting ill natured commentators upon her conduct as well as upon that of the other french ladies just mentioned.

But let me now tell you a little piece of news which has occupied all Charleston for the last four days. Miss Bell Middleton, third daughter of Mrs. M. eloped the other night with Mr. Daniel Huger,[183] brother to the young ladies who lived at Col. Morris'. He has been paying his addresses during eighteen months, and was refused by Mrs. M.'s orders in rather a rougher style than he thought his respectful offer deserved. He went to Rhode Island with his Sisters, & on his return employed his rhetoric so well that she consented to leave the maternal roof & be his. They were married at Mr. Barnard Elliott's,[184] & the next day after receiving a friendly visit from her Brother & two of her Sisters she accompanied her husband to Accabee, seven or eight miles from Town. It is to be hoped that the Mother will soon be persuaded to forgive, & receive them. At present she cannot bear to hear them named.

I heard a person lament very feelingly last night that Mr. D. P. was not here. Perhaps he may recollect a Mr. Moses Franks[185] in Philadelphia. He is now here with his Wife. They left the Bahamas for their health, & leave us in a few days. He is an Englishman, & Chief Justice of the Bahamas. She is a West Indian, in other words a Creole, & upon reflection, not unlike Mme. Bournonville.[186] Do you want to know more? She was covered with broad lace, & ornaments. A propos I will certainly send you a little model of a gown which I lately received from England. I have not yet worn it, not having been in Company for many months until last night, & then we made a party à la hâte [hastily] for these Bahamians. If I can procure the materials, I hope too to send you a true & faithful copy of a hat or bonnet which is to be mes delices [pleasure] this winter. One of my head dresses is a very pretty hat of black satin with steel spots, & a handsome steel button, & loop in front, & a plume of blue, & white feathers. Every thing is to fit the head exactly, & as flat as possible. They have sent me some pretty ceintures.[187] I will endeavor to give you an idea of them. . . . Mrs. Pinckney is now in Town. She is well, but in great dread of a return of her disorder. . . . Our gentlemen are all at Columbia,[188] of course the Town is tolerably dull. I did party last night. . . .

Mrs. du Pont to Mrs. Manigault (in French)

20 Dec. 1800

. . . Once again, receive my sincere and tender congratulations on the happy arrival of your handsome little boy, whose name I have yet to learn. Raise him, I beg you, as well as the others so he will not unduly fatigue you. . . .

The Wilmington trip had some consequences, for it is not a circumstance of indifference in the life of a reasonable woman (at least one who has some pretentions of reason) to acquire a friend. A friend, you are going to exclaim. Made a friend in a week spent shopping and being entertained? A modern Greek would not be more ridiculous! I agree, and to justify myself and make the matter less extraordinary would take a page of reasoning and two or three of explanation. So I am sorry to have confessed this, especially if you are not a physionomist, and if you do not agree that there sometimes exist certain points of contacts in character and feelings that attract you involuntarily and assume real consistency when one sees them shared. That is what happened. On leaving Wilmington I said to Mr. D. P. that of the whole collection of amiable women the one who pleased and attracted me the most was the elder Mrs. Bauduy.[189] She seems charming. I would like very much for us to be close friends. When he returned from Phila-

---

[183] Isabella Middleton, daughter of Arthur Middleton, signer of the Declaration of Independence, married Daniel Huger, planter-lawyer and later U.S. Senator, on November 26, 1800. The young couple resided in 1801 on Legaré Street. *Charleston Directory*, 1801.

[184] Mr. Barnard Elliott, planter, lived on St. Philip Street.

[185] Moses Franks was the son of David Franks, a prominent Philadelphia Jewish merchant. Educated at the University of Pennsylvania, he was subsequently admitted to the bar in London and pursued a distinguished legal career in the Bahamas. Jacob R. Marcus, *The Colonial American Jew 1492–1776*, 3 vols. (Detroit: Wayne State University Press, 1970), 2:545.

[186] Mme. Bournonville's husband was secretary to Genêt.

[187] Belts. Crewel, crochet, painted fabric, cording, and metallic bands were all popular, as were sashes.

[188] Columbia, S.C., the state capital, where the legislature was in session. Except for the Charleston French, most of the gentlemen in the Manigault circle were politically involved.

[189] Hélène Cruon Bauduy, widowed mother of the Wilmington, Delaware, Bauduys.

delphia, he said on that subject: Rest easy. Mde. B. said the loveliest things about you, wants you to spend the summer in Wilmington and pretends that if you cannot decide to do so, then she will come to New York. Is that not amazing on both parts!! . . .

What do you think of that fine motion which, nine hundred miles apart, pushes us both to the generous sacrifice of part of our European treasures as a kind of competition between London and Paris. I greatly fear that the amaranth may lose, for it is not nearly as imposing as your black velvet scattered with steel. Fortunately there is no need to draw back nor to unwrap it, for in my national pride I would have been woman enough to substitute for it a turban of white satin and crape trimmed in silver with a kind of drapery which falls from the left side of the fichu. I enclosed only some parisiennes in person [fashion prints] who will defend themselves as they can. I am keeping some to copy, but I shall send them to you soon. Despite their thin appearance some are very pretty indeed. Once again, renounce your blond circlet for the present. Thirty times I have sent to the maker, but there is no way to get anything from him. He pretends that the hair he had set aside for us was burned in the oven! What a misfortune! What a calamity for the New York belles. So how do you manage? Can it be that you would still have the courage to use your own hair. Pretty as it is, it seems impossible to me to use now. The revolution is complete here—wigs and no powder at all! But they are for the most part curled and stiff. There are still very few like mine, although mine are pronounced very attractive. The assemblies are beginning. The other evening we had a very brilliant party—all the Ch[urch family], Hamilton, Cra[w]-ford, Stoughton and many others, not counting a Mlle. Dhomme. By the mantel three game tables. It has been talked of, and in a complimentary manner. Our salon is very pretty. It lacks only mirrors and a grand piano. Mde. Church told me yesterday that one of your cousins, Mde.—Livingston[190] had asked her for an introduction to me. You must realize, I am eager to know her. I intended to go to see Mde. Go[o]ld yesterday to get news of your aunt. I have not yet found time. Perhaps she is in town. Belle et bonne, ever faithful, was truly charming last night. She had a percale dress em-

broidered in front with two rows of flat gold rings, the little fichu and an arm matching, with a bonnet fashioned after my "bonnes femmes" with buckles and chains. I wore a gray taffeta redingote edged with white fur, a charming white straw hat garnished with a buckle and a type of steel fringe from the little box, an orange muslin shawl trimmed with black fur. That toilette was a success. Mme. Ch. appeared with a superb diamond buckle on her négligé of point, a shawl of the same stuff originating from a lilac-lined falbala[191] nonchalantly attached by means of a crescent of brilliants. As for the others, you have seen them a thousand times. The gathering was at Mrs. Stoughton's. We had a loo, but what a loo, my dear friend. Imagine, they only put in 5 when one was loo, and the ante was a quarter. One could die of boredom. . . .

Mrs. Manigault to Mrs. du Pont
(in French)
Charleston   24 Dec. 1800
. . . My children keep me very busy—instructing the oldest, feeding the little one, busying the others, teaching them to read, to work, &c. But I would rather steal from my sleep (And you know how I like it) than to miss such a sweet, such a precious correspondence.

<u>26.</u> There is but one way, that will be to write a little at a time, to recommence often. I thought I had two good hours before dinner, because M. M— is dining in Town. But I had a small group to dinner, and we laughed so much, ate so many jellies, dressed so that now it is almost midnight. Here we are in our great holidays. These are the Saturnals of the Romans. All our domestics have their heads turned. They dream only of drinking, eating, dancing, & amusing themselves well during the three days they are given. It is very entertaining for them. And assuredly those who serve us well during the rest of the year merit at least this little vacation. Also we try to add to it all the joys possible. But in these times (you understand me) we are not perfectly in a state of security and repose. You have doubtless heard talk of the Virginia affair, [which] happily failed.[192] They sent us in-

[190] Which of the many Livingston ladies is meant is unclear.

[191] Rows of plaiting, or a puckered flounce.

[192] The Gabriel Conspiracy (August 1800) occurred in Henrico County, Virginia. The blacksmith Gabriel was said to be prepared to lead a thousand slaves in a march on Richmond when warnings to the whites and a severe storm quashed the revolt. Kenneth Stampp, *The Peculiar Institu-*

numerable troops of those wicked faces who were indiscreetly received in the interior of the country. Our sages and our soothsayers have talked so much of it that I avow the cry "Fire" heard at two o'clock in the morning last night gave me a terrible start. I am sick from it today. But my fright was baseless. There was only one house burned, and order and tranquillity were immediately reestablished. . . . I am going to spend the evening with Mme. Pinckney, where my husband dined, and I must at least make a little toilette.

Here I am returned. We took our tea very smartly, we chatted, we played Nain Jaune [a card game], which is in no way worth that unfortunate Loo which is so disdained. We supped very wisely too. And here we are. (I am) in my Bergere[193] at my fireside. . . .

The conformity of our tastes and our feelings has often brought me the greatest pleasure. I am presently enjoying the coincidence that made us act the same way at the same time. You were assembling for me the kind little extract from the box that arrived from France, while I was copying for you the contents of a case that came from London. You were telling me of Colonel de V. while I was announcing to you Captain Pelor of the [ship] South Carolina. That Captain Pelor made me work like a horse to complete dressing my good little Amelie's doll. She would have been prettier if I had not insisted on wanting to give you a dress pattern which I assure you has a great deal of merit. It came to me in the latest case, and you will like it. The doll's is very ample throughout, and too short in front. It should have three rows of lace instead of two. I am not enthused over the back, but it is very much better in full size. And the demoiselle's back does not lend itself very well to the charm of its drapery. The sleeves are very pretty, and new. As for the hat, I am ashamed of the lace. But in truth all of Charleston could not supply me with the right kind. But you have some no doubt, and you can change it. It is the proper width, and in all

respects the hat is faithfully copied, and I love it madly. Tell me honestly if you agree with me. I made one in violet Crepe, trimmed with a lovely blond [crepe], and decorated with one of the pretty flowers you sent me. The poor Doll looks like a sack, but her little mistress has not yet begun to criticize outfits. I announce to you that the lady is of Wax, so that you may unpack her very gently and with great caution. I did not want to take one with eyes that closed, because I have found them extremely disagreeable. They spoil and become frightful. . . .

I very sincerely share in your chagrin over the departure of Mr. D. P. . . . Will I tell you that M. M. is at this very moment decided on making a trip north? . . .

Monday 29. I have just wrapped my little package. Besides the doll and that hat there is a band. You will readily see that the corner makes the fichu, that it is attached with a pin, that the two small knots are found on the shoulders. But instead of the little pin that holds the crossed ribbon, a buckle or a gold ornament is needed. You surely have one. And then after crossing it on the chest, it is knotted in the back. The little veil on the hat can be worn over the eyes or else lifted up as it is, and that is the way I like it. I beg M. *Charles* to accept the little Cabriolet with a kiss on his two rosy cheeks. I hope a barrel of sweet potatoes, which I am having put on board, will succeed better than the last time, and that those dear children will like them because of their country. . . . Mlle. Washington de Poissure[194] has just married. She wed a big animal, former overseer, and has greatly angered her Brother. A man named LaLande[195] has just ruined most of the French who are left with us. He took bankruptcy. M. de Pestre lost some. That poor Mme. Remoussin lost 200 pounds. And an infinity of others I know only by name. The Wasp is no longer seen, as I believe I told you. The favorite I told you about has returned [Comte de Fierbeau]. . . . He is said to resemble M. D. P. in the face, and he even has something of his appearance and manners—with this difference, that he makes all possible efforts to please while M. D. P. rather lets things take their course and perhaps pleased no less with that. There

tion, *Slavery in the Ante-Bellum South* (New York: Knopf, 1956), p. 135. An unrecorded number of the conspirators apparently sought refuge in the less settled inland region of the Carolinas.

[193] "The arm chair, or *fauteuil*, with *upholstered* instead of *open* sides was introduced into the suite of tapestry furniture and the term by which it is known, '*chaise bergère*,' seems to be a sign of the fashion of the day." Frederick Litchfield, *Illustrated History of Furniture* (Boston: The Medici Society of America, 1922), p. 236.

[194] Possibly the daughter of William Washington, South Bay, Charleston.

[195] The bankruptcy of Mr. Lalande, whose name is not listed in existing Charleston directories, occurred when the business community of the city was prospering, and may have been related to unsettled conditions in the West Indies.

have arrived here a M. and Mme. Millet, with a lady who is supposed to be a prodigy. She dances and sings like an angel, and it is said that she intends teaching. That M. Millet was sent to St. Domingo by Bonaparte. And Toussaint[196] did not wish to receive him. The other day I was told that M. de la Chapelle had made more than 40,000 pounds since his sojourn in Santo Domingo, and that he has spent it all. And how? By playing the gallant for two personages of yellow and livid tint whom you could have seen here at the home of another old man who offered lunch.

I am no longer sending my letter by Captain Pelor. He is delaying too much. A man who has rented a house from M. M— is taking charge of my little box, my potatoes and my letter. He promises to deliver them to you. He is called Jessop. It is he who has made the first ices here, and he even goes to New York to load his little ship with it.[197] As he is returning here immediately, I think the opportunity excellent. His vessel is called The Rising Sun. . . . We have established a Whist Club where women are admitted. Notice that I say admitted. The first meeting will be here next Friday. It will meet every Friday, at the home of all the members who have houses, in turn. . . .

I have nothing new in Music. Bradford no longer

knows how to order or have anything of value. We have some pretty little airs for Harp by Guilbert. But nothing at all for the Piano. I almost never play it now. My little Piano is no longer any good; my Grand is in the large salon where there is not always a fire. I told you I was degenerating. . . .

Mrs. Manigault to Mrs. du Pont
(in English)
Charleston 31 Dec. 1800 for the last time.

In five minutes this Century will be no more—The Clock now strikes twelve—It is gone! May the New year, may the new Century bring nothing but happiness, & prosperity to you, my amiable Friend! I finished a letter of five sheets to you [MS torn] Evening—That goes by the letter bag. This by a Mr. Jessop. He keeps a Coffee house here, & goes to N. York for a Cargo of Ice. Our Winter is so delightfully mild that he has no chance of supplying himself here: He also takes charge of a little box, & a barrel of sweet Potatoes. . . .[198]

Good Night. Or rather Good Morning. My bed gown is thin, & I am cold, not cold in heart sweet Lady—but very warmly Yours

M. I. M.

---

[196] Toussaint Louverture, a native of Haiti, was chief of the Santo Domingo insurgents from 1796 to 1802.

[197] Possibly Jeremiah Jessop of 12 King Street. *Charleston Directory*, 1801.

[198] To ship these sweet potatoes, Margaret Manigault packed the cooked product in the lower half of a barrel, and then placed raw sweet potatoes on top. Only the top portion arrived unspoiled and was enjoyed by the du Pont children.

A Most Perfect Resemblance at Moderate Prices

The Miniatures of David Boudon

Nancy E. Richards

WHEN DAVID BOUDON arrived in America in late 1794 or early 1795, the list of French émigré miniaturists already in residence included such names as Jean-Claude Imbert, Philip Parisen, Pierre Henri, Jean Belzons, Peter J. Meance, Henri Elouis, Thomas de Valdenuit, and Charles Févret de Saint-Mémin. Some had fled the political upheavals in Europe; others were refugees from the holocaust in Santo Domingo created by an uprising under the leadership of Toussaint Louverture. Whatever their origins all came hoping to earn a livelihood by painting portraits. America offered a singularly attractive location to practice their trade: political stability, a dearth of competent artists, and a growing and increasingly well-to-do public ready to buy works of art.

The historical background of the portrait miniature and its significance in eighteenth- and nineteenth-century society have been assessed by several authors.[1] Although the term "miniature" is used today to identify any small-scale painting, eighteenth-century artists differentiated between miniature portraits painted in oil or watercolor on ivory, profile likenesses painted in watercolor on vellum or paper, and profile shades or silhouettes drawn and cut from paper. The first required the skills of a painter to create form with tone and value. The second emphasized drawing technique, using line to develop form. The third was a mechanical proc-

ess of shadow tracing, employing a pantograph to capture outline. Boudon was particularly skilled in drawing, and his works include many profile portraits drawn in silverpoint on vellum.

David Boudon is an elusive figure. Although he worked in America for more than twenty years, the details of his career must be pieced together from the inscriptions on surviving portraits and a few newspaper advertisements. At least fifty-one portraits, each meticulously annotated, stand as a record of his work. Each has inscribed on the reverse in French (Fig. 1) or English (Fig. 2) his name, his place of origin, the provenance of the portrait, and its date. Rarely does an artist provide such complete documentation. Yet Boudon's work is known to only a few scholars and collectors.[2]

If details concerning his years in America are scant, even less is known of his career in Europe. He was born in Geneva, Switzerland, on July 11, 1748, the son of David and Anne (Farinière) Boudon. At the age of twelve he was apprenticed to the Genevan copperplate engraver Jean-Daniel Dupré.[3] As part of his apprenticeship he received two

[1] Theodore Bolton, *Early American Portrait Painters in Miniature* (New York: Frederick Fairchild Sherman, 1921); Harry B. Wehle, *American Miniatures 1730–1850* (New York: Garden City Publishing Co., 1937); Torben Holck Colding, *Aspects of Miniature Painting, Its Origins and Development* (Copenhagen: F. E. Bording, 1953); Daphne Foskett, *A Dictionary of British Miniature Painters* (London: Faber & Faber, 1972).

[2] No mention of David Boudon appears in either the comprehensive lexicon by Emanuel Bénézit, *Dictionnaire Critique et Documentaire des Peintres, Sculpteurs, Dessinateurs, et Graveurs* (Paris: Gründ, 1948–55) or Ulrich Thieme and Felix Becker, *Allgemeines Lexikon der bildenden Künstler von der Antike bis zur Gegenwart*, 37 vols. (Leipzig: E. A. Seeman, 1907–1950). Boudon is mentioned briefly in William Dunlap, *History of the Rise and Progress of the Arts of Design in the United States*, 2 vols. (1834; reprint ed., New York: Dover, 1969), 2: pt. 1, p. 227; "The Editor's Attic," *Antiques* 21, no. 1 (Jan. 1932): 12; Anna Wells Rutledge, *Artists in the Life of Charleston* (Philadelphia: American Philosophical Society, 1949), note p. 125; George C. Groce and David H. Wallace, *The New-York Historical Society's Dictionary of Artists in America 1564–1860* (New Haven: Yale University Press, 1957), p. 68.

[3] C. Roch, "David Boudon," *Pages d'Art* (1924): 295.

FIG. 1. Silverpoint inscription from Boudon's portrait of *Mrs. William Moore* (Fig. 3). (Collection of Mrs. Joseph Carson: Photo, Charles P. Mills & Son Photography.)

FIG. 3. David Boudon, *Mrs. William Moore* (Susannah Bolton). Savannah, Ga., Apr. 1795. Silverpoint and watercolor on vellum; H. 3½", W. 3⅛". (Collection of Mrs. Joseph Carson: Photo, Charles P. Mills & Son Photography.)

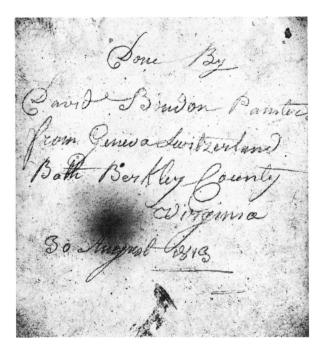

FIG. 2. Silverpoint inscription from Boudon's portrait of *Aberdy Gustin* (Fig. 19). (Collection of William T. Hassett, Jr.: Photo, Raup Photographic Studios.)

years of instruction in drawing and design, which he probably took at the municipal art school in Geneva.[4] His "academic" training included a program of copying drawings from books, of drawing from plaster casts of antique and baroque sculpture, and of drawing from life. He would have had some exposure to painting techniques, but primary emphasis was placed on drawing.

Because of his training with Dupré, it is assumed that Boudon began his professional career in Geneva in the late 1760s as a copperplate engraver or etcher, although no examples of his work have been identified. In fact, fewer than ten works dating from the fifteen-year period between the end of his schooling and his emigration to America have been

[4] This school was chartered in 1751 by Pierre Soubeyran to provide practical instruction for commercial artists. In the original charter Soubeyran stated: "I am here not speaking of a school suitable for the education of architects, sculptors or painters, in the proper sense, but of one that regards it as its proper task to improve the work and manufactures most usual in commerce and everyday life." Nicholas Pevsner, *Academies of Art, Past and Present* (Cambridge: At the University Press, 1940), p. 157.

located.[5] By 1780 his artistic accomplishments included metalpoint drawing. His earliest documented work is a metalpoint portrait of an unidentified man shown writing at a table. The figure is seen in full-front view with his head turned three-quarters to the viewer's right. Above the subject's left arm is the inscription: "David Boudon fecit/Geneva avril/1780." The portrait shows that Boudon was an excellent draftsman. The planes of the figure's face are finely modeled in a stipple technique, and the surrounding space and the texture of the costume are defined by a series of overlapping lines. The portrait of an unidentified woman, drawn at Nîmes, France, in 1786, employs a similar technique.[6] In this instance, the figure is shown in profile against a neutral background. By this method of presenting the figure, Boudon minimized problems of foreshortening and utilized a less complex method for indicating spatial volume. As in the earlier portrait, he concentrated on the face, using the stipple technique to mold facial planes, and reduced the delineation of costume to a series of lines.

To an artist trained in the use of engraving or etching tools, the transition to metalpoint is not a difficult one. In both techniques design is achieved by laying line against line, or line over line, to develop shadow and depth of tone. In both, the line must be deliberate and decisive; errors cannot be removed without reworking a prepared ground. In metalpoint, a stylus is used to lay a line on the prepared ground, whereas engraving requires a graver or burin to gouge a line into the surface, and etching employs a needle to draw a line on an acid-resisting ground. Metalpoint lends itself to drawings that invite examination at close range and are enjoyable for the delicacy of their detail. It produces precisely conceived images that are highly linear and have little suggestive shading.

Nothing is known of Boudon's work in the years between 1786 and his arrival in America in 1794 or 1795. Later advertisements suggest that he spent those eight years studying in Italy. Boudon was forty-seven when he emigrated to America, propelled by political events in Europe and enticed by the hope of a quickly made fortune. A trained artist, he arrived in this country with a fully developed style—a style that did not vary perceptibly throughout the rest of his career. While most contemporary miniature painters were creating form with opaque colors, Boudon's technique was linear with color used as a transparent wash. In appearance his portraits relate to line engravings or etchings. Throughout his career, he thought of himself as a draftsman, a limner rather than a painter. Nowhere is this more clearly stated than in his first newspaper advertisement, which appeared more than two years after his arrival in this country.

DAVID BOUDON, limner, from Geneva in Switzerland, Draws any picture upon Vellum in imitation of Miniature, at Six Dollars each. He Draws it with the hands in it, even when composed with several family pictures. Specimens may be seen at Mr. Bossee's Hotel, No. 50 South Fifth Street, and at Messrs. Houards and Frontis's Tailors, No. 9, South Front street.
N.B. He also draws in Miniature upon Ivory.[7]

Despite the availability of a wide variety of metallic substances—silver, gold, lead, tin, brass, or bronze—that could be used for making drawing styluses, Boudon seems to have preferred to work in silverpoint. This technique employs a line that is light gray when applied but, under normal exposure to the air, it turns a delicate light brown.[8] He specialized in bust-length portraits although he produced an occasional half-length figure. Of the total group of surviving American portraits, more than three-fifths are silverpoint profile likenesses and about one-fifth are silverpoint portraits showing the figure in three-quarter or full-front view. The remaining paintings are watercolor portraits on ivory.

Boudon chose Charleston as his first American headquarters, a logical selection since Charleston was a cosmopolitan center with a high proportion of European contacts and a long history of French emigration. As the social and commercial capital of the South, it was the home of a large group of influential merchants, bankers, lawyers, and planters. Among his first patrons were William Gui-

---

[5] Among Boudon's European works are the portraits of an unidentified man, probably his brother, François (Geneva, 1780); David-François Montandon (1781); his two-year-old niece, Anne-Françoise Boudon (Nîmes, 1786); his year-old nephew, Jean-March Boudon (Nîmes, 1786); an unidentified woman (Nîmes, 1786); and an unidentified man (Nîmes, 1786). All these portraits are metalpoint on vellum. An undated portrait of an unidentified woman is the only known example of an oil portrait on ivory by Boudon. Roch, "David Boudon," pp. 297–98.

[6] Roch, "David Boudon," pp. 297–98.

[7] *Aurora* (Philadelphia), Dec. 4, 1797.

[8] Technical information on metalpoint drawing is available in James Watrous, *The Craft of Old-Master Drawings* (Madison: University of Wisconsin Press, 1967), pp. 3–33.

gnard Richardson and William Coffin, both members of families engaged in mercantile trade.

The possibilities for commissions were numerous, but the limited number of works surviving from this first period in Charleston suggest that Boudon encountered more competition than he had anticipated. Certainly, there were three well-known miniaturists already settled in Charleston when he arrived. Jean-Claude Imbert had emigrated from Nantes in 1793 and was providing "miniature painting in exact likenesses, on very reasonable terms." Philip Parisen, visiting from New York, advertised "strong likenesses in profile at the moderate price of three guineas each." And Jean Belzons, Thomas Sully's brother-in-law, advertised that he "had established his price at 5£ for a likeness and will furnish [a] plain elegant gold setting for the additional price of 2£."[9]

Like most artists, Boudon had to move frequently in search of commissions. Surviving portraits confirm that by April of 1795 he was in Savannah. Since no advertisements appeared in the Savannah newspapers, probably his Savannah commissions were the result of letters of introduction from prominent Charlestonians. Boudon's fixed fee for each portrait was six dollars. If surviving examples are any indication, he preferred to do portraits of several members of a family. This afforded him some semblance of financial security and reduced the constant problem of locating individual sitters.

Boudon spent about three months in Savannah. During that time he executed portraits of at least two family groups. Three-quarter face portraits of Mrs. William Moore (Fig. 3) and her son, Mauve John Moore (Fig. 4), were completed in April. For an artist seeking patronage, Susannah Moore, the socially prestigious widow of a prominent local merchant, was an ideal client, one who could provide entrée to equally prominent mercantile families along the eastern seaboard. She was the sister of Robert Bolton, Jr., a Savannah merchant with business connections in Chestertown, Maryland, and New York City. Later commissions in New York and on the Eastern Shore may have been a direct result of this early contact.

Also dating from the Savannah visit are a pair of profile likenesses of Robert James Mossman Houstoun (Fig. 5), aged ten, and his eleven-year-old

sister, Priscilla (Fig. 6). They were the two youngest children of Sir George Houstoun, a wealthy merchant who traded in indigo. In both portraits, the profile outline of the face and neck is delicately drawn with meticulous care. The hair and the costume have been laid in with heavier brush strokes of water color.

A portrait of Stephen Van Wyck (Fig. 7) survives as the only record of Boudon's brief trip to New York late in 1795. As in the portraits of Susannah Moore and her son, Van Wyck is shown almost full front. Boudon took great care with the delineation of the face, but despite the suggested bulk of the costume, the body of the figure seems flat. Boudon used color only as a tinting medium, not for purposes of modeling.

On the trip back to Charleston, Boudon stopped for several months on the Eastern Shore of Maryland. Between February and September of 1796 he was working in Talbot County near Easton. His return to Charleston in October was marked by a commission for a portrait of Elizabeth Anne Horry (Fig. 8), the young daughter of Jonah Horry, a

Fig. 4. David Boudon, *Mauve John Moore*. Savannah, Ga., Apr. 1795. Silverpoint and watercolor on vellum; H. 3³⁄₁₆″, W. 2⅝″. (Collection of Mrs. Joseph Carson: Photo, Charles P. Mills & Son Photography.)

⁹ *The City Gazette & Daily Advertiser* (Charleston), Aug. 3, 1793; Oct. 21, 1795; June 16, 1795.

FIG. 5. David Boudon, *Robert James Mossman Houstoun.* Savannah, Ga., May 1795. Silverpoint and watercolor on vellum; H. 2¾″, W. 2⅜″. (Collection of Edith D. Johnston Papers, Georgia Historical Society.)

FIG. 6. David Boudon, *Priscilla Houstoun.* Savannah, Ga., June 1795. Silverpoint and watercolor on vellum; H. 2⅞″, W. 2⅜″. (Collection of Edith D. Johnston Papers, Georgia Historical Society.)

planter with vast land holdings in South Carolina. For this portrait Boudon chose the profile pose he had used so successfully with the Houstoun children. No other Charleston portraits have come to light, although Boudon probably remained there until mid-1797. His second departure from Charleston marked the end of the first phase of his American career. In his first two years in this country, he had painted portraits of several prominent families, and his contacts had included many wealthy merchants and members of the southern gentry. It is interesting to note that many of his commissions came from the same prominent families that had patronized Henry Benbridge half a generation earlier.

What prompted Boudon's move to Philadelphia in late 1797 is not known. Potentially, Philadelphia was an artist's paradise filled with wealthy families, visiting celebrities, and diplomats. Like Charleston,

it was a focus of French influence; in fact, after the Revolution it was the great center for French émigrés. But in Philadelphia Boudon certainly encountered more competition than he had faced in Charleston. Several lesser-known miniaturists were firmly established: Samuel Folwell, a miniaturist, silhouettist, and engraver; Lewis Pise, an Italian miniaturist; John Roberts, a portrait and miniature painter and engraver visiting from New York; and Lawrence Sully, the older brother of Thomas Sully. But his major competition came from the Peale family. For more than twenty-five years Charles Willson Peale had controlled portraiture in Philadelphia. Now Peale was devoting his major interest to the management of the Peale Museum, and most commissions for miniature portraits were granted to his brother James or to his sons Rembrandt and Raphael.

Boudon arrived in Philadelphia sometime be-

FIG. 7. David Boudon, *Stephen Van Wyck*. New York City, Sept. 1795. Silverpoint and watercolor on vellum; H. 3″, W. 2⅜″. (Collection of Mrs. Daniel F. Larkin: Photo, Arthur J. Kiely, Jr.)

fore December 4, 1797, when his first published advertisement appeared.[10] He probably spent two or three years in the area using Philadelphia as his headquarters. In September 1798, he visited Harrisburg, Pennsylvania. While there he completed a profile likeness of John Bayly (Fig. 9), a silversmith who worked primarily in Philadelphia. While this portrait of a craftsman seems to break with Boudon's established practice of seeking commissions from the gentry, Bayly was sufficiently successful to be considered the economic equal of many of Boudon's other patrons.

The appearance of Charles Févret de Saint-Mémin in Philadelphia in the winter of 1798 must have caused Boudon some concern. Saint-Mémin, an artist of established reputation, carried letters of introduction from the first families of New York to the leaders of Philadelphia society. Moreover, while the Peales' miniatures were executed in a painterly tradition with form molded by juxtaposing color, Saint-Mémin's engraved portraits (Fig. 10) had a visual similarity to the linear technique

[10] *Aurora* (Philadelphia), Dec. 4, 1797.

used by Boudon. Saint-Mémin was prepared to provide an original full-size crayon portrait, the engraved copperplate, and twelve copies of the engraving at a cost of $25.00 for gentlemen and $35.00 for ladies. Twelve additional engravings could be purchased for $1.50.[11] This was considerably less than the $6.00 fee Boudon charged for one of his silverpoint drawings.

Faced with economic competition of this kind, Boudon withdrew to the south. During the next few years he spent much of his time traveling. In 1801 and again in 1804, he was working in Alexandria, Virginia. By late November 1804 he was in Raleigh, North Carolina.[12] Early the next year he

[11] Fillmore Norfleet, *Saint-Mémin in Virginia: Portraits and Biographies* (Richmond, Va.: Dietz Press, 1942), pp. 24–25.

[12] Boudon offered his services in Raleigh through the shop of J. B. Dumoutet, a jeweler from Philadelphia. *Raleigh Register*, Dec. 3, 1804.

FIG. 8. David Boudon, *Elizabeth Anne Horry*. Charleston, S.C., Oct. 1796. Silverpoint and watercolor on vellum; H. 1¾″, W. 1³⁄₁₆″. (Collection of Richard J. Bryan: Photo, courtesy of William Buggle.)

FIG. 9. David Boudon, *John Bayly*. Harrisburg, Pa., Sept. 1798. Silverpoint and watercolor on vellum; H. 2⅛″, W. 1¹¹⁄₁₆″. (Collection of Yale University Art Gallery.)

FIG. 11. David Boudon, *Gabriel Du Brutz*. Fayetteville, N.C., Jan. 1805. Pencil on paper; dimensions unknown. (Collection of Alston family of North Carolina and Virginia: Photo, courtesy of Mrs. Charles Green Summers.)

FIG. 10. Charles Févret de Saint-Mémin, *Mr. Allen Smith*. Philadelphia, 1801. Engraving; H. 2⅝″, W. 2½″. (Winterthur 65.3073.1.)

was commissioned to do portraits of Gabriel Du Brutz (Fig. 11) and his wife in Fayetteville, North Carolina. By late 1805 he returned to Baltimore where he completed the portrait of Peregrine Welch, newly appointed clerk of the city commissioners. This pattern of constant travel suggests that his financial position was less than sound. His fortunes changed somewhat in mid-1806 when he was commissioned to draw the likenesses of Anthony-Charles Cazenove and his family. Cazenove was a Swiss émigré whose banking and shipping business in Alexandria, Virginia, had prospered. Between July and September, Boudon completed likenesses of Cazenove (Fig. 12), his wife (Fig. 13), and their four children (Figs. 14–17). The portraits finished, he returned once more to Baltimore.

Despite the fortunes made in trade in early-nineteenth-century Baltimore, for artists the economic climate of the city was precarious. Several portraitists had already left the city and even Rembrandt Peale, who certainly enjoyed a major share of local patronage, was forced to go elsewhere in search of

FIG. 12. David Boudon, *Anthony-Charles Cazenove*. Alexandria, Va., Sept. 16, 1806. Silverpoint and watercolor on vellum; H. 2¹³⁄₁₆″, W. 2⅝″. (Winterthur 69.158.)

FIG. 13. David Boudon, *Mrs. Anthony-Charles Cazenove* (Ann Hogan). Alexandria, Va., Sept. 17, 1806. Silverpoint and watercolor on vellum; H. 2½″, W. 2¼″. (Winterthur 69.156.)

commissions. It is indicative of the impending economic depression that Boudon felt compelled to reduce his price for a likeness from six dollars to three. Further, in an effort to establish some broad base of financial security, he opened a school to teach drawing.

DAVID BOUDEN [*sic*], (late of Geneva) feeling himself adequate, from his long study and experience, both in Europe and America, proposes to teach MINIATURE AND OTHER PAINTING, in all the various branches, and respectfully solicits the patronage of those ladies and gentlemen who wish to be taught the above art; assuring them that no pains on his part shall be wanting to make them proficient. He will also draw, with water colors, Profiles on vellum, for 3 dollars each, and requires no payment without a likeness. Ladies and gentlemen who will honor him with their confidence, are desired to apply to Mr. Charles Avisse Merchant & perfumer, No. 34 North Howard street.[13]

Boudon probably did not offer a full art academy curriculum; rather he provided instruction in those fundamentals of drawing and painting that were considered part of a genteel social education.

Boudon spent the next few years in Maryland. Baltimore was his headquarters, but on frequent

occasions he journeyed to Annapolis to complete commissions. Perhaps the paucity of available work encouraged him to advertise his skills.

David Boudon LIMNER FROM GENEVA Has the honour to inform the public, that having now received his complete Port Folio, and a collection of studies and principles proper for teaching to draw and paint Flowers, Landscape, Figures, &c. &c., so that if by subscription he can procure a sufficient number of scholars to form an academy, he offers to teach with rapid success.

He also paints MINIATURES at moderate prices. Likewise PROFILE PORTRAITS, colored on vellum at three dollars each, all warranted likenesses.

He assures the public that his profiles are not produced by machinery, but are the effects of his acquirements, from close and attentive application to the study in the best schools of Italy. His extensive practice in his profession he hopes will entice him to the patronage of a generous public.[14]

No record of his academy appears in either the Baltimore or Annapolis directories. Still he must have been able to stimulate sufficient interest to justify remaining in Baltimore until 1810.

Early in 1810 the prospect of patronage in the new "Federal City" lured him to Washington. Although several well-known artists—Rembrandt

[13] *American and Commercial Daily Advertiser* (Baltimore), Nov. 13, 1806.

[14] *Maryland Gazette* (Annapolis), Nov. 5, 1807.

FIG. 14. David Boudon, *Eliza Frances Cazenove*. Alexandria, Va., July 21, 1806. Silverpoint and watercolor on vellum; H. 2⅞", W. 2³⁄₁₆". (Winterthur 69.160.)

FIG. 15. David Boudon, *Charles John Cazenove*. Alexandria, Va., July 31, 1806. Silverpoint and watercolor on vellum; H. 2⅞", W. 2³⁄₁₆". (Winterthur 69.159.)

FIG. 16. David Boudon, *Ann Marie Cazenove*. Alexandria, Va., Aug. 1806. Silverpoint and watercolor on vellum; H. 3", W. 2⅜". (Winterthur 69.155.)

FIG. 17. David Boudon, *Pauline Cazenove*. Alexandria, Va., Sept. 17, 1806. Silverpoint and watercolor on vellum; H. 2¹³⁄₁₆", W. 2¼". (Winterthur 69.157.)

Peale, Gilbert Stuart, and Saint-Mémin among them—already had established studios in the city, Boudon's most serious competition came from the silhouettist, I. Todd. Using a patented physiogno-trace, the ubiquitous Todd and other enterprising silhouettists offered profile likenesses at the minimal cost of four for a quarter. This was even less expensive than the Saint-Mémin engravings that cost twelve and a half cents each. The miniaturists Nicholas and Dominic Boudet provided additional competition. Although the Boudets' miniatures and Boudon's silverpoint likenesses were very different, the similarity in names and the relative scarcity of available commissions prompted Boudet to publish a clarifying statement.

Mr. Boudet, Historical, Portrait and Miniature Painter, from the Academy of Paris.
  Respectfully informs the inhabitants of this City, Georgetown, and the vicinity that he has opened a Painting Room on the Capital hill, where he offers his professional services, and at the same time informs them that in the consequence of his not wishing to have his paintings taken for those of Mr. Boudon's and Mr. Boudon's for his, he acquaints them that Mr. Boudet is not Mr. Boudon, and Mr. Boudon is not Mr. Boudet.[15]

Apparently Boudon's share of the potential market was less than he had hoped, and he was forced to look for other ways to supplement his income. He had not abandoned his plans for a drawing school when he moved to Washington. In fact, soon after his arrival he informed the public that "he has opened a drawing school for young ladies and gentlemen at the house of Mr. John Gardiner on the Pennsylvania Avenue next door to Mrs. Lee's Academy." Although he continued to take portraits, much of his energy seemed to be directed toward this school.

DAVID BOUDON PAINTER FROM GENEVA, Informs the public, that he draws Profiles in water colors, on vellum, and Family Groupes in the same manner. He likewise executes Miniatures on Ivory; and also undertakes Oil Painting of every description connected with his branch of the Art.
  Being in possession of a considerable and very valuable collection of Drawings, of his own execution in the most celebrated Academies of Europe, he intends to devote them to the advancement of Pupils, by establishing a Drawing School, in which they will be displayed for the inculcation of correctness and taste among scholars. He will, meanwhile, appropriate a portion of his time to private instruction, in the different kinds of Drawing.
  Amateurs are invited to an inspection of his collec-

FIG. 18. David Boudon, *Mrs. Henry Fogler*. Frederick, Md., Mar. 23, 1813. Silverpoint and watercolor on vellum; H. 2⅞″, W. 2⅜″. (Collection of Stoll D. Kemp.)

tion of pictures (of the first masters) which he will with pleasure exhibit at any time in his leisure hours.[16]

When neither the sale of portraits nor the income from his school provided financial security, Boudon left Washington and moved to western Maryland.

His decision to abandon the eastern seaboard could have been predicted. In the coastal cities, large numbers of painters vied for patronage; further west the relative scarcity of trained artists eased competition. His choice of western Maryland is not surprising; several of his earlier clients had business connections in the area. The relative ease of transportation coupled with the general economic expansion of the area were added inducements.

With his move to Frederick, Maryland, early in 1813, Boudon began the third phase of his career in America. By far, the largest group of surviving portraits is from this period. He stayed in Frederick from March through July drawing likenesses of

---

[15] *National Intelligencer* (Washington, D.C.), Aug. 10, 1810.

[16] *National Intelligencer* (Washington, D.C.), July 20, 1810; Oct. 3, 1812.

Henry Fogler, a prominent tavern keeper, and his wife (Fig. 18), and portraits of the sons of two prominent Frederick merchants. August and September 1813 found him at the spa at Bath, Berkeley Springs, West Virginia. While there he did portraits of Aberdy Gustin (Fig. 19) and his wife. Boudon spent the years 1813 and 1814 traveling between Frederick, Hagerstown, Bath, and Charles Town. He returned to Frederick in October and remained there until mid-March 1814. That spring he took a brief trip to Charles Town, West Virginia, but returned to Hagerstown in the fall. While in Hagerstown he again advertised that he would teach:

Drawing, Painting Flowers, Landscapes, Figures, Groups, &c. at ten Dollars per quarter, three lessons per week, two hours each lesson. The lessons will be given in the afternoon for the convenience of the pupils who may be employed in the morning with other branches of Education.

Fifteen pupils are required before the School is opened. Those who wish to become subscribers will please make immediate application to Mr. Johnston, Watch and Clock-Maker or Mr. D. Boudon, at Mr. Saylor's Tavern.[17]

In the spring, Boudon made a brief trip to Frederick, and summer found him in Bath again. Late in 1815 he moved farther west. His last recorded commission was a portrait of Eliza Villette (Fig. 20) completed in April 1816, in West Virginia, probably at Wheeling. Later that year, a newspaper advertisement for his drawing school records his presence in Chillicothe, Ohio.

He will give lessons to those Ladies and Gentlemen who may be desirous of acquiring the knowledge of that noble art. His terms will be Ten Dollars per quarter, or Thirteen dollars, thirty-three cents for four months, at the option of the pupil. The Academy will open so soon as twenty pupils shall have subscribed.

Subscriptions received at this office or at the Eagle Tavern until the evening of Saturday, the 23 instant; and the time of instruction will be from two o'clock until four, three afternoons in each week.

N.B. If the weather permit, Mr. Boudon will give a

[17] *Maryland Herald and Hagerstown Weekly Advertiser,* Nov. 24, 1813.

FIG. 19. David Boudon, *Aberdy Gustin*. Bath, Va. (now Berkeley Springs, W.Va.), Aug. 30, 1813. Silverpoint and watercolor on vellum; H. 2¹³⁄₁₆″, W. 2¹⁵⁄₁₆″. (Collection of William T. Hassett, Jr.: Photo, Raup Photographic Studios.)

FIG. 20. David Boudon, *Eliza Villette*. W.Va., probably Wheeling, Apr. 1816. Watercolor on ivory; H. 2¾″, W. 2⅛″. (Collection of Mr. and Mrs. Charles Duncan Miller, Jr.: Photo, courtesy of Frick Art Reference Library.)

concert this evening, Nov. 2 [?] at the Masonic Hall at seven o'clock. Admitance fifty cents.[18]

Boudon disappears from public record in late November 1816, at the age of sixty-eight.

Historians have not been particularly kind in their assessment of Boudon's work. In his monumental *History of the Rise and Progress of the Arts of Design in the United States*, William Dunlap described Boudon as "a French refugee, who painted in an indifferent style. He [also] figures in the triple capacity of painter, musician, and dancing master."[19] And except for an occasional reference in a modern encyclopedic work, Boudon's painting has been ignored.

The deliberate selection of silverpoint separated Boudon from the bulk of late eighteenth- and early nineteenth-century miniature painters. Although art historians have relegated this technique to a minor position, silverpoint requires no less technical skill than does painting in oil. Because of his training as a draftsman, Boudon was most comfortable working in a linear style. Within the two-dimensional format, he used line to define form and to suggest shallow relief. His profile portraits are his most successful works. In contrast, his handling of three-quarter and full-face portraits is less adroit. Using the same linear technique, he was able to suggest the volume of a head, but he had difficulty indicating the space surrounding the head and establishing the volume of the body. The color wash on the body seemed to flatten the figure instead of modeling it. Only in his watercolor portraits on ivory (Fig. 20) does Boudon work in a painterly tradition using color rather than line to develop form.

While the more fashionable miniaturists looked to statesmen, politicians, and wealthy families for patronage, Boudon's clients were frequently members of the middle or upper middle class. Most of his subjects were businessmen or merchants and their families, including two merchant silversmiths. Many of his early patrons were Swiss or French émigrés or their descendants. It is significant that in all his advertisements and on each portrait Boudon specified Geneva, Switzerland, as his home. Perhaps this identification helped to distinguish him from the large number of French miniaturists working in America in the same years. His portraits are al-

[18] *Scotio Gazette* (Chillicothe, Ohio), Nov. 28, 1816.
[19] Dunlap, *Rise and Progress of the Arts of Design*, 2: pt. 1, p. 227.

FIG. 21. David Boudon, *Sophia Schley*. Frederick, Md., Jan. 20, 1814. Silverpoint and watercolor on vellum; H. 3½", W. 2⅝". (Collection of Mrs. George Chaplin: Photo, courtesy of Stoll D. Kemp.)

ways strong likenesses. It would be difficult to mistake the sitter for anyone else. Boudon recorded each sitter in appropriate attire. Young ladies were shown in their best dresses with their hair suitably styled in the latest fashion (Figs. 20, 21, 22). Dignified matrons were more modestly attired and their hair was partially hidden under a lace mobcap (Fig. 3). Older women covered their heads with close-fitting mobcaps and swathed themselves in shawls leaving little visible but their features (Fig. 18). As might be expected, there is less variation in the dress of male sitters. With rare exceptions men are dressed in the latest fashion with short hair, frilled shirts, high white muslin stocks, and broadcloth coats with deep collars (Figs. 11, 12, 23, 24).

Like many miniature painters, Boudon probably sold his portraits in frames. Although many have been reframed over the years, several survive in their original frames. Occasionally Boudon used a stamped metal frame consisting of a gadrooned border with a row of beading on the interior edge (Figs. 3, 4, 7, 23). Other portraits were set in plain gold lockets (Figs. 8, 9). Toward the end of his career, Boudon adopted a third type of frame. In it

FIG. 22. David Boudon, *Amelia Schley*. Frederick, Md., Mar. 9, 1815. Silverpoint and watercolor on vellum; H. 3⅝", W. 2¾". (Collection of John F. Byerly: Photo, courtesy of Stoll D. Kemp.)

FIG. 24. David Boudon, *Osborn Sprigg*. Western Md., ca. 1800. Watercolor on ivory; H. 2", W. 1⅝". (Collection of Maryland Historical Society: Photo, courtesy of Frick Art Reference Library.)

FIG. 23. David Boudon, *Woolman Gibson III*. Talbot County, Md., Sept. 1796. Silverpoint and watercolor on vellum; H. 2⅞", W. 2¼". (Collection of Maryland Historical Society: Photo, courtesy of Frick Art Reference Library.)

the portrait was matted with a black and gold eglomise panel and edged with a simple ogee-molded gold frame (Fig. 18).

Overshadowed by such well-known miniature portraitists as Elouis, Saint-Mémin, Edward Malbone, and the Peales, David Boudon's contribution to American miniature painting deserves reappraisal. His career serves as a good barometer of artistic practice in the 1790s and 1800s. His periodic migrations from place to place in search of commissions provide insight into the difficulties encountered by many of his contemporaries. Working in a little-used technique, Boudon was able to capture an accurate likeness without using a physiognotrace or pantograph. An excellent draftsman, his portraits are uncompromising; he does not try to glamorize or idealize his sitters. Working in a highly competitive field, Boudon's patrons were members of the gentry—a segment of society frequently overlooked by artists in search of more prestigious clients. At a time when painters were charging $100 for a full-length portrait, $50 for a half-length figure, $6 to $20 for a miniature on ivory, $6 to $8 for a profile likeness, and six cents for a silhouette, Boudon's prices were moderate.[20] David

[20] Prices were obtained from newspaper advertisements appearing in Charleston; Philadelphia; Baltimore; Washington, D.C.; Frederick and Hagerstown, Maryland; and New Bern, North Carolina, during the period in question.

Boudon is not a major figure in the history of American miniature painting, but by providing an accurate record of middle and upper middle-class Americans at a reasonable price, Boudon anticipated the need for true likenesses that photography would satisfy later in the nineteenth century.

Checklist

This checklist contains the available information on all of the American portraits by David Boudon that have been discovered to date. For convenience the portraits are grouped geographically. Chronological sequence within each geographical area has been maintained except to permit comparison of family portraits. Entries include the name of the sitter, provenance, date, medium, dimensions, inscription, and present location. Biographical information about the sitter has been included when available. Portraits not examined by the author are indicated by an asterisk (*).

South Carolina

*1. *William Guignard Richardson,* bust-length profile portrait; Charleston, S.C., 1795
    Medium: Silverpoint and watercolor on vellum
    Dimensions: H. 2¼″, W. 1¾″
    Inscription: [on obverse] Boudon f [on reverse] Made by David Boudon Limner / of Geneva / Switzerland / Charleston South Carolina / March 1795
    History: William Guignard Richardson (1770–1847) was the eldest son of William and Anne Magdaline (Guignard) Richardson. His father, a Charleston merchant, had moved to Bloom Hill plantation outside of Sumter, South Carolina, about 1772. After his father's death in 1786, Richardson returned to Bloom Hill to administer the property for his mother, brothers, and sisters. In 1798 he married Harriet Eveliegh, who died in 1804 leaving four children. Four years later, in 1809, he married Emma Corbet Buford. In his later years,

Richardson served as state senator for his district.
    Portraits of Richardson's father and his grandmother, Mrs. Edward Richardson, were painted by Jeremiah Theus. These portraits were copied in miniature by Henry Benbridge about 1780.
    Collection: Mrs. Eugene Hartley
    References: Elizabeth Buford Richardson, *Genealogical Records and Reminiscences of the Richardson Family* (Macon, Ga.: J. W. Burke Co., 1906); Anna Wells Rutledge, *Artists in the Life of Charleston Through Colony and State from Restoration to Reconstruction* (Philadelphia: American Philosophical Society, 1949); Edward Richardson to the author, Nov. 20, 1971
    Exhibited: Carolina Art Association, *Exhibit of Miniatures Owned in South Carolina and Miniatures of South Carolinians Owned Elsewhere Painted Before the Year 1860* (Charleston: Carolina Art Association, 1936), no. 10.

*2. *William Coffin,* waist-length three-quarter face portrait; Charleston, S.C., 1795
    Medium: Watercolor on ivory
    Dimensions: H. 1½″, W. 1″
    Inscription: [Not available for examination.]
    History: Captain William Coffin was the son of Ebenezar Coffin, a Charleston merchant. The only record of this portrait is a photograph owned by the Frick Art Reference Library. It shows Coffin dressed in a style similar to that worn by William G. Richardson (checklist no. 1). What makes this portrait so unusual is the fact that Boudon included the figure's right arm and hand. This portrait is the only known American example substantiating Bou-

don's claim that he drew likenesses "with the hands in it."

Collections: Dr. George E. Brewer (1931); unknown

References: Mrs. Francis J. H. Coffin to the author, Feb. 7, 1972

*3. *Patrick Coffee*, Charleston, S.C., 1795
History: Although this portrait his disappeared, reference to it appears in a letter written by Mr. M. Mayers of Brooklyn to Mr. Robert Whitelaw.
Collections: Unknown
References: Mrs. Francis J. H. Coffin to the author, Feb. 7, 1972

*4. *Elizabeth Anne Horry*, bust-length profile portrait; Charleston, S.C., 1796 (Fig. 8)
Medium: Silverpoint and watercolor on vellum
Dimensions: H. 1¾", W. 1³⁄₁₆"
Inscription: [on reverse] D. Boudon f / 8ber 1796
History: Elizabeth Anne Horry (1789–1856) was the daughter of Jonah and Sarah (Burnet) Horry. Her father was a wealthy landowner whose estate at the time of his death included about fifteen thousand acres and between two hundred and three hundred slaves. In 1809 Elizabeth Anne Horry married John Herbert Dent, commander of the sloop *Hornet*. Portraits of other family members include a miniature of her father painted by Henry Benbridge and a chalk drawing of her husband by Saint-Mémin executed in Charleston about the time of their marriage. The portrait of Elizabeth Anne Horry is in its original gold locket.
Collections: Mrs. Samuel Wragg (1896–1912); Richard J. Bryan (1936–)
References: The Carolina Art Association, *Exhibition of Miniatures from Charleston and Its Vicinity Painted Before the Year 1860* (Charleston: Carolina Art Association, 1935), no. 30; Fillmore Norfleet, *Saint-Mémin in Virginia: Portraits and Biographies* (Richmond, Va: Dietz Press, 1942), p. 51; interview with Helen McCormack, Nov. 30, 1970
Exhibited: South Carolina Society of Colonial Dames of America, 1896; The Carolina Art Association, 1912; The Carolina Art Association, *Exhibition of Miniatures from Charles-*

ton and Its Vicinity Painted Before the Year 1860 (Charleston, S.C.: Carolina Art Association, 1935)

Georgia

5. *Mrs. William Moore* (Susannah Bolton), bust-length three-quarter face portrait; Savannah, Ga., 1795 (Fig. 3)
Medium: Silverpoint and watercolor on vellum
Dimensions: H. 3½", W. 3⅛"
Inscription: [on obverse] Boudon f [on reverse] Fait a Savannah Georgie / Par David Boudon Peintre / de Geneve en Suisse / avril 1795
References: See checklist no. 6

6. *Mauve John Moore*, bust-length three-quarter face portrait; Savannah, Ga., 1795 (Fig. 4)
Medium: Silverpoint and watercolor on vellum
Dimensions: H. 3³⁄₁₆", W. 2⅝"
Inscription: [on reverse] Made in Savannah / Georgia / By David Boudon Limner / of Geneva Switzerland / April 1795
History: Susannah Bolton Moore (1748–1810) was the eldest child of Robert and Susannah (Mauve) Bolton. Her maternal grandparents, Matthew and Jane Mauve, emigrated to America from Switzerland early in the eighteenth century. Her father, Robert Bolton, was a successful saddler whose land holdings at his death included properties in Savannah, Hamsted, Brunswick, Hardwick, and St. Paul's Parish. On October 8, 1766, Susannah Bolton married William Moore, a prosperous Savannah merchant. After his death, about 1791, she continued to operate the business with the help of her son Mauve John Moore. Her youngest brother, Robert Bolton, Jr., also a prosperous Savannah merchant, maintained business connections with mercantile firms on the eastern shore through his marriage to Sarah McClear of Chestertown and with firms in New York City through his cousins John and Curtice Bolton.
Mauve John Moore (d. 1797) the only son of William and Susannah (Bolton) Moore (checklist no. 5), was a merchant and property

owner in his own right. He married his cousin Nancy Bolton of Chestertown, Maryland, on December 17, 1791. In March 1795 he was elected an alderman of Savannah. His untimely death occurred on September 30, 1797, on a trip to Charleston. The stamped brass frames on the portraits are probably original. The inscription on the backboard of Moore's portrait, "Likeness of Mr. Jn Moore/Savannah," is reported to have been added by his widow.

Collection: Mrs. Joseph Carson

References: Robert Bolton, *Genealogical and Biographical Account of the Family of Bolton in England and America* (New York: privately published, 1862); interview with Mrs. Joseph Carson, Feb. 9, 1972

Exhibited: The Pennsylvania Society of Miniature Painters, *Golden Jubilee Fiftieth Annual Exhibition of Miniatures Antique and Contemporary* (Philadelphia: Pennsylvania Academy of the Fine Arts, 1951), nos. 253, 267

7. *Robert James Mossman Houstoun,* bust-length profile portrait; Savannah, Ga., 1795 (Fig. 5)
    Medium: Silverpoint and watercolor on vellum
    Dimensions: H. 2¾″, W. 2⅜″
    Inscription: [on obverse] Boudon f [on reverse] Made By / David Boudon Limner of / Geneva Switzer-land / May 1795 / Savannah Georgia
    References: See checklist no. 8

8. *Priscilla Houstoun,* waist-length profile portrait; Savannah, Ga., 1795 (Fig. 6)
    Medium: Silverpoint and watercolor on vellum
    Dimensions: H. 2⅞″, W. 2⅜″
    Inscription: [on obverse] Boudon f [on reverse] Made By / David Boudon of / Geneva Switzer-land / Savannah Georgia / 795 Juin
    History: Robert Houstoun (1785–1818) was the eighth and youngest child of George and Ann (Moodie) Houstoun. His father was a prosperous indigo merchant. Robert Houstoun served briefly on the Savannah city council in 1809. Priscilla Houstoun (1784–1837), an older sister of Robert was eleven when this portrait was painted. Other Houstoun family portraits were painted by Henry and Hetty Benbridge.

Collections: Mrs. Macarten C. Kollock and Susan M. Kollock; Edith D. Johnston (1941); Georgia Historical Society

References: Edith Duncan Johnston, *The Houstouns of Georgia* (Athens: University of Georgia Press, 1950), p. 142

New York City

9. *Stephen Van Wyck,* bust-length three-quarter face portrait; New York, N.Y., 1795 (Fig. 7)
    Medium: Silverpoint and watercolor on vellum
    Dimensions: H. 3½″, W. 2½″
    Inscription: [on obverse] Boudon f [on reverse] Made / By David Boudon Limner of / Geneva Switzerland / New York 7ber 1795
    History: Stephen Van Wyck (1775–1860) traced his ancestry to Cornelius Barentse Van Wyck, who emigrated from Holland in 1660. Between 1796 and 1828, Van Wyck was listed in the New York directories as a clock- and watchmaker. Newspaper advertisements indicate that he also functioned as a wholesale and retail merchant. At the time the portrait was painted he maintained a shop at 275 Pearl Street.
    Collections: G. W. Blunt White; Mrs. Daniel F. Larkin
    References: Frick Art Reference Library; interview with Mrs. Daniel F. Larkin, July 17, 1972

Maryland

*10. Unidentified man, bust-length three-quarter face portrait; Easton, Talbot County, Md., 1796
    Medium: Silverpoint and watercolor on vellum
    Dimensions: H. 2⅞″, W. 2⅜″
    Inscription: [on obverse] Boudon f [on reverse] Made by David Boudon Limner of Geneva Switzerland Eastown Talbot County Md February 7, 1796
    History: When this portrait was exhibited at the Virginia Museum in 1941, the subject was identified as Charles Carroll MacKubin. J. Hall Pleasants questioned this attribution noting that the MacKubins were residents of Anne Arundel County. He could find no evi-

dence to suggest that any members of the family lived in Talbot County.

Collections: Mr. George MacKubin (1928); Mrs. George MacKubin (1941); unknown

References: J. Hall Pleasants, "Studies in Maryland Painting," manuscript notes on deposit at Maryland Historical Society, no. 1130; Virginia Museum of Fine Arts, *An Exhibition of Virginia Miniatures* (Richmond: Virginia Museum of Fine Arts, 1941), p. 15

Exhibited: Virginia Museum of Fine Arts, *An Exhibition of Virginia Miniatures* (Richmond: Virginia Museum of Fine Arts, 1941), no. 11

11. *Woolman Gibson III,* waist-length three-quarter face portrait; Talbot County, Md., 1796 (Fig. 23)

Medium: Silverpoint and watercolor on paper

Dimensions: H. 2⅞″, W. 2¼″

Inscription: [on reverse] Made / by David Boudon Limner / of Geneva Switzerland / in Talbot County / 7ber 1796

History: Woolman Gibson (ca. 1750–98) was the third son of John and Elizabeth (Porter) Gibson. During the Revolution he served as a lieutenant in Captain Robert Goldsborough's Talbot militia. This portrait is in its original frame.

Collections: W. Hooper Gibson (1927); Maryland Historical Society

References: Anna Wells Rutledge, "Handlist of Miniatures in the Collections of the Maryland Historical Society," *Maryland Historical Magazine* 40, no. 2 (June 1945): 125; Pleasants, "Studies in Maryland Painting," no. 1133

*12. *Osborn Sprigg,* bust-length profile portrait; western Md., ca. 1800 (Fig. 24)

Medium: Watercolor on ivory

Dimensions: H. 2″, W. 1⅝″

Inscription: [The Maryland Historical Society has been unable to locate this miniature for examination.]

History: Osborn Sprigg (ca. 1762–1815) was the second son of Joseph Sprigg. The elder Sprigg was a prominent barrister in Prince George's County, Maryland, until just before the Revolutionary War when he moved to western Maryland. Young Sprigg grew up in Washington County, Maryland, and is said to

have lived there until he moved to Virginia about 1800. An unusual feature of this portrait is the inclusion of a shadow behind the figure to indicate depth. The gold locket is probably original.

Collections: Mrs. Robert R. Henderson; Maryland Historical Society

References: Rutledge, "Handlist of Miniatures in the Collection of the Maryland Historical Society," p. 132

13. *Peregrine Welch,* bust-length profile portrait; Baltimore, Md., 1805

Medium: Silverpoint and watercolor on vellum

Dimensions: H. 3″, W. 2¼″

Inscription: [on reverse] David Boudon / Painter / Geneva Switzerland / Baltimore / City Maryland / [illegible] 1805

History: Peregrine Welch (d. 1826) was the son of Robert Welch of Londontown, South River, Anne Arundel County, Maryland. Welch moved to Baltimore about 1805 and was appointed clerk of the city commissioners. In 1807 he married Lydia Richardson of Baltimore.

Collections: J. Clinton Perrine; Maryland Historical Society

References: Eugenia Calvert Holland and Louisa Macgill Gray, "Miniatures in the Collection of the Maryland Historical Society," *Maryland Historical Magazine* 51, no. 4 (Dec. 1956): 353

*14. Unidentified man, bust-length profile portrait; Anne Arundel County, Md., ca. 1807

Medium: Silverpoint and watercolor on vellum or heavy paper

Dimensions: H. 3″, W. 2⅛″

Inscription: [Artist's name is reported to be on the reverse.]

History: J. Hall Pleasants tentatively identifies the sitter as a member of the Murray or Clapham families because the last known owner was a descendant of Dr. William Murray (1752–1852) and of Jonas Clapham (1763–1837). No positive identification is possible.

Collections: Mrs. William H. Murray; unknown

References: J. Hall Pleasants, "Studies in Maryland Painting," no. 1039

*15. *Cos Gibson,* Annapolis, Md., 1807
    Medium: Silverpoint and watercolor on vellum
    Dimensions: H. 2$^{15}/_{16}$″, W. 2$^5/_{16}$″
    Inscription: [on reverse] Done By / David Boudon / Limner / of Geneva Switzerland Annapolis / Maryland 17th ——— 1807
    History: The subject of this painting is identified tentatively by a nineteenth-century ink inscription that appears on the reverse of the portrait: "Cos Gibson/Marengo/Talbot Co. Maryland."
    Collections: Corrine L. Melchers; unknown
    References: Virginia Museum of Fine Arts, *An Exhibition of Virginia Miniatures,* p. 15
    Exhibited: Virginia Museum of Fine Arts, *An Exhibition of Virginia Miniatures,* no. 14

*16. *William McParlin,* bust-length profile portrait; Annapolis, Md., 1807
    Medium: Silverpoint and watercolor on vellum
    Dimensions: H. 2$^3/_4$″, W. 2$^1/_4$″
    Inscription: [on reverse] Made by David Boudon / Limner of Geneva / Switzerland in Annapolis Maryland State / 13 December 1807
    History: William McParlin (1780–1850), the Annapolis silversmith, was born in Loughbrickland, County Down, Ireland, and came to Maryland about 1798. He was apprenticed to the Annapolis silversmiths William Faris and his son Charles Faris. McParlin opened his own shop in 1803 or 1804. A man of some importance, he was elected to the city council in 1819. He worked as a silversmith, jeweler, and clockmaker until his death in 1850. This portrait is known only through a photograph in the J. Hall Pleasants collection at the Maryland Historical Society.
    Collections: Unknown
    References: Pleasants, "Studies in Maryland Painting," no. 1734; J. Hall Pleasants and Howard Sills, *Maryland Silversmiths 1715–1830* (Baltimore: Lord Baltimore Press, 1930), pp. 60–61

17. *Richard Owen,* bust-length profile portrait; Annapolis, Md., 1808
    Medium: Silverpoint and watercolor on vellum
    Dimensions: H. 2$^3/_8$″, W. 2$^3/_{16}$″

Inscription: [on reverse] By / David Boudon Limner of Geneva / Switzerland / [illegible] / 1808
History: A later nineteenth-century inscription identifies the sitter as a Richard Owen (ca. 1745–1822), aged sixty-four. He is said to have been a Methodist minister who also taught writing and mathematics at St. John's College in Annapolis.
Collections: Mary H. Maynard and Mrs. William Ross Howard; Maryland Historical Society
References: Holland and Gray, "Miniatures in the Collection of the Maryland Historical Society," p. 350

18. *Mrs. Henry Fogler,* bust-length profile portrait; Frederick, Md., 1813 (Fig. 18)
    Medium: Silverpoint and watercolor on vellum
    Dimensions: H. 2$^7/_8$″, W. 2$^3/_8$″
    Inscription: [on reverse] Done By / David Boudon Painter from / Geneva Switzerland / In Frederickstown & County / Mar. 23, 1813
    References: See checklist no. 19

19. *Henry Fogler,* bust-length profile portrait; Frederick, Md., 1813
    Medium: Silverpoint and watercolor on vellum
    Dimensions: H. 2$^5/_8$″, W. 2$^3/_8$″
    Inscription: [on reverse] Done By / David Boudon Painter / Geneva In Switzerland / In Frederickstown / Maryland / Mar 27 1813
    History: Margaret Fogler (1754–1822) was the wife of Henry Fogler (1754–1840) who was born in Rothen, Germany. At the time this portrait was painted, Fogler kept the Washington Inn at the upper end of Market Street in Frederick. These portraits retain their original pine frames.
    Collection: Stoll D. Kemp
    References: Interview with Stoll D. Kemp, Feb. 24, 1972

20. *Samuel Markell,* bust-length three-quarter face portrait; Frederick, Md., 1813
    Medium: Silverpoint and watercolor on vellum
    Dimensions: H. 3$^7/_8$″, W. 3″
    Inscription: [on reverse] Done By / David

Boudon painter, from / Geneva In Switzerland / In Frederick Town / 11 June 1813
Collection: John F. Byerly
References: See checklist no. 21

21. *Jacob Markell,* bust-length profile portrait; Frederick, Md., June 1813
Medium: Silverpoint and watercolor on vellum
Dimensions: H. 3½″, W. 2⅝″
Inscription: [on reverse] Done By / David Boudon Painter / From Geneva Switzerland / In Frederickstown / Maryland June 1813
History: These portraits are from a series of likenesses of members of the Markell and Schley families painted by Boudon. Samuel Markell's family were merchants and had extensive land holdings in Frederick County. Samuel (1796–1846) married Amelia Schley (Fig. 24, checklist no. 23), and they were the parents of John J. Markell (1820–1844), a painter who worked in the Frederick area. Jacob Markell (1767–1847), a cousin of Samuel, married Sophia Schley (Fig. 21, checklist no. 22), half sister of Samuel's wife, Amelia. Samuel Markell's portrait is still in its original pine frame. There is an ink inscription in the artist's hand on the backboard that reads "David Boudon Fecit / Frederick Town [illegible] June." A piece of newspaper with an article bearing an Annapolis, Maryland, dateline for January 13, 1813, was used as a separator.
Collection: Mrs. George M. Chaplin
References: Interview with Stoll D. Kemp, Feb. 24, 1972

22. *Sophia Schley,* bust-length profile portrait; Frederick, Md., 1814 (Fig. 21)
Medium: Silverpoint and watercolor on vellum
Dimensions: H. 3½″, W. 2⅝″
Inscription: [on reverse] Done By / David Boudon Painter / From Geneva Switzerland / In Frederickstown / Maryland / 20 January 1814
Collection: Mrs. George Chaplin
References: See checklist no. 23

23. *Amelia Schley,* bust-length profile portrait; Frederick, Md., 1815 (Fig. 22)
Medium: Silverpoint and watercolor on vellum
Dimensions: H. 3⅝″, W. 2¾″
Inscription: [on reverse] Done By / David Boudon Painter / from Geneva Switzerland / In Frederickstown / Maryland / March 9 1815
History: Sophia Schley (1793–1816) was the daughter of George Thomas Schley, a Frederick businessman, and his first wife, Anna Marie Getendanner. Sophia's grandfather, John Schley, had emigrated from Germany to Frederick about 1746. In 1815 Sophia married Jacob Markell (checklist no. 21). Amelia Schley (1796–1870), the daughter of George Schley and his second wife, Katherine Weisingen, married Samuel Markell (checklist no. 20). Sophia's portrait was probably painted about the time of her twenty-first birthday. Both girls are shown wearing the same necklace, locket, and hair ornaments.
Collection: John F. Byerly
References: J. Thomas Scharf, *History of Western Maryland,* 2 vols. (Philadelphia: L. H. Everts, 1882), 1:485; interview with Stoll D. Kemp, Feb. 24, 1972

24. *Barbara Lowe,* bust-length profile portrait; Frederick, Md., 1814
Medium: Silverpoint and watercolor on vellum
Dimensions: H. 3⅛″, W. 2½″
Inscription: [on reverse] Done By / David Boudon Painter / from Geneva Switzerland / in Fredericks Town / Maryland / February 23, 1814
Collections: W. B. Stottlemeyer (1939); Stoll D. Kemp
References: See checklist no. 25

25. *William Lowe,* bust-length profile portrait; Frederick, Md., 1814
Medium: Silverpoint and watercolor on vellum
Dimensions: H. 3¼″, W. 2⅞″
Inscription: [on reverse] Done By / David Boudon Painter / from Geneva Switzerland / In Frederick Town / 5 March 1814
History: The portraits of Mr. and Mrs. Lowe are still in their original frames. On the portrait of Barbara Lowe, Boudon inscribed the backboard "David Boudon [illegible] / Fecit / February 1814 / Mrs. Barbara Loue [*sic*]." A fragment of a memorandum or date book written in French was used as a separator be-

tween the vellum and the glass panel. Unfortunately, not enough of it remained intact to be translated. The backboard of the portrait of William Lowe (1788–1858) is inscribed in Boudon's hand "David Boudon Fecit / March 1814." Of particular interest is a fragment of paper with the partial inscription in a similar hand ". . . files on vellum [missing] 3 dollars . . ." used as a separator.
Collection: Stoll D. Kemp
References: Interview with Stoll D. Kemp, Feb. 24, 1972

*26. *John Van Swearingen,* bust-length profile portrait; Washington County, Md., 1813
    Medium: Silverpoint and watercolor on vellum
    Dimensions: H. 2½", W. 2"
    Inscription: [on reverse] John v Swearingen / done by David Boudon Painter / from Geneva Switzerland / 7 8ber 1813
    History: John Van Swearingen (also spelled Van Swearingan) was the son of Charles Van Swearingen and his wife Susannah Stull. Van Swearingen (1778–1849) was born in Washington County, Maryland, and lived there all his life. In 1803 he married Elizabeth Bond. At the time of this portrait he was serving as collector of revenue for the Seventh District of Maryland (Washington County).
    Collections: Rose Bond Green (pre-1932); Mr. and Mrs. John Green (1932); Mrs. John Martin Green (1947); Daughters of the American Revolution Museum
    References: *Antiques* 21, no. 1 (Jan. 1932): 12; Pleasants, "Studies in Maryland Painting," no. 1301

27. Unidentified woman, waist-length profile portrait; Hagerstown, Md., 1814
    Medium: Silverpoint and watercolor on vellum
    Dimensions: H. 3⅛", W. 2¼"
    Inscription: [on reverse] Done By / David Boudon Painter / from Geneva Switzerland / in Hagerstown / Washington County Md / 16 7ber 1814
    References: See checklist no. 28

28. Unidentified man, bust-length profile portrait; Hagerstown, Md., 1814

    Medium: Silverpoint and watercolor on vellum
    Dimensions: H. 3", W. 2⁵⁄₁₆"
    Inscription: [on reverse] Done By / David Boudon Painter / from Geneva Switzerland / In Hagerstown / W County, Md / 18 7ber 1814
    History: Nos. 27 and 28 are a pair.
    Collections: Mrs. Frank W. Mish, Jr.; Frank W. Mish, Jr. (1971); William T. Hassett, Jr.
    References: Interview with William T. Hassett, Jr., Feb. 23, 1972

Pennsylvania

29. Unidentified woman, bust-length profile portrait; probably Pennsylvania, ca. 1797–98
    Medium: Silverpoint and watercolor on vellum
    Dimensions: H. 2¾", W. 2⅛"
    Inscription: [The picture cannot be removed from its frame for inspection.]
    History: Although the sitter has been identified by the Historical Society of Pennsylvania as Elizabeth Graff (b. 1773), the author is unable to confirm this attribution. The lady portrayed is obviously considerably older than the twenty-five-year-old woman Elizabeth Graff would have been at the time of this portrait. This is possibly a companion piece to the portrait of John Bayly painted by Boudon in Harrisburg in 1798 (see checklist no. 30). This portrait appears to be in its original locket frame.
    Collections: Anna Bella Townsend (1919); Historical Society of Pennsylvania
    References: William Sawitzky, *Catalogue Descriptive and Critical of the Paintings and Miniatures in the Historical Society of Pennsylvania* (Philadelphia: Historical Society of Pennsylvania, 1942), pp. 49, 272

30. *John Bayly,* bust-length profile portrait; Harrisburg, Pa., 1798 (Fig. 9)
    Medium: Silverpoint and watercolor on vellum
    Dimensions: H. 2⅛", W. 1¹¹⁄₁₆"
    Inscription: [on reverse] Executed by / David Boudon / Limner / of Geneva Switzerland / in Harrisburg / 7ber 1798
    History: John Bayly or Bailey (d. 1805), a sil-

versmith, worked primarily in Philadelphia. Advertisements for his shop appear in the Philadelphia newspapers as early as 1750 and continue through at least 1785. The extent of his clientele and the variety of items produced suggest that Bayly's business was sufficiently profitable to classify him as a craftsman-merchant. One unusual feature of the portrait is a braided queue shown pinned up the back of his head. The portrait of William McParlin, an Annapolis silversmith (checklist no. 16), reveals a similar hair style. The portrait is mounted in a gold locket made by Samuel Ford, a silversmith working in Philadelphia in 1797, who later moved to Baltimore.

Collections: Walter M. Jeffords; Yale University Art Gallery

References: John Marshall Phillips, *Yale University Portrait Index 1701–1951* (New Haven: Yale University Press, 1951), p. 9

*31. *Mary (Ewalt) Funk,* bust-length three-quarter face portrait; Bath, Bedford, Pa., 1815
Medium: Watercolor on ivory
Dimensions: H. 3⅝″, W. 2⅞″
Inscription: [on reverse] Done By / David Boudon Painter / from Geneva Switzerland / in Bath Bedford Penn / 12 July 1815
History: The only known photograph of this portrait is at the Frick Art Reference Library.
Collections: Mrs. John C. Lyon; unknown

Virginia

*32. *Samuel Gordon,* bust-length three-quarter face portrait; Va., ca. 1800
Medium: Watercolor on ivory
Dimensions: H. 2¾″, W. 2⅛″
Inscription: [Not available for examination.]
History: Samuel Gordon (1759–1843) was born in Scotland and came to Falmouth, Virginia, in 1783 with his brother Basil. Gordon is reported to have amassed a large fortune exporting tobacco. On December 14, 1798, Gordon married Susannah Fitzhugh Knox of Culpepper County, Virginia. He purchased Kenmore, the estate of Fielding Lewis near Fredericksburg, where he spent the remainder of his life.
Collections: Mrs. Clarence C. Whiting (1933); unknown

References: J. Hall Pleasants, "Studies in Maryland Painting," no. 1490; Frick Art Reference Library

*33. Unidentified child; Alexandria, Va., 1801
Medium: Silverpoint and watercolor on vellum
Dimensions: H. 2⅛″, W. 1⅝″
Inscription: [on reverse] Desine par / David Boudon peintre / de Geneva Cä devant / en Suisse Alexandria Etat da Virginie / 1801
Collections: Victor E. Burnett (1941); unknown
References: Frick Art Reference Library

*34. Unidentified man, bust-length three-quarter face portrait; probably Alexandria, Va., 1804
Medium: Silverpoint and watercolor on vellum
Dimensions: H. 2⁹⁄₁₆″, W. 2″
Inscription: [on reverse] David Boudon / fecit Feb 1804
History: When this portrait was exhibited at the Virginia Museum of Fine Arts in 1941, the sitter was erroneously identified as James Alexander Seddon of Sabot Hill. Seddon (1815–80) served two terms in the House of Representatives and was secretary of war under the Confederacy. The portrait is that of a man too young to be Seddon's father, Thomas Seddon. Although the identity of the subject remains unknown, an inscription scratched on the case, "Adam Lynn Alexandria / Jan 16, 1804," does record the maker of the locket. A silversmith, jeweler, clockmaker, and hardware merchant, Lynn (1775–1836) worked in Alexandria from about 1791 until his death. Active in civic affairs, his honors included clerk of the Common Council (1809), first vestryman of St. Paul's Church (1810), lieutenant colonel of militia in the War of 1812, and justice of the peace (1824). His portrait was engraved by Saint-Mémin in 1805 in Alexandria.
Collections: Mrs. Robert Nelson (1941); unknown
References: Virginia Museum of Fine Arts, *An Exhibition of Virginia Miniatures,* p. 15; *Dictionary of American Biography;* Virginia Historical Society, *The Bruce Family Genealogy* (1904; reprint ed., New York: Kraus Reprint Corporation, 1968), pp. 442–43; Alexandria Association, *Our Town: 1749–1865, Likenesses*

*of This Place and Its People Taken from Life
by Artists Known and Unknown* (Alexandria,
Va.: Alexandria Association, 1956), p. 44;
George Barton Cutten, *The Silversmiths of
Virginia* (Richmond, Va.: Dietz Press, 1952),
pp. 14–17; Norfleet, *Saint-Mémin in Virginia,*
p. 187
Exhibited: Virginia Museum of Fine Arts, *An
Exhibition of Virginia Miniatures,* no. 17

35. *Anthony-Charles Cazenove,* bust-length profile
portrait; Alexandria, Va., 1806 (Fig. 12)
Medium: Silverpoint and watercolor on vellum
Dimensions: H. 2 13/16″, W. 2 5/8″
Inscription: [on reverse] Dessine Par / David
Boudon, Peintre de / Geneve en Suisse / a
Alexandrie / en virginie / 16 7ber 1806
Collections: Ann Lee Cole; The Henry Francis du Pont Winterthur Museum
References: See checklist no. 40

36. *Mrs. Anthony-Charles Cazenove* (Ann Hogan),
bust-length profile portrait; Alexandria, Va.,
1806 (Fig. 13)
Medium: Silverpoint and watercolor on vellum
Dimensions: H. 2 1/2″, W. 2 1/4″
Inscription: [on reverse] Dessine Par / David
Boudon Peintre / de Geneve en Suisse. / A
Alexandrie / Stat de Virginia / 17em 7ber 1806
Collections: Elisabeth Packard; The Henry
Francis du Pont Winterthur Museum
References: See checklist no. 40

37. *Eliza Frances Cazenove,* bust-length profile portrait; Alexandria, Va., 1806 (Fig. 14)
Medium: Silverpoint and watercolor on vellum
Dimensions: H. 2 5/8″, W. 2 3/16″
Inscription: [on reverse] Dessine Par / David
Boudon peintre / de Geneve devant / Suisse /
Alexandrie Etat de / Virginie / 29 Juillet 1806
Collections: Ann Lee Cole; The Henry Francis du Pont Winterthur Museum
References: See checklist no. 40

38. *Charles-John Cazenove,* bust-length profile portrait; Alexandria, Va., July 31, 1806 (Fig. 15)
Medium: Silverpoint and watercolor on vellum

Dimensions: H. 2 7/8″, W. 2 3/16″
Inscription: [on reverse] Dessine Par / David
Boudon Peintre / de Geneve & devant / Suisse
/ a Alexandrie / virginie / 31 Juillet 1806
Collections: Ann Lee Cole; The Henry Francis du Pont Winterthur Museum
References: See checklist no. 40

39. *Ann Marie Cazenove,* bust-length profile portrait; Alexandria, Va., August, 1806 (Fig. 16)
Medium: Silverpoint and watercolor on vellum
Dimensions: H. 3″, W. 2 3/8″
Inscription: [on reverse] Dessine Par / David
Boudon Peintre / [partially obliterated] Geneve en Suisse / Alexandrie / Etat Virginia /
Aoust 1806
Collections: Mrs. Cazenove G. Lee; The Henry
Francis du Pont Winterthur Museum
References: See checklist no. 40

40. *Pauline Cazenove,* bust-length profile portrait;
Alexandria, Va., 1806 (Fig. 17)
Medium: Silverpoint and watercolor on vellum
Dimensions: H. 2 13/16″, W. 2 1/4″
Inscription: [on reverse] Dessine Par / David
Boudon Peintre / de Geneve en Suisse / A
Alexandria / Etat de Virginia / le 17em 7bre
1806
History: Anthony-Charles Cazenove (1775–
1852) emigrated to America from Switzerland
during the French Revolution. He lived briefly
in Philadelphia where he met Ann Hogan
(1776–1843), the daughter of Edmund Hogan.
They were married on June 29, 1797, and
moved to Alexandria, Virginia, where late in
that year he established a banking and shipping business. He also served as Swiss counsel
for the middle and southern states. The Cazenoves had four children. Eliza (1798–1857)
married William C. Gardner of Newport,
Rhode Island, in May 1817. Charles-John
(1801–1834), who served as an escort for Lafayette on his visit in 1824, married Sarah
Greenleaf of Boston on September 19, 1826,
and resided in Boston until his death. Ann
Marie (1803–1859) married Archibald Henderson. Pauline (1806–1891), only two months
old when her portrait was made, married
Lieutenant Colonel John Fowle of Watertown,
Massachusetts, on May 26, 1831.

Collections: Ann Lee Cole; The Henry Francis du Pont Winterthur Museum

References: John Askling, ed., "Autobiographical Sketch of Anthony-Charles Cazenove, Politial Refugee, Merchant and Banker, 1775–1852," *The Virginia Magazine of History and Biography* 78, no. 3 (July 1970): 295–307; Alexandria Association, *Our Town: 1749–1865*, pp. 52, 97–98 (refers only to Anthony-Charles Cazenove)

Exhibited: Alexandria Association, *Our Town: 1749–1865* (only the portrait of Anthony-Charles Cazenove)

*41. *Dandridge Spotswood,* bust-length three-quarter face portrait; probably Virginia, ca. 1810–12

Medium: Watercolor on ivory

Dimensions: H. 2⅝″, W. 2⅛″

Inscription: [The picture cannot be removed from its frame for inspection.]

History: The son of John and Sarah (Rowsie) Spotswood, Dandridge Spotswood (1789–1849) was born at Orange Grove near Fredericksburg, Virginia, and died at Petersburg, Virginia. The portrait appears to be in its original locket.

Collections: Mrs. Frank Nash; Martha Dunlop Spotswood (1956); Virginia Museum of Fine Arts

References: Virginia Museum of Fine Arts, *An Exhibition of Virginia Miniatures,* p. 15

Exhibited: Virginia Museum of Fine Arts, *An Exhibition of Virginia Miniatures,* no. 18

North Carolina

*42. *Gabriel Du Brutz,* bust-length three-quarter face portrait; Fayetteville, N.C., 1805 (Fig. 11)

Medium: Pencil on paper

Dimensions: [Not available.]

Inscription: [reportedly on reverse] Made by David Boudon, Limner of Geneva, Switzerland, Fayetteville, North Carolina, Jan. 1805

References: See checklist no. 43

*43. *Mrs. Gabriel Du Brutz* (Deborah Montgomery) (1770–1825), bust-length three-quarter face portrait; Fayetteville, N.C., February, 1805

Medium: Pencil on paper

Dimensions: [Not available.]

Inscription: [reportedly on reverse] Made by David Boudon, Limner of Geneva, Switzerland, Fayetteville, North Carolina, February 1805

History: A native of Bordeaux, Gabriel Du Brutz (1763–1824) had served with the French fleet at the Battle of Yorktown. After the war he returned to France, but emigrated to Santo Domingo in 1783. The following year he left Santo Domingo and moved to Fayetteville, N.C., where he operated a very successful import-export business with France and the West Indies. In January 1792 he married Deborah Montgomery (1770–1825), the daughter of John and Mary (Willcox) Montgomery, of Mill Creek Hundred, New Castle County, Delaware, and Chatham County, North Carolina. Born in Mill Creek Hundred on March 3, 1770, she died May 18, 1825, in Marengo County, Alabama. These portraits are known only through photographs; the miniatures have disappeared. The quality of the drawing suggests the possibility that these were preliminary sketches for watercolor portraits on ivory.

Collections: The Alston family of North Carolina and Virginia; unknown

References: Mrs. Charles Green Summers to the author, Feb. 1, 1972; Frick Art Reference Library

Washington, D.C.

*44. *Andre Joseph Villard,* bust-length profile portrait; Washington, D.C., 1810

Medium: Silverpoint and watercolor on vellum

Dimensions: H. 2¹³⁄₁₆″, W. 2⅜″

Inscription: [on reverse] Dessine Par / David Boudon Peintre / de Geneve, Department / du Lac Leman / a Washington City / May, 1810 / District of Columbia

History: Nothing is known about Andre Villard. However, the use of the French inscription on the portrait suggests that he was Swiss or French.

Collections: Frederick W. Cron; National Collection of Fine Arts, Smithsonian Institution

*45. Unidentified woman, bust-length three-quarter face portrait; Washington, D.C., 1811

Medium: Watercolor on ivory

Dimensions: H. 2$^{11}\!/_{16}$″, W. 2$^1\!/_8$″
Inscription: [on reverse] David Boudon fecit /
W. City, D.C. Ocber 1811
Collections: Bernard H. Cone (1942); National
Collection of Fine Arts, Smithsonian Institu-
tion
References: Pleasants, "Studies in Maryland
Painting," no. 2791

*46. Unidentified man, Washington, D.C., 1812
Medium: Silverpoint and watercolor on vel-
lum
Dimensions: H. 2$^5\!/_8$″, W. 2$^1\!/_{16}$″
Inscription: [on reverse] Done by / David
Boudon Painter / from Geneva Switzerland /
In Washington City / District of Columbia /
1812
History: The subject of this portrait is listed
in the file of the National Portrait Gallery as
"General Southerland." This tentative iden-
tification resulted from misreading "Geneva
Switzerland" in the inscription.

West Virginia

47. *Mrs. Aberdy Gustin* (Eleanor Chew), waist-
length profile portrait; Bath, Va. (now Berkeley
Springs, W.Va.), 1813
Medium: Silverpoint and watercolor on vel-
lum
Dimensions: H. 3″, W. 2$^{11}\!/_{16}$″
Inscription: [on reverse] Mrs Gustin / Done
By / David Boudon Painter / from Geneva
Switzerland / Bath Berkley County / Virginia
/ 27 August 1813
References: See checklist no. 48

48. *Aberdy Gustin,* bust-length three-quarter face
portrait; Bath, Va. (now Berkeley Springs,
W.Va.), 1813 (Fig. 19)
Medium: Silverpoint and watercolor on vel-
lum
Dimensions: H. 2$^{13}\!/_{16}$″, W. 2$^5\!/_{16}$″
Inscription: [on reverse] Done By / David
Boudon Painter / from Geneva Switzerland /
Bath Berkley County / Virginia / 30 August
1813
History: Aberdy Gustin (1780–1855) was the
son of Alpheus and Margaret (Strange) Gus-
tin. The family had moved from New York
State to Berkeley, Virginia, near Clarksburg

about the time of the Revolution. His grandfather had owned vast tracts of land in the
area; these were later lost.
Eleanor Gustin was the daughter of John
Chew of Loudoun County, Virginia.
Both the Gustin portraits are in their original frames. On the backboard of Gustin's portrait Boudon inscribed "David Boudon Fecit /
Bath Berkley County / 30 August 1813." The
name "Aburdy [*sic*] Gustin" appears in ink on
the frame. On the backboard of Mrs. Gustin's
portrait in the artist's hand is the inscription
"David Boudon Fecit / Bath August 1813 /
virginia." A further ink inscription on the
frame identifies the sitter as "Eleanor Gustin
1813."
Collection: William T. Hassett, Jr.
References: Gustine Courson Weaver, *The
Gustine Compendium* (Cincinnati: Powell &
White, 1929), p. 170; interview with William
T. Hassett, Jr., Feb. 23, 1972

*49. *Miss Ogden,* Bath, Va. (now Berkeley Springs,
W.Va.), 1813
Medium: Silverpoint and watercolor on vel-
lum
Dimensions: H. 3″, W. 2$^1\!/_{16}$″
Inscription: [Not available for examination.]
History: This notation came from the files of
the National Portrait Gallery. No copy of the
miniature has been located. Possibly the sitter
is Miss Sarah Ogden who married Colonel
Robert Gustin (1778–1839) of Bath, an older
brother of Aberdy Gustin (checklist no. 43).
Collections: Mrs. F. G. Leonard (1937); un-
known
References: Weaver, *Gustine Compendium,* p.
170

*50. *Mrs. J. Russell,* Charles Town, W.Va., 1814
Medium: Silverpoint and watercolor on vellum
Dimensions: H. 3$^3\!/_4$″, W. 3$^1\!/_2$″
Inscription: [on reverse] Done By / David
Boudon Painter, from / Geneva in Switzerland / In Charleston / Jefferson County Virginia / 4 May 1814
History: The sitter has been identified by the
inscription on a small paper label attached to
the original backboard. Boudon inscribed the
backboard "David Boudon Fecit / May 1814."
The painting is in its original frame.

Collections: John W. Russell (1909); Miss Dallas Russell (1909–71); Robert T. Eilertson, Jr.
References: Robert T. Eilertson, Jr., to the author, Jan. 12, 1972

51. *Eliza Villette,* bust-length three-quarter face portrait; probably near Wheeling, W.Va., 1816 (Fig. 20)
Medium: Watercolor on ivory
Dimensions: H. 2¾″, W. 2⅛″
Inscription: [on original backboard] David Boudon Fecit / April 1816
History: Eliza Villette (1796–1878) was the daughter of Captain John Villette and Patience Taylor Tillinghast of Newport, Rhode Island. She married James Duncan on July 21, 1816. Duncan, a New Englander, had made his fortune as a merchant captain. About 1815 he moved to Wheeling, West Virginia. After their marriage they settled near Kendall, Ohio. This portrait was painted just prior to her marriage. Although the painting has been reframed, the original backboard has been preserved.
Collections: Mrs. Charles Duncan Miller, Sr.; Mr. and Mrs. Charles Duncan Miller, Jr.
References: Interview with Mrs. Charles Duncan Miller, Jr., Apr. 12, 1972

Without a Blush

The Movement toward Acceptance of the Nude
As an Art Form in America, 1800–1825

E. McSherry Fowble

FOR A BRIEF PERIOD at the end of the eighteenth century and the beginning of the nineteenth, it appeared that progress in the fine arts in the United States would gain new vigor and direction from the Francomania that followed the Revolutionary War. While many American bourgeois, self-conscious in their new freedom and wealth, looked to France for intellectual and social styles, exiled French aristocrats in New York, Philadelphia, and Baltimore encouraged patronage of the arts as one accouterment to the manners of the genteel tradition. After their example it became a matter of fashion among a few of the intellectual elite to collect art, take drawing lessons, and visit art galleries. In contrast to Paris where Napoleon Bonaparte and Vivant Denon had recently opened the great galleries of the Louvre, the principal American cities in 1800 could not boast a single public collection of any significance. Nor was there an academy for the training of artists or the advancement of the arts, such as those that enjoyed royal patronage in London (Fig. 1) and Paris. While a few Americans enjoyed the privilege of classical studies, the public was for the most part far removed from historical and moral traditions that had been a ready source for subject matter among European artists.[1] Furthermore, with the exception of those Americans who had taken the grand tour or those who had the opportunity of seeing the European graphic reproductions after Renaissance and baroque masters, most Americans had never seen an artist's interpretation of a historic or classical subject, especially one that presented the nude figure.

In the years between 1790 and 1800, a few artists and patrons of the arts seemed motivated to overcome this cultural deficiency. From the vantage of an opportunity to read seventeenth- and eighteenth-century publications on art theory and a basic education in classical studies,[2] these individuals moved to bring to America an improvement in arts that would reflect the most ancient and noble ideals of mankind. Based on an appreciation of the classical art of Greece and Rome, this effort introduced the nude to the American public as an ideal expression in sculpture and painting.

In the last decade of the eighteenth century a number of prominent New Yorkers gathered to plan an institution, modeled after the Louvre, that would provide the public with an opportunity to see replicas of the most famous of the ancient Greek and Roman sculptures. Robert R. Livingston, a prominent financial and social figure in New York and United States minister to France, was chosen to seek advice from Vivant Denon on the purchase of a suitable collection of plaster casts from antique sculpture. As a result, twelve casts, which were to form the nucleus of the collection of the newly formed American Academy of Fine Arts, arrived in New York from Paris in 1802.[3]

[1] Sir Kenneth Clark, *The Nude: A Study in Ideal Form* (New York: Pantheon Books, 1956). In this study of the nude as an aesthetic statement, Kenneth Clark considers the various concepts that have been applied to the nude as a vehicle of artistic expression throughout history.

[2] Henry Adams and Worthington Chauncey Ford, *A Catalogue of the Books of John Quincy Adams Deposited at the Boston Athenaeum* (Boston: for the Athenaeum, 1938), pp. 26–27. To the man who wished to introduce himself to European circles as a gentleman of taste and breeding a knowledge of the classics was essential. Cicero and Juvenal, like a knowledge of languages, "placed him on an equality with all, breaking down even the barriers of British reserve and opening a way to free and confidential intercourse as profitable to his country as to himself."

[3] Nancy E. Richards, "The American Academy of Fine Arts, 1802–1816; New York's First Art Academy" (M.A. thesis, University of Delaware, 1965).

FIG. 1. Johann Zoffany, *The Academicians of the Royal Academy.* LONDON, ca. 1772. Oil on canvas; H. 39¾″, W. 58″. (The Royal Academy. By gracious permission of Her Majesty the Queen.)

Aware of the general public's lack of familiarity with classical studies and concerned about the average citizen's ignorance of artistic expressions other than the utilitarian and ubiquitous portrait, Livingston wrote from Paris in December 1802 to advise his son Robert G. Livingston to use appropriate precautions in the public presentation of these casts. "Though these statues are viewed by the most delicate women here without a blush, yet the modesty of our country women renders a covering necessary and I beg you that you begin by preparing one before you suffer them to be exhibited— This is done by getting from the broker [?] a small concave shell of fig leaf which you paint white and hang with a small white pach [piece/patch of?] thread around the waist."[4] Livingston's precaution in deference to provincial modesty was well taken,

for the exhibition at the American Academy received favorable editorials; and for a while New Yorkers, eager to prove their sophistication, visited the gallery. From the initial response it appeared that the American public might be educated to the sublimity and universality of art, particularly as presented in the art of the nude.[5] What was needed was the art itself and a carefully planned program of gradual enlightenment.

Although new to public awareness at the beginning of the nineteenth century, the nude in art was not entirely new to America. Stimulated by a desire for sophistication and encouraged by the continuous arrival of European-trained painters, a few eighteenth-century colonial patrons of art had demonstrated a tentative willingness to tolerate, even

[4] Robert R. Livingston to Robert G. Livingston, Dec. 23, 1803, Robert R. Livingston MSS, The New-York Historical Society, New York (hereafter N-YHS).

[5] For the purpose of this paper the nude will be considered as a visual representation of the human figure in any state of undress that exceeds the contemporary requirements for public appearance.

to support, a classical view of the nude in art as a symbol of truth and beauty.

When he brought his collection to Boston for display in his gallery and painting room after 1730, the English painter, John Smibert (1698–1751), may have been the first person to exhibit a nude in that city. The collection that contained his own copies of Renaissance and baroque masterpieces, including Titian's *Venus and Cupid,* casts from the antique after the *Venus di Medici* and, possibly, the *Laocoön,* as well as a large number of "Valuable PRINTS, engrav'd by the best Hands, after the finest Pictures in Italy, France, Holland and England," was advertised for sale in May 1735. There remains a question as to Bostonians' readiness to buy these items for their personal collections. The fact that the sale was extended to June "at the request of several gentlemen who were hindered the last week from being present"[6] indicates that there were at least some interested purchasers. Although Smibert's collection was an initial source for Renaissance and baroque art in Boston, how much of it, especially that featuring the nude, was purchased for private collections can only be surmised.

Characteristically, the few scattered art patrons in eighteenth-century America were modest in mentioning their collections. That such collections existed is apparent only in notes, letters, diaries, and, more particularly, in the personal papers of aspiring colonial artists who were eager to search out every opportunity to familiarize themselves with the art of Europe. John Singleton Copley (1738–1815), through contacts made at his step-father's Boston print shop, gained access to private collections and to conversations among collectors. His letters mention "a fine Coppy of the Titiano Venus" and a "Niobe," both classical subjects, the former traditionally presented as a nude, which he had seen at the home of William Allen, Chief Justice of Pennsylvania, as well as a copy of the *Aurora* by Guido Reni (1575–1642), which he purchased while in Italy for a Mr. Palmer of Boston.[7] Account books occasionally provide other references to private art collections; as an example, a 1774 entry

made by Colonel Edward Lloyd of Maryland indicated that he paid Charles Willson Peale (1741–1827) thirty-five pounds for a picture of "Venus rising from the sea."[8]

If the available documentary evidence is an accurate indication, prints were a more widespread medium for transmitting European representations of the nude to American audiences than were paintings or sculpture. Engravings were available to colonial travelers who took the grand tour, and those who remained at home could buy graphic reproductions through colonial print shops. Prints were relatively inexpensive to produce and transport, and they were suitable for storage in a folio in a gentleman's library. Indeed, the provincial conservatism and moral values that seemed to have figured in the collectors' penchant for anonymity may have been responsible for making the library a cache for that part of the collection that featured the nude, whether a plaster cast of the antique, a painting, or a print.[9]

In eighteenth-century America, books with line engravings, including the Earl of Shaftesbury's *Characteristicks,* first published in 1723, which presented a nude in the title page engraving portraying the *Judgment of Hercules* (Fig. 2), or the freely illustrated *Antiquities Explained,*[10] were principal

[6] *Boston Weekly News-Letter,* May 15 to May 22, May 29 to June 5, 1735.

[7] Guernsey Jones, ed., *Letters and Papers of John Singleton Copley and Henry Pelham: 1739–1776, Massachusetts Historical Society Collections* 71 (Boston: Massachusetts Historical Society, 1914): 163, 332 (hereafter *Letters of Copley and Pelham*).

[8] Cash Book, 1774–89, Mar. 15, 1774, Lloyd Papers, Maryland Historical Society, Baltimore (hereafter MHS). Location of painting unknown.

[9] Art historians since the mid-nineteenth century have tended to attribute the popular reluctance to accept the nude in art to both ignorance and a persistent religious restraint. Henry T. Tuckerman called the public's reaction to the nude "ignorant prudery"; see *Artist's Life: Sketches of Eminent American Painters* (2d ed.; New York: D. Appleton & Co., 1849), p. 67. Lorado Taft implied religious overtones when he explained that Hiram Powers's sculpture *Greek Slave,* ca. 1840, was critically examined by a "committee of clergymen . . . in the interest of public morals," who subsequently gave her "character"; see *The History of American Sculpture* (New York: Macmillan, 1925), p. 61. With few exceptions, recent scholars explain the public reaction as based upon values commonly held by the provincial middle classes, without designating a specific religious discipline or tradition; see Edgar P. Richardson, *Painting in America: From 1502 to the Present* (New York: Thomas Y. Crowell Co., 1965), p. 125.

[10] Anthony Ashley Cooper, Earl of Shaftesbury, *Characteristicks of Men, Manners, Opinions, Times,* 3 vols. (5th ed.; Birmingham, England: John Baskerville, 1773), 3: title page; see also pp. 347–91 for an essay on painting based upon the engraving on the title page. There were several editions of *Characteristicks* and the essay on *Judgment of Hercules* was printed separately by J. Darby, of London, as early as 1714;

FIG. 2. Simon Gribelin, engraving of *Judgment of Hercules*. Detail from the title page of Anthony Ashley Cooper, Earl of Shaftesbury, *Characteristicks of Men, Manners, Opinions, Times,* vol. 3 (Birmingham, 1773). H. 1⁵⁄₁₆″, W. 3⁹⁄₁₆″. (Winterthur Museum Libraries.)

pictorial sources for the nude as art. The 1741 catalog of the Library Company of Philadelphia and the post-1751 catalogs of James Logan's library show the number of publications available that were concerned with appreciating the art of the ancients.[11] There can be little question that these and other European publications had some impact on even the most urbane of Americans who, in their colonial outpost, were far removed from the accumulation of a centuries-old art tradition that

was an everyday experience for their contemporaries in London, Paris, and Rome.[12] Although a small portion of eighteenth-century patrons were able to accept the place of the nude on a philosophical basis, the practical problem of finding artist's models to pose for such idealistic portrayals was not easily overcome.

Before 1750 the majority of artists practicing in America had received their training in London and Rome. They brought with them the skills acquired

---

George Ogle, *Antiquities Explained: Being a Collection of Figured Gems Illustrated by Similar Descriptions Taken from the Classics* (London: James Bettenham for Cl. Du Bosc, 1737). Benjamin West is listed as one of the original subscribers to this publication.

[11] In the *Catalog of Books Belonging to the Library Company of Philadelphia* (facsimile of the 1741 ed.; Philadelphia: Library Company of Philadelphia, 1956) the following publications were listed: *The Satyrs of Juvenal and Persius: Translated by Dryden . . . Adorned with Sculptures* (5th ed.; 1726); *Cicero's Three Books Touching the Nature of the Gods . . . with Notes and Illustrations* (London, 1683); *Antiquity Explained, and Represented in Sculptures. By the learned Father Montfaucon* (London, 1725). James Logan's library and that of his son, Dr. William Logan, formed the foundation of a public library for the citizens of Philadelphia. It opened in 1794 and thereafter was added to by purchases by the trustees. Although most of the library was related to religion and the practical sciences, some attention was given to the fine arts and antiquity. Included was the beautifully illustrated *Vitruvii de Architectura libri cum not variorum Henr. Wotton elementa Architecturae . . .* (Amsterdam, 1649); as well as Charles du Fresnoy's *Art of Painting* (Dublin, 1783).

[12] Jules Prown in *John Singleton Copley,* 2 vols. (Washington, D.C.: National Gallery of Art, 1966), and Grose Evans in *Benjamin West and the Taste of His Times* (Carbondale, Ill.: Southern Illinois University Press, 1959), have suggested that colonial isolation was in part responsible for the intensity with which some Americans read and accepted the treatises on art theory published abroad. Removed from an actual knowledge of artist-patron relationships in England and on the continent, Copley and West were profoundly influenced by the idealistic discourses that elevated the purpose of art to a stated responsibility of uplifting moral and spiritual values. Consequently, they, like others in America who read Charles Alphonse du Fresnoy, *De Arte Graphica,* trans. Dryden (London: J. Heptinstale for W. Rogers, 1695), or later works such as Sir Joshua Reynolds's *Discourses on Art,* 2 vols. (London: Edmund Malone, 1797), seized the theory that history painting—the classical and Renaissance presentation of man performing a noble deed—was art at its highest level. The common practice of portraiture was most acceptable when the subject was an individual of great moral stature. Indeed, the portrait artist was encouraged to present his subject in a heroic or serene attitude. Charles Willson Peale in a mezzotint of William Pitt went even further to aggrandize his subject; he dressed Pitt in the accouterments of an ancient Roman senator.

by long hours of copying antique and Renaissance masterpieces and drawing studio life models. Some artists like John Smibert and Gustavus Hesselius (1682–1755) bought their own copies and large portfolios of European engravings for reference. Only as the first generation of American painters began to mature did the limited possibilities in the colonies for valid instruction in their craft become so painfully obvious.

The youthful artist who aspired to the fine arts found many obstacles in his way. He was handicapped by lack of academic instruction, a serious shortcoming in the pursuit of a career that demanded a high degree of technical skill. If he was fortunate enough to know a European-trained painter who would give lessons or criticism, he was still denied the most direct source of study, since the life model was discouraged, if not forbidden, by colonial morality. At best he had only a few casts, some European medical anatomy books, and engravings for imitation. The particularly fortunate student had the direct encouragement of a collector who was willing to share his books and objets d'art. But on the other hand, the young artist found that the critical, status-conscious colonial connoisseur interested in historical or classical themes chose to buy European work. The few scattered examples of the nude in American painting before the Revolutionary War are silent testimony to the arid climate for this form of domestic expression. Nonetheless the colonial aesthete, as he joined with émigré artists from Europe to acknowledge the need for life study in the training of art students, became a pivotal figure in encouraging the first generation of native American painters to shift their attention from portraits to more sublime and romantic subjects.

In terms of the actual native product, the introduction of the nude into the vocabulary of the fine arts in eighteenth-century America came about in an uneven manner through a few timid, self-conscious exercises, beginning with the *Judgment of Hercules* by Robert Feke (ca. 1707–1751), painted about 1744. Feke apparently undertook the *Judgment of Hercules,* which was copied from Simon Gribelin's engraving for the title page of Shaftesbury's *Characteristicks,* in order to gain a clearer understanding of the aesthetic theory the engraving was intended to illustrate. The degree of success that Feke, a birthright Quaker, achieved in imitating Gribelin's sensual interpretation of the subject can only be imagined since the sole surviving

documentation of Feke's painting is a notation in Alexander Hamilton's *Itinerarium.*[13]

Like Feke's, John Singleton Copley's early ideas about art came from books and engravings supporting the art theory that all forms of painting were not equal, especially that history painting was a more worthy expression than the popular portrait. Three of Copley's earliest paintings attest to the impact of these eighteenth-century treatises and to the native artists' dependence on engravings of European works as training devices. *The Return of Neptune, The Galatae,* and *Mars, Venus, and Vulcan* were painted in Boston in 1753 and 1754.[14] In each of these studies Copley exercised his own invention and strengths; all three are interesting for their gaiety, bold and decorative use of color, and striking reflection of new rococo influences.

The determination of artists to understand the structure of the human body continued in spite of domestic opposition to the use of live models or cadavers. Even in Boston, where he had access to private collections and limited professional criticism, Copley copied from a book of anatomical drawings with painstaking care.[15] In Philadelphia the obstacles and frustrations were much the same. There were no studio models for the study of anatomy or figure composition. Furthermore, European-trained artists were occupied with portrait commissions and had little time to pursue less profitable historical or allegorical themes. As a result, there were few opportunities, if any, for the student to learn from example.

Benjamin West (1738–1820), like Copley, depended on treatises for encouragement to pursue history painting instead of portraiture. It was this interest in the application of published theory that

[13] Alexander Hamilton, *Hamilton's Itinerarium,* ed. Albert Bushnell Hart (St. Louis: W. K. Bixby, 1907), entry for July 16, 1744.

[14] *The Return of Neptune* (Metropolitan Museum of Art), probably painted in 1753, was based on an engraving made in 1749 by Simon François Ravenet after a design by Andrea Casali. See A. T. Gardner, *American Painting I* (New York: Metropolitan Museum of Art, 1956), pp. 38–39. *The Galatae* (Museum of Fine Arts, Boston), painted in 1754, was taken from an engraving entitled *Galataë Triomphe Sur L'Onde.* The design source for *Mars, Venus, and Vulcan* (Collection of Mrs. James F. Chapman, Pueblo, Colo.), painted in 1754, is believed to be an eighteenth-century print. See Prown, *John Singleton Copley,* 1:18.

[15] Prown, *John Singleton Copley,* 1:19. See also Prown, "An 'Anatomy Book' by John Singleton Copley," *Art Quarterly* 26, no. 1 (Spring 1963): 31–46.

led to one of West's early interpretations of a historical subject and accounted for a very early use of the naked model in America. Having chosen the death of Socrates as a theme and determined that the poison-bearing slave should be naked, West further decided that he "had only to look into nature for models which would impart grace and energy to his delineation of forms."[16] With the help of a friend, West found a model, and the young man was posed, naked to the waist. Although far from the total nakedness of European artists' models, this nonetheless was a monumental achievement for the colonial artist. It was the beginning of a career that led West to continue his studies in Europe and to pursue a style of painting in which history was sublime. For West the hero became an embodiment of the ideal of physical beauty with all the appropriate manifestations of moral character necessary to supply the beholder with a sense of spiritual elevation. And in the loves of gods and goddesses, West found the opportunity to paint the idealized human body for the sake of moral beauty.[17]

Beginning with Benjamin West, it became clear to young men who wanted to become accomplished artists that only in Europe could they find opportunities for the training that was necessary to bring refinement to American painting. From the vantage of his studio in London and his connections in Rome, West inspired the succeeding generation of American artists to look to nature for their models and to copy classical examples for refinement of technique. It is difficult to conceive that any colonial artist who took the opportunity to study abroad could have escaped the late eighteenth-century direction toward classicism; but it was due in large part to the attitude of West and the atmosphere of his atelier that a number of these young students found themselves copying the classical nude. Even those who remained in Philadelphia were subject to West's influence. West, who favored Titian's "gift to the Human figure [of] truth of color which surpassed all other painters," made several copies after Titian. One of these, a *Venus,* came to Philadelphia. Copley had seen this or another *Venus* on his trip to Philadelphia in 1771. Charles Willson Peale considered the arrival

of the *Venus* as a measure of artistic advancement in Philadelphia and encouraged his brother, St. George Peale (1745–78), to copy the painting.[18]

In some respects the interruption. of the Revolutionary War brought a temporary reversal in the progress of the nude in colonial art. Many of the patrons associated most closely with the European aesthetic who were more likely to support the advance of a catholic art lost their influence because of their political sympathies. With popular patronage limited to portrait commissions, American artists were left to their own devices and the encouragement of very few private collectors. There were surprising exceptions. Perhaps the most unusual was the commission given to William Clarke (w. 1785–1806) in July 1793 by Thomas Wright of Centreville, Maryland. Wright employed the Philadelphia-based artist to paint an overmantel panel for the dining room in his home at Reed's Creek. The subject, taken from Tasso's epic poem *Gerusalemme Liberata,* illustrates the idyll from book 16 where the heroic Rinaldo was led away from the Crusades by the seductive, half-naked Armida.[19]

By the last decade of the eighteenth century, training opportunities for young artists were no better than they had been for Copley or West. William Dunlap (1766–1839) recalled that prior to his 1784 visit to West's studio his knowledge of art had came from making "Indian" ink copies of books and prints generously shared by Thomas Barlow of New Jersey.[20] Charles Willson Peale had returned from West's atelier enthusiastically stating that "one rude line from nature is worth an hundred from coppys—enlarges the ideas and makes one see and feel such [sensations]—as are worthy of the author."[21] In America the life model was still prohibited, and plaster casts from classical sculptors were not available for regular study in the classroom. By the time Peale's own sons were old enough to begin a systematic study of drawing and

---

[16] *The World of Benjamin West* (Allentown, Pa.: Allentown Art Museum, 1966), p. 19. The painting *Choice of Hercules,* 1764, is in the Victoria and Albert Museum, London.

[17] Evans, *Benjamin West,* pp. 40–47.

[18] *Letters of Copley and Pelham,* pp. 307, 163; Charles Willson Peale, "Letterbook I," Peale-Sellers Papers, American Philosophical Society (hereafter APS), p. 32.

[19] E. McSherry Fowble, "Rinaldo and Armida: An Example of Classical Nudity in Eighteenth-Century American Painting," *Winterthur Portfolio* 5 (Charlottesville: University Press of Virginia, 1969), pp. 49–58. Painting owned by Mr. and Mrs. Bradford Smith, Centreville, Maryland.

[20] William Dunlap, *A History of the Rise and Progress of the Arts of Design in the United States,* ed. Frank W. Bayley and Charles E. Goodspeed, 3 vols. (Boston: C. E. Goodspeed & Co., 1918), 1:290.

[21] C. W. Peale, "Letterbook I," July 18, 1771, p. 18, APS.

painting, Peale's interest in establishing an appropriate training facility occupied much of his time.

Reconciled to the fact that he would be some time in overcoming local resistance to using live models in his studio, Peale pointed out the value of using the one model available—the plaster cast. "A good painter of either portrait or History, must be well acquainted with the Grecian and Roman statues to be able to draw them at pleasure, by memory, and account for every beauty [and] must know the original cause of beauty in all he sees."[22] It was on this premise that he began the training of his son, Rembrandt. The class was opened to others; but, initially, only Jeremiah Paul (d. 1820) shared the experience. The ever-enterprising, always perceptive Charles Willson Peale knew that the promise of a model would bring better attendance in his class. One of the more hilarious, or pitiful, incidents at this early school was reported by Rembrandt Peale when he recalled his father's desperate effort to procure a studio model for the young draftsmen. The older Peale hired a younger baker who, in the conduct of his daily occupation, was accustomed to being stripped to the waist; however, Peale failed to anticipate the model's self-consciousness as "the object of a dozen pair of scrutinizing eyes." The baker fled; and Peale, himself, partially disrobed to "serve as the first academical model in America."[23]

Charles Willson Peale was the generating force behind the formation of the Columbianum in Philadelphia in 1795. It was a futile effort to bring artists together to establish a school and exhibition facility. Divided by political rifts and operating in a city where, according to John Vanderlyn's 1794 observation, there was not a plaster cast of any importance, the organization collapsed.[24] Not until the formation of the Pennsylvania Academy of the Fine Arts in 1805 was a permanent gallery provided for the Philadelphia public, and not until the establishment of the Society of Artists of the United States in 1810 did working artists have a cohesive organization.[25]

The barrenness of training opportunities for artists in Philadelphia, Boston, or New York was evident when compared with the conditions John Vanderlyn (1775–1852) found in Paris in 1796. In many respects Vanderlyn was the exception to the rule among the second generation of American painters abroad. Like so many of his contemporaries he recognized that an American artist's only option to study anatomy was to go to Europe. Unlike the majority who went to London, usually to West's studio, Vanderlyn went to Paris where he found not only accomplished draftsmen for inspiration but also life models for study. In 1796 he wrote of the attractions of studying art in Paris. "I am every day at drawing scholl [*sic*] from breakfast untill dinner where I draw after chalk drawings, plaster figures of men & after living naked men who are kept for that business & from 5 to 7 in the evening by candle light so that by next summer I think I shall be pretty well acquainted with the human figure which seems to be the only thing they draw in schools." A year later Vanderlyn wrote of his attendance at anatomy lectures that were "given gratis for the artist." Whatever his hopes were for the development of adequate professional training in America, he was quick to note that the artist's freedom in Paris was the result of a prevailing attitude alien to American moral discipline. "Here are at Paris upwards of 30 Places of public amusement such as the theatres &c the grandest of which is the Opera, the machinery, musick, acting & dancing are perfection, the dancers are almost naked when they represent Nymphs Gods &c which might shock the modesty of Americans though it is not noticed for the dress here is very licentious & expect nothing else but Greek customs or dress will take place in some time here."[26]

Despite the obvious momentum a major change

[22] C. W. Peale, "Letterbook I," p. 34, APS.

[23] Rembrandt Peale, "Reminiscences: Exhibitions and Academies," *The Crayon* 1, no. 19 (May 9, 1855): 290.

[24] Richardson, *Painting in America*, pp. 134–35; Robert Grosman, "Biographical Sketch of John Vanderlyn, Artist," Reverend Roswill Randall Hoes Collection, MSS, N-YHS, reproduced in Louise Hunt Averill, "John Vanderlyn" (Ph.D. diss., Yale University, 1949), Appendix B, pp. 292–338.

[25] The Pennsylvania Academy of the Fine Arts was founded in 1805, chartered in March 1806, and opened to the public shortly thereafter. Helen W. Henderson, *The Pennsylvania Academy of the Fine Arts* (Boston: L. C. Page & Co., 1949), pp. 1–13. The Society of Artists of the United States, according to the constitution published for that organization in 1810, described itself as a "Society of Artists and Amateurs, founded on liberal principles" responsible for the establishment of a "Drawing School" and "annual Exhibitions." *The Constitution of the Society of Artists of the United States* (Philadelphia: T. L. Plowman, 1810), pp. 4ff.

[26] John Vanderlyn to Nicholas N. Vanderlyn, Dec. 30, 1796, MSS, N-YHS, quoted in Averill, "John Vanderlyn," p. 193; John Vanderlyn to Peter Vanderlyn, Mar. 10, 1798, MSS, N-YHS, quoted in Averill, "John Vanderlyn," p. 196; John Vanderlyn to Peter Vanderlyn, Aug. 14, 1797, MSS, N-YHS, quoted in Averill, "John Vanderlyn," p. 194.

in favor of the fine arts in America was not to coincide with the beginning of the new century. For much of the decade before 1810, the second generation of American-born artists were in Europe. Some traveled back and forth. John Vanderlyn returned for a brief period in connection with the opening of the American Academy, and Rembrandt Peale (1778–1860) made three visits to Europe before 1810. Others remained abroad for long periods of study. Washington Allston (1779–1843) and Samuel F. B. Morse (1791–1872) did not return to America until the second decade of the nineteenth century. An exception was Thomas Sully (1783–1872) who did not leave Philadelphia until he went to England in 1809–10. All of the Americans who left to study in Europe did so with high ambitions. Primarily, they were motivated by a desire to improve the standard of art in America by returning with art skills that reflected new European trends in painting. And, ultimately, they hoped to stimulate a shift in popular interest from portraiture to history painting.

For the figure painter, the greatest advantage of European training was the availability of life models. Rembrandt Peale recalled that during his 1802–03 stay in London he had been expelled from his drawing classes at the Royal Academy for an ill-advised prank, but he made up for the classes when he and other students hired the academy models for their private study.[27] Peale made no mention of the scarcity or reluctance of the models to pose, nor did he note any public objection to the practice. Thomas Sully and Charles King (1785–1862), in London in 1809 and 1810, used casts and live models at the Academy during the day and hired models "to stand in their painting rooms" in the evenings.[28] And in Paris, John Vanderlyn found artists' models possessed of "composure" and "unaffected modesty."[29]

In Europe the American artist was free to examine the centuries of artistic accumulation that served as the basis for eighteenth-century treatises on improvement of the arts. He saw the ancient sculptures from Rome and Greece, paintings by the masters of the Italian Renaissance, and he enjoyed an art in which portraiture was only one element, not the major thrust. With this introduction to new forms and concepts in painting and with exposure to the writings of Charles du Fresnoy or Sir Joshua Reynolds, it was inevitable that the artist would imitate what he saw. It was likely, too, that he would recognize an articulate, expressive rendering of the human figure as the supreme test of his skill as an artist. Success in this endeavor would certainly secure his recognition and establish his reputation. Thus motivated, many American students undertook difficult figure and group compositions while abroad.

During the first decade of the nineteenth century, American artists made only limited use of the nude in their work; the few surviving examples indicate just how sparse and widely scattered the practice was. A large proportion of these early studies of the nude from history or mythology are associated with Benjamin West, who continued as a principal source of inspiration and encouragement for American students. In London, West was available to all who sought his advice, and in America his theories were supported by Charles Willson Peale. West's absolute conviction that the artist must first have a thorough knowledge of anatomy was stated in a letter he addressed to Peale. "Correctness of outline, and the justness of character in the human figure are eternal; . . . color, manners, and costume: they are the marks of various nations; but the form of man has been fixed by eternal laws, and must therefore be immutable."[30] Undoubtedly, West emphasized these same tenets to the students who studied in his atelier and copied the master's latest paintings, which were hung in galleries adjacent to West's painting rooms. After his arrival in London in 1809, Thomas Sully made a copy of West's *Pylades and Orestes*, which he recorded in his register along with his earlier, independently designed, study of a Venus.[31] For some years following, Americans continued to refer to West's studies of the nude and to their own sketches and copies after West.

Artists outside of West's direct influence also painted the nude while in Europe. Washington Allston, in London in 1808, completed *Cupid and Psyche*, a composition he prized so highly that he decided against sending it to America until he could bring it across the Atlantic with his personal

[27] R. Peale, "Reminiscences: Exhibitions and Academies," p. 290.

[28] Dunlap, *Arts of Design*, 2:261.

[29] R. Peale, "Reminiscences: Exhibitions and Academies," p. 290.

[30] Dunlap, *Arts of Design*, 1:93.

[31] Edward Biddle and Mantle Fielding, eds., *The Life and Works of Thomas Sully: 1783–1872* (Philadelphia: The Wickersham Press, 1921), p. 379.

FIG. 3. John Vanderlyn, *Ariadne Asleep on the Island of Naxos.* Paris, 1812. Oil on canvas; H. 68″, W. 87″. (Pennsylvania Academy of the Fine Arts.) The second version of the subject. The first—a draped version—is in the Edward C. Coykendall Collection, Senate House Museum, Kingston, N.Y.

baggage. In Paris in 1809 John Vanderlyn copied Correggio's *Antiope* for John Murray, a New York patron.[32] Shortly thereafter he began *Ariadne* (Fig.

3), the most celebrated painting of his career. Another artist recalled the early preparatory studies for it. "In Paris I drew, with Vanderlyn, and another American, from one of the five models he [Vanderlyn] employed to finish his beautiful picture of *Ariadne.* She reclined, with apparent composure, on her couch, until her breakfast was announced, she rose, and covered herself with every indication of unaffected modesty, although our other American was angry that she could bear the scrutinizing gaze of three artists."[33]

The *Ariadne,* a study of the mythological princess who was abandoned on the isle of Naxos by her lover, Dionysus, was completed in 1810. Vanderlyn

[32] "The Picture I have consent to copy is Antiope asleep with Cupid along side of her & Jupiter in the form of a Satyr by Corrigio, you probably recollect the picture, its size is 5 feet seven inches by 4 feet. . . . I have already dead coloured my copy which is the size of the original & hope in the course of two months to be able to finish it, however I am determined to spare no time nor pains to make a good copy in the public opinion. . . . I am not sure the subject will please you so as to be desirous of possessing it for it is perhaps not chaste enough for American eyes, at least to be displayed in the dwelling of any private individual to either the company of a Parlour or Drawing room." John Vanderlyn to John R. Murray, June 12, 1809, draft in MSS, Senate House Museum, Kingston, N.Y., quoted in Averill, "John Vanderlyn," pp. 219–20.

[33] R. Peale, "Reminiscences: Exhibitions and Academies," p. 290.

produced subsequent versions of the subject, the second of which is believed to be the undraped version painted in 1812, now in the collection of the Pennsylvania Academy of the Fine Arts. Sometime between 1812 and 1818 Vanderlyn made a watercolor and crayon sketch in preparation for an engraving of the undraped version. The prints were issued and Vanderlyn presented one as a "discreet reminder of past favors" to Mrs. James Monroe.[34]

The encouragement and success American painters found in Europe, in combination with the excellent training opportunities in London, Paris, and Rome, served to heighten their determination to improve the atmosphere at home. Through correspondence or in person after their return to America, the artists joined the company of other native artists and gentlemen connoisseurs agitating for the establishment of institutions to train artists and to stimulate popular awareness of the many facets of art. At the beginning of the century there was a sincere desire on the part of patrons and artists alike to charter and to support academies for the visual arts. Yet, however united the laymen and professionals were in their enthusiasm for building suitable institutions, they were seriously divided in their support of the various objectives of such organizations.

Professional artists wanted a teaching academy, and to a limited extent the dilettanti were in agreement. The artists hoped to create an academic situation that would imitate the European model, much like one Vanderlyn found in Paris in 1797 or the West atelier and Royal Academy in London. In this atmosphere the student in New York or Philadelphia would be able to learn basic skills by drawing from casts and later refine these skills by studying a live model. While artists lent their support to the establishment of an academy to provide a continuing training facility, patrons considered the academy principally a dispensary for culture. Most of these intellectual laymen were also businessmen who equated the cultural opportunities of Europe with social status. By their terms Napoleon's Louvre was a repository for the arts and a monument to taste and power. Some of the patrons appreciated art as an aesthetic experience, but they were few.

The gentlemen of the committee that organized and directed the opening of the American Academy of Fine Arts in 1802 were typical. First they asso-

ciated themselves with Richard Livingston and, through him, with Denon and the Louvre. Then they ordered a fine array of casts made in France from antique sculptures: the *Apollo Belvedere* and the *Venus di Medici,* on the basis of West's recommendation that these two works represented the ideal male and female figures; the *Laocoön,* unsurpassed as a study of the body in tension; and an assortment including *The Gladiator, Silenus, Grecian Cupid, Castor and Pollox, Venus of the Bath,* and *Niobe.*[35] When the collection was opened, the New York public was invited to come and bask in the atmosphere of the glorious past. The artist-student, too, was invited to come and make drawings—provided, of course, he did not become obtrusive or interfere with the pleasures of the audience. No matter how the committee had worded the original objectives of the organization, interpretation of these objectives proved unsympathetic to the young painter.

Joseph Hopkinson of Philadelphia was one of those who viewed the New York academy exhibition of 1802 with genuine enthusiasm. He convinced several Philadelphians that the city's nominal academy (the sculpture gallery and painting rooms Charles Willson Peale maintained in Independence Hall after the failure of the nation's earliest training academy, the Columbianum), could not benefit the public or the artist without being moved to a building suitable for the exhibition of casts. A charter for the Pennsylvania Academy of Fine Arts was granted in 1806, and by April of that year, Philadelphia had "an elegant and appropriate building" as well as the promise of a substantial purchase of European casts. But the new organization, directed by a committee of laymen, did not represent the artists' interests in sufficient measure to satisfy the professional membership.[36]

The continued emphasis on the collection of casts and the imitation of classical figures drew the attention of George Murray, who voiced the artists' opinions in *The PortFolio* of September 1810: "The study of the antique, though important to the pupil, has nevertheless been carried much farther than what is necessary. . . . The grand object

[34] Averill, "John Vanderlyn," p. 100.

[35] Dunlap, *Arts of Design,* 2:105n. See also Richards, "The American Academy," p. 49.

[36] Burton Alva Konkle, *Joseph Richardson* (Philadelphia: University of Pennsylvania Press, 1931), pp. 146–51; *The PortFolio* 1, no. 6 (June 1809): 462–63; Edward J. Nygren, "Art Instruction in Philadelphia, 1795–1845" (M.A. thesis, University of Delaware, 1969).

. . . ought to be to establish a school of the arts, founded on plain and simple principles." More specifically, he declared the proper use of the antique was only to prepare the student for a "more important study of Nature in all her varieties."[37] Three years later on May 3, 1813, a Philadelphian wrote to Samuel F. B. Morse: "Our Academy of Fine Arts has begun the all important study of the live figure. Mr. Sully, Mr. Peale, Mr. Fairman, Mr. King and several others have devoted much attention to this branch of the school, and I hope to see it in their hands highly useful and improving."[38]

The live model, however, was still not readily available in Philadelphia, New York, or Boston. Training opportunities for artists remained relatively unchanged until the National Academy of Design instituted regular classes with life models in the late 1820s. There were earlier scattered incidents of art students' being admitted to anatomy classes at medical colleges. John Wesley Jarvis (1780–1840) was allowed this privilege. His medical instructor was Dr. John Augustine Smith; and through the generosity of Dr. John W. Francis, who lent Jarvis a "splendid edition of Galt and Spurzheim," the artist was able to study the "science" of anatomy at his leisure.[39] For the majority of art students, however, casts were the chief source for study and were available only to male students.

Notwithstanding the substantial increase in the number of cast collections by 1826, these models belonged to academies, athenaeums, or private collectors, and they were generally inaccessible to students. Artists were required to make special arrangements with librarians, keepers, or other officials to draw from the collections, and some keepers were notoriously indifferent to the needs of students. The problem was particularly acute at the New York Academy of the Fine Arts. Formerly known as the American Academy, this institution had stipulated that its cast collection be made available for study. Yet, even with a sympathetic keeper, the hours set aside for student use were few, and these were scheduled in the early morning. As a result the collection was seldom used.[40]

The restrictions and frustrations that the artist found in America in the 1820s when he attempted to advance his study were summed up by John Neal. "He [the artist] has no academy figures—no people trained to stand and set as he requires—no works in plaster if he wants a hand made permanently, for some particular study. And what is yet worse, nobody, whom he can prevail upon to sit. So that his men and women are nine times out of ten, even in their anatomy, the literal creation of his own brain."[41] Neal's comments on the condition of the arts in America are recognized generally for their incisiveness and a sarcasm bordering on insult. In this instance, perhaps, they reflected a dire situation.

As the artists who had been abroad to study returned home with their paintings, they were faced with the immediate problem of finding a facility for public exhibition. For some the problem was twofold: first, the academies in New York and Philadelphia were committed to the art of the antique rather than to exhibitions of works by contemporary Americans; and second, with due consideration to propriety, the lay academicians were reluctant to permit the exhibition of a contemporary study of the nude. At length, the artists were left to their own devices in getting their work before the public.

The painter's desire to exhibit his work was founded on the hope for popular recognition and acclaim, but, more directly, his decision to display his work in the public arena grew out of financial necessity. There was only a limited chance that he would find a private buyer in a country that generally viewed the nude as a statement of questionable morality rather than a statement of artistic theory. Then, even if he found a buyer who would accept the nude in principal, there was the very practical problem of size. Heroic subjects that lent themselves most readily as a vehicle for the nude were best suited to art on a grand scale. There were no palaces in America, and few private residences would accommodate large-scale works of art. At best, the artist could hope to make a reasonable financial gain from the quarters and half dollars that bought the curious observer a ticket of admission to a gallery.

[37] "Progress of the Fine Arts," *The PortFolio*, n.s. 4, no. 3 (Sept. 1810): 260. Probably George Murray of Philadelphia, who became noted as a bank note engraver for Murray, Draper, Fairman and Company.

[38] Edward Lind Morse, ed., *Samuel F. B. Morse: His Letters and His Journals*, 2 vols. (New York and Boston: Houghton Mifflin Co., 1914), 1:101.

[39] Dunlap, *Arts of Design*, 2:214.

[40] Dunlap, *Arts of Design*, 3:51.

[41] Quoted from John Neal's two-volume novel, *Randolph*, published in 1823, in Harold Edward Dickson, ed., "Observations on American Art: Selections from the Writings of John Neal," *The Pennsylvania State College Bulletin* 37, no. 6 (Feb. 5, 1943): 22.

FIG. 4. John Vanderlyn, *Bacchante and Satyr*. Paris, 1812–18. Oil on canvas; H. 44″, W. 59″. After a painting by Annibale Carracci. (The New-York Historical Society.)

The number of works in America that lent themselves to this type of exhibition was growing. Despite the fact that the nude was the featured subject in a relatively minor portion of American artistic output, there were apparently more than enough examples to satisfy the public appetite. By the middle of the second decade of the nineteenth century, the majority of artists who had gone abroad in the first wave were on their way home with graphic proof of their accomplishments. In addition to the *Ariadne,* which Vanderlyn had designed for exhibition or sale in America, he brought back the *Bacchante and Satyr* (Fig. 4), begun in 1812 and finished in 1818, and the *Antiope* (after Correggio), which he copied for John Murray, who finally refused it on the grounds that it

was morally unsuitable for display in his home.[42] Charles Leslie's 1810 copy of Benjamin West's *Amor Vincit Omnia* was brought to America before 1820. So was Samuel F. B. Morse's small terra-cotta statuette of *The Dying Hercules* (Fig. 5), for which he had received a gold medal in 1812 and which he used as a preparatory study for the painting *Dying Hercules* (Fig. 6).[43] In 1816 Washington Allston's *Dead Man Revived,* a study of a partially nude figure, was in Philadelphia. Morse, a student and

[42] Averill, "John Vanderlyn," p. 219; Dunlap, *Arts of Design,* 2:162. The *Antiope* is now owned by the Century Association, New York.

[43] Dunlap, *Arts of Design,* 2:262n. Both the terra cotta and the painting are in the collection of Yale University Art Gallery.

Fig. 5. Samuel Finley Breese Morse, *The Dying Hercules*. London, 1812. Terra cotta; H. 20½", W. 9", L. 22½". (Yale University Art Gallery.) Preliminary study for the painting shown in figure 6.

friend of Allston's, remarked that the Pennsylvania Academy of the Fine Arts had purchased it "for the sum of thirty-five hundred dollars, Bravo for our Country." Another copy by Charles Leslie (1794–1859) of a West painting, *Musidora Bathing,* was included in the third annual exhibition in Philadelphia.[44]

Surprisingly, in spite of the difficulty of finding suitable models at home,[45] there was a proportional increase in the number of domestically produced works featuring the nude. Rembrandt Peale painted a study entitled *Dream of Love* or *Io* in 1812, and in 1813 he exhibited a moral essay *The Grecian Daughter,* or *Roman Charity,*[46] which though not a nude was based on a theme that stim-

[44] Morse, *Samuel F. B. Morse,* 2:73. "Third Annual Exhibition," *The PortFolio* 3rd. ser. 2, no. 2 (Aug. 1813): 128.

[45] John Neal, "American Painters—and Painting," *The Yankee; and Boston Literary Gazette,* n.s., no. 1 (1829): 48–51. As quoted in Dickson, *Observations,* p. 42: "They [American painters] are better than we deserve; and more than we know what to do with. Their progress, too, is altogether astonishing, if we consider the disadvantages under which they have laboured, with no models, no casts, no academy figures, and little or no opportunity for them ever to see the old masters gathered, where they could be either copied or studied with impunity."

[46] R. Peale, "Reminiscences: Adolph Ulric Wertmüller," *The Crayon* 2, no. 14 (Oct. 3, 1855): 207. *Roman Charity,* which is privately owned, has recently been on loan exhibition at the Peale Museum, Baltimore. For a discussion of its history and rediscovery, see Wilbur H. Hunter, "Rembrandt Peale's *The Roman Daughter,*" *Antiques* 102, no. 6 (Dec. 1972): 1073–74; see Dunlap, *Arts of Design,* 2:183n.

FIG. 6. Samuel Finley Breese Morse, *Dying Hercules.* London, 1812–13. Oil on canvas; H. 96¼″, W. 78½″. (Yale University Art Gallery.)

ulated an intense emotional response from the public.[47] Thomas Sully, a Philadelphia painter better known for his portraits, was very much involved with painting the nude following his return from England. In 1813 he made his own copy of the *Musidora,* using the *Venus Bathing; Musidora,* which Charles Leslie had copied from the original painting by West. The subject, represented as a three-quarter length study of the nude, was taken from William Thomson's *Seasons,* a popular eighteenth-century work. Either the theme or the visual expression of the subject had particular appeal for Sully, for two years later, in 1815, he began a sec-

---

[47] The tradition of the *caritas Romana* includes in its subject two of the seven acts of mercy: the feeding of the hungry and the visit to the imprisoned. The subject is frequently represented as a woman, Pero, breast-feeding an aged prisoner, Simon. The acts of mercy are found in Matthew 23:35, 36. The theme is also found in Valerius Maximus, *Factorum ac Dictorum Memorabilium,* book 5, chapters 4 and 7. It is represented in Caravaggio's *Seven Acts of Mercy.* Walter Friedlander, *Caravaggio Studies* (New York: Schocken Books, 1969), pp. 207–18.

ond copy of the *Musidora,* which he completed in 1835.[48]

When faced with the problem of finding a suitable place to exhibit paintings of the nude, American artists were influenced, no doubt, by a combination of financial and historical precedents. If an artist exhibited his work in his own gallery or painting rooms, he stood to realize all the profit from the admission charge. Above all, the value of privately sponsored exhibitions had been proven in practice, beginning with John Smibert's Boston Gallery. More recently the private exhibition had been utilized by Adolph Ulrich Wertmüller (1751–1811) who, in 1806, arranged the first public exhibition in America of a monumental-size painting of a nude female. According to Wertmüller's New York advertisement, the exhibition of his monumental work *Danaë and the Shower of Gold* (Fig. 7) was to be held in a special room of a house on Filbert Street and would be open to the public every day of the week—Sundays excepted. Monday would be appropriate "for the accommodation of ladies exclusively. Admission 25 cents."[49] If scruples obliged some people to disapprove, curiosity or urbane broad-mindedness caused others to hasten to see just what it was that should be considered offensive. The artist's receipt books for the four-year period of the *Danaë*'s public exhibition indicate that the patronage was considerable.

Danaë, a mythological beauty imprisoned in a cell, was visited by her lover, Zeus, who transformed himself into a shower of gold so he could sift on the light as it passed through the small opening in the room. Wertmüller's life-size representation of *Danaë* is reported to have been a creation of the ideal feminine form for which three of the most beautiful ladies of the court of Louis XVI posed. Stylistically, it was in opposition to the movement toward romanticism that was gaining popularity in the United States; but inasmuch as the *Danaë* was painted in Paris it was not unusual that Wertmüller would have followed the precise drawing and clearly defined contours characteristic of the prevailing French style.

Even before its exhibition in New York, the *Danaë* had a reputation for attracting the curious.

---

[48] Gardner, *American Painting,* pp. 161–62. The second version of the *Musidora* is now in the collection of the Metropolitan Museum of Art.

[49] Franklin D. Scott, *Wertmüller—Artist and Immigrant Farmer* (Chicago: Swedish Pioneer Historical Society, 1963), p. 19.

In his diary, written while he was at Naaman's Creek, Wertmüller recorded a steady stream of Philadelphia visitors to his country studio where he kept either the original canvas or one of the known copies. The Peale sisters and brothers, an innkeeper, some other ladies, a Miss Juliane Robinson and a Mrs. Penrose Robinson, as well as a Philadelphia art collector visited the studio before August 1806. The point to be made is that the *Danaë* attracted a large and varied audience. Whatever their reasons, people came to see the Parisian nude and, in so doing, provided the artist with financial success. An 1812 circular for the sale of the painting claimed that it had an annual earning power of eight hundred dollars or more, with occasional daily receipts from fifty to seventy-five dollars.[50]

Eager to find a justification for the paintings they knew would not be suitable in private homes and possibly encouraged by the monetary rewards realized from the exhibition of the *Danaë*, other artists seemed to interpret the curiosity of the gallery audience as a sympathetic, embryonic interest in art for art's sake. From their point of view, this interest was to be encouraged and enlarged. Although Vanderlyn, in a letter to John Murray in 1809, recognized the uncertain situation of the arts, he allowed his own ambitions of introducing a concept that would elevate art in America to obscure his vision. Still, he must be credited for his recognition of the shift in emphasis that soon characterized the new republican society's approach to the nude in art. In the democratic surge of the nineteenth century the studio nude, placed in the public arena, became an object of curiosity. Vanderlyn resigned himself to the fact that the artist who painted nude subjects, and who intended to have his paintings provide his income, would have to rely on public exhibition. On the basis of hearsay reports he received in Paris, he put aside his fear of criticism and planned to return to America with a public exhibition of his painting from which he anticipated a "handsome compensation."

In 1816, six years after Vanderlyn finished his first version of the *Ariadne,* and with the permission of DeWitt Clinton, he opened a gallery of his paintings in quarters that had been assigned to the American Academy. Exhibited there were the *Marius Amid the Ruins of Carthage, Ariadne, Antiope* (after Correggio), *Danaë* (after Titian), and other copies of works by Raphael, Jordaens, and Veronese. Vanderlyn's hope that the nude studies of *Antiope* and *Ariadne* would serve as drawing cards in the way Wertmüller's *Danaë* had done seemed realized.[51]

Rembrandt Peale, like many of his contemporaries, favored the new interest in paintings of the nude form and, like Vanderlyn, Peale conceived the idea for such paintings with public exhibition in mind. So far as can be determined the *Dream of Love* or *Io* was painted soon after Peale's return from Paris in 1810; it was certainly finished by 1813. The painting remained in Peale's collection for "a few years" until the artist had realized "some reputation, and a sufficient profit" for the work. It was then sold to a Broadway exhibitor who, through his own carelessness, lost the painting in a fire. The only surviving evidence of its existence is literary, the chief sources being the writings of John Neal and Rembrandt's comments in his reminiscences. According to Peale's account, after Wertmüller's death in 1812 the "*Danaë* increased in popularity, and 'bustling connoisseurs' declared that its beauty of coloring could not be exceeded by any American painter. The imputation, being chiefly against me, stirred up my pride," Peale wrote, "and I painted a picture the size of life to compete with it. . . . My painting was the 'Dream of Love' founded on a slight French engraving, but varied and finished from nature."[52] Peale gave his reason for painting *Io,* and John Neal described what he saw in the painting: "He painted his DREAM OF LOVE; or as he called it at first, his JUPITER AND IO. Originally, the face of Jupiter was pressed to hers—and no other part of his body could be seen, through the smoke and cloud that enveloped them. It had a bad effect. . . . The head was afterward blotted out; and a naked cupid, painted over the face of Io. The whole is now passionately, purely beautiful."[53]

[50] Scott, *Wertmüller,* pp. 18, 19, 34, 79, 108; Michel N. Benisovich, "Further Notes on A. U. Wertmüller in the United States and France," *Art Quarterly* 24, no. 1 (Spring 1963): 25, n. 27. As late as 1864, the *Danaë* was reported to be kept upstairs by its owner, "under a curtain, and shown with caution or seen by stealth."

[51] John Vanderlyn to John R. Murray, June 12, 1809, draft in MSS, State House Association, Kingston, New York, quoted in Averill, "John Vanderlyn," pp. 219–20; see also pp. 104–5.

[52] R. Peale, "Reminiscences: Adolph Ulric Wertmüller," p. 207.

[53] John Neal, *Randolph,* 2:120–40, as quoted in Dickson, *Observations,* p. 20.

graver's art; however, in the second decade the public gallery for the engraving became the magazine illustration. One of the first line engravings of the nude to appear in an American-published magazine was a copy of Veronese's *Perseus and Andromeda* by Cornelius Tiebout (ca. 1773–1832), which appeared in the *PortFolio*, May 1812. In July of that year Guido Reni's *Dejanira and Nessus* was engraved for that same magazine.[58] These illustrations accompanied articles in a series on the fine arts designed to develop the reader's familiarity with art and art masterpieces.

For as long as the nude had remained secluded in the private collections of a few educated and wealthy eighteenth-century Americans who were determined to follow in the established tradition of the European upper classes, its presence in America was relatively unheeded. But once the nude was thrust before the public, its existence and purpose were unprotected. The public too, for that matter, was unprotected. Having no precedent to follow, any citizen with the price of admission was faced with an art object and a philosophy foreign to his experience.

Some gentlemen, following the tradition of the eighteenth century, had earlier taken available opportunities to enjoy the nude in painting, prints, and sculpture in private collections. But for most women public exhibitions brought them their first opportunities to see the nude in art. Certain that female audiences would be subject to greater self-consciousness than men and, thus, more reluctant to visit galleries, institutions made special addresses to the distaff. The situation at the Pennsylvania Academy, discussed by Joseph Hopkinson in his *Annual Discourse,* was typical.

Our collection of painting and statuary, from its first exhibition, has been visited by our ladies, with a consistency which acquits them of the motive of mere curiosity, and an ardour which could be found only in the minds well improved, touched with the fire of genius. . . . It must be admitted, too, that the objects of this institution were so novel in this country, as well as the exhibition, that it required no considerable share of good sense and fortitude in a lady to countenance them. But intelligence, and genuine modesty bore down ignorance, prejudice, and affection, without in the least, impairing that delicacy which is the most fascinating attraction of fascinating women.[59]

If Hopkinson's remarks tended toward flattery, it was understandable. From his position as a layman-academician he perceived the potential social obstacles in the way of displaying the nude to the American public. If artists were ever to realize the patronage they sought for their studies of the nude, it would be because men and women were truly educated to the nude as an artistic expression.

The public response to contemporary painting was far different from that given to a display of casts from the antique. Perhaps the larger scale and the use of natural color in paintings lessened the distance between the gallery visitor and the work of art. Generally ignorant of the intellectual theories that related the nude to classical art forms, the popular visitor responded to paintings through his senses. He was vulnerable to feelings of self-consciousness, awkwardness, and exposure. His offense at his own identification with the painting was voiced in periodic charges of indecency, indecorousness, and immorality directed at the artist.

Wertmüller's *Danaë* had been the first jarring note. Alien to anything previously exhibited before the American public, it was at once famous for its nakedness and became the most discussed painting of its day. It is curious that while the painting received high commendation from David and others, it does not appear to have been publicly exhibited in France.[60] In America the honors received by the painting in Paris were valuable in stimulating early gallery attendance, but they did little to form the average American's opinion of the painting. The success of the *Danaë* was soundly criticized by a large portion of the American public who had neither the desire nor the sophistication to remain detached. William Dunlap noted that the *Danaë* had made a "great noise in our cities." And, although it was the artist's "greatest and most splendid production," in accord with other popular editorials of the time Dunlap wrote, "it offends alike against taste and morality of art."[61] Controversy over the painting continued. Each time one voice decried its indecency, another praised the painting for its virtues.

In the final analysis, whether the *Danaë* was an encouragement or a detriment to the popular acceptance of the nude in America, the painting stimulated public awareness of art for art's sake

---

[58] *The PortFolio* n.s. 7, no. 5 (May 1812): facing 469; *The PortFolio* 8, no. 1 (July 1812): facing 73.

[59] Joseph Hopkinson, "Annual Discourse," quoted in *The PortFolio* n.s. 4, no. 6 (Dec. 1810): 34.

[60] Scott, *Wertmüller*, p. 18.

[61] "Wertmüller," *Analectic Magazine* 5 (June 1815): 490–93.

more than any work that preceded it. Perhaps John Neal summed up the controversy when he wrote in 1824: "We never saw . . . *Danaë*. It has been spoken of as a masterpiece . . . nay, as a picture, dangerous even for a woman to look at. The plain truth is . . . we believe . . . that such a naked woman, so full of languor, richness, and beauty, has not often been met with in this world."[62]

When Vanderlyn's *Ariadne* arrived in New York in 1815 after a successful European exhibition, the American public was still piqued over the moral invasion of Wertmüller's *Danaë* and still divided in opinion as to the social propriety of the nude and its legitimacy as art. The public leveled its disapproval at both the artist and the painting. In many instances, the *Ariadne* suffered a verbal assault that had its stimulus in the affectation and the naughtiness of the *Danaë*. Although Wertmüller's celebrated work had been removed from public view to the seclusion of an artist's studio, the painting was still accessible. From time to time moral purists felt the compulsion to write of the painting's assault on public decency; and, thus, they managed to keep this alleged outrage before the public. And as long as the public's approach to art was primarily emotional, it could readily transfer its reactions from the *Danaë* to the *Ariadne* with little loss of intensity.

On the other hand, many who came to see the *Ariadne* left with admiration for the artist and his work. John Neal wrote in 1823, "Ariadne is very beautiful." His objection to the painting was that it did not stimulate a stronger sense of involvement in the spectator; "you feel no emotion, no trembling, . . . which you ought to feel when trespassing upon the sleep of even a *picture* woman in her innocence, timidity, and loveliness."[63] By March 1821, Vanderlyn had taken the *Ariadne* to New Orleans, but there is no evidence that the artist was particularly pleased with the success of his exhibition in that city. In other southern cities the reports were more favorable. Rembrandt Peale, who leased the right to exhibit the *Ariadne* in Baltimore, wrote to Vanderlyn in 1820 that the "ladies behaved very handsomely on their Mondays." In Baltimore, a city where ladies and gentlemen held an obvious delight in the language, costume, manners, and society of France, the showing had

grossed over "199 dollars."[64] The *Charleston Courier* of 1822 commented that the *Ariadne*'s "crimson lips, teeth of pearls, and pure white skin made the southern gallery visitors subjects of eager attraction and awakening interest."[65] In Savannah, in February 1822, George Schley found the ladies somewhat reluctant to visit the exhibition of the *Ariadne*. He invited several to visit the gallery and hoped that they would overcome the "ridiculous fastidiousness," which he felt made them backward. The success of the exhibition depended upon female acceptance in a city where Schley determined that "fashion more than taste governs."[66] Finally, when the *Ariadne* and *Marius* were exhibited in Boston, an announcement in *Bowen's Boston News-Letter, and City Record* for July 25, 1826, noted there was "no amusement" in all of Boston any more popular.

If the public could not make up its mind about the rationale behind the use of the nude in art, neither could some artists. Most practicing artists were aware of the necessity of the nude as a training vehicle, but many others, divided in their approval of the exhibition of the nude, responded negatively to the *Ariadne* and similar works. Benjamin Latrobe offered the opinion that popular prejudice toward art was rooted in the sociopolitical character of the United States, and he soundly warned professionals that arguments against this prejudice would be in vain.[67] The warning was either unheard or unheeded. John Rubens Smith (1775–1849), who appropriated rooms adjoining Vanderlyn's in the American Academy for his drawing school, demanded the removal of the "indecent pictures" from Vanderlyn's apartment, and his demands triggered silent pressures that finally caused Vanderlyn to move.[68]

The most venerable and, possibly, the most colorful of the professional protagonists was Charles Willson Peale. In spite of his earlier enthusiasm for using nude models in his short-lived academy,

[62] Quoted in Dickson, *Observations*, p. 33.

[63] Quoted in Dickson, *Observations*, p. 22.

[64] Rembrandt Peale to John Vanderlyn, Mar. 3, 1820, MSS, N-YHS, quoted in Averill, "John Vanderlyn," p. 258.

[65] As quoted in Marius Schoonmaker, *John Vanderlyn: Artist 1775–1852, Biography* (Kingston, N.Y.: Senate House Association, Inc., 1950), p. 26.

[66] George Schley to John Vanderlyn, Feb. 13, 1822, quoted in Averill, "John Vanderlyn," p. 265.

[67] Benjamin H. Latrobe, "Anniversary Oration Pronounced Before the Society of Artists of the United States, May 8, 1811," Supplement to *The PortFolio* n.s. 5, no. 6 (June 1811).

[68] Dunlap, *Arts of Design*, 3:49–50.

Peale on one occasion tried to prevail on his son Rembrandt to give up painting the nude. In a letter addressed to Thomas Jefferson, recorded in his letterbook for 1811, Peale restated his position that the nude was for study only, and he continued, "however well I love the art of Painting in my present Ideas I think that we should guard against familiarizing our Citizens to sights which only excite a blush in the most modest." He concluded, "therefore, at our last exhibition at the Academy of Arts I advised and procured some old pictures of nudities to be put out of sight." Peale could accept the impersonal white cast, but he seemed to object to the use of color in portraying the nude; "the artist may always find subjects to show his excellence of colouring &c. without choosing such as may offend modesty." One of Peale's last attacks was against Washington Allston's *Rebecca at the Well,* a "showy picture" of a "naked female figure carrying her child taken from a picture of Titian [which] ought not to have found a place in an American Exhibition."[69]

For all the disquieting discussion among members of their own profession, some artists continued to choose the nude as a subject for their art, and visitors still paid modest admission fees to see the results. What the patron did not do was to buy the figure study or to commission a similar work for his own collection. "I am in general proud of the spirit of my countrymen, but there is too little attention paid to the fine arts," Samuel F. B. Morse wrote to his wife in the spring of 1814. "Man here is weighted down by his purse, not by his mind. . . . A fine painting or a marble statue is very rare in the houses of the rich in this city [New York]." He further lamented that "individuals who would not pay fifty pounds for either, expend double that sum to vie with a neighbor in a piece of furniture."[70] In a society leaning toward materialism and free-spending, the artist was forced to realize a return from his art by hanging it as a curiosity in a makeshift gallery.

Just as the accumulation of wealth did not automatically create the desire to invest in sculpture or painting, the price of admission did not necessarily stimulate a genuine understanding of art. George Murray remarked in Philadelphia in 1812: "It is rather unfortunate for the progress of the arts that a number of pretend connoisseurs and amateurs, instead of encouraging living artists have the temerity to direct them. . . . We hope," Murray continued, "that the time is not too distant when it will become fashionable for the public to buy as well as look at pictures."[71] But for the first quarter of the nineteenth century, the public was content to look and to be amused.

In the years from 1800 to 1825 it became increasingly apparent that if the public were to give any substantial encouragement to the progress of the arts in America, laymen would first have to learn to interpret the work before them. For the citizen who had not enjoyed travel in Europe and whose education had not included a command of classical literature, the nude was truly an enigma. Depending as it did on classical or mythological references for its moral and artistic justification, the study of the nude continued to have little meaning to a general audience. Realizing this, many leading Americans joined with artists in an effort to advance the education of the potential patron. In the first quarter of the nineteenth century, this united endeavor toward the refinement of popular taste, in addition to a heightened desire to improve professional standards, brought about the opening of the academies in Philadelphia and New York, the organization of the annual exhibition of the Society of Artists of the United States, and numerous publications, the most influential possibly being the "Fine Arts" series in the *PortFolio* published in Philadelphia.

By 1825 American painters were far from the goal they had set themselves at the beginning of the century. Perhaps, in a limited way, they had encouraged the public to outwardly view the nude without a blush. Inwardly, the usual gallery visitor had not yet acquired the necessary understanding of the nude in art. Subdued, if not defeated, the artists who had held such lofty standards twenty years earlier gradually moved to more profitable applications of their craft; and a new generation of painters turned away from history toward nature in the presentation of the romantic and monumental. It remained for those who chose sculpture as a vehicle of artistic expression to bring new vigor and direction to the movement that would establish the nude as an acceptable art form in America.

[69] C. W. Peale, "Letterbook XII," p. 13, APS.
[70] Morse, *Samuel F. B. Morse,* 1:100.

[71] G. Murray, "Review of the Second Annual Exhibition," *The PortFolio* n.s. 8, no. 1 (July 1812): 17–23.

The Account Book of Thomas Appleton of Livorno

A Document in the History of American Art, 1802–1825

Philipp Fehl

THE CLIMATE in which American art developed was necessarily conditioned by the importation of works of art and artifacts from Europe to this country. The history of this influential trade in works of art is still largely unexplored, nor is it easy to collect material on a more than impressionistic scale for such a study. It is therefore particularly pleasant to come upon the account book of Thomas Appleton (1763–1840) who, for many years while the United States Consul in Livorno, Italy, concerned himself with commissioning and exporting works of art to the United States. Appleton's account book gives us a view of how such an enterprise worked. It provides a wealth of examples that indicate the artistic values of American collectors and the prices they were willing to pay for imported works of art, and it may also afford us an opportunity to see with greater clarity how the business not only reflected an existing taste but also subtly helped to change it.

Appleton was in many respects a pioneer and one of the most inventive, if not enterprising, traders in works of art in his time. A review of the remains of his correspondence shows him to have been a frustrated and lonely man, yet also a lover of art who was sure of his taste and who did what he could, when occasion presented itself, to contribute to the advancement of the fine arts in the United States. His great model in this respect was Thomas Jefferson whom he knew and for whom he executed several important commissions. But it should be kept in mind that Appleton thought of himself first and foremost as a general merchant. He dabbled in any trade that came his way, and, as his accounts and his continuous complaints to his superiors in the foreign service show, he remained by and large impecunious. The entries in his account book that relate to his trade in works of art, important though they are, make up only a small fraction of the entries in the book.

Appleton was a member of an old Boston family. He descended from Samuel Appleton of Suffolk County, who came to America in 1635. Certain members of the family became remarkably wealthy in the course of the nineteenth century and were prominent in Boston society.[1] Our Appleton belonged to the honorably poor. His father, Nathaniel, was a small, unsuccessful merchant who eventually made a living as Intendant of the United States Loan Office at Boston. The most prosperous relative with whom Appleton dealt was Thomas

[1] I am grateful to the trustees of the Boston Public Library for their permission to publish the account book and to John Alden, Keeper of Rare Books, for his kind assistance. Professor A. C. Land of the University of Georgia was most generous in his assistance to me in matters monetary and commercial. As are all students of the correspondence of Thomas Jefferson, I am deeply indebted to the work, and the courtesy, of Professor Julian Boyd. I also wish to express my gratitude to the directors of the State of North Carolina Department of Archives and History, the Maryland Historical Society, the Massachusetts Historical Society, the Library of Congress, and the National Archives for many kindnesses I was shown in the course of my work and for their permission to publish from manuscripts in their collections. The White House, the Capitoline Museum in Rome, the New York Public Library, and the Maryland Historical Society have generously allowed me to publish works of art in their collections. I am also indebted to Mrs. Marilyn Caldwell, who helped me in setting up the form of the transcript of the account book and in checking the accounts, to Dr. Ellen Wiese who compared the final typescript against the manuscript, and to Dr. Alan Fern, and professors H. W. Janson and Miles Chappell for procuring some of the photographs. On Appleton's family connection see Isaac Appleton Jewett, *Memorial of Samuel Appleton, of Ipswich, Massachusetts; with Genealogical Notices of his Descendants* (Boston: privately published, 1850), pp. 1–36, and William Sumner Appleton, *A Genealogy of the Appleton Family* (Boston: T. R. Marvin, 1874).

Perkins, his brother-in-law, who appears in the account book as his most important partner or agent in the trade in works of art.[2]

In 1786 Appleton went to France, presumably to advance himself there as a merchant. He bore a noncommital letter of introduction from Governor James Bowdoin of Massachusetts to Thomas Jefferson, who was then American minister to France. In 1789 Appleton was one of eight members of the American colony in Paris, who, on July 4, signed a declaration in which they expressed their loyalty and fervent gratitude to Jefferson.[3]

In 1797 Jefferson was instrumental in securing for Appleton the post of United States Consul at Livorno. It was far from the position of emolument Appleton had hoped to obtain from the government. He had dreamed of Paris, and then, more modestly, of Hamburg. Only when the President offered him a choice between the two very insignificant posts at Dunkirk and Ostend did Appleton elect to sue for Livorno, and was glad to obtain it.[4] It was Appleton's fate to remain stationed at Livorno for the rest of his life. In fact, he established

there a record (for his time) of having been in office longer than any other American consul.[5] He made several attempts to be transferred to Paris, but they were halfhearted and he was given no encouragement. By and large, he seems to have responded with a certain relieved eagerness to the opportunities of a semiretirement from active life and of sponsoring the arts (as well as using them in commercial ventures) that the seaport of Livorno, serving the city of Florence, so richly offered him. Thomas Jefferson summed up Appleton's career in these terms:

while I lived in Paris, I became acquainted with Thomas Appleton of Boston, then a young man, and recommended him to the old Congress as Consul of Leghorn [Livorno], & he was appointed. on the commencement of thé new government he was confirmed by Genl. W. [Washington] at my request. he has been now about 30. years in possession of the office, has conducted himself with integrity & diligence and never done an act to incur blame from the government.

From the time of his appointment, he appears never again to have set foot on American soil or, for that matter, to have traveled farther than Paris.[6]

[2] Appleton is described as "honorably poor" by Thomas Jefferson in a letter to Governor Gabriel Holmes of North Carolina. See Robert D. Connor, *Canova's Statue of Washington* (Raleigh: North Carolina Historical Commission, 1910), p. 55. Thomas Perkins was the husband of Appleton's sister Charlotte. He should not be mistaken for Thomas Handasyd Perkins, a wealthy merchant and philanthropist of Boston. Jewett, *Memorial of Samuel Appleton*, p. 36.

[3] Bowdoin to Jefferson, July 22, 1786, Julian Boyd, ed., *The Papers of Thomas Jefferson*, 17 vols. to date (Princeton: Princeton University Press, 1960–), 10:160. The letter refers to the bearer only as "Mr. Appleton," and the editors refrain from an identification, but Thomas Appleton must be the person meant. Thomas's older brother John was known to Jefferson as early as 1785, see Boyd, *Papers of Thomas Jefferson*, 8:58, and eventually became United States Consul at Calais. Bowdoin's letter states merely that Appleton is "in the mercantile line" and goes on to speak of the father, Nathaniel, as "a worthy character, expressing a desire that his son might be introduced to you." See also Nathaniel Appleton to Jefferson, May 27, 1788, Boyd, *Papers of Thomas Jefferson*, 13:207, in which Nathaniel Appleton thanks Jefferson "most sincerely for the kind notice you have been pleased to take of my son since his arrival in Paris" and sends him, at the request of his son Thomas "eight boxes of Spermaceti Candles." In consequence of this shipment Thomas Appleton repeatedly had occasion to address Jefferson about difficulties with the import duty. See Boyd, *Papers of Thomas Jefferson*, 13:367, 421, 429, 543, 560; for the declaration of loyalty, 5:239–41. A significant portion of Jefferson's and Appleton's extended (but primarily commercial) correspondence is preserved in the Jefferson Papers in the Library of Congress. See also Constance E. Thurlow and Francis L. Berkeley, Jr., *The Jefferson Papers of the University of Virginia: A Calen-*

dar (Charlottesville: University of Virginia Library, 1950), p. 294; Connor, *Canova's Statue of Washington*, pp. 25–26, 55–56.

[4] For the confirmation of the appointment see Feb. 8, 1798, Consular and Agents' Commissions to Foreign Countries from February 10, 1790, to August 18, 1829, State Department Papers, National Archives, Washington, D.C. (hereafter NA); for Jefferson's letters referring to Appleton's search for an appointment, see Jefferson to Mr. Barrett, Dec. 15, 1791; Jefferson to an unidentified correspondent, July 15, 1815, Coolidge Collection, Massachusetts Historical Society, Boston; for negotiations concerning other posts see Nathaniel Appleton to John Adams, Oct. 16, 1797; Thomas Appleton to John Adams, Dec. 7, 1797, and Jan. 22, 1798; Nathaniel Appleton to Timothy Pickering, Oct. 16, 1797, State Department Papers, PG59, NA.

[5] J. B. Sartori to the Secretary of State, Apr. 30, 1840, "Miscellaneous Correspondence from 1798–1850," entry in the index to Leghorn, State Department Papers, NA. John B. (Giovanni Battista) Sartori is frequently referred to in Appleton's account book. He was United States Consul at Rome from 1797 to 1823, and from 1829 to 1841 acted as Consul General of the States of the Church in the United States while he resided in Trenton, N.J. When Appleton wrote to President Monroe, Aug. 15, 1814, he was already in a position to state that "as a native Citizen and Consul, my Commission is antecedent to every American Consul in Europe, excepting Mr. Bourne of Amsterdam." State Department Papers, C59, NA.

[6] See Appleton's letters to Jefferson, Aug. 29, 1803, and Dec. 12, 1808; to James Monroe, Oct. 10, 1813, and Aug. 15, 1814; to James Madison, Dec. 26, 1814, State Department Pa-

Appleton's diplomatic activities were meager. With the exception of the Napoleonic Wars, when he had occasion to address several excited communications to Washington, there was nothing to report except that trade was declining. In 1814 Appleton found it necessary to explain his lassitude to James Monroe: "If I have suspended, Sir, almost intirely during the past few years, that regular correspondence which, I trust I faithfully perform'd while our commerce continu'd in any degree in the Mediterranean, it has been owing to its total extinction with the port of Leghorn." Appleton probably was not a good administrator, certainly not in his last years. Some time after J. B. Sartori had taken over temporary administration of the consulate after Appleton's death Sartori complained "about the confused state, that I found the Books and Papers of that Consulate, kept by the late Consul Appleton."[7]

Consular officers of the period did not receive a salary. Appleton had a very small income from the consular fees that he collected from time to time, and he probably derived marginal benefits from occasional commissions, which he executed for the government, such as the purchase of clothing for destitute seamen.[8] It was taken for granted that he would make his livelihood, if not his fortune, as a merchant—but neither his talents nor the circumstances of his time and place equipped him to prosper.

In the papers left behind by Thomas Jefferson, we find that Appleton functioned more or less as Jefferson's Italian agent, a matter that was of no small consequence in either man's life. Among the principal objects of their business with one another were works of art and architectural sculpture that Appleton sent (or offered to send) to Jefferson, and —with naturally far greater regularity—the wines that Appleton shipped to Jefferson, a service much appreciated by Jefferson and one requiring careful discussion, since the care taken in shipping bore a direct relation to the taste of the product upon arrival.[9]

The letters by Appleton that follow are characteristic of his correspondence with Jefferson and indicate clearly the kind of services Jefferson called on him to perform. Appleton appears in the correspondence not only as a reliable merchant but also as a familiar acquaintance, a man who could take pleasure (if not pride) in passing on to Jefferson interesting bits of gossip, who knew he was Jefferson's equal as another American but who also knew how to respect the distance that naturally separated their stations in life. The first letter shows Appleton as a purveyor of sundry goods; the others are chiefly concerned with works of art.[10]

---

pers, NCRD 226, NA. Jefferson to an unidentified correspondent, July 15, 1815, Coolidge Collection; he must have erred in recalling the date of Appleton's appointment since all relevant documents in the National Archives agree in placing Appleton's petition for the appointment in December 1797. For Appleton's status as an amateur see Philipp Fehl, "Thomas Appleton of Livorno and Canova's Statue of George Washington," in *Festschrift Ulrich Middeldorf*, ed. Antje Kosegarten and Peter Tigler (Berlin: De Gruyter, 1968), pp. 523–52. The visit to Paris is recorded in the account book, Oct. 12, 1813, to June 7, 1814.

[7] United States Office of Naval Records and Library, *Naval Documents Related to the United States Wars with the Barbary Powers*, 7 vols. (Washington, D.C.: Government Printing Office, 1939), 1:353, 472, 483–85, 613, 620, 624–25. Appleton's official diary is preserved in the State Department Papers. The title on the cover of the book, in Appleton's hand, reads "Register of Events in the Consulate of Leghorn containing events such as arrival of vessels of war &c., Deposits, etc., from Commencement of the Consulate to 1828." The subjects of the entries are generally indifferent and in the later years far apart from each other in date. Appleton's reports to the Secretary of State on the affairs of the consulate were written at irregular intervals. See "Despatches from Consuls in Spain, Portugal, Sicily, Italian States: September 12th, 1812, to December 25th, 1853" and Appleton to Monroe, Aug. 15, 1814, State Department Papers, NCRD 1328, NA; Sartori to J. Binda, Jan. 6, 1841, "Leghorn, Miscellaneous Correspondence from 1798–1850," State Department Papers, NCRD 1329, NA.

[8] On the conditions of the consular service at the time see William Barnes and John Heath Morgan, *The Foreign Service of the United States: Origins, Development and Functions* (Washington, D.C.: Historical Office of the Department of State, 1961), pp. 26–68. There are regular entries for minor government commissions in the account book.

[9] Jefferson's most formidable commission to Appleton involving works of art required Appleton to furnish capitals and various units of marble needed for the building of the University of Virginia. See William B. O'Neal, *Jefferson's Buildings at the University of Virginia: The Rotunda* (Charlottesville: University Press of Virginia, 1960), pp. 28–30, 35–39. For an example of Jefferson's tact in turning down an unwelcome offer of marble busts for Monticello, together with a rather affecting description of his need for wine, see his letter to Appleton, Jan. 14, 1816, in Andrew A. Lipscomb, ed., *The Writings of Thomas Jefferson*, 20 vols. (Washington, D.C.: Thomas Jefferson Memorial Association, 1903–1904), 19:228–31. There are a number of entries concerning materials for the university and of bills for wines made out to Jefferson in the account book.

[10] The three letters reproduced here are in the Coolidge Collection, Massachusetts Historical Society.

1st Jan 1807

Sir

About two months since I receiv'd a letter from Mr. Cathalan,[11] requesting me to purchase for your use, some smyrna raisins without seeds, a parmesan cheese, and a small quantity of macaroni. —I have delay'd forwarding the two latter articles, which I have with much ease procur'd, in hopes that the raisins would soon arrive from the Levant; but various disastres have happened to the vessels bound here, and it has therefore been impossible to procure them for this conveyance.

I have then, sir, concluded to send a box Neapolitan macaroni, the best we have in Italy, and your account, as Mr. Cathalan desir'd I should draw on him for the amount. —I purchas'd during the last autumn about 200 bottles of Montepulciano wine, from the same grounds as that which on a former occasion you found so agreeable to your taste;[12] but it cannot arrive here before the next month; it shall therefore be forwarded early in March, in order to avoid the inconvenience you suggested, which attends transporting light wines to America, in the warm seasons—

Agreeably to your directions, I sent to Mr. Joseph Barnes[13] the sum you pointed out as the suppos'd value of the wines he sent you, and I now enclose you his reply. I have thought, Sir, that in consideration of his intention of speedily returning to the U. States, it was most proper to leave this little affair as it now stands, until he waits on you in person

Mr. Mazzei[14] who I saw yesterday, enjoys his usual share of health; but as he scrupulously avoids reading newspapers, or other political conveyance, and thus by degrees prepare his mind for those great events, which he cannot at last prevent coming to his Knowledge, so

[11] Stephen (Etienne) Cathalan, a merchant of Marseilles, and Mme Cathalan and Cathalan *fils* appear in Jefferson's correspondence as his agents and are, on occasion, named (as a business house) in the account book. See Boyd, *Papers of Thomas Jefferson*, 10:173–74, 197, 547, 11:358–59, 601, 12: 131–32, 198, 207–8, 464, 534–35, 639–40.

[12] The wine is presumably the same Montepulciano that was "produced on ground formerly belonging to the order of Jesuits and sold for the benefit of the government in 1773 at the time that that institution was abolished. I hope it has preserved its reputation and the quality of its wines." Jefferson to Appleton, Jan. 14, 1816, Lipscomb, *Writings of Thomas Jefferson*, 19:228–31. See also Fehl, "Thomas Appleton of Livorno and Canova's Statue," p. 526.

[13] Unidentified. Possibly John Barnes, a resident of Powhatan County, whose name appears in the Jefferson correspondence. See Boyd, *Papers of Thomas Jefferson*, 11:360n.

[14] Philip Mazzei (1730–1816) was a Florentine physician. In 1773 he emigrated to Virginia to introduce there the culture of grapes, olives, and other useful fruits. He lived not far from Monticello and was a friend and confidant of Jefferson. During the American Revolution he was agent of the state of Virginia in Europe. After a short second stay in America he returned to Europe in 1785. From about 1796 he resided at Pisa where he also died. See *Dictionary of American Biography*, ed. Dumas Malone, 22 vols. (New York: Scribner's, 1928–40), 12:469–70.

he bears them with much impatience inasmuch as, he conceives they rather tend to increase the general map of misery in Europe, than to alleviate its sufferings.—

he continually mentions both his desire and purpose to finish his days in America; but the truth is, that he has a very rich cousin many years older than himself, to whom he is the legal heir at last—but if appearances are good grounds to justify an opinion on, my own is that the older cousin will outlive the younger. —Mr. Philip Mazzei about a year since, in rising from his bed in the morning, fell suddenly on the floor where he remain'd (he thinks) some minutes, in a senseless state, and in attempting to rise fell a second time; however, by a fort'night's attention and diet, he was again restor'd to health.—he himself attributes this event to his mind having been long agitated, by frequently thinking on the distress'd state of Europe—his friends who judge perhaps more sanely, view it as an omen of a lethargic disposition.—

Accept Sir the assurance of the high respect with which I have the honor to be your devoted Servant.

Th. Appleton

Leghorn 8 May 1825

dear Sir

I greatly regret it was not in my power, to comply with your wishes, that your chimney-mantles might be Sent, by a different vessel, from that which carries the bases & the paving squares [for the University of Virginia]; but there was no other vessel in port, at the time. —I have mention'd to Mr. Thompson, the Collector, those cases which are for your private account, and they are so mark'd, that there can arise no confusion. —great labour & skill were exercis'd by the Sculptor, in the workmanship & selection of the various marbles, and I hope they will be found Satisfactory. —The Sculptor, far from making any profit on them, assures me, that on any other occasion, he must have added 50 Dollr. to the price in the amount. —Since Shipping the marble works, the Brig. Wm. Gray, Captn. Mc.Keever. has arriv'd, & is up for freight for New York. by this vessel I shall send the Capitels, & will sail in one month.—

I call'd a few days ago, on madame Pini, at Pisa, when I found her confin'd to her bed, and rapidly approaching dissolution—her disorder is on the lungs, & her physicians have pronounc'd her malady, past all remedy— She will leave three children, & a husband who is devotedly attach'd to her. —I have long observ'd a tendency to this fatal disorder, for she was produc'd by the expiring effort, of an ill-tim'd marriage, as her father [Philip Mazzei] had pass'd three score & ten, before he took his wife, and which injudicious connection evidently hasten'd the period of his life—She was a comely woman, and there was precisely, half a century, difference in their ages. —Mr. Pini, is earnestly pressing the arrival of his funds, for the reasons, I have mention'd in my preceding letters; to wit, that he has bought a small farm, contiguous to some lands he owns, in the environs of Pisa.—

as you have not mention'd anything, in your last letters, in relation to the capitels for the interior of your fabric, of which, I wrote you the prices in marble or in wood,

I presume, you have found, a better mode of supplying this want, in the United-States. —If in the progress of your edifice, you should have occasion for any further architectural works, your instructions shall be scrupulously attended to. —Raggi,[15] will undoubtedly wait on you, in order to obtain some work, for he is reduc'd, I believe, to his last cent. I think him an honest & well-intention'd man, but he is so vague & flighty in his projects, that one would judge either that he is not yet arriv'd at maturity, or that he is returning into a second childhood. in short, he is now only fit for dayly labour, if he is even fit for that—now, that he sees, the injudicious agreement he made for the bases, he gives the most ridiculous reasons for doing so: to wit, "for fear of giving offense."—

Your chimney mantles are, as follows

	2—Mischio	
2. call'd mischio	1—Statuario	Smaller
Large	1—Bardiglio fiorito	Size
Size	1 common,	

1—venato muvolato

[The different types of marble are *mischio* ("mottled"), *venato muvolato* ("veined"), *statuario* ("sculptor's"), and *bardiglio fiorito* ("streaked").]

with the Sincerest Sentiments of esteem & respect Y. Ob. Serv.

Th. Appleton

Leghorn 22 June 1825

Dear Sir,

I now inclose your private account with me, balance due me 178 Dollr . . 50-Cts[16] I am hourly, in expectation of the piedestal, for your own use, which my sculptor has made, as Raggi had not, even the means to execute this trifle if it arrives, before sailing of the vessel, it shall be now sent. otherwise, it shall be forwarded by the first for New York. —You will perceive it is included in your private account. —Raggi, being determin'd to return to the U. States, he has, through my intercession, obtain'd a

[15] Among the persons repeatedly mentioned in the Jefferson–Appleton correspondence and in the account book are Michele and Giacomo Raggi, two stonecutters whom Appleton had found at Jefferson's request and sent to America. They arrived in Charlottesville early in July 1819, but discovered almost immediately that they could not turn the native stone into suitable capitals. The work progressed miserably, and they repeatedly proposed to return to Italy. In September 1823 Jefferson commissioned Giacomo Raggi to obtain in Italy the ten Corinthian capitals and two pilaster bases called for by the design of the porch of the Rotunda. The price agreed upon was $65.00 for each capital and $32.50 for each pilaster; marble of Carrara was specified, and Raggi was to work under Appleton's direction. Raggi did not carry out his commission, but Appleton eventually supplied the desired marbles as well as several marble chimney pieces and a marble pedestal for Jefferson's private account. Thurlow and Berkeley, *Jefferson Papers*, nos. 1615, 1703, 1709, 1711, 1714, 1715, 1717, 1739, 1804, 2028; Philip Alexander Bruce, *History of the University of Virginia, 1819–1919: The Lengthened Shadow of One Man*, 5 vols. (New York: Macmillan, 1920–22), 1:172, 254–55, 265–68.

[16] See Appleton account book, June 14, 1825.

passage for New York, at less than half the customary price—I hope he may, there find bread, for here, he would soon want it. —he carries with him, a trifling paccotile [parcel of goods], which he has obtain'd on credit, payable 3 months after his arrival, and which, I believe will never pay the cost & charges.—In my next letter, which will be in July, I shall be able to fix the precise balance due me, from your university, which amount, together with the balance of your private account, may be remitted, as heretofore, to Mr. Williams of London, or if it should be more convenient, remit both to Thomas Perkins of Boston, adding, whatever, may be, the then rate of exchange on London. —I hope you may find the chimney-mantles, much to your satisfaction, for no pains were spar'd, either in procuring beauty of marble, or in their execution. —with constant wishes. Sir, for your happiness, believe me, with great sincerity your devoted servant

Th. Appleton

Thomas Jefferson, of Monticello, to Thomas Appleton of Leghorn—Dr.
1825

		Dollars
June	To a piedestal of white statuary marble agreeable to instructions given to Giao. Raggi	40.—
	To case, freight from Carrara duties & porterage	6.—
		46.—

Dr. Thomas Jefferson in accot. currt. with Thos. Appleton Cr.
1825

		Dollr Cts
June	To bala. Due me in accot. of May, as transmitted you by Ship Caroline.	132.50
	To a piedestal of Statuary marble as above	
		178.50

1825   Doll
June by bala. due me 178.50

Leghorn 22 June 1825
E. E.
Th. Appleton

[The following entry in pencil is in Jefferson's hand:]

1824. surplus of 500D this year	42
1825 do . . . . this year say	56
	98
	178.50
balance due T. A.	80.50

In 1816 Jefferson, responding to an inquiry from the legislature of North Carolina, which desired "a fullsize statue of General Washington of the best marble and workmanship to be procured and put up in the Capitol of the State," urged earnestly that Antonio Canova be asked to execute the statue: "No artist in Europe would place himself on a line with him; and for 30 years, within my own knowledge, he has been considered by all Europe as without a rival." Jefferson also recommended Appleton ("a man of worth and taste") as agent in the business of negotiating with Canova: "None so ready, or so competent as Mr. Appleton himself. He has relations with Canove, is a judge of price, convenient to engage the work, to attend to its progress, to receive and forward it to N. Carolina."[17] Appleton in consequence was commissioned to approach Canova on behalf of the state, to supervise the making of the statue, and eventually to ship it and to handle the complexities of the monetary transactions involved in the payment for the work. As soon as he was asked, Appleton threw himself into this work with much energy and was quite successful, not only in the execution of his commission but also in the invention of a program rich in figures for the relief on the pedestal of the work. He also managed to secure the commission for the execution of the pedestal reliefs for Raimondo Trentanove, a young sculptor whose talent he much admired and to whom he was bound by close familial ties through his Italian wife, Vincenza Maria Raimonda Trentanove. After the destruction of Canova's statue—and its pedestal—by fire in 1831, Appleton tried unsuccessfully to secure for Trentanove the commission for a new and, as he thought or pretended, even better monument to Washington.[18] The memory of Canova's work is fortunately

preserved in a full-size plaster model from Canova's studio (Fig. 1). A modern replica of it was recently unveiled in the old State Capitol in Raleigh, North Carolina.

However commercial Appleton's interests were, there is no doubt that he also cared seriously about the advancement of his country in the arts. He cooperated with Philip Mazzei (though not always seeing eye to eye with him in the matter) in bringing Italian workmen to America to work on the United States Capitol, and he attempted, unsuccessfully, but evidently entirely for patriotic reasons, to secure the emigration of the sculptor Lorenzo Bartolini to the United States.[19]

In another instance involving a lesser artist, the Austrian die cutter Moritz Furst, he was successful—and lived to regret it. Furst (or Fuerst, as he spelled his name before coming to America) arrived in the United States in 1808. He worked chiefly for the United States mint in Philadelphia and won acclaim with a series of twenty-eight portrait medals (commissioned by Congress) in honor of American heroes of the War of 1812. Despite his success he never rose above the position of assistant to the engraver at the mint. Soon after 1824 when the post of engraver to which he had aspired was given to another man, Furst initiated proceedings against the United States government in which he claimed redress for the damage he suffered because he had been lured to America by promises—which were not kept—made him by Appleton in the name of the United States. He also published his grievances in a pamphlet entitled *Proceedings of the Engagement Between Thomas Appleton, Esq., Consul for the U.S. at Leghorn and Mr. Moritz Furst, Engraver on Steel.*

[17] Jefferson also refers to the "bust of Genl Washington in plaister" by Giuseppe Ceracchi, which was in Appleton's possession and "is the only original from which the statue can be formed." Jefferson to Nathaniel Macon, Jan. 22, 1816, Lipscomb, *Writings of Thomas Jefferson*, 14:408–12; Connor, *Canova's Statue of Washington*, pp. 23–26, 28–33; Fehl, "Thomas Appleton of Livorno and Canova's Statue," pp. 525–29, 532–38.

[18] Raimondo Trentanove (1792–1832) was born at Rimini, the son of Antonio Trentanove, himself a sculptor and worker in stucco. Raimondo studied at the Academy of Carrara where he received his instruction in sculpture from Lorenzo Bartolini (1777–1850) who, in a manner altogether radical for his time, tempered the Empire classicism of his art with a fresh and affecting observation of nature and a corresponding study of quattrocento Florentine sculpture. In 1815 Trentanove went to Rome to study with Canova and soon became one of his assistants. He was looked upon, in his own time, as an artist of distinct merit and promise, especially for his figure of a seated *Amor* (in the collection of the Duke of Devonshire), a *Venus and Amor*, and a number of funerary monuments worked in relief. Trentanove's early death caused by consumption was much lamented in Rome where he had been one of the ornaments of polite society. The best account of Trentanove's life is by Carlo Secondo Azario in Joseph Michaud, *Biographie Universelle Ancienne et Moderne*, 45 vols. (Paris: Desplaces, 1843–65), 42:127; see

also Ulrich Thieme and Felix Becker, *Allgemeines Lexikon der bildenden Künste von der Antike bis zur Gegenwart*, 37 vols. (Leipzig: Engelmann, 1939), 33:778. For further information on Appleton's dealings with Trentanove, see Fehl, "Thomas Appleton of Livorno and Canova's Statue," pp. 532–41. Vincenza Trentanove's name is first mentioned in an entry in the account book for Oct. 11, 1813, where Appleton refers to her as his housekeeper. On Aug. 9, 1823, and Oct. 29, 1827, he recorded some of the provisions of his last will and testament in the account book. Vincenza Trentanove appears there in the character of his wife (or common-law wife) and Raimondo Trentanove—probably her brother—is named as one of his executors.

[19] The sculptors imported to work on the Capitol were Giovanni Andrei and Giuseppe Antonio Franzoni; account book, July 17, Aug. 17, Sept. 5, Nov. 22, 1805; Fehl, "Thomas Appleton of Livorno and Canova's Statue," pp. 525–26, 545 n.22.

In this pamphlet Furst describes his encounter with Appleton as follows:

About the latter part of May or beginning of June, 1807 Francis Wittenberg, now residing in the City of New York, who transacted my business in Italy, was several times requested by Thomas Appleton, Esq. Consul for the United States at Leghorn, to introduce me to him, with which this Mr. Wittenberg complied, and introduced me to the Consul according to the Consul's request. After some conversation, the Consul showed me a gold coin and requested my judgment about its execution, and we, both the Consul and myself, found it to be badly done. In the meantime the Consul, Mr. Appleton, represented to me that he was authorized by his government, to engage an Artist, as a Die Sinker or Engraver for the United States Mint, and said, that in case I should be willing to enter into such an engagement, and to go to the United States, I should get a fixed salary of $2000 per annum, from the Mint, besides extra work from the Government of the United States; so, to make my fortune in a short time, after some consideration I accepted his offer and engaged with him accordingly, in presence of Mr. Wittenberg.[20]

In consequence of this complaint Appleton received a rather annoyed communication from the Department of State asking for an explanation. His response is not preserved, but we know that Furst's action was not successful. He returned to Europe about 1840.[21]

After Appleton's death in April 1840 his official papers were turned over to his successor by his daughter Minerva Eufrosina, his heir. These included Appleton's "Register of Events in the Consulate of Leghorn . . . from Commencement of Consulate to 1828," which is now in the National Archives, and the account book. The latter was evidently considered government property because it contained, besides Appleton's commercial notations, records of his official expenditures and receipts. In 1890 William T. Rice, who was then United States Consul at Livorno, turned the book, which "had been ordered destroyed by several of my predecessors," over to Appleton's relatives in Boston. Though it appears that the historians of the family did not regard the career of Thomas Appleton with much esteem or interest, the book found its way to the Boston Public Library, as a gift of Nathan Appleton.[22]

The account book is an ordinary notebook, 10¾ by 8½ inches, with cardboard covers bound in vellum. It contains on 256 pages covered with a small, efficient, tightly compressed script—except for a few passages in which the handwriting is exuberantly irregular—the record of by far the better part of Appleton's commercial career. The first entry is dated March 10, 1801, the last, in a trembling hand, March 13, 1835. There, together with all sorts of references to consular business and speculations in lottery tickets, to loans of money on interest, to trade in amber beads, wine, umbrellas, and an improbable variety of other objects, are the records of Appleton's trade in works of art.

The most enterprising and, for his time, extraordinary of Appleton's ventures in the art business were two shipments of "old masters," paintings that are recorded under the dates of February 15 and May 31, 1817. The entries abound with names such as Guercino, Parmigianino, and Tintoretto, but it may be taken for granted that Appleton's attributions as well as his distinctions between copy and original are casual, at best. A number of these alleged old masters may well still survive in the basements of American museums.

Among the works of sculpture shipped by Appleton, the number of busts of George Washington is remarkable (Fig. 1). They owe their iconographic authenticity to a cast—or, perhaps, as Appleton claimed, "the original plaister model" of Giuseppe

[20] For details on Furst's life (1782–after 1840) and work see Georgia Stamm Chamberlain, *American Medals and Medalists* (Annandale, Va.: Turnpike Press, 1963), pp. 26–47, figs. 22–28. See also Joseph Florimond, Duc de Loubat, *The Medallic History of America: 1776–1876*, 2 vols. (New York: privately published, 1878), 1:xxiv–xxv, 166–277, 2:pls. 27–52; James Ross Snowden, *A Description of the Medals of Washington, of National and Miscellaneous Medals* (Philadelphia: Lippincott, 1861), pp. 69–74, 79–88; William Dunlap, *History of the Rise and Progress of the Arts of Design in the United States,* ed. Alexander Wyckoff, 3 vols. (New York: Blom, 1965), 2:374–75, Thieme-Becker, *Allgemeines Lexikon,* 12:562–63; Cornelius Vermeule, *Numismatic Art in America: Aesthetics of the United States Coinage* (Cambridge, Mass.: Harvard University Press, Belknap Press, 1971), p. 30; Patterson du Bois, "Our Mint Engravers," *American Journal of Numismatics* 18, no. 1 (July 1883): 12–13. Furst's pamphlet was discovered by Daniel Parish, Jr., and republished under the title, "A Bit of U.S. Mint History," *American Journal of Numismatics* 43, no. 1 (July 1908): 45–50.

[21] Daniel Brent of the Department of State to Thomas Appleton, Jan. 4, 1826, "Dispatches to Consuls," vol. 2 (Mar. 12, 1817–May 31, 1828), State Department Papers, NA; Dunlap, *Rise and Progress of the Arts of Design,* p. 375; Du Bois, "Our Mint Engravers," p. 14; George C. Groce and David H. Wallace, *The New-York Historical Society's Dictionary of Artists in America: 1564–1860* (New Haven: Yale University Press, 1957), p. 247.

[22] Account book, Aug. 9, 1823; undated inscription by Rice on the first page of the account book; the account book is identified as follows: Accession 26, 937; Manuscript Shelf no. G. 31. 44. Presented to The Boston Public Library by Nathan Appleton, Oct. 22, 1891.

FIG. 1. Antonio Canova, *George Washington*. Rome, 1820. Plaster model. (Gipsoteca Canoviana, Possagno, Italy: Photo, Gabinetto Fotografica Nazionale, Rome.)

Ceracchi's portrait of George Washington, which was in Appleton's possession (Fig. 2). Appleton had bought the plaster from a fellow consul, William Lee, then at Bordeaux, who previously had engaged, to a modest extent, in the identical business of multiplying the likeness. A number of these busts, passing under the name of Ceracchi, were probably adaptations by Appleton's protégé Raimondo Trentanove, or copies of them. A fine example of such a work is in the White House (Fig. 3). A signed and dated original composition by Trentanove survives in the New York Public Library (Fig. 4).[23]

[23] Fehl, "Thomas Appleton of Livorno and Canova's Statue," pp. 526, 535, 545 n.20, 547 n.4, 550 n.85; Connor, *Canova's Statue of Washington,* pp. 29–31; account book, Oct. 13, 1803, Apr. 19, 1809. For work by Ceracchi and the probable original of Appleton's "plaister model," see Ulysse Desportes, "Giuseppe Ceracchi in America and His Busts of George Washington," *Art Quarterly* 26, no. 2 (Summer 1963): 140–79. The White House bust of Washington probably represents the type Appleton called "plain"—as opposed to "bust

Another work of patriotic significance that appears repeatedly in the account book is the bust of

with heroic garb," a description which, in turn, fits the bust in the New York Public Library. See account book, Sept. 9, 1817; June 16, 1818, nos. 19, 20. The White House bust was originally "one of three purchased in 1817"; *The White House: An Historic Guide* (Washington: White House Historical Association, 1964), p. 31. In 1822 Appleton states with some pride that Trentanove's "likenesses of Washington are in the hands of many of our citizens in America." In 1831 he says in turn that "not less than a dozen of the busts of Washington are in those cities [Baltimore, Philadelphia, New York, and Boston], for he has greatly improved the likeness of Washington, from that formed by Canova, in several journies to London and Paris, and which are universally acknowledged to approach so near the original features of the hero, as to remain unrivalled by any European artist." One of the purposes of Trentanove's travels, in other words, was to compare Ceracchi's authentic portrait, on which Canova had based his version of Washington's face, with other authentic portraits not available in Italy. The bust in the New York Public Library clearly bears the marks of this "improved likeness." For Appleton's letters see Fehl, "Thomas Appleton of Livorno and Canova's Statue," pp. 538, 550 n.85; and Connor, *Canova's Statue of Washington,* p. 59.

FIG. 2. Giuseppe Ceracchi, *George Washington*. Philadelphia, 1795. Marble. (Metropolitan Museum of Art, Bequest of John L. Cadwalader, 1914.)

Fig. 3. After Giuseppe Ceracchi, *George Washington*. Ca. 1817. Marble. (White House Historical Association.)

Fig. 4. Raimondo Trentanove, *George Washington*. Rome, 1824. Marble. (New York Public Library: Photo, H. W. Janson.)

Christopher Columbus. Again, it is likely that Trentanove was responsible for the invention of the head. A *Christopher Columbus* by Trentanove is now in the Protomoteca of the Capitoline Museum (Fig. 5). This work was originally placed, together with the busts of other great men, in the Pantheon in Rome. Like most of the other busts it had been commissioned by Canova, who in this way at once contributed toward the realization of a cherished dream—to make the Pantheon a memorial church (or temple) for men of genius—and offered young and needy sculptors the opportunity to gain experience and earn money in the execution of a noble task.[24]

Christopher Columbus was a somewhat lonely explorer in the Pantheon; the great majority of the busts of heroes collected there were artists and men of letters. Trentanove's and, perhaps, even Canova's interest in the unusual subject may well have been awakened by Appleton who, as an American, as an admirer of Thomas Jefferson (who had been one of the first Americans to procure for himself the portraits of its first discoverers),[25] and as a man of business, had a natural stake in the matter.

Appleton and Trentanove also cooperated in supplying visitors to Italy with portrait busts of themselves. The Maryland Historical Society is in possession of two of these works. One of them is of General Robert Goodloe Harper (Fig. 6) whose name appears among the receipts listed in the account book.[26]

[24] Valentino Martinelli and Carlo Pietrangeli, *La Protomoteca Capitolina* (Rome: L'Erma di Bretschneider, 1955), p. 65, no. 21; see Luigi Huetter, *Iscrizioni della Città di Roma*, 3 vols. (Florence: Instituto di Studi Romani, 1959), 2:623; *Memorie Enciclopediche sulle Antichità e Belle Arti di Roma* ser. 2 (1817): 36; Vittorio Malamani, *Canova* (Milan: Hoepli, n.d.), pp. 249–50.

[25] Boyd, *The Papers of Thomas Jefferson*, 15:xxv–xxxvi, 526, 545 n.21, plates facing p. 425.

[26] Account book, May 1, 1823, a retrospective balancing of accounts with Trentanove. The date of the receipt of payment from Harper is July 8, 1822; the bust according to the inscription on it was made in 1819. The work is also men-

FIG. 5. Raimondo Trentanove, *Christopher Columbus.* Rome, 1817. Marble. (Capitoline Museums, Protomoteca, Rome: Photo, Oscar Savio.)

Appleton's largest trade was in the field of the minor arts. There are frequent bills of shipment for ornamental vases, candelabra, and small sculptured genre pieces after the antique or, occasionally, after favorite pieces by Canova (Figs. 7, 8), which were mostly made of alabaster. More constant yet was his trade in marble chimney pieces. It appears from the account book that the bulk, if not all, of the marble work Appleton sold came to him from workmen located at Carrara.

The persons most frequently referred to in the account book as Appleton's agents or partners in the United States are members of his family. They are, besides Thomas Perkins of Boston, Perkins's son, Thomas, Jr., also of Boston, and two other

FIG. 6. Raimondo Trentanove, *Robert Goodloe Harper.* Rome, 1819. Marble; H. 20″. Signed: R. Trentanove, Fece / Rome 1819. (Maryland Historical Society.)

nephews, N. W. and C. H. Appleton of Baltimore.[27] In Philadelphia he dealt with the firm of David Ware.

The monetary systems and values of Europe, and especially those of the Italian states, with which

_____
tioned in Appleton's correspondence; Fehl, "Thomas Appleton of Livorno and Canova's Statue," p. 535; General Harper also owned one of Trentanove's busts of Washington, p. 538. The second bust by Trentanove in the Maryland Historical Society is of Lloyd N. Rogers (1787–1860). Robert Goodloe Harper (1765–1825) was a politician and major general of the Maryland troops in 1814. See *Dictionary of American Biography*, 8:285–86.

[27] The two nephews were sons of Nathaniel Walker Appleton, Thomas's oldest brother. In 1817 or 1818 one of them returned to Boston because of ill-health, and Appleton in consequence used the services of Thomas Perkins, Jr., in receiving the payments for Canova's statue of Washington. In 1819 Perkins, Jr., went bankrupt, a circumstance that caused the state of North Carolina to lose three thousand dollars. Appleton, on his own account with Perkins, Jr., lost about fifteen hundred dollars. Appleton to Governor John Branch, June 1, 1820, in Fehl, "Thomas Appleton of Livorno and Canova's Statue," pp. 535–36; account book, page preceding the date Feb. 15, 1816; Jan. 4, 1817.

Appleton had to operate, were bewilderingly complex. He seems to have moved in this jungle of figures with serene competence: it was the arena of his pride and marginal profit as a merchant. His trade in works of art was a simpler affair. Next to the use of dollars and, occasionally, pounds sterling, his transactions required only the use of the currencies of Tuscany and the Papal States. The table will be immediately helpful to the reader of

who is not ambitious of passing for an Englishman of fashion, may enjoy . . . every convenience of life except a carriage at an expense of no more than a hundred pounds sterling a year including dress, pocket expenses, etc." In 1815 they were told, in almost identical words, that the cost would be £150 (i.e., about 666 American dollars). In Rome, between 1830 and 1850, "a *baiocco* was about a cent, a *paul* a dime, a *scudo* a dollar; $1000 was deemed

Table of Comparative Monetary Values

Florence (Tuscany)			Rome (Papal States)	
1 quattrino		= 0.3 cents		
3 quattrini = 1 soldo (copper)		= 0.9 cents		
5 quattrini = 1 crazia (copper)		= 1.5 cents		
8 crazie = 1 paul [paolo, pavolo] (silver)		= 12 cents =	10 baiocchi (copper) =	1 paul (silver) [9.5 cents]
69 crazie = 1 pezza della Rosa or Livornina (silver)		= $1.03 =	1 scudo (silver)	= 10 pauls [95 cents]
10 pauls = 1 scudo or francescone [franceschino] or crown (silver)		= $1.11 =	[1 Spanish dollar (silver)]	= 10 pauls
20 pauls = 1 zequin [sequin, zechino] (gold)		= $2.22 =	1 sequin (gold)	= 20 pauls [$2.07]
60 pauls = 1 ruspone [ruspono] (gold)		= $6.66		
			1 doppia (gold)	= 32 pauls [$3.04]
			1 old louis d'or	= 44 pauls [$4.18]

the account book. The exchange in dollars is computed on the fairly steady value of the dollar between the years 1815 and 1834. In the same period the English pound could be bought for approximately 4.44 American dollars. The approximate correspondences between Tuscan and Roman values are those indicated in old guide books. The dollar values are given in greater exactitude and indicate the margins of profit (or loss) that mattered to traders. The spelling of the Italian values is that favored by Appleton.[28]

The real values of the currencies changed constantly, but not altogether drastically. English travelers in 1791 were advised that "a prudent person

enough to see an American artist through for a year; many tried it for half that amount." At that time the customary charge for room and board (on a modest scale) in a city like Richmond, Virginia, was between $10 and $20 a month. The cost of a room (with four or five big meals included) in the most celebrated hotels of the big cities was $2.50 to $3.00 per day; in other places the customary charge in first-class hotels was about $2.00. A standard workingman's budget—for a man supporting a family—in New York City came to about $600, total annual expenditures. A typical New York businessman in turn was expected to spend about $1,330 for the same purpose ("a frugal family of four with an annual income of $1500").[29]

[28] Compiled from William Brockendon, *Road Book from London to Naples* (London: John Murray, 1835), pp. 99, 126; Heinrich A. O. Reichard, *Itinerary of Italy* (London, 1819), pp. 43–44; Giovanni Carboneri, *Monete e Biglietti in Italia dalla Rivoluzione Francese ai Nostri Giorni*, vol. 1 of *La Circolazione Monetaria nei Diversi Stati* (Rome: Unione, 1915). The computation of the dollar values is the work of Professor A. C. Land. Appleton's quotation of the exchange rate, when presenting a bill in America, appears to have been tipped slightly to his advantage. See the account book, Feb. 23, 1820, and May 4, 1821, where the zequin comes to $2.37. The practice of charging a little more in transactions of the kind was (and is) common enough and was, indeed, legitimate when the posts were slow and the tending of a bill amounted to the extension of a short-term loan.

[29] Thomas Martyn, *A Tour through Italy* (London, 1791), pp. xviii–xx; Henry Coxe, *Picture of Italy* (London: Sherwood, Neely & Jones, 1815), pp. xxxi–xxxvii; see also Giuseppe Vallardi, *Itinerario Italiano* (Florence, 1806), pp. 19–27; Heinrich A. O. Reichard, *Handbuch für Reisende aus allen Ständen* (Leipzig, 1793), pp. 89–91; James Aug. (Jacques Augustin) Galiffe, *Italy and Its Inhabitants: An Account of a Tour in That Country in 1816 and 1817*, 2 vols. (London, 1820), 1:197–99, 2:411; Giuseppe Prezzolini, *Come gli Americani Scoprirono l'Italia (1750–1850)* (Milan: Treves, 1933); Margaret Thorp, *The Literary Sculptors* (Durham: Duke University Press, 1965), pp. 16–17; Paul D. Converse, "How a Family Lived in the 1830s," *Current Economic Comment*,

The account book itself contains many interesting clues for a comparison of the true value of prices in Italy and America. It is only fitting that we leave the last word on the subject to Appleton himself. On July 20, 1822, he addressed the following complaint on behalf of the American consuls abroad to John Quincy Adams, then the secretary of state: "if we are desirious of availing ourselves of every legal means to increase the miserable emoluments of our Offices, it will not appear unaccountable to you when you are inform'd that my consular fees do not exceed four hundred Dollars annually, and that Leghorn is, by far, the most resorted to, by Americans in the Mediterranean; while a decent Apartment, or a floor of a house, in this City, costs three hundred Dollars."[30]

In the following transcription of Appleton's account book entries concerning works of art, Appleton's spelling has been preserved throughout, but not the division or the layout of his entries on the (unnumbered) pages of his book. Raised letters, for example, have been lowered to the line of type. The entries can easily be identified by the dates under which they are recorded. On occasion Appleton did not give the date of a transaction. Whenever the date could be reconstructed by a comparison with other entries on the page it has been added and enclosed in brackets. The same device is used to indicate the date of an entry that was excerpted from notations having nothing to do with Appleton's trade in works of art. Eliminated is the place reference Leghorn (Livorno), which, on occasion, precedes the date as given by Appleton. All of his entries relating to business may, in fact, be understood as being dated at Leghorn.

It remains to be said that there survives in Appleton's file in the State Department papers a letter by a Baltimore physician, Dr. Patrick Macaulay, in which he asks Appleton to supply him with chimney mantelpieces in marble for his house. It is dated November 30, 1839.[31] Appleton was evidently too old and too ill to take on the commission.

FIG. 7. Henry Moses, engraving after Canova's *Hebe.* From *The Works of Antonio Canova,* vol. 1 (London: Septimius Prowett, 1824). (Photo, Winterthur.)

Feb. 1950, pp. 1–2; Edgar W. Martin, *The Standard of Living in 1860* (Chicago: University of Chicago Press, 1942), pp. 153, 394–95.

[30] "Despatches from U.S. Consuls in Leghorn, 1793–1906," State Department Papers, NA.

[31] "Leghorn: Miscellaneous Correspondence from 1798 to December 1850," State Department Papers, NCRD 1329, NA. Dr. Patrick Macaulay was a member of the Academy of Sciences and Belles-Lettres at Baltimore. He is mentioned in "The Diary of Robert Gilmor," *Maryland Historical Maga-*

FIG. 8. Henry Moses, engraving after Canova's *Venus*. From *The Works of Antonio Canova,* vol. 1 (London: Septimius Prowett, 1824). (Photo, Winterthur.)

There is, at any rate, no entry relating to it in the account book. The letter will serve to acquaint us with a typical order in Appleton's trade with works of art. Its politesse is joined to a not uncertain taste and a businessman's caution. Appleton, it would seem, was just the man to rejoice in such a correspondence and to carry out commissions of the kind with understanding and a sense of integrity.

> Sir
> After some conversation here with my friends Robert Gilmor Esq. & Mr. R. Dorsey[32] I have taken the liberty to desire you to let me know at what price I can obtain at Leghorn Marble Mantles for a principal story—say for Library, Drawing room, Dining room, Parlor & Hall, also six for Chambers in the same house. I do not wish them too highly ornamented, but of very neat and *well* carved patterns; those sent to Mr. Dorsey may be considered good sample and I am anxious to know what the cost will be and the freight came to from Leghorn. Your attention to this matter will much oblige me and should I determine to import them the order will be sent to you next spring.
>
> With Great respect
I remain
Yr obt Servt
P. Macaulay
>
> Marble Mantles are now very cheap in this Country owing to the introduction of Machinery in cutting Marble, but the patterns are not so *recherche* as I could wish—if not too dear I should prefer on this account to import.

---

zine 17 (1922): 249; his full name appears in the index [spelled Macauley in keeping with Gilmor's spelling], p. 424.

[32] Robert Gilmor, Jr. (1774–1848), was a merchant of Baltimore and a leading member of the board of managers responsible for the erection of the Washington Monument at Baltimore. See "The Diary of Robert Gilmor," pp. 231–68, 319–47. Richard Dorsey was Gilmor's brother-in-law: "the son of a respectable country gentleman. . . . He was brought up in my father's compting house, and was much esteemed by him" (p. 234, n.4). Gilmor also mentions Charles Carroll Harper, son of Robert Goodloe Harper (see note 26) as a distant relative. Note also Gilmor's account of his relations with Mr. Flandis, a picture dealer from New York, pp. 346–47. On Gilmor, see also J. Jefferson Miller II, *The Washington Monument in Baltimore* (Baltimore: The Peale Museum Historical Series, Jan. 1966), p. 4.

The Account Book
Entries
Pertaining to Appleton's Trade in
Works of Art

[Facing the page opening with the date April 2, 1802]

On the 27th of March (1802) made an agreement with Giuseppe Luciani of Carrara to be delivered me in Leghorn the following pieces of marble at the prices annexed. Viz.

			Zequins	
10 Marble Chimney pieces	@	6.	60.–
10 ditto	do [ditto]	@	8.	80.–
6 do	do	@	10.	60.–
Marble pavements of different Colours & sizes for				50.–
in white Marble tables or Slabs from 3 @ 5 Zequins for				50.–

Zequins in Silver.–300.–

To be paid on the delivery in Leghorn & which is not to exceed the month of June.

8th [Apr. 1802]

Giuseppe Luciani Dr. To Cash pd. Ba [Battista] Pisani[33] agreeably to his letter & on acct. of Marbles he is to deliver————Pauls 200–

8th June 1802

Giuseppe Luciani of Carrara Dr to Cash pd Luigi Salluci as per his order & on acct of marbles to be deliver'd to him   24 Crowns   Pauls 240–

16th [June 1802]

Made an Agreement this day (being at Volterra) with Settimio Guadaroli e Cie for 50 pair of Alabaster Vases. to be from 10 to 12 inches in heighth and at the rate of 3 Zequins the pair, the whole to be delivered me in Leghorn in all July at which period he is to be paid.

[33] Probably Giovanni [Battista] Pisano who, with his brother Pietro, ran a statuary shop in Florence. G. B. Pisano and other members of his family are referred to repeatedly in the account book under the surname Pisani. The two brothers Pisano claimed in 1803 that they owned the bulk of Cerrachi's life portrait busts of America's founding fathers and the sketch for his proposed monument to George Washington. See Desportes, "Giuseppe Ceracchi in America," p. 141.

4th August [1802]

p'd this day Settimo Guadaroli of Volterra for 100 Vases of Alabaster agreeably to his letter of 29 July. to be pd. to Francisco Milani. Say 50 pr [pair] @ 60 Pauls.–3000–
p'd for Case   36–

Pauls –3036–
p'd transporting from Volterra.   — 26–

The above was shipped on board The Philadelphia Capn Raser for Phila. and there consigned to Saml. Emery to be sold for my Accot.

12th [Aug. 1802]

This day shipped on board the Ship Philadelphia Bernard Raser Master 52 Cases containing 27 Marble chimnies 5 Tables & 800. Squares for paving, on my Account and Consigned to Saml Emery at Phila for Sale.–

N.B. there were no bills of Lading signed on account of there being no marks or numbers on the Cases. I have therefore only the Capt. [Captain's] receipt in the form of a letter of this date.

13th [Aug. 1802]

Giuseppe Luciani Dr to Cash paid Luigi Bibilino for money lent him by sd Bibilino 400" [denomination not given] and for freight of 52 Cases Marble from Carrara. as per order of sd. Luciani

viz.————————————484"
as the vessel was in the
road for extra trouble   20   Pauls
504" ————   756–

25 [Aug. 1802]

Giuseppe Luciani Dr. to Cash
p'd M. Benedetti being the bala. due on Marble Chimnies etc. after I shall have pd. the acceptance of 51:1/2 crowns

	Zequins.	Pauls
& 140 Do————	94.	9–

29th [Sept. 1803]

Received this day from George Pollok by bill of Excha drawn by Donati Orsi Merriman on J. Ulrick. fifty Zequins in Silver, which is for the purpose of erecting a marble monument over the grave of his late brother Thos. Pollok. who was lately interred in the english burying ground of Leghorn

13th [Oct. 1803]
Settimo Guadarolli Dr To Cash p'd him for four busts
of Genl Washington in Alabaster   26 Crowns

June 5th [1804]
Giuseppe Luciani Dr. To Cash Niccola Lambro on
accot. 2 Chimnies to be delivered   33-Zequins

26 June 1804
Giuseppe Luciani (of Carrara) Dr. To Cash p'd J. B.
Pisani on accot. of two chimnies   12 francesconis

[June 26, 1804]
Thomas Perkins (Brother-in-law). Dr. To 2 Marble
Chimney pieces purchased by his desire, and forwarded
by the Ship Bonetta Capt. Osgood for Salem.—Cost at
Carrara—Spanish Dollars. 126 one hundred and twenty
six Spanish dollars

10 [July 1804]
Giuseppe Luciani (of Carrara) Dr. To Cash p'd Bte.
Pisani as per his Order in letter. the bala. due on two
Chimnies sent to Bror. [Brother-in-law] Perkins
                              frano   Pls [Pauls]
                              28.   2½

[Feb. 13, 1805]
Giuseppe Luciani Dr. to Cash p'd Madme Pisani on
accot. of 2 Chimnies for Mr. Perkins—
                              8 Zequins—16 fraconi

26th [Mar. 1805]
Giuseppe Luciani of Carrara. Dr To Cash p'd Madme.
Pisani by his desire on accot, of two chimnies to be de-
liver'd and which are by the order of Mr. Thos Perkins—
                              Eight Zequins-16-Crowns

7. May 1805
Giuseppe Luciani Dr To Cash pd. B. Pisani on accot. of
Chimnies to be deliver'd.   9 Zequin   Pauls 180–

June 10 [1805]
J. N. Millingan Dr. To Cash paid freight of
2 cases of Vases from Naples   Pauls 78.6
to p'd duties, porterage etc. etc. —21.6   21.6
[The following was added later to complete
the bill:]

July 8	To p'd freight of 4 Cases from Naples		157.4
	To p'd porterage duties etc. etc.		28.–
Aug. 2	To p'd porterage on bd [board] felucca for Marseilles and french Consuls fees—35.		35–
Sept. 9	To p'd freight of 4 Cases from Naples—	Pauls 174	210–
	To p'd duties porterage & Boatage etc.	36	
Oct. 9	To p'd French consuls fees on shipping of 4 Cases together with porterage		20–
	To p'd Storage of all the above Cases at different times		30–
	equal to Livres of France—354 Livres—590 say-Pauls		590

Drawn in favr of Cathalan for the Amt paid. 11. Oct.

27. June 1805 [excerpt]

	Pauls
St.[?] Cathalan [merchant of Marseilles] Dr. To Cash p'd on alabaster bust of Genl Washington Dd. *P. Argent*	120
To Cash p'd P. d'Argent as per his order	63.4
	183.4

July 17 [1805]
The Secretary of the treasury Department of the U.
States Dr To thirty five Zequines paid to Ph. Mazzei on
accot of his expences to Rome, to hire Sculptors for to
be sent to America [to work on the Capitol building in
Washington]. Say Pavolis 700.
[A later insertion]
Septr 5 [1805]
The Secretary of the Treasury Department of
U. States Dr To Cash p'd Philip Mazzei on
accot. of his expences to Rome for to procure
Architects for the Govt of the U. States   Zequines
Sixty five Zequines—   65–

[July 31, 1805; excerpt]
Statement of my Account Settled with Thomas Perkins
of Boston. To Ballance due me from my late fathers estate, as likewise my mother's.   Dollars
                                        5003.5

also 2 chimney pieces sent last year   94.26
To bala. due T: Perkins.   Dollars 5097.31

13. August 1805
Thomas Perkins (bror. in: law.) Dr. To Cash p'd G. Luciani for very elegant Statuary Marble: Chimney:pieces
agreably to directions. Amt. 91 Zequins   Crowns 182–
To Sundry charges making in all One hundred & Ninety
four Spanish Dols.—sent by the Brig. Calisto to Cap. St.
Clair

17. Augt 1805
Giuseppe Luciani Dr. To Cash p'd Carlo Prizzi Agree-
ably to his order 115 scudi—
On Accot. of two chimnies rec'd and forwd. to Bror.
Perkins pr Brig Calisto Cap S Clair   francesconi 115–

[Aug. 17, 1805; a second entry:]
Govt of the U. States Dr To Cash p'd to Ph. Mazzei for
his expences to Rome

	Zequines Pauls	Zequines Pauls
5. Sept	65.—	
17. July	34.7	
		99.7
16th Septr To an order on florence for 260 francesconis. destin'd for the use of the 2 Sculptors—	130.—	
Octr 25 To Cash p'd Ph. Mazzei for So much he advanc'd to Sculptors 60. francesconis	30.—	
Novr 16 To Cash p'd the two Sculptors on accot of their salaries—65 francesconis	32.10	
[Nov] 18 To Cash p'd the Sculptors to Compleat the month	2.10	
To Cash p'd board of Sculptors as per rec. of Mazzei	77.8	
To Cash p'd for Bed. linnen etc. for the passage	24.9	
To do. p'd board of Sculptors, after Mazzei rec.	5.8	
To divers small expences, transporting etc. etc. etc.	3.8	
	405–	
To my comn. [commission] for advg [advancing] 5 pct.	20.5	
	425.5	

22 Nov. 1805
Govt of the U. States. Dr. To Certain Expences for
Sculptors as appears three pages back.—[in the entry for
Aug. 17, 1805]   Zequines 425.5

[Feb. 22, 1807]
On the 22. february John Walley Langdon left this port
in the Brig Dispatch. Elijah Nickerson Master for Phila–
I propos'd to him a copartnership in trade Vizt [vide-
licet?] myself. G. L. Giera & he I. W. Langdon.—the
benefits to be divided into thirds. Giera on the arrival of
a vessel to make any advances that may be requir'd the
benefits of adva to be for him—this principle he ac-
ceeded to, so far as to say that on his arrival in America,
in case his Unkle [*sic*] did not oppose it, he would accept
it and in all events he would return here in July or August that he would write me immediately on his arrival
in America. if he accepts. . etc.

22 Oct [1807]
Giuseppe Luciani Dr to Cash p'd Gardanni as pr his
order on acct of Marbles purchas'd   Zequines 39.

Nov. [1807, the day is not given. The entry immediately
   follows the entry for Oct. 22, 1807.]
Tobias Lear (Consul at Algiers) To Cash p'd for a tomb
stone for the late Consul Dodge at Tunis.   Dollars
                                                   78
78 Dol. (p'd by Degen and Purviani Jan. 7.)[34] The above
monument is in the Store of Dunna [Duppa?] Brothers.

Nov. 25 [1807; excerpt]
Statement of account with Luciani (Carrara)   Pezzi
To Cash p'd him in Sept.   25 Zeq.   57.19.5–
To acc. of coat p'd for him—£136 Zarnona [?]   28.10.
[Later entry added:]
1808 To Cash p'd his ord. Fontana. 39 Zequins   90.8.8
Aug. 1 To do p'd bill of Excha. for marble
purchas'd on joint accot. and now in Leghorn
440 franc   510.2.2
                                                   Pezzi 687.0.11

                    Cr
By half of a quantity of marble purchas'd on   Pezzi
joint a/c & now in Leghorn. my half   382.8.3
By a marble Tomb for Tripoli   69.11.3
By Cash rec'd 6. augt by a draft on Leghorn   236.10.5
                                                   Pezzi 688.9.11

[34] Dr. James Dodge, surgeon, U.S.F. *Constitution*, was ap-
pointed chargé d'affaires at Tunis in 1805. U.S. Office of
Naval Documents and Library, *Naval Documents Related to
the United States Wars with the Barbary Powers*, 6:237.
Appleton was involved in the complicated negotiations over
the bankruptcy of the firm of Degen, Purviance and Co.,
Appleton to James Monroe, Oct. 10, 1813, State Department
Papers, NCRD 2261, NA.

[Aug. 1808; the entry is in the middle of the page dated
1st Augt 1808]
To Remember—The Monument or Tomb Stone for Mr
Dodge late Consul at Tunis, made by Order of Coll:
Lear Consul at Algiers & Paid for by M. Degen is lodg'd
in the Magazine of Degen & Guebhard in order to be
embark'd when oppo. offers—
[Later entry added:] Monument sent to Tunis & rec'd by
M. Coxe Consul. / To remember. The chimney piece
made by order of N. W. Appleton for his friend at Boston is lodg'd in the Magazine of G. L. Giera

April 19 [1809; this added entry is recorded on the page
headed by the date 20. Aug. 1808, Tobias Lear, Consul
at Algiers, Dr To Cash]
To do p'd Porters, Boatage, Custom-house fees etc etc.
on the marble Tomb Stone Sent to Tunis
£37..6:4
To p'd primage to Captain —2—

                                    59 Pavolis

[July 1809; directly below July 8]
Bust of Washington made by Cerrachi ariv'd on the 10th
of June from Wm Lee of Bordeaux—1809
p'd freight from Marseilles   £40
July 25. p'd postage of Certificates from
Wm Lee   7   £47
p'd Cathalan for expences at Marseilles   60

July 1809 [On the page facing the entry dated July 21]
Giuseppe Luciani of Carrara—Dr   Pezzi
1809 To my half of proffits on chimney   18.16.10
To my acceptance for 100 francs [francesconi]
  the 28 June payable the last of September
  ensuing   115.10.10
                                         ─────────
                                         134.15.8
      Bala. due Luciani   71.1.5
                                  Pezzi 205.17.1
Cr
By bala due him in accot. Settled 25 Nov 1807 1.9—
By cash p'd his brother for my account   4.8. 1
By accot of a chimney   200.—
                                         ─────────
                                            205.17.1

[Apr. 1812; on the page facing the entry dated 17. April
1812]
[A long "Statement of Account with Saml Emery of
Phila as sent to Thos Perkins the 15. April 1812"; the
following items relate to works of art:]

1802 August To 50 pair Alabaster Vases
cost   [Dollars] 350
  To 52 Cases Marble Containing
    29 Chimnies
    5 Slabs   Cost   650
    800 Squares for Paving

[July 1812; immediately following the entry dated July
18]
Statement of Acco. Currt [Current] with Giuseppe Luciani, Carrara   Pezzi
1809 June 28. To half proffit on chimney 18.16.8
               To cash p'd frat. [fratelli]
               Brizzi pr your order   115.18.10
1812 March 3   To Cash p'd for Massimiliano
               Ravenna   34.19.2
1808 31 July   To Cash p'd you for Marbles
               which you never deliver'd   382.8.3
               To Intst [Interest] on the
               above to 31. July 1812   91.15
                                          ─────────
                               Pezzi   643..17..14
          Cr
1808   My bala due you 31. July   1.9
1809 June My Cash p'd Gaud. Luciani   4..8.1
1812   By amt of chimney piece   200—
          By Cash p'd Vincenza Trentanove   2.6.4
                                          ─────────
                                           208.3.5—
          Balance due me this 1 July 1812 435.14.6—
                                          ─────────
                               Pezzi   643.17.11

14 [July 1815]
This day made an agreement with Saml Purviance in
legal form before Advo [Advocato] Vannucchi for the
payment of P [Pezzi?] 3636.12.5 due Tobias Lear, late
Consul of Algiers, in behalf of the U. States, which including interest to the present time, & the enregistering
of former sentence & advo [advocat's] fees, amounts now
to P 5272.9.10– [the entry continues at length describing
the rate of payment.]
N.B. The above sums, or rather what was rec'd was accounted for & paid to Colll [Collonel] Lear in money &
4 busts Deliver'd & Sold him in Balto. by N & C. Appleton.—

[July 1815; on top of the next page]
Giuseppe Luciani of Carrara—Dr.

                                          Pezzi
1815 6 June To bala. of account settled
      1st July 1812—   435.15.4
             To interest to the present time 27.12.—
          Cr.   Pezzi: 463.7.4

	Pezzi
By ½ value of 3 busts sent to Paris	69.11.3
By amt. of 6 Busts of Washington,	
Vespucius & Columbus rec'd in Leghorn	278.5.2
	347.16.5
say	347.16.5
Balance due	115.10.9

Aug. 9 [1815]
N & C Appleton Dr To 3 Cases, containing
     6 Busts— 2 of Washington
               2 of Vespucius Americanus
               2 of Crisofe Colomb—Sent by the Scho
               [Schooner] Adeline.
Captn Jenkins for Baltimore, to Sell for my Account.

[Feb. 1816, following the entry for 7 February, as part of a page titled "My accounts unsettled are as follows."]
My account unsettled with Giuseppe Luciani of Carrara. See this book July 1815. balance due me.
                            —Pezzi 115..10..9—
[Listed in the same entry, but added 20 July 1819, is the following:]
unsettled account with Thomas Perkins Jun. of Boston— for which see different charges in this book & memo book.—
[Below, in different ink, a still later addition:]
The above account has not been settled, as he became a bankrupt & Debtor to me about—1500-Dollars.[35]

9 [Dec. 1816]
Paid a Massimiliano Ravenna, of Carrara 100 francesconi on Account of Busts of Washington to be Deliver'd & Afterwards to be sent to the U.S.—on our joint account
                                £666.13.4

4 January 1817
N. W. & C. H. Appleton. of Baltimore U.S. Dr
           To amn [amount] Sales of an invoice, of umbrellaes—Sent 9. January 1816 as per 10 pages back & Sold by you as per your a/c   U.S. Dr
                                 495.65
To 6 Marble Busts of Washington,

[35] This debt involved money that the state of North Carolina paid for the statue of Washington by Canova. The state sent $4,346 in partial payment to Perkins, to be forwarded to Appleton who, in turn, would pay Canova. The debt eventually had to be paid a second time by the state. See Fehl, "Thomas Appleton of Livorno and Canova's Statue," p. 536.

Vespucius & Columbus Sold Coll Lear at
80-Doll.-each   480.–
                               975.65
     Your Comsn 2 pct   19.50
                Dollrs 956 Cts 15
Cr.
                         Dol
May 15. By Cash p'd Coll. Lear.—   189–
        By 6 Busts do Coll. Lear amt   480.–
                     Doll   669
        By Sundry Charges on the
above as per your accot 287.15 956.15 Dollrs
N.B. The foregoing Settles all accounts whatsoever with the sd N. W. & C. H. Appleton of Baltimore; and it is my intention that this shall be the last in life.
Memorandum, I gave an order in favor of Tobias Lear on N. W. & C. H. Appleton for Doll. 944.23 cts. —bala. of my accot. with him, as appears 4. Dec. 1815—but as sd. Appletons did not think proper to pay only the amt they held of mine, which was

	Doll	
	189—in Cash	
6 Busts	480	
making	669	there remains due to
sd. Lear Doll.	275.23—Doll. 944.23	

January 15. 1817 [excerpt]
Advanced to Luigi Cajano, of florence in 3 different payments—

Viz–	1st journey	35 francesconi
	2nd do	30 pls [pauls]
	3 do	15—
	p'd for corniches	1.3
	p'd him 3rd journey	6.0
	p'd in Leghorn, corniches	8..8.–
	p'd L. Cajano 7 feb	8
	p'd ditto 8 feb	6
	p'd Legnioulo	2
	p'd Cajano 11 feb.	12
	p'd do for a Carraci[36]	6–1–
	p'd do for cornici & c.	8–
	p'd do for repg [repairing]	
	corniches	7–
	p'd do for cornishes	5.5
	p'd for Case Cord etc. portore	
	[porterage]	6–
	p'd Cajano for himself	12
	p'd Gums, acqua raggia	
	[turpentine] &c	2.6–
	francesconi	165

[36] Uncertain reading. A painting, or its copy, attributed to Annibale Carracci or his school may be meant.

Sums paid for pictures Sent Thos Perkins as on the opposite Side [i.e. the entry following], & all the attendant expences until on board. N.B. —124 fransesconi was paid him which is to be deducted from his 1/3 of nt proffits

15. february 1817.
Thomas Perkins. Bror-in-law of Boston— Dr
To 1—Marble Chimney-piece Sent per Ship Heroine. Captn Smith in 4 Cases marked T+P— no. 1. 2. 3. 4. to be sold for my a/c Cost   Dollars
                                                               160–0
to 1 Case containing pictures No 5. to be sold for my a/c– marked T+P one third of Nt proceeds, excepting Nos. 6. 29. 30–37. which appertain to me intirely, the rest, 2/3 & for my benefit, & one third for the benefit of Luigi Cajano of florence, after deducting the Sums paid him & which appears on the last page.—
No 1. By Albano— Subject the three Marys at the tomb. Holy family.
2. —Pontormo—1st Scholar of Andrea del Sarto—do
3. Guercino. Rebecca at the fountain
4. a Scholar of Bartolomeo. Master of Raphael— Holy family
5. Salvator Rosa.–a Marine Subject—great merit
6. John Bolanger,[37] Scholar of Guido Rene—birth of Christ
7. a Scholar of Raphael.—Holy family—
8. Guido Rene—Christ on the cross—great merit
9. Parmegianino—1st Scholar of Corregio—Virgin, Child, Catha. [St. Catharine] & Angel
10. Fiamingo[38]—a beautiful Vase of flowers.
11.   do ———— do
12. Cigoli, florentine professor—St Appoline, protectress of teeth.
13. Fiamingo.—Flowers & Fruit
14.   do ———— do
15. Van dyke.—a female portrait great merit
16. Teniers, the elder. a Chymist at work in his laboratory great merit
17. Guelardo delle Notti[39]—an old woman Killing fleas by night great merit

18. Veyx.[40] flemish a celebrated master. dead birds & various fruits. merit
19. Bronzino. Scholar of Michael Angelo—the Annunziation
20. a scholar of Claude Lorraine—paysage—landskip.
21. Carlo Dolci's daughter[41]—Goddess Flora
22.   idem ———   idem
23. Fiamingo— a Saint distributing to the poor
24. Andrea Del Sarto—a Bust of St Joseph
25. Domenichino. a do. of St Jerome
26. a female portrait. by Vandyke
27. Death of St Catha Guido Reni
28. Communion of St Peter & St Marguarite   Do.
29. fine Magdalen La Syranis[42] Scholar of Do
30. Sa Veronica Do
31. Landskip. Salvator. Rosa
32.   Do   Do
33. Chaste Joseph. Martinelli[43]
34. Decapitation of So John by Luini
35. a [illegible] Pietro Perugino, it was an admirable painting but has a little Suffer'd.
36. Christ, give unto Cesar &c. by Tintoretto—
37. a beautiful small Virgin & Child by Carlo Maratti, the head is equal to Raphael—

March 9th [1817]
Luigi Cajani Dr To Cash on accot of 8 paintings left with me, for the purpose of forming a collection for a 2nd pacotilla [parcel of goods] in America.—ten Zechines & a half.

20. May 1817.—
Shipp'd this day onboard the Ship Ann, Capn Church. bound to Buenos Ayres, & to the address of M. Le Chev. Laurinsany, owner on board the Same, 20. pictures representing batels, Sea pieces &c. which I have requested him to Sell for my account & invest in *mercha.* of that *country* to bring me on his return.
[added later] his receipt is in file of papers. See Letter book of this Date. Case mark'd B & T+A No. 1—

---

[37] Jean Boulanger (1566–1660), court painter in Modena. The identification of the "old masters" in this and another shipment of Appleton's is restricted to the clarification of difficult entries. For additional details, cf. Thieme-Becker, *Allgemeines Lexikon.*
[38] Perhaps Michele Desubleo, called Il Fiammingo (d. 1676).
[39] Gerrit van Honthorst, called Gherardo della Notte (1590–1656).

[40] Probably Jan Weenix (1640–1719) or his father, Jan Baptist Weenix.
[41] Agnese (or Maria) Dolci (d. 1670).
[42] Elisabetta Sirani, daughter of Giovanni Andrea Sirani (1610–1670). Her less well-known sister, Anna Maria, also painted in the manner of Guido Reni.
[43] Giovanni Martinelli (ca. 1610–1659), Florentine painter.

31. May [1817]

This Day Shipp'd on board the Ship Genl Smith, Capn Thomas Beavon for Baltimore and consign'd to Richd Smith esq., passenger on board and of Phila to be by him Sold for my account & the nt proceeds thereof to be remitted to Thomas Perkins esq. Boston.—

& pack'd in a large Case, mark'd No 1. T+A—and are as follows—

No 1– A large picture representing living and dead animals by Impali[44] scholar of Andrea del Sarto—

2. A large painting representing a naked Venus by Padovanino first Scholar of Titian

3 The Chaste Susannah (3 pictures in the painting)[45] Size of life, and by Paul Veronese

4 A holy family by francesco Salviati, Scholar of Andrea del Sarto—

5 A Sybil copied from the famous Sybil of Guercino

6 an annunziation to the Shepherds, by Basano—

7 Sa Catharine by George Vasari Scholar of Michael Angelo—

8 a battle by Bourgogni[46]

9 A Shepherd & animals by Monsr. Rosa—

10 Judith—by Carravaggio—

11 A holy family by a Scholar of Parmigianino—

12 a Magdalen by Cigola,[47] chief of a florentine School

13 portrait of the celebrated painter Moroni. copied from the original

14 a landscape by Torrigiani[48] Scholar of Salvator Rosa

15 fruits—Fiamingo

16 a holy family by Pontormo 1st Scholar of Andrea del Sarto

17 fruits and instruments of musick—Fiamingo

18 a landscape by Monsr Rosa

19 2 Saints adoring the virgin Mary—School of Bologna

20 Virgin & child by a Scholar of Andrea del Sarto—

21 a beautiful figure of the virgin in prayer—by Carlo Dolci

22 a Magdalen.—by the Same.

23 a holy family of the School of Andrea del Sarto

24 a portrait of Raphel copied from the original painting

25 portrait of a child by the celebrated Paul Veronese—

26 Sa Catharine by Tintoretto

27 a Small holy family by Sghedoni,[49] Scholar of Corregio

28 a Sepulchral painting of the florentine School—

29 St Jerome of the Bolognese School

30 An angel by Parmigianino. a fine Venetian painter

31 & 32 2 Muses. Terpsichore & Clio. both of the florentine School.

33 & 34 in one frame No 33 is Arethusa Companion of Diana pursued by a river-God; is rescued by the Goddess & transform'd into a fountain. No 34 is a triton seizing on a bathing Vestal of Bacchus, both of the florentine School—

35 A femal Saint by Onorio Marinaro.[50] florentine School—

36 a Ditto.   —by Ditto.—

N.B.—No 1. I was compell'd to take from the Case, as it was too large for the hatches of the Ship—the rest were sent. for charges on ditto See memorandum book. The Sum pd. Luigi Cajano for the above & for those sent as appears four pages back. is in all 225 francesconi which he has acknowledg'd, as per his rect. [receipt] in file of papers to be in full for the value of the whole: he is, however to receive one third of the Nt proceeds in the U.S. deducting therefrom the sd. 225 frani. & his proportion of the expences p'd by me in Leghorn as appears 4 pages back; & in Memo book—

The numbers— 1. 5. 9. 33. 34. belong'd to me personally & on which Luigi Cajano is not to partake the benefits.—

2 June 1817

An Invo for the foregoing pictures being necessary in order to pay the duties in America, I made the following [illegible] to Rd. Smith in whose charge they are

Invo of 35 paintings shipped onboard the Ship Genl Smith Thomas Beavon master bound for Balto. & consign'd to Richd Smith seq. of Phila passenger onboard Sd. Ship & for my a/c.

No. 1 T+A.

		Dolls
3 large paintings @ 30 Dolls each		90–
6 smaller do	—18	108
15 less do	— 5·	75
11 do do	— 3	33
		306

Charges	
To Consl 2 p Ct	6.22
To various charges here	42
Doll.	354.22

---

[44] Perhaps Jacopo Chimenti, called Jacopo da Empoli (1554–1640). He painted the ceiling of the duomo in Livorno.

[45] A painting with three figures—Susanna and the two elders.

[46] Jacques Courtois, called Il Borgognone (1621–75).

[47] Lodovico Cigoli (1559–1613).

[48] Probably Francesco Torriani (1612–81).

[49] Bartolomeo Schidone (ca. 1570–1615).

[50] Onorio Marinari (1627–1715).

25 [July 1817]

Cr. His Excellency Gov Miller of No. Carolina by my drafts of this day on Daniel Cromelin & sons Amsterdam

for 2000 guilders Pezzi

$$\left.\begin{array}{r}1900 \\ 1800 \\ 1700 \\ 1600\end{array}\right\} \quad 3750$$

[This description of exchange transactions continues: "equal to 6653; £6.10.8 Spanish Dollars" and ends: "which at the then exchanges were equal to 6654 Spanish dollars."]

The above is on a/c of Statue to be sculptur'd by Canova of Roma. [The reference is to the statue of Washington]

Sept. 9 [1817]

Thos. Perkins of Boston Dr To 2 Busts of Washington Sent by Bulah Capn Morgan for Boston

No. 1—larger than life. plain. Cost—	60
No 2. Do. Heroic garb.	90
	150
To an ord. on Astolf of Phila.	8.
	158—

[No date, immediately following entry for Sept. 9, 1817.] Thos Perkins Jun. of Boston. Dr to 8 Cases of Alabaster work cosign'd to him for my a/c & shipp'd onboard Brig Gossypeim [?] for Boston amounting as per Invo. & as per bill of Chiani to 408 francesconi.—which when Sold, he is intitled to one third the Nt. proffits for his trouble in Sale, the remr: is to be remitted me in white India Sugar or any other article he may judge from my price currt. will be more beneficial to me.

[added later:] N.B. produc'd me net for my part—695—Dollrs.

18 [Oct. 1817]

Shipp'd onboard this day of the Brig Columbia Capt Lowe for Balto 5 Cases of Alabastre Vases &c. & consign'd to John Donaghey of Norfolk Mercht. & passenger onboard, to be Sold for my account, & the Nt proceeds to be invested in Mercha. if he should determine to return here in the Spring, or otherwise to Send a bill on London for the Nt. Sales.

marked J + D Doll. cts
      A

No 13. 14. 15. 16. 17. amounting to 264. 20 for particulars of Articles see Chiani's bill of this date amg [amounting] 125 Zechi & ½—letter book—

27 [Nov. 1817]

Paid this day Giaco. fr. [Giacomo Francesco?] Chiani balance due him for Alabaster works bought & shipp'd for U.S. & in full of all accounts to this day as per rect. Book & on Accounts 329½ Zechini Zechini 329½

Dec 13 [1817]

Thomas Perkins (Bror. in law) of Boston Dr To a marble hearth rec'd from Luciani of Carrara, & shipp'd on board Ship Hamilton Captn Greenough for Portsmouth to the care of N. A. & I. Haven merchants there.

13. Decem. 1817

[The following entries occur in an account mostly concerned with stocks and notes. "Thos Perkins Esq. of Boston (bro. in law) Dr"]

	Dollars
1817 July To amt of a marble chimney	240—
1817 18 Jan By expences on chimney & pictures per Ship Heroine frt. [freight] Duties etc.	112.15

26 December 1817 [excerpt]

Invoice of nine Cases of Alabaster works Shipp'd on board the Brig Wilmot John Devereux master for Philadelphia & there consigned to David Ware mercht for Sale on my account viz.—

[inserted later] Sail'd 6th January 1818

D.W.	Case no. 1	Dolls
no. 1 @ 9	an elegant plateau consistg. of 53 pieces	54
	Case no. 2	
	6 pair of large vases @ 12 Doll	72
	Case no. 3	
	14 pair of oval vases small	20—
	Case no. 4	Doll
	6 pair of vases work'd with flowers @ 3	18
		164
		Doll.
	Amt. brot. forward	164
	Case no. 5	Doll
	2 pair of Globes for Lamps. @ 10	20
		Doll
	6 pair of small vases no. 7—@ 3	18
	2 pair of do. no. 8—@ 3.50	7
	Case no 6	
	4 pair of vases no. 8 @ 3.50	14
	6 pair of Do. no 9. @ 3.75	22.50
	1 pair large open vases no. 10	15.
	1 pair Do. Do. no. 11	17—
	Case no 7	
	1 pair of vases no 12	8
	1 Do. Do. 13.	10
	1 Do. Do. 14	9
	Dol	
	2 Do. Do. 15. 5	10
	1 Large Lamp for Entry No. 16—	5
	1 Pair of [ditto] No. 18.	4

46

Case No. 8

1 pr of openwork'd vases no. 17.   5
1 pr with flower covers. no. 19   — 4
2 Small clock cases—No. 20   — 2
8 pr of candlesticks—No. 21   — 8   } 46
1 pr. Large vases—no. 23.   —   16
1   Do. Do. no. 24.   —   8
2 writing Stands   no. 26. 27—   3

Case no. 9

2 Small. Statues. Herculaneum
Dancers by Canova[51] . . . .   24—
4 pr. Candlesticks—no 21   4
                                                  _____
                        Dollars   415.50

N.B. The above is the real invoice & cost by adding about 30 Dollrs for charges & Difference of money.—I sent a 2nd. invce that he might show to buyers amg. to Doll 600.— The Nt proceeds to be remitted to Thos. Perkins junr. of Boston

10. January 1818

Governor Miller, of North Carolina—Dr. To Cash p'd this Day the order of Anto. Canova of Rome for the first third of the Statue of Washington to wit in gold—2448.9.6—Pezzi. which amounts to 2260 francesconi—or —2369—Spanish Dollars.

N.B. this bill of Excha. is in red pocketbook This Sum was equal to 1000 golden Roman Zechines.

26 [Jan. 1818]

Thomas Perkins, junr. (my nephew) of Boston—Dr. to 8 marble chimney pieces, Shipped on board the Brig Adamant Captn. Covil for Boston, to be sold for my account—the Ntt Amount of which he is to remit me, except one third of the proffits, which I have agreed with him he shall be intitled to for his trouble in selling, remitting &c. &c. to wit—2 white elegant Statuary marble chimnies in 7 Cases mark'd No. 1 @ 7 T—P—A—@ 115 Doll.   Dollars 230
6 Common Marble do 4. white & 2 blue in 13 Cases
    mark'd T-P. as each 2 Cases contains a chimney
    they are number'd from No. 1 @ 6—No. 7
    Contains all the hearths tho' of different forms
    & ornaments, they cost all together.—   140

[51] Probably the "dancer with the finger at her chin" and the "dancer with cymbals." There is also a third dancer by Canova "with her hands on her hips." The models Canova wished to emulate with these works are the famous dancers from Herculaneum, in the Museo Nazionale, Naples. The works Appleton lists are undoubtedly small-scale copies. The price is far too low for a replica from Canova's studio. Malamani, *Canova*, pp. 162–63, 176–77.

In my letter to T. P. junr I say the chimneys *really* cost me
    The 2 fine ones—230
        ordinary ones   170   400—Doll.
N.B. The invo. sent which is for the Custom house is made out
    2 chimnies @ 100 — 200
    6   Do.   @ 20 — 120
                        _____
            Dollrs   320

18 March 1818

Gov. Miller of north Carolina Dr To Cash p'd Raimondo Trentanove on a/c of piedestal of Statue of Washington—200 franci.—equal to Spanish Dollars—210—See red pocketbook for bill
This day shipp'd on board Ship Pallas I. T. Heartte master for Baltimore ten Cases of alabasters on my account & consign'd to John Donaghey of Norfolk for Sale to the Care of John Myers & Co. of Balto. to be by them forwd. to Sd. Donaghey

J.D   Dollrs
1 @ 10
No. 1   1 Statue of Hebe[52] on a piedestal   14.60
 "   2   1   do. Venus of Medicis large size   14.60
 "   3   9   do. representing Hercules, Apollo,
             Antinous, Ceres, Venus of belles
             feces;[53] Venus by Canova of Rome,
             Diana & the two female dancers by   94.50
             Do. & copies from those found in
             Herculaneum[54] @ 10.50 each
 "   4   1 large & elegant Statue of Mercury
             with the foot on a Zephyr, copied
             from that in the gallery[55]   25.20
 "   5   4 elegant vases   33.60
 "   6   2 large Bases grecian meanders   18.90
 "   7   2 large & highly wrought columns
             for Lamps[56]   11.55

[52] Canova made four statues of Hebe (Fig. 7). Malamani, *Canova*, pp. 74–77. Again we must have to do with "freelance" replicas, as suggested in the account book entry for Dec. 26, 1817.

[53] Venus des belles fesses, the *Venus Kalipygo*s ("with the beautiful buttocks") in the Museo Nazionale, Naples.

[54] For Canova's *Venus* (Fig. 8), see Malamani, *Canova*, pp. 166–67. See also Hugh Honour, "Canova's Statues of Venus," *Burlington Magazine* 114, no. 835 (Oct. 1972): 658–70. "Diana and the two female dancers" must be Canova's *Three Dancers*. See note 51 *supra*.

[55] Giovanni da Bologna's *Mercury*, now in the Bargello in Florence.

[56] Read: ". . . columns for Lamps." Items 7 and 8 belong together.

"	8	2 ditto plain	9.50
"	9	6 clock cases	7.35
"	10	2 Vases of Egyptian drawings[57]	6.30
"	11	2 Do. large & plain for lights and flowers	6.30
"	12	4 Do. for Lamps	15.75
"	13	15 pair of candlesticks	11.55
"	14	2 large & elegant vases with fruits	14.70
"	15	2 oval vases with festoons of pearls & fruits	8.40
"	16	2 large do. Damask'd	15.75
"	17	2 Smaller do with heads of Bacchus	8.40
"	18	2 Do with greek ornaments	6.30
"	19	2 Do — Chinese — Do	6.30
"	20	2 beautiful agath Globes	10.50
"	21	2 vases for flowers	6.30
"	22	3 pair vases Rafael figures	15.75
"	23	3 pair do without engravings	12.60
"	24	1 very large ornamented Lamp	24.15
"	25	100 fruits & Eggs	3.15
		Dollars	402.—

[later entry:] Sailed 29 March

26 March 1818
Thomas Perkins junr (my nephew) of Boston. Dr. two marble chimney pieces shipp'd onboard the Scho. Pinguin Capt. Bartlet Holmes to be sold for my Account.

	Dollars
Cost—115 Dollars each say	230 —

marked T. P. in 6 cases   No 1 @ 6
[added later:] Sailed 29 March by the way of Palermo

26th June 1818
David Ware, of Philadelphia Dr. To the following merchandize Sent by the Brig John Burguin Captn. Perry to be Sold for my account and the nt. proceeds remitted to me.—Viz.—

	Doll—
D. W. No 1. 2. 3.—three cases contg a fine marble Statuary chimney piece	80.—
No. 4. 5. 6. 7. 8. 9. Six cases contg 3 chimney pieces & cost together	80.—
No. 10. 11. 12 three cases contg one chimney piece similar to No 1. 2. 3.	80.—
No. 13 @ 14 Two Cases contg a chimney piece from Massmo—Ravenna.	32—
No. 15 @ 21 Seven Cases contg to wit—	
No 15 Bust of Washington larger than life[58]	56
16 Do Do	56
17 contains Busts of Vespucius & Columbus @ 36	72

18	Bust of Washington larger than life	56
19	Bust of Do Colossal & plain	52
20	Bust of Do Colossal with heroic garb	92
21.	Bust of Do larger than life	56.

No. 22. a Case contg 97 Straw hats & as many extra crowns from No 34 @ 47 as per accon. of G. Semiani   639
D. W
No. 1 @ 12   Twelve Cases of Alabaster works amg as per Invoice of Chiani & as by Detail'd Invo. Sent to D. Ware   462

                                    Dollars   1813.

N.B. To the above Invoice ought to be added 5 pct. as I have plac'd Dollars for what cost me [amount omitted] Francesconis. & about 25 Dollars in divers expences on the Same, making in all together.—about 117 Dollars.— The adventure therefore costs me really here, about 1930 dollars.— See letter-book of this date, in which I instruct David Ware of Philadelphia to Sell the Same, & remit the Net proceeds for me to Saml. Williams mercht. London.—

[July 9, 1818; excerpt]
David Ware, of Philadelphia. Dr. To 12 Cases of Alabaster works, as p Invo. of Chiani, Shipp'd on board Schooner Fame, Captn Robbins for Phila. to be by sd. Ware Sent to New York for Sale, or to be Sold in Phila. for my account, as he shall judge expediant

	Dollars
D+W. No 1 @ 12 Twelve Cases amt to	474

The proceeds to be remitted to Saml Williams No 13 Finsbury Square London for my a/c. May be added about 35 Dollars expences here including difference of money between francesconi & Dollars.
[added later:] Sailed 14 July

13th July 1818
Gov. Miller of No Carolina—Dr To Cash p'd Raimondo Trentanove on a/c of Piedestal of Washington.—204 Francesconi— . . . 214 Spanish Dollrs—75 cts.
[added later:] Rect in file papers relating to Statue Cr Thomas Perkins jun. (of Boston) by his letter Cr on Saml Williams of London for £316.12s Stg [Pound 316.12 Shilling Sterling] which has produc'd here 1309 francesconi & 7 pauls.—which it appears by letter from his father was for Sale of Alabaster & bill on Jefferson equal to Doll. 1421 . . 32
[excerpt from another entry, same day:]
Thomas Perkins, Bro. in law, Boston. Dr. To cash p'd you by Graham of n York –$17.— To nt proceeds paintings sent to n York 181. .84

---

[57] Vases decorated with designs in the Egyptian manner.
[58] See note 23.

14 [July 1818]

Raimondo Trentanova, (Sculptor Roma) Dr To Cash p'd his ordr. in favr. of Scultheist & endorsed to P. & A. fellichj [?] for 500 francesconi on a/c of Piedestal of Washington   Francesconi 500–
accepted 14 [July] payable in 10 days.

1st October 1818

Thomas Perkins jun. (nephew Boston) Dr. To the following articles Shipp'd on board the Brig Amsterdam Packet, George Soule Master bound to Baltimore & directed there to the Care of James Sterret Merchant, to be by him Shipp'd to Sd Perkins of Boston & be by him Sold for my account; one third the net *proffits* thereof appertaining to him for his trouble in Selling &c. as per agreement made between us.–to wit.–

T+P. 9 Cases of alabaster works from
No. 1 @ 9   Dollars

No			
1	2 Large Vases or one pair		23 00
2	2 Ditto Do		16 —
3	2 Do.		9
4	2 Do.		6
5	2 Do. with flowers		6
6	2 Do. with grape Vines		6
7	2 Do. Do		7
8	2 Do. Smaller		2
9	2 Do. with flowers		9
10	2 Do. Do		6
11	2 Do.		6
12	2 Large Do.		12
13	2 Smaller		3
14	1 Lamp for a table		3
15	2 Vases with grape vines		6
16	2 Do. with vines		8
17	2 Do. Do		8
18	2 Do. Smaller		6
19	2 Do. large with flowers		23
20	2 Do. large Do		17
21	2 Do. large Do		17
22	2 Do. Do with Basso Relievo		13
23	2 Do. with engravings		6
24	2 Large Columns for Lamps with incisions		21
25	2 Large Globus for Do with Do		13
26	2 Do. Do with cover, of flowers		12
27	2 Grand Vases with leaves		16
28	2 Do. smaller with Do		5
29	2 Do. Do		5
30	1 Large Lamp for an entry with leaves		9
	carrd forward		299 Dollars
	Amount brought forward		299 Doll
No 31	2 Small vases plain		3
32	2 Columns for lamps plain		5

33	2 oval vases with fruit		10
34	6 pair of vases with flowd tops @ 3		18
35	6 pair do Small 3		18
36	2 Globes with pearl'd edges		5
37	2 Small vases with leaves		4
38	2 Ditto with urnes		3
39	6 writing Stands		7
40	6 beautiful figures female @ 8		48
41	2 Venus of Medicis		10
	Dollars		430

The above were the prices in francesconis there being a difference of 5 pCt.   21.50
                                                    Dollars   451.50
To which I added 10 pCt for different Charges   43
                                                    Dollars   494.50
To one chimney piece representing a Bacchante with attributes   130
                                                    Dollars   624.50.

27 [Jan. 1819; excerpt]

Thomas Perkins Jun: (nephew) Dr. of Boston To 3 chimney pieces (marble) to be sold for my a/c. Shipp'd onboard Brig. New. Packet. Joseph Thacher, master & bound for Boston.–Viz.

T. P. No. 1 @ 8.   2 chimneys. representing emblems
                      of Bacchus @ Doll. 150.–   300
     No. 9 & 11   1 Do. with ornaments of flowers   80
                                                      380

N.B. The above were shipp'd by Edd Swords to avoid the inconvenience of my appearing to take the oath to myself. No. 11 contains pieces belonging to No 5. 6. 7. 8. 9. 10.–

february 20 1819.

Ths Perkins Jun. of Boston (my nephew) Dr To a Draft on John Hollins of Balto. for so much advd. to 2 Architects [to work on the University of Virginia buildings] for /a/c Thos Jefferson

                                                   Doll   cts
                                                   444.   41
also Dr. To an Order on Colll [Collonel] Lane Com. of publick buildings at Washington for 4 marble tables for Madme. Monroe as per letter & order of Wm. Lee.[59] See file of letters.   75– Dollars   75.–

30 May 1819

Statement of Account with Raimondo Trentanove. Rome
1818   francesconis
    18 March To Cash   200

[59] William Lee was U.S. Consul at Bordeaux.

13 July	To Dr.	204	first 1/3
14	To Dr. p'd ord. to Scultheis	500	
		904	francs
			francesconis

18 Augt Paid Serrafino Bargigli —4 9
for Do for journey 5
To p'd 12 pauls pr week to
Madme Bargigli 15 weeks 18
30 Nov. To p'd Mad. Bargigli. pr
order 7–2

1819

3 Feb	To p'd Do	6.1½
8 March	To p'd ordr to Scultheis	150
	To p'd Mad. Bargigli	6.1½
8 April	To p'd ordr to Scultheis	250.–
11 "	To p'd Mad. Bargigli	6.1½
28 —	To p'd — Do	5.1
28 May	To p'd — Do	6.1½

francci 463.9
bala. due for 2nd portion for statue 440.1
francesconis 904

[later entry:] Sent 28 May bala paid. For Settlement & payment of the 3rd & last portion, vide account book 23 february 1820 & his triplicate rects in file of papers relating to Statue of Washington—

June 4 [1819]

David Ware, of Philadelphia. Dr To. Cases, containing 2 Marble Chimneypieces. Shipp'd by the Schooner Nymph, Capt. Kennedy for Philadelphia, to be sold for my account, & the proceeds remitted to Saml Williams of London, marked D. W. No 1 @ 8 inclusive.

francesconis

No 1. 2. 3. 4.—a chimney peice with
emblems of Baccants. Cost 150.–
5. 6. 7. a ditto.—highly
ornamented with flowers 80.–
230 francesconis

No. 8 2 hearths for the above.—
Sailed 16 June

20. August 1819.

Henry F. Green & Co—of New York Dr To 9 Cases of Marble works contg. 2 Chimney-pieces representing the Goddess Ceres & her Attributes.

Dollars

No 1 @ 9. Cost here 150 Dollars each 300.–
Shipp'd on board Brig Orleans Captn. Ths. E. Brown & Consd. to Sd H. F. Green & Co to be sold for my accot. & the proceeds to be remitted in good bills to Sam. Williams, London.

23d february 1820

Governor Miller of North-Carolina—Dr To Cash paid Raimondo Trentanove. Sculptor of Rome. for the com-
pleat pedestal, together with the ornaments & bassi-rilievis for the Statue of Washington by Canova of Rome, Sculptur'd by Order of the Sd. Governor Miller, to wit, *One thousand Seven Hundred Roman Zechines* as appears by the triplicate receipts of Sd. Trentanove in file of papers relative to Sd. Statue & in date of 16 february——*1700 Roman Zechines in gold—Dollrs 4044.*—[60]

25 January 1821

Cr Government of North Carolina, on accot of Statue of Washington, for 4,346 Spanish Dollars, rec'd of Robrt & Will Pealsford of London by a draft in Paris (Sold to Viollier & Co) in franci—23633. Dollars are at £6.10—£28.441.7.4. franci 4263 = £2.13.4-

March 13 [1821]

Anto Canova, Sculptor. Rome Dr To Cash p'd his order on me for 3000 francesconis, on accot of Statue of Washington for the State of North Carolina—francesconis 3000.— See order in file of papers for Statue.—

10th April 1821

Government of North-Carolina, on accot of Statue of Washington—Dr. To Cash p'd Raimo. Trentanove for expenses for case, cloth, straw, packing &c. of piedestal 43 Roman scudi—say— Roman Scudi 43

To Cash p'd Anto Canova for government duties on exportation, for case, cloth, packing, Porterage &c. &c.—of statue say 80.90
To Cash p'd M. Des Plas, American Vice Consul for express Transp. of Statue &c. from Rome to Civita Vecchia .. 17½ say 17.50
Scudi 141.40

4 May [1821]

Anto Canova, Sculptor of Rome. Dr To 2 Drafts on Rome for balance of Statue, & expences of Case, Duties &c. &c.

Scudi—850—of Jullien & La Coutura— 2nd p'd 15 June } Ceded to me
Do —580.33 of Asdenti e Caprano @ 30 days date } by Walser.
Scudi 1430.33 @ soldi 127 pr pezzo 1504..16. Gold
Aggio 7 pt [percent?] 105.6.8
1610.2.8 Silver

Francesconis 1388—£4.18.8
The above remited by this days' post to Canova, as p'r Letter—
[added later] 7th May paid Walser for the above Bills as pr rects in file. See Canova's receipt in full in file. —2

[60] The words italicized here are written in a different ink and were obviously added later. For the text of Trentanove's receipt see Fehl, "Thomas Appleton of Livorno and Canova's Statue," p. 535.

receipts Sent to Govt.— The Govt of State of No Carolina to Thomas Appleton Consul Leghorn Dr 1821.

To cash p'd Anto Canova of Rome for a Colossal Statue of Washington, in marble, as pr. order of Govr Miller of Sd. State in the year 1816.—3000 Roman Golden Zechines as pr. inclos'd receipt. which at the excha on Leghorn in Silver are   Spanish Dollars   7.107.–

To Cash p'd Raimondo Trentanove of Rome, first Scholar of Canova, for the Piedestal of Sd Statue, with the bassi rilievi on the four Sides & sculptur'd under the Direction of Canova, 1700–Roman golden Zechines, as pr inclos'd rect which at the excha on Leghorn are equal in Silver to Dollars   4044.–

	Spanish Dollars	11.151.–
amount brought from last page		11.151

1821	*Charges*	Dollars
To Cash p'd Anto Canova for Govt Duties on exportation of Statue, Case, Cloth, Cords, packg & porterage to Tyber		85.5
To Cash p'd Raimondo Trentanove for Case, Cloth, packing & porterage of the Piedestal to the Tyber		45.5
To p'd transporting both to Civita Vecchia		18.40
To p'd transporting from Carrara, Colossal Bust by Cerracchi, to Serve as a model for the Statue		5.–
To p'd postage during four years to & from Roma relating to Statue; to Amsterdam, London &c on remittances amounting to 127 Letters receiv'd, or frank'd in reply, on the Subject of the Statue		60.–
To expenses to engage the Statue & emblems		122.–
		336.50

Spanish Dollars   11.487.50

Credit

1817

By cash receiv'd for my Drafts on Daniel Cromelin & Sons of Amsterdam, for 17.304.3 florins, being the net amount. they informed me was at my Disposal, for acct of State of No Carolina, & which produced here at the then exchange Spanish Dollars   6654.—

1821

By cash receiv'd of R & W. Pulsford of London, as pr. this letter, authorising me to draw on them for 4346. Dollrs   4346

	Dollars	11000
paid—Bala. due to Thos. Appleton		487.50
		11.487.50

Leghorn 18. April 1821	above account sent to
E. E. Th. A	Govt by duplicates. with Duplicate vouchers of Canova, and Trentanove.[61]

[61] For the cover letter and the bill as received at Raleigh, see Connor, *Canova's Statue of Washington*, pp. 47–52.

original—Sent by Augusta Captn Lee for Salem. 22 June & prints of Statue.

Duplicate—. by Ranger Capt. Hodge. Salem 10. July.—

[Later entry:] The above bala of 487.50 was remitted to I. I. Astor & Son by them remd in a bill to S. Williams & by him to me on Cook & Co 8 December 1821.

April 1823

Thomas Jefferson, of Virginia. U. S. A. Dr.	Dollars
To 18 Corinthian & Ionic Capitals	1850.
To Cases for the above	50
To Custom. house Duties, expenses on Shipping and postage	13
	1913
To bala. Due & held to your order	189.75
Dollars	2102.75

Credit

By cash rec'd in two remittances	2102.75

N.B. the above settles all accounts to the present 2. April.

1 May [1823]

Raimondo Trentanove, Sculptor Roma in accon. with T. A.—Dr

1822

5 July To Amt bala Due to me as Settled this Day & by your note	Franci 324..6.–		
7 Augt To p'd your order to Mad: Bargigli	3 Scudi..		2.8.1½
20 " To p'd " " Do	3	"	2.8.1½
2 Octr To p'd to the wife of Bargigli	8..		7.6.–
10 Novr To p'd to Mad. Bargigli	3	"	2.8.1½
1823			
15 Feb. To p'd to Do	3	"	2.8.1½
6 Apl To p'd to Do	3	"	2.8.1½
18 " To p'd to Serafino Bargigli	2	"	1.9–
		francesconis	348.7.1½

Balance due Trentanove this 1. May 1823	34.8.1½
francesconis	383.6.–

Credit

1822

8 July By Cash rec'd from Genl Harper of U. S. A...[62]	98.6.–
1823	
May By amt of 2 Sette of mosaics for Daughter of Prest. Monroe Scudi 300	285.–.–
francesconis	383.6.–

[62] See note 26.

May 1823 [excerpt]
Statement of Account with Thos Perkins junr: as recd from his father T. P. sen.

1818		1818		
Oct 26		Oct 26		
To amn Sales $				Dollars–
adamant [?]	271.67	By postages		2.44
To Do by				
Pinguin	94.88	By bala due me		1193.64
To Do for				
Alabaster sold				
by Mr. Ware,				
Phila	697.53			
To Amn ord				
[ordered] on				
J. Hurd	132.–			
Dollars	11 96.8–			

1818		1819		
To bala bro.		Apl By p'd duties		
down	1193.64	on 3		
To cash rec'd		chimnies...		63.96
of Blake &		By Do pd		
Cunningham,		Sterrit. Balto		
auctioneers	80.–.–	freight &		
To proceeds 9		charges in		
cases Alabaster		alabaster &		
by Amsm Packet		marble by		
by Balto by		Amsterdam		
accn Sales Blake		Packet		169.45
& Cunning.	529.13	By postages		3.75
Dollars	1802.77	Dollars		237.16
		1820		
		feb. 28–		
		Bala due me		1565.61
		Dollars		1802.77

Account in red pocket book.

16 July [1824]
[excerpt from an entry headed "Thomas Perkins, of Boston, bror in law in accot Current. Dr"]

		Dollars
1824, May 3rd	To a marble bust of	
	Washington	100.–

20. March 1825
[excerpt from an entry headed as above]
23 Nov [1824]   To a marble Slab   /$/ 10.–

4. May 1825
Thomas Jefferson esq. of Monticello   To Thomas Appleton of Leghorn—Dr T+J No 1 @ 19   To 19 Cases contg 1400 marble squares for paving @

Doll.		Dollars
22½ the hundd		315.–
No 20 @ 31	To 12 Cases contg ten whole	
	& two half marble bases for columns	866
	[later corrected to 865]	
	Dollars	1181

Charges

To 31 Cases @ £7—each	£217.	
To Custom-house Duties		
at £2—each	62–	
To boatage and porterage		
to Ship	52	
	£331 @ £6 1/3 each are	52.25
	Dollars	1233.55

Shipp'd on board Ship Caroline, Capt. Farmer & to the Care of Jona Thompson, Collector of New York

Dr. Thomas Jefferson, in account current with Thomas Appleton   Cr

1825		1823	
	Dollars		Dollars
To am. of above		April By bala Due	
account of sculp-		you, as pr accot	
tur'd marble		render'd of this	
works	1233.25	Date	189.75
To bala Due you,		1824	
carried to the Cr		Jany By 3 Setts of	
of the Capitals:	2875.50	Excha from	
Dollars	4108.75	Saml Williams	
		of London,	
		which after	
		Deducting var-	
		ious to Do &	
		postages pd by	
		me, & Discount	
		here as They	
		were at 3 Mos	
		noted	3919.–
		Dollars	4108.75

Thomas Jefferson's private Account with Thomas Appleton.   Dr
1825

May	To 8 Chimney-mantles of various Colours	Dollars
	& qualities of marble, contain'd in 6	
	Cans from No 32 @ 37. inclusive	
	mark'd T. J./M Cost	180
	Charges	
	To 6 Cases for the above	
	@ £7 each £42.–	
	To Custom house Duties	
	@ £2 " 12.–	

To porterage & boatage
onboard   12.–

£66. @ £6 1/3 each are 10.50

Dollars 190.50

Credit

1823

26 Aug   By bala. due you on bill sent for
M. Pini   Dollars—16.–

1824

10 Dec   By bala. due you, on bills sent
for Do   42

58

Bala. Due me   132.50

190.50

14 June 1825

Massimiliano Ravenna, Sculptor Carrara   Dr
To Cash p'd him at different times
agreably to his Drafts on me, & are in
file; & agreably to his receipt in full.
of all Demands, to this Day for
Capitals, Bases, Squares of Marble &   franci — Pls
a Piedestal for Mr Jefferson as pr reco.
in file to wit—francesconis—4982&   4982. .   4-
4 pavolis   4982.4

Credit   franci   Pls

By bala Due on old accot of Capitels   32.   –
By 10 whole & 2 half capitels as pr
Contract   4004.
By 1400 Squares for paving—£1400   210.–
By 8 Chimney Mantles for Mr.
Jefferson's private accot   120.–
By 12 Bases for College   578. .4
By a Piedestal for Mr. Jefferson's
private accot   4982.4   38   4982.4

N.B. In the above account, was paid
to this Day   4667. .8½
Cash p'd Massno Ravenna this day   245. .5½
Cash p'd for freight from Carrara
24 Cases   69.–

francesconis   4982.4

Thomas Jefferson of Monticello. U. S. America   Dr

1825

14 June   To 10 Corinthian Capitels of 32 4/10
inches Diminish'd Diameter   Dollrs   Dollars

@ 550   5500

To 2 half Do for pilasters @ 290   580

T. J.   6080

38 @ 61   *Charges*

To 24 Cases.—@ 4½ Doll each   108.–

To Custom house fees.—@ £3. 3. 4
each case   12.–
To Detention of vessel from Carrara
10 Days as the american Vessel was
in quarantine & to avoid a much
greater expence of landing. at
3 Dollars @ 3 Dollr per day   30.–
To p'd American Captn the customary
fee in Leghorn £1 per case . . . £24
To p'd on 31 cases by Ship
Caroline omitted in that
accot call'd Signing
money   31   }   £255   40.77
To p'd frt. from Carrara of
the bases omitted in last
accning 200.–

6270.27

Thomas Jefferson's Private account   Dr
1825   To a Piedestal of white Statuary marble,
June   agreably to instructions given to
Giaco Raggi   Dollars   40
Case, freight, duties & porterage   6

Dollars   46.–

Dr Thomas Jefferson in account current with Thomas
Appleton Cr.   Dollars   Cts
1825   To Amo. [Amount] of 10 whole &
June   2 half capitels as pr within accon.
[account]   6270.   77
1825   Dollars
June   By bala due you in accon rendd in
May last   2875. .50
[a later entry now follows:] By bill excha. remd.
S. Williams London, but as I have not yet
rec'd amn. I cannot fix this precise sum,
but I presume will be about 3000 Doll:
Dr. Thomas Jefferson's private account with Thomas
Appleton . . Cr.
1825   To bala. Due   1825   Bala. due
June   me in accn. of   June   me   Dollrs. 178.50
May   Doll.   132.50
To a piedestal
of Statuary
marble with
the charges   46.–

178.50

12th [June 1825]
Dr Thomas Jefferson of Virginia in accon. currt. with
Thomas Appleton Cr

1825 To am. of 10 whole	1825		
June & 2 half capitels as	May		
pr accon. render'd		By bala Due	
Doll. cts		you in acco.	Doll.–
6270. . 27		of May	2875.50
Leghorn 12 July 1825	July		
T. A.		By a bill of	
		Excha remitted	
		me by S. Wil-	
		liams, London	
		which bill due	
		28 Septr when	
		paid will	
		produce	3032.–
			5907.50
		Bala. Due me	362.77
		The above bala	
		was paid to	
		T. Perkins &	
		credited in his	
		accon 6	
		march.	6270.27
		[Later entry:] All accounts	
		are settled & paid with the	
		late Thos Jefferson—[63]	

[63] The entries that follow are almost entirely concerned with the management of Appleton's account with the banking firm of André and Cottier, Paris. The subject is primarily the transfer of money.

Artifact Study
A Proposed Model

E. McClung Fleming

EVERY CULTURE, however primitive or advanced, is absolutely dependent on its artifacts for its survival and self-realization.[1] The earliest records of man include objects made to satisfy his many needs—to extend his physical and psychic power over nature and his fellow man, delight his fancy, affirm his sense of form, and create symbols of meaning. If a basic wonder about man is his capacity for building culture, certainly the next wonder is his astounding capacity for making things as part of his culture. In this he surpasses the animal a thousand times in cunning, power, imaginativeness, beauty, destructiveness, and grandeur. To know man we must study the things he has made—the Parthenon, the Panama Canal, Stonehenge, the computer, the Taj Mahal, the space capsule, Michelangelo's *Pietà*, the highway cloverleaf, the Great Pyramid, Rembrandt's self-portraits. The artifacts made and used by a people are not only a basic expression of that people; they are, like culture itself, a necessary means of man's self-fulfillment.

Study of artifacts is therefore a primary humanistic study. Along with the study of man's physical constitution, his ideas, and institutions, the physical settings in which he has lived, and the records of his actions in time, there is an obvious, natural, universal fascination with the things man has made. Kenneth Clark has popularized a dictum of Ruskin's: "Great nations write their autobiographies in three manuscripts, the book of their deeds, the book of their words, and the book of their art. Not one of these books can be understood unless we read the two others, but of the three the only trustworthy one is the last."[2] Nevertheless, the exploration of the things man has made may be one of the least developed of our humanistic studies. Utilizing Leslie A. White's three main subdivisions of culture—material, social, and mental—it can be argued that material culture[3] has received less systematic attention than the other two.

Certain academic disciplines do, to be sure, center their attention on artifacts. First in popularity is art history, with its study of those works of man having a relatively high aesthetic component—architecture, sculpture, painting, graphics, and decorative arts. Second, perhaps, is archaeology, prehistoric and historic, with its examination and analysis of the entire spectrum of man-made objects recovered from the earth. A more recently organized discipline is the history of technology, which gives serious attention to artifacts made to perform work. Far less organized than these three disciplines in its approach to artifacts is cultural history, which in many instances has made effective use of

[1] The word *culture,* as used in this paper, can be defined as "that complex whole which includes artifacts, beliefs, art, all the other habits acquired by man as a member of society, and all products of human activity as determined by these habits." Clyde Kluckhohn and W. H. Kelly, "The Concept of Culture," *The Science of Man in the World Crisis,* ed. R. Linton (New York: Columbia University Press, 1945), pp. 78–106; see also A. L. Kroeber and Clyde Kluckhohn, *Culture: A Critical Review of Concepts and Definitions* (New York: Vintage Books, 1963). The word *artifact,* as used in this paper, can be defined as "a product of human workmanship," *Webster's New Collegiate Dictionary* (1959), or "anything made by man at any time," Ivor Noël Hume, *A Guide to Artifacts of Colonial America* (New York: Alfred A. Knopf, 1970), p. 4.

[2] Sir Kenneth Clark, *Civilisation: A Personal View* (London: British Broadcasting Corporation, 1969), p. 1.

[3] Leslie A. White, *The Science of Culture* (New York: Farrar, Straus & Giroux, 1969), pp. 364–65. The term *material culture,* as used in this paper, can be defined as the totality of artifacts in a culture. See Melville J. Herskovits, *Cultural Anthropology* (New York: Alfred A. Knopf, 1963), p. 119.

both practical and artistic objects, but which has not, as yet, developed either models or a methodology for the analysis and interpretation of this kind of primary source material. The first and only session devoted to material culture as such by the American Historical Association was at its 1964 annual meeting, and by the Organization of American Historians at its 1972 annual meeting. Other disciplines analyzing and interpreting material culture include cultural geography and folk culture. A very few universities offer introductions to American culture—notably the University of Pennsylvania, George Washington University, Brown University, the University of Delaware, and St. Mary's College in Maryland—but the use of material culture by historians and social scientists is minimal.

Related loosely to the preceding disciplines but concentrating on specific types of material culture are museums. Of the 6,000 museums in the United States and Canada, some 2,200 might be classified as natural history museums and about 3,600 as cultural history museums. The latter include museums of science and technology, art, and history, though more and more museums—such as historic house museums and outdoor, "living" museums—cannot be neatly classified under these headings. The American Association of Museums defines these institutions chiefly by their collections of artifacts. Their mission is the acquisition, cataloging, conservation, exhibition, study, and interpretation of artifacts. It would be logical to assume that a substantial contribution to the study of material culture should come from the community of numerous and rapidly growing cultural history museums in this country.

Important progress has been made in analysis of the physical properties of museum objects and in methods of preventing their physical deterioration. Important progress, also, has been made in exploring the different ways in which the encounter of observer and object can be promoted through imaginative attention to angles of vision, lighting, and use of multimedia communication. At the information level, techniques are constantly being improved for identifying and cataloging objects in museum collections, moving toward more standardized methods of classification, better methods of material analysis, and devices for faster information retrieval. There has not been equivalent progress in differentiating the information level from the conceptual level in the museum scholar's research with collections, and it is especially on these con-

ceptual levels, which this paper will call cultural analysis and interpretation, that more work remains to be done. For example, the interrelationship of the artifact and its culture is implicit in all that museums say and write about their collections, but relatively few contributions have been made to a theoretical understanding of the ways in which the artifact explicitly implements, expresses, and documents a particular way of life. In short, museums have paid relatively little attention to developing a discipline of artifact study.

A Proposed Model for Artifact Study

THIS PAPER is an attempt to present a model for artifact study.[4] Hopefully, it is a model that can identify many of the possible approaches to the subject, provide a framework relating them to each other, and thus suggest the outlines of a program of collaborative research for all who are engaged in study of the artifact. The model has been developed in the context of the study of early American decorative arts. With this background it doubtless bears the special impress of thinking oriented toward cultural history, but it should be equally applicable in other areas of study. The model utilizes two conceptual tools—a fivefold classification of the basic properties of an artifact and a set of four operations to be performed on these properties (Fig. 1). The model will be applied to a seventeenth-

[4] For one of the few other models suggested see Craig Gilborn, "Pop Pedagogy: Looking at the Coke Bottle," *Museum News* 47, no. 41 (Dec. 1968): 12–18.

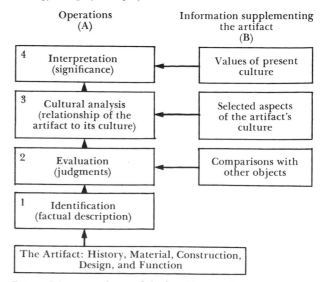

FIG. 1. Diagram of a model of artifact study.

FIG. 2. Court cupboard, Salem, Mass., 1680. H. 57¾″, W. 50″, D. 21⅝″. (Winterthur 66.1261.)

century American court cupboard (Fig. 2) in the Winterthur Museum collection.

The five basic properties provide a formula for including and interrelating all the significant facts about an artifact. These properties of an artifact are its history, material, construction, design, and function. History includes where and when it was made, by whom and for whom and why and successive changes in ownership, condition, and function. Material involves what the object is made of—woods, fibers, ceramic bodies, metals, glass, and so on. Construction has to do with the techniques of manufacture employed, workmanship, and the way parts are organized to bring about the object's function. Design includes the structure, form, style, ornament, and iconography of the object. Function embraces both the uses (intended functions) and the roles (unintended functions) of the object in its culture, including utility, delight, and communication.

The four operations to be performed on the five properties yield answers to most of the important questions we want to ask about an artifact. These operations are identification (including classification, authentication, and description), which results in a body of distinctive facts about the artifact; evaluation, which results in a set of judgments about the artifact, usually based on comparisons with other examples of its kind; cultural analysis, which examines the various interrelationships of an artifact and its contemporary culture; and interpretation, which suggests the meaning and significance of the artifact in relation to aspects of our own culture. Each of these operations may involve each of the five properties of the artifact, and each successive operation is dependent upon those preceding it. Identification is the foundation for everything that follows; interpretation is the crown. A further word about each of these four operations is in order.

Identification: Identification should begin with the question, What is it? The answer is classification—specification of the general class to which the particular object under consideration belongs. Most current systems of classification are unsystematic. Many are based on function (chair, floor covering, coffeepot, firearm), some on material (textile, glassware), others on construction (painting, print), or on iconography and subject matter (map). The adoption of a more uniform and exact classification scheme for artifacts should be considered a major item of unfinished business in the development of a rigorous discipline of material culture study.

The second step in identification is authentication,[5] to determine whether the object is genuine. Is it actually what it purports to be in date, provenance, authorship, material, and construction? Is it a fake or forgery made with a deliberate intent to deceive or a reproduction made without intent to deceive? Is this log cabin the one in which Daniel Boone actually lived? Is this sword truly the one worn by Washington at Yorktown? Was this silver tankard, with its Paul Revere mark, really made by Revere? The skills of connoisseurship or laboratory analysis, or both, may be used in authentication, which is sometimes referred to as "external criticism." Authentication is the precondition for accurate identification. Another element in identification is description, possibly by both words and images. Description often begins with measurements that specify the dimensions and sometimes the weight of the object. The essence of description is the concise and orderly delineation of the physical aspects of the object.

The chief objective of identification is to provide accurate information about the five properties of the artifact. This information must obviously be based on authentication and will either precede or follow description. Since it is the rare artifact that fully identifies itself with a maker's mark or label, a date, an owner's initials, and that remains (like a building or a gravestone) in the place of its origin, this information must be hunted out. Finding it can involve a combination of connoisseurship and extensive, painstaking research utilizing not only a number of primary and secondary verbal sources (probate records, family records, bills of sale, newspaper advertisements, design books, emblem books, travel accounts, city registers, and so forth), but also a growing range of sophisticated technical hardware. The tools of the scientist are increasingly employed by museums to reveal physical and chemical properties not apparent to the naked eye. Authentication can hinge on the results of these investigations, which necessarily require a knowledge of what was technologically feasible in various historical periods.

Identification can be simple and brief—as in the case of picture captions, exhibit labels, and catalog cards, or it can be extended and detailed. Extended

[5] Oscar Handlin, ed., *Harvard Guide to American History* (Cambridge: The Belknap Press of Harvard University Press, 1955), pp. 22–25.

identification might involve discovering biographical details about the maker, the purchaser, or the owner of the artifact; the cultural geography of its place of origin; the sources and characteristics of the material; the origins and antecedents of the techniques of construction or the design motifs employed; the history of the functional form; or the meaning of the iconography. An important type of extended identification contributed by art historians is the location of a center from which the style or ornament of an artifact was originally diffused, and the modifications this style underwent.[6] It is obvious that the amount of extended identification that can be undertaken is unlimited. And the fruits of this research can be embodied in monographs that are not artifact studies in themselves, but can form part of, or contribute to, the identification operation in artifact studies. One property of the artifact—function—so obviously involves the whole artifact rather than its details and so uniquely relates the artifact to its culture that the extended identification of function is considered to be part of the operation of cultural analysis discussed below.

Evaluation: Although our understanding of an artifact must begin with the identification of its properties, it can be greatly extended by the evaluation of those properties in terms of our culture's value standards. There are two kinds of evaluation. One has to do with judgments of aesthetic quality and workmanship, i.e. appropriateness of material and texture, skill and taste of craftsmanship, effectiveness of overall design (proportion, balance, unity), and expressiveness of form, style, and ornament. Such judgments result in a ranking of the artifact's qualities, for example excellent or poor, and depend on a subjective exercise of the observer's taste and discrimination. The other kind of evaluation consists of factual comparisons of one object with others of its kind in quantifiable terms such as relative size, cost, rarity, or temporal primacy as determined through objective research. If extensive, this research may become the operation of cultural analysis as defined below. Evaluation can result in applying to the object such adjectives

as similar, unique, early example, avant-garde, *retardataire,* and so on. Evaluation might compare the given artifact with other artifacts made by the same craftsman, or it might compare the given artifact with similar ones made by other craftsmen in the same subculture. An artifact made in one region might be compared with a similar one made in another region.[7]

Identification and evaluation constitute the special province of connoisseurship and curatorship. When these operations are accomplished through direct perception—the trained eye and knowing touch matured by the special kind of artifact expertise resulting from extensive experience in examining and comparing objects—and the findings are interpreted by a well-stocked memory bank of precise images, we are in the presence of the connoisseur.[8] When connoisseurship is supplemented by additional skills in the cataloging, care, conservation, exhibition of objects, and scientific examination, we are in the presence of the curator. Identification, and to a lesser extent evaluation, provide the essential building blocks for conceptual generalization about the artifact. These generalizations represent the fruit of the third and fourth operations, cultural analysis and interpretation.

Cultural Analysis: The third operation, cultural analysis, begins where identification and evaluation leave off. It is found in any one of a dozen different kinds of artifact study that seek to examine in depth the relation of the artifact to aspects of its own culture. Certainly it embraces the largest potential of artifact study.

One important form of cultural analysis deals with the functions performed by the artifact in its culture. Unlike the other artifact properties of material, construction, and design, function involves both the concrete and the abstract aspects of the artifact, the reasons for its initial manufacture, its various intended uses, and its unintended roles. Functional analysis, indeed, reveals the essential importance and meaning of the things man has made. Ordinarily the most obvious and simplest function of an artifact is its utility as a tool. Discussion of the utility function will necessarily involve discussion of the human behavior associated

[6] See, for example, R. Peter Mooz, "An Art Historian's View: A Commentary on Style in Country Art," in *Country Cabinetwork and Simple City Furniture,* ed. John D. Morse (Charlottesville: University Press of Virginia, 1970). Erwin Panofsky uses the term "iconographical analysis," as distinguished from "iconological interpretation," for the extended identification of the influence of style centers. Panofsky, *Meaning in the Visual Arts* (Garden City, N.Y.: Doubleday, 1955), pp. 35–40.

[7] For example see Charles F. Montgomery, *American Furniture: The Federal Period* (New York: Viking Press, 1966), p. 229; Alan Gowans, *Images of American Living* (Philadelphia: J. P. Lippincott, 1964), pp. 69, 97.

[8] Montgomery, *American Furniture: The Federal Period,* pp. 48–49.

with the artifact and the social groups of structures engaging in that behavior. The artifact also functions as a vehicle of delight through its form and decoration. Finally, by means of its materials, construction, design, and use of signs and symbols, the artifact functions as a vehicle of communication conveying status, ideas, values, feelings, and meaning. In some cases functional analysis will indicate the ways in which the artifact became an agent of major change within its culture.[9]

Related to functional analysis are several kinds of historical analysis that further seek to indicate the place of the artifact in its culture. For example, the esteem in which an object was held by its culture might be determined from learning the quantity produced or imported, prices paid, and allusions to the particular form in both pictorial and verbal documents of the period. Research in these areas would suggest the social function of the artifact and whether its use was confined to one class or subculture or more widespread.[10] Whatever meaning it held for its culture and how it conveyed that meaning is an essential part of cultural analysis.

Other forms of cultural analysis that may yield significant conceptual generalizations are sampling operations involving a body of related artifacts. For purposes of cultural analysis, artifacts may, for example, be grouped according to one or more of the following criteria: their identification with a specific culture or subculture, geographical area, a single maker or a group of makers, a unique set of physical and aesthetic characteristics, and so on.

The purpose in cultural analysis is to isolate characteristics common to the group that enable the researcher to make inferences of a general nature about the society that produced and/or used the body of artifacts. On the basis of one type of sample, cultural analysis might establish a chronology of construction techniques or design traits. The chronology might focus on whether design traits found in one region predated or followed similar design traits found in other regions. Relationships determined from a sample could be graphed to indicate chronological sequences, expressed in tabular form to clarify types and subtypes, or subjected to statistical analysis.[11]

Cultural analysis can carry artifact study beyond description toward explanation by "the explication of those critical links that exist between human behavior and its material products."[12] Some of these links, termed "real intersections," were discussed by George Kubler in a passage in which he underlined the importance in art history of going beyond identification to cultural analysis:

In the history of art, which is a young discipline, it has long been necessary to restrict attention to manageable questions like artistic biography and catalogues and iconography. It is now apparent that those tasks have been accomplished and that we need not repeat them over and over. . . . Many more new tasks lie in connecting the history of art with other fields of thought, by finding intersecting lines of investigation where thought renews both itself and the fields it illuminates. In other words, the history of art can look beyond its own well-worn road to intersections with other roads. These intersections, however, are of two kinds. There are real intersections, as when economic history and silversmithing connect in the use of coin silver. But there are also virtual intersections which exist only in the beholder's

[9] For three examples of functional analysis dealing with the utility function see Rodris C. Roth, "Tea Drinking in Eighteenth Century America: Its Etiquette and Equipage," *Contributions from the Museum of History and Technology* (Washington, D.C.: Smithsonian Institution, 1961); Frank H. Sommer III, "The Functions of American Church Plate," in *Spanish, French, and English Traditions in the Colonial Silver of North America* (Winterthur, Del.: The Henry Francis du Pont Winterthur Museum, 1969); Charles F. Hummel, *With Hammer in Hand: The Dominy Craftsmen of East Hampton, New York* (Charlottesville: University Press of Virginia, 1968). A good example of an analysis of the function of the artifact as a culture symbol is Alan Trachtenberg, *Brooklyn Bridge: Fact and Symbol* (New York: Oxford University Press, 1965). For a treatment of artifacts as agents of cultural change see Marshall McLuhan, *Understanding Media: The Extensions of Man* (New York: McGraw-Hill Book Co., 1965).

[10] See Bruce R. Buckley, "A Folklorist Looks at the Traditional Craftsman," in *Country Cabinetwork and Simple City Furniture*, ed. John D. Morse (Charlottesville: University Press of Virginia, 1970), pp. 265–76.

[11] For an example of a design chronology, see Margaret Burke, "Massachusetts High Chests, 1710–1780: Regional Characteristics and a Chronology of Design" (seminar report for History 802, University of Delaware, 1972). For examples of typology and seriation see Craig Gilborn, "Pop Pedagogy"; James Deetz and Edwin Dethlefson, "Death's Head, Cherub, Urn, and Willow," *Natural History* 76, no. 3 (Mar. 1967): 28–37; James Deetz, *Invitation to Archaeology* (Garden City, N.Y.: Natural History Press, 1967), pp. 26–33. For examples of statistical analysis see Anthony N. B. Garvan, "American Church Silver: A Statistical Study," in *Spanish, French, and English Traditions in The Colonial Silver of North America* (Winterthur, Del.: The Henry Francis du Pont Winterthur Museum, 1969), pp. 73–104; Barbara G. Teller, "Ceramics in Providence, 1730–1800: An Inventory Survey," *Antiques* 94 no. 4 (Oct. 1968): 570–77.

[12] James J. F. Deetz, "Ceramics from Plymouth, 1620–1835: The Archaeological Evidence," in *Ceramics in America*, ed. Ian H. G. Quimby (Charlottesville: University Press of Virginia, 1973), p. 15.

mind. . . . They exist as possibilities, and it is in them that we can hope to discover some latent system of relations far more instructive than those revealed by the study of real problems.[13]

Kubler's real intersections between the component subsystems of a culture suggest a host of interesting and important research possibilities, most of them of an interdisciplinary nature. This interdisciplinary approach to cultural analysis explores parallels or relationships between the expressive products of one cultural subsystem and similar patterns in other subsystems, e.g. how an artifact relates to the religious beliefs, ideas, standard of living, and politics of its subculture. Panofsky regarded this comparison of the "intrinsic meaning or content" discovered in different cultural subsystems as the ideal meeting ground of the various humanistic disciplines.[14]

Research along these lines, which Richard Sykes argues could be the unifying theme of American studies, is beginning to appear. The intersections between the old silver of American churches and denomination, type of piece, church location, and so on, have been explored by Anthony Garvan with the aid of a computer; and the same scholar has traced relationships between the iconography of New England porringers and Puritan ideas of love and marriage. Intersections between the iconography of Edward Winslow's silver sugar boxes and concepts of courtly love, marriage, and fertility have been suggested by Edward J. Nygren; and Barbara Teller has examined intersections between ownership of four types of imported ceramic forms and three income levels in eighteenth-century Providence. Henry Glassie has studied Anglo-American material culture of the eighteenth century in relation to the Georgian mind-set, and Alan Gowans has pointed out connections between Federal-Adamesque architecture, Federalist politics, and new mercantile wealth. Other real intersections throw light on "the dynamics of change in material objects as a function of changes in the society which produced them," as in the investigation of changes in gravestone iconography in relation to changes in

religion, population, social values, and social organization in early New England by Edwin Dethlefsen and James Deetz.[15]

Kubler's virtual intersections, which can throw a brilliant light on the larger character of the artifact, consist of noncausal, unprovable but possible correspondences and conformities between artifacts and cultural constructs. Examples are studies correlating the pattern of ceramic usage in early Plymouth with that of the Stuart yeoman foodways subsystem; relating living room styles to intergenerational mobility, frequency of church attendance, and political party preference; and hypothesizing that the development of eighteenth-century American Georgian architecture conforms to six principles of maturation.[16]

Two reciprocal methods of procedure in discovering the real and virtual intersections of an artifact with its culture are product analysis (the ways in which a culture leaves its mark on a particular artifact) and content analysis (the ways in which a particular artifact reflects its culture). From the standpoint of product analysis, every artifact—in its history, material, construction, design, and function—is a product of its culture. "Every epoch, everywhere," Edgar Kaufman asserted, "creates the objects it needs in its own spirit, its individual character unmistakably stamped on them." From the standpoint of content analysis, every artifact is a document bearing some content of evidence about its culture, and in this role it can serve as primary source material for the cultural historian.

[13] George A. Kubler, "Time's Perfection and Colonial Art," in *Spanish, French, and English Traditions in the Colonial Silver of North America* (Winterthur, Del.: The Henry Francis du Pont Winterthur Museum, 1969), pp. 8–9.

[14] For an attempt to trace parallel patterns in architecture, painting, sculpture, literature, and music, see Frederick B. Artz, *From the Renaissance to Romanticism* (Chicago: University of Chicago Press, 1962); Panofsky, *Meaning in the Visual Arts*, p. 39.

[15] Richard E. Sykes, "American Studies and the Concept of Culture: A Theory and Method," *American Quarterly* 15, no. 2, part 2 (Summer 1963, supplement): 263–70; Garvan, "American Church Silver"; Garvan, "The New England Porringer: An Index of Custom," in *Smithsonian Annual Report* (Washington, D.C.: Government Printing Office, 1958), pp. 543–52; Edward J. Nygren, "Edward Winslow's Sugar Boxes: Colonial Echoes of Courtly Love," Yale University Art Gallery *Bulletin* 33, no. 2 (Autumn 1971): 39–52; Barbara G. Teller, "Ceramics in Providence"; Henry Glassie, "Architecture as Cognitive Process" (public lecture, American Civilization Department, Brown University, Dec. 1971); Gowans, *Images of American Living*, pp. 206–9; Dethlefson and Deetz, "Death's Head, Cherub, Urn, and Willow"; Dethlefson and Deetz, "Death's Head, Cherub, Urn and Willow Trees: Experimental Archaeology in Colonial Cemeteries," *American Antiquity* 31, no. 4 (Nov. 1966): 502–10.

[16] Deetz, "Ceramics from Plymouth"; Edward O. Lanmann and James S. House, "Living Room Styles and Social Attributes: The Patterning of Material Artifacts in a Modern Urban Community," *Sociology and Social Research* 54, no. 3 (Apr. 1970): 321–43; Gowans, *Images of American Living*, pp. 173–78.

"It is easy to overlook the data afforded by physical survivals and objects of material culture," warns the *Harvard Guide to American History,* "yet such vestiges of the past may be quite as revealing as written records." Artifacts are not only natural facts in themselves, but the evidence they contain can be read to establish historical facts on which the structure of historical interpretation can be raised. These historical facts may indicate the technological level of a culture, the materials at its command, its taste and form preference, quality of craftsmanship, trade relations, standard of living, social usage, popular enthusiasms, and life-style.[17] When the scholar's research subject is a particular artifact, he will probably concentrate on explaining how the shaping influence of the culture made the artifact what it is. When the scholar's subject is a particular culture, he will probably concentrate on extracting evidence from the artifact about the character of its culture.

It is evident that both product and content analysis equally involve the interrelationship of artifacts and culture. Of the two, the former is the more readily accepted and carried out. Content analysis, on the other hand, is a less familiar concept. The general proposition that the structures, tools, dress, jewelry, settlement patterns, and art of a people help us to understand that people is universally accepted: it is the chief basis of all foreign travel and museum visitation. But when the specific question is raised as to just what these objects tell us, the proposition often seems less clear. Little has been written on the specific question as to whether and how artifacts (nonverbal documents) constitute evidence of a culture in the same way as written texts (verbal documents).[18] In fact, procedures in reading the content of a nonverbal document parallel those in reading the content of a verbal document. In each case the would-be reader must start

by being literate. In the case of the verbal document, he must understand the vocabulary of nouns, adjectives, verbs, and prepositions and how they are put together. In the case of the nonverbal document, he must understand the vocabulary of material, construction, design, and function and how they are put together.

Assuming one is literate in the language of the document to be read, it is necessary to begin with identification. The unidentified document is worthless as evidence. Sometimes a document carries its own identification. A letter may indicate where and when it was written, by whom, and to whom; a silver tankard may bear a maker's mark that gives a good clue as to who, where, and when, or a coat of arms that indicates for whom. At other times the document does not identify itself, and extrinsic aids must be used—a comparison of the unidentified item with identified ones, the resort to handwriting experts and connoisseurs of craft construction, the consultation of calendars, atlases, dictionaries, encyclopedias, and handbooks of heraldry. Moreover, not only the general character of the document, but its terms will have to be identified—proper names, place names, reference to events, ornament, and iconography that can be clarified only with the help of outside references. If sound identification is finally made, it does not matter whether it was made by the use of reference tools or not. Certainly no assumption is implied, with either the verbal or the nonverbal document, that the document must "speak for itself" and be self-identifying.

Once validated as authentic and identified, the document can be read for content. The content of each document will be formulated in a series of statements. The artifact is actually a bundle of facts, and its content is, in theory, the sum total of all the statements that result from combining what we know about its properties with what we know about its history. In practice, content is only those statements that seem relevant to our investigation.

Once the content is available, it will normally be evaluated for its importance. Does it constitute new evidence? Does it confirm or contradict existing evidence? In all these steps in reading the content of the artifact, the scholar using the nonverbal document is proceeding through the same operations employed by the scholar using the verbal document. He stands under the same imperative to be objective, to be skeptical, to use public standards, and to use intuition with caution. The conclusions of the one need be no more impressionistic than those of the other.

[17] Edgar Kaufman, *An Exhibition for Modern Living* (Detroit: Detroit Institute of Arts, 1949), p. 40; Handlin, *Harvard Guide to American History,* pp. 61–63; see E. McClung Fleming, "Early American Decorative Arts As Social Documents," *Mississippi Valley Historical Review* 45, no. 2 (Sept. 1958): 276–84. For an example of historians' use of artifacts as evidence see John Demos, *A Little Commonwealth: Family Life in Plymouth Colony* (New York: Oxford University Press, 1970), pp. 36–51.

[18] For a discussion of this problem see William B. Hesseltine, "The Challenge of the Artifact," *The Present World of History* (Madison, Wisc.: The American Association for State & Local History, 1959); Fleming, "Early American Decorative Arts As Social Documents"; John Chavis, "The Artifact and the Study of History," *Curator* 7, no. 2 (1964): 156–62.

Interpretation: The last of the four basic operations involved in artifact research is interpretation. Whereas cultural analysis was concerned with the relations of the artifact to its culture, interpretation is concerned with the relations of the artifact to our culture. More specifically, interpretation focuses on the relation between some fact learned about the artifact and some key aspect of our current value system, and this relation must be sufficiently intense or rich to have self-evident meaning, significance, or relevance. Interpretation does not result in a statement of fact that can be documented, but a statement of relationship born of what Panofsky calls "synthetic intuition" and imagination that goes beyond documentation. As in content analysis, an artifact is not subject to just one "correct" interpretation, but many. Interpretation will vary as the personal, class, ideological, and national interests of interpreters and their audiences vary. Whatever the audience aimed at, interpretation will suggest the particular values held by it that are represented by the object under consideration. The study of the artifact is not complete until an interpretation of its significance has been offered.

The particular facts about the artifact that interpretation singles out for our attention may have come from the operations of identification, evaluation, or cultural analysis. It might be an association with some famous person or event in history; the use of some costly, rare, or novel material; some innovative technological principle embodied in construction; the superlative quality of design; the strategic character of symbolic function; the cultural changes effected by use; or the way the artifact expresses the life-style of the age or culture in which it originated. The value to which an object relates may be our love of statistical "firsts." Thus the significance of an artifact might be interpreted as the fact that it was the largest or tallest or costliest or first one of its kind. For an American audience, other relevant values to which facts about an artifact might be related are upward social mobility, American nationalism, American superiority or uniqueness, urbanization, ecology, democracy, mechanization, black power, or women's liberation. One might interpret the significance of the Model T Ford to be the pioneering application of the assembly line to mass production, its improvements on the internal combustion engine, or its provision of cheap transportation. On the other hand, its significance might be found in the fact that it was a particular instance of the general democratization

of technological benefits, or that it created a revolution in the life-style of rural America. Or its significance might be found in its effects and consequences, such as the increased mobility of the American people, the liberalized sexual ethics of the middle class, or air pollution. The balance of this paper will apply the concept of the five properties and the four operations to a specific example of seventeenth-century American furniture.

Application of the Model to an Early American Court Cupboard

Identification: Identification of this object begins with its denomination as a court cupboard, a classification based on function. A court cupboard can be defined as an open three-tiered structure of equal-size shelves for the display of plate, a form introduced in England toward the end of the sixteenth century.[19] Curatorship authenticates the court cupboard as genuine, and for the most part original. Simple identification yields a body of concise facts about its five properties. Some of these facts are derived from connoisseurship, some from laboratory analysis, some from documents.[20]

Beginning with the history of the cupboard, the artifact itself tells us its date and original ownership. On the front case below the upper drawer are the incised characters "P 1680 WҒ" (Fig. 3). Such initials and numerals conform to fairly widespread practice in the ornamentation of case furniture of the period. Curatorship affirms that the "1680" numerals are original and probably represent the date of construction; that the "PW" initials are original and represent the first owner, and that the "Ҡ" (J) represents a later addition. Connoisseurship provides the judgment, based on a comparison with documented examples, that the provenance is Essex County, Massachusetts. Assuming the accuracy of the family records of a modern owner and with the help of genealogical records, Irving P. Lyon concluded that the "PW" denoted Peter Wood-

[19] Louise Ade Boger, *The Complete Guide To Furniture Styles* (New York: Charles Scribner's Sons, 1959), p. 207; Benno M. Forman, "The Seventeenth Century Case Furniture of Essex County, Massachusetts, and Its Makers" (M.A. thesis, University of Delaware, 1968), p. 188; Peter Thornton, "Two Problems," *The Journal of the Furniture History Society* 7 (1971): 62.

[20] I am indebted for several points made in the following discussion to the friendly assistance of Benno M. Forman and to seminar papers written by Winterthur fellows of the classes of 1971 and 1972.

FIG. 3. Court cupboard, Salem, Mass., 1680. Detail of panel between drawers. (Winterthur 66.1261.)

bury. Benno M. Forman concluded that the "I" denotes Woodbury's son, Josiah, who inherited half of his father's house and its contents in 1704. Simple identification of the history of this court cupboard thus results in the statement that it was made in 1680 in Essex County, Massachusetts, probably in the Salem-Beverly area, for Peter Woodbury, by an unknown joiner.[21] Wear and tear over the years have resulted in the necessary restoration of the right rear foot, most of the knobs, and replacement of some of the applied moldings, one of the pendles, and the top; the drawer dividers and cloth lining are modern (Fig. 4).

Extended identification of the history of this court cupboard shows that the first owner, Peter Woodbury, was a resident of Beverly, Massachusetts. He was born in 1640, the eldest son of John Woodbury, who was one of the original proprietors of the Dorchester Company and a founder of Salem in 1628. Peter Woodbury became a freeman in 1668 and a sergeant of militia in 1685. He was married first to Sarah Dodge, daughter of Richard Dodge; his several children included Peter by his first wife and Josiah by his second. Part of his home is still

extant in a structure located at what is now 82 Dodge Street in Beverly. A yeoman farmer, Woodbury owned considerable land and at his death in 1704 left an estate worth nearly a thousand pounds, which made him one of the dozen wealthiest men in Beverly. His inventory lists "one Wincut Cubard," which is valued, along with "one long Table, one bench, and two gined [joined] stooles" at four pounds. The value of the cupboard in 1704 could be estimated at around two pounds, but in 1680 it was probably worth more. At the time of Woodbury's death or that of his second wife, the cupboard appears to have passed to their son Josiah, who may have added the "I" to the right of the "W." Resident in Beverly was a joiner named Ryce Edwards who had the skills to make this court cupboard.[22]

Proceeding to material, inspection supported by microanalysis of wood samples ascertains that red oak was used for the framing of the case, drawer fronts, and drawer sides; sycamore for the drawer bottoms, drawer front moldings, two remaining original shelves, and back of the enclosed section. Three kinds of decorative wood were used—hard

[21] Irving P. Lyon, "The Oak Furniture of Ipswich, Massachusetts," *Antiques* 33, no. 6 (June 1938): 325; Charles Levi Woodbury, *Genealogical Sketches of the Woodbury Family* (Manchester, N.H., 1904), p. 83; Forman, "Case Furniture of Essex County," p. 119. The attribution of this cupboard to Thomas Dennis cannot yet be dismissed.

[22] James Savage, *A Genealogical Dictionary of the First Settlers of New England*, 4 vols. (Baltimore: Genealogical Publishing Co., 1965), 4:635–36; Forman, "Case Furniture of Essex County," pp. 118–19; Lyon, "Oak Furniture of Ipswich," p. 325; Registrar's Object File, 66.1261, Winterthur Museum.

FIG. 4. Court cupboard, Salem, Mass., 1680. Detail of drawer showing construction and modern cloth lining. (Winterthur 66.1261.)

FIG. 5. Court cupboard, Salem, Mass., 1680. Detail of drawer bottom showing mill saw marks. (Winterthur 66.1261.)

maple for the turned columns and split spindles, black walnut for the applied ornament on the door, and poplar for the dated panel between the drawers. Other materials included iron nails used in the drawers (Fig. 4) and glue and sprigs, which hold on the applied half spindles.[23]

[23] Catalog card for 1680 court cupboard (66.1261), Winterthur Museum.

Regarding construction, we can see that the oak was riven; regularly spaced parallel saw marks on the sycamore indicate that it was mill-sawn (Fig. 5). The carcass was framed with mortise and tenon joints, which are pinned with wooden pegs. Panels were inserted into the frames. The sycamore boards of the drawer bottoms were fitted to each other longitudinally with a tongue-and-groove, and the drawers were side hung (Fig. 4). Many of the decorative elements are of the split-spindle type made by turning on the lathe. The applied moldings and spindles were originally attached to the surface with glue. The drawer sides were nailed to the drawer fronts rather than dovetailed. Extended identification of construction indicates that oak could be easily riven but was hard to saw. Riving was a much older technique than mill sawing, although there was more mill sawing in New England than in England.[24]

Extended identification of the court cupboard form indicates that the form was found in many countries of western Europe during the sixteenth and seventeenth centuries.[25] The New England court cupboard was derived from the English court cupboard, a furniture form representing the last phase of the medieval plate cupboard, which functioned as a serving table with open shelves.[26] As the English upper classes turned from the medieval hall in favor of the new dining parlors, where they could take their meals apart from the servants, the plate cupboard underwent a change, becoming a piece of wall furniture designed for these new rooms. Thus the new design of plate cupboards—now called court cupboards—became fashionable around the mid-sixteenth century. Although the new court cupboard, like the plate cupboard, started with open shelves (Fig. 6), some cupboards were fitted with enclosed areas by the middle of the sixteenth century. The court cupboard enjoyed its greatest popularity in the seventeenth century and declined in fashion toward the end of the century, its functions being replaced early in the eighteenth century by the corner cupboard, the long

Fig. 6. Court cupboard. England, early seventeenth century. (Victoria and Albert Museum.)

side table or sideboard table, and the mantle tree. The eighteenth-century court cupboard was, according to Ralph Fastnedge, "the unfashionable product of the country joiner."[27]

In the American colonies seventeenth-century probate records note eighty-one examples of court cupboards in New England, quite a number in the South, and none in New York.[28] The largest number of surviving examples, about fifty, are from New England and particularly from Essex County. A few Southern examples are known, but none from the Middle Colonies have been identified. In the typical New England form, the enclosed cabinet is above; in the only southern one, it is below. The examples surviving in American museums and

[24] Benno M. Forman, "Mill Sawing in Seventeenth Century Massachusetts," *Old Time New England* 60, no. 4 (Spring 1970): 110–30; Forman, "Continental Furniture Craftsmen in London: 1511–1625," *The Journal of the Furniture History Society* 7 (1971): 94–120.

[25] For German examples of mid-sixteenth-century court cupboards see the painting *The Marriage at Cana* by Ludger Tom Ring the Younger in Otto von Falke, *Deutsche Möbel des Mittelalters und der Renaissance* (Stuttgart: Verlag Julius Hoffmann, 1924), pp. 28–29. For a French example of a mid-seventeenth-century court cupboard see Jean Dubreuil, *La Perspective Pratique* . . . Premier Partie (2nd ed.; Paris: Chez François L'Anglois, 1651), p. 100. Some furniture historians believe that the English court cupboard is related to the Continental dressoir and the French armoire.

[26] R. W. Symonds, "The Evolution of the Cupboard," *Connoisseur* 112, no. 490 (Dec. 1943): 95; L. G. G. Ramsey, "Foreword," *The Connoisseur Period Guides: The Stuart Period, 1603–1714*, ed. Ralph Edwards and L. G. G. Ramsey (New York: Reynal & Co., 1957), p. 9.

[27] Symonds, "Evolution of the Cupboard," p. 95; Symonds, "The Dyning Parlor and Its Furniture," *Connoisseur* 113, no. 491 (Mar. 1944): 15, 17; Boger, *Complete Guide to Furniture Styles*, p. 207; Ralph Fastnedge, "Furniture," in *The Connoisseur Period Guides: The Stuart Period, 1603–1714*, p. 35; Luke V. Lockwood, *Colonial Furniture in America* (New York: Charles Scribner's Sons, 1901), p. 85; Thornton, "Two Problems," p. 61; Forman, "Case Furniture of Essex County," passim.

[28] Irving W. Lyon, *Colonial Furniture in New England* (Boston: Houghton Mifflin, 1892), p. 35; Lockwood, *Colonial Furniture*, pp. 85–86. It should be noted that very few New York probate records survive.

private collections all seem to indicate a date of construction during or after the last quarter of the seventeenth century.[29]

The 1680 court cupboard is designed as a rectangular, open structure consisting of three shelves separated by corner supports that form two cases: an upper case with a recessed trapezoidal cabinet between the top shelf and the middle shelf; and a lower case fitted with two long drawers just below the middle shelf. The top and bottom shelves are completely open. The upper case and the two drawers form a three-sided overhang (two sides and rear). The design is clearly architectural in such elements as the base, column supports, cornice effect, overhang, and some of the ornament.

The style of the case is late medieval, the latest phase of the evolving medieval plate cupboard. On this basic medieval form, was superimposed a vocabulary of Anglo-Dutch mannerist ornament that characterized much Elizabethan-Tudor and early Jacobean furniture. Examples include the distortion of classical proportions, the transformation of classical columnar supports into bulbous or vase-like balusters, the use of split spindles to simulate columns that support nothing, and the arches with carrot-shaped pendant drops that express a delight in manipulating gravity-defying plastic form (Fig. 7).[30] By no means can this court cupboard be considered part of the New England plain style, rather it was self-conscious emulation of the fashion then up-to-date among the rural yeoman class in England.

Six types of ornament give the cupboard a rich decorative effect: the architectural element of the cornice on three sides of the top shelf; the overhang of the central shelf on both sides and rear; the application of moldings, split spindles, and bosses in geometrical patterns; the turning of the vertical supporting members; the use of black paint to simulate ebony on the decorative columns, pendants, split spindles, and some of the moldings; and the use of contrasting woods. The recessed cabinet surfaces are decorated with applied moldings that form double-arched panels with keystone headings; long, central, carrot-shaped drops; and blanking

FIG. 7. Court cupboard, Salem, Mass., 1680. Detail of side panel on cabinet. (Winterthur 66.1261.)

bosses. There is none of the carving that marks somewhat earlier case furniture (Figs. 8, 9).

Extended identification of the ornament indicates that applied moldings and split spindles in geometrical patterns were introduced into English furniture late in the sixteenth century, were in wide use in England by the middle of the seventeenth century, and appeared on New England court cupboards in the last quarter of the century (Figs. 10, 11), replacing the earlier preference for ornament carved in low relief and occasional inlay (Figs. 8, 9).[31] This new mannerist decoration, such as the turned half-pendants that are broader at the top and taper towards the bottom, came into the Anglo-American tradition from the Flemish Netherlands. The bulbous vase-shaped balusters, borrowed by the English from the Dutch in the sixteenth century, were used as supports on tables and bedsteads as well as court cupboards. And the use of black paint on bosses, spindles, and columns may be an adaptation of the German imitation of southern European use of ebony. By the time of the settlement of Massachusetts Bay Colony in the 1630s, these and other Renaissance motifs were well known to craftsmen in the American colonies

---

[29] Forman, "Case Furniture of Essex County," p. 118.

[30] Margaretta Lovell, "Background of the Court Cupboard in Seventeenth Century America" (seminar report for History 802, University of Delaware, 1971); Deborah (Dependahl) Waters, "The 1680 Court Cupboard" (seminar report for History 802, University of Delaware, 1971).

[31] Helen Park, "The Seventeenth Century Furniture of Essex County and Its Makers," *Antiques* 78, no. 4 (Oct. 1960): 355; Forman, "Case Furniture of Essex County," pp. 76, 89–90.

FIG. 8. Parmenter court cupboard, 1640–60. (Wadsworth Atheneum.)

FIG. 9. Court cupboard, probably Virginia, 1640–60. (Wadsworth Atheneum.)

and, indeed, were used in the colonies after they were outmoded in Europe.[32]

Evaluation: An evaluation of the 1680 court cupboard begins with a comparison of court cupboards in general with other American furniture forms of the period. Four conclusions can be formed. First, the court cupboard was one of the largest, most intricate, most profusely ornamented, and most sophisticated pieces of furniture made at this time. Second, it was the most expensive American-made furniture form of the period.[33] Third, in its vocabulary of ornament, the court cupboard might well have been "the most impressive manifestation of Renaissance ideas (however distorted) that found its way into seventeenth-century New England parlors." Fourth, no other American furniture forms of this date show a more developed sense of the early Jacobean style. Therefore, by Essex County standards of 1680, the 1680 court cupboard can be considered avant-garde. As a result the 1680 court cupboard and its fellows were the most important pieces of seventeenth-century furniture made in New England.

Compared to other court cupboards of the same quarter century (Figs. 9, 10, 11), the 1680 court cupboard stands out as one of the largest, most imposing, and most handsomely designed and ornamented of all these examples, with perhaps the finest workmanship. The 1680 court cupboard does share a number of decorative details with other Essex County court cupboards and chests of the same date. Three so closely resemble it in their overhanging central shelves with pendants that Irving P. Lyon concluded that they all "came from the same hand." Richard H. Randall calls attention to three others (Fig. 10) that closely resemble it in having similar balusters and ball feet and a similar arrangement of molded panels and split spindles. One other court cupboard and a chest from Essex County have been found with exactly identical paneled door designs.[34] Indeed, there seems to

[32] Frederick S. Robinson, *English Furniture* (London: Methuen & Co., 1905), p. 91; Joseph Aronson, *The Encyclopedia of Furniture* (New York: Crown Publishers, 1965), p. 187; Lockwood, *Colonial Furniture,* p. 96; Helen Comstock, *American Furniture* (New York: Viking Press, 1962), p. 13.

[33] Bed "furniture," often consisting of important fabrics, could be worth five times as much as a court cupboard Lovell, "Background of the Court Cupboard," p. 2.

[34] Lyon, "Oak Furniture of Ipswich," pp. 322–23; Richard H. Randall, Jr., *American Furniture in the Museum of Fine Arts, Boston* (Boston: Museum of Fine Arts, 1965), p. 29.

FIG. 10. Thomas Dennis (attributed), court cupboard. Ipswich, Mass., 1684. H. 53⅝″, W. 48½″, D. 20⅜″. (Winterthur 57.542.)

FIG. 11. Court cupboard, Essex County (Ipswich-Beverly area), Mass., 1680–90. H. 55½″, W. 49⅛″, D. 19⅞″. (Museum of Fine Arts, Boston, Bequest of Charles Hitchcock Tyler.)

have been a school of Essex County case furniture utilizing applied ornament in the last quarter of the seventeenth century.

All the court cupboards show a strong family resemblance to somewhat earlier English work. Compared to similar pieces made in western Europe, the 1680 cupboard is somewhat provincial, less sophisticated than work done in Antwerp one hundred years earlier, in Amsterdam fifty years earlier, or London twenty-five years earlier. Yet the American forms exhibit some divergences from European pieces. The overhang, which adds a dramatic shift of planes to the Essex County court cupboard, has not yet been found in English examples.[35]

Cultural Analysis: Cultural analysis of the 1680 court cupboard focuses on its functions, five of which can be identified. Randle Holme, in his *Academy of Armory* of 1688, lists the court cupboard as among those "things necessary for and belonging to a dineing Rome." Inventories also place it in the other rooms, halls, parlors, and chambers where eating took place. Its utility function was threefold—to provide surfaces for the display of decorative eating and drinking vessels; to act as a service table; and to provide storage space. George Chapman's comedy of 1611, *May Day,* suggests what some of the vessels displayed might be. "And so for the feast, you have your court cupboards planted with flagons, cans, cups, beakers, bowls, goblets, basins, and ewers." Nicholas Davison's inventory, Charlestown, Massachusetts, 1664–65, mentions "A Court Cubboard with Cubbord Cloath, glases and Earthenware."[36] Indeed the court cupboard assumes the possession of a number of household articles worthy of display. The storage function, for utensils, not food, was provided by the enclosed area and the two drawers, which were probably designed to contain tablecloths and napkins. Some of the enclosed storage spaces were fitted with locks to prevent theft (Figs. 2, 8, 10).

In addition to its utility function, the court cupboard served as a "vehicle of delight."[37] The power and beauty of its design, the variety and imaginative richness of its ornament, and the textures of its woods all made it an object that "demands to be experienced aesthetically."[38] Third, the court cupboard had an important communication function in its statement of status. In England, many late-Tudor and Jacobean court cupboards were made of walnut and richly carved and inlaid "as befitted ceremonial pieces." In New England inventories these forms were found only among the better sort —magistrates, clergy, merchants, large landowners, and so on. Court cupboards were expensive, large, highly ornamental, stylish, quite likely the most striking object in a room, and certainly the most important piece of case furniture that a New Englander could own. They connoted wealth, sophistication, luxury, business success, possibly to the Puritan even election to salvation. They did not represent an efficient utilization of space—the trapezoidal enclosed area limited storage—and one furniture historian has referred to the court cupboard as "that rare, expensive, and virtually useless piece of vanity furniture." Wallace Nutting suggested that "people aspired to own a court cupboard as a token of assured position in society." Charles Montgomery liked to call the court cupboard "the Cadillac of the seventeenth century." To Peter Woodbury's guests, the court cupboard said, "This is what I, Peter Woodbury, have achieved."[39]

Beyond its communication of status, the court cupboard served, through its style and ornament, as a vehicle of expression of the early Jacobean aesthetic and ethos with its special combination of late-medieval forms and Renaissance-mannerist ornament. "It spoke of contemporary English and Continental decorative developments as no other artifact of its date did or could."[40]

Finally, the court cupboard in Essex County may well have served as a symbol of the New Englander's participation in the English heritage, a substantial affirmation of ties with English culture and society at its middle class best that were not broken but were merely transplanted. Thus it served as a means of transforming the impersonal new environment of New England's "howling wilderness"

---

[35] Forman, conversations with author.

[36] Fastnedge, "Furniture," p. 35; Symonds, "Dyning Parlor," p. 16; Lyon, *Colonial Furniture of New England,* pp. 35, 38, 42, 44.

[37] Theodore Meyer Greene, *The Arts and the Art of Criticism* (Princeton: Princeton University Press, 1940), p. 7.

[38] Panofsky, *Meaning in the Visual Arts,* p. 39.

[39] Fastnedge, "Furniture," p. 35; Lyon, *Colonial Furniture,* pp. 35, 42; Forman, "Case Furniture of Essex County," p. 74; Wallace Nutting, *Furniture Treasury,* 2 vols. (Framingham, Mass.: Old American Co., 1928), 1:190; Montgomery, lecture on the seventeenth century for Art History 801, University of Delaware.

[40] Lovell, "Background of the Court Cupboard."

into a personal setting of rich cultural meaning that offered reinforcement and security.

Cultural analysis of the 1680 court cupboard can be extended in several ways by a sampling operation. Since drawer construction is a key variable in identifying the provenance, maker, and possibly even the dating of case pieces, the 1680 court cupboard might be classified through a typology based on this construction feature.[41] In this example the fifteen pieces of seventeenth-century New England case furniture in the Winterthur collection are used as a sample of New England case furniture of the period. Of the seven or eight possible characteristics that might be used in analyzing drawer construction, two important ones are how the sides of the drawer are joined to the front and rear. The joinery techniques involved can be described and graphed in terms of nine variables (Tables 1, 2).

The representation of drawer construction leads to the hypothesis, duly qualified by the small size of the sample and the limited number of variables selected, that the drawer construction of the 1680 court cupboard (rabbeted-overlap) represents one of the two most common forms used in seventeenth-century New England case furniture. Since all court cupboards did not utilize exactly the same techniques of drawer construction (the three in the sample fall into three different categories, with the single cupboard in a fourth), the analysis suggests a considerable lack of standardization in craft practice, although all of the five examples positively identified as of Essex County (including Salem) provenance fall into two of the nine categories, i.e. either the rabbeted-overlap or the rabbeted-rabbeted (which together make up 59 percent of the total). The rabbeting technique was the one preferred during that period since drawer sides in 86 percent of the sample were joined to the front by rabbeting rather than by dovetailing.

A sample could also be used to form a chronology of court cupboards, which might yield interesting conclusions about changes and priorities in the selection of woods, construction techniques, design, and size, and might identify regional preferences of construction. With a large enough sample of court cupboards and enough identifying data, a

statistical analysis could produce extremely useful correlations between court cupboard ownership and income, occupation, religious affiliation, rural-urban residence, and geographical location.

Product analysis of the 1680 court cupboard seeks to account for its material, construction, design,

Table 1: Variants of Joining Drawer Sides to Drawer Front and Rear in Seventeenth-Century New England Case Furniture

---

Variant AB: How the sides of the drawer are joined to the front

a. rabbeted (by letting a rabbet into the front, and the side let into the rabbet and nailed).

b. rabbeted from higher (same as above but with the front an inch or two higher than the sides or rear).

c. 1 dovetail (the use of one large dovetail, wherein the wedge-shaped tenon is on the side and the mortise is cut into the end of the front).

Variant AC: How the sides of the drawer are joined to the rear

a. rabbeted (the side can be rabbeted into the rear).

b. overlap (the side to overlap the rear, butted and nailed).

c. overlapped (the side to be overlapped by the rear, butted and nailed).

---

and function by exploring how each of these was conditioned by its culture. Essex County, Massachusetts, in the late seventeenth century, can be described as a homogeneous, English, yeoman, Puritan culture rooted in the life-style of provincial, rural England, perhaps especially of East Anglia. Conservative reliance on tradition was the rule, innovation the exception. The plans of its towns, the style of its architecture and painting, the spirit of its laws, the organization of its family life, its language, literature, and religion expressed a conscious continuity with what had been known in the home country. What had been known in rural England was strongly marked by late medieval traditions and forms surviving in Tudor-Jacobean design.

In the case of the material of the court cupboard, the choice of oak for the predominant wood resulted chiefly from the Essex County joiner's reliance on English traditional preference for oak, the choice of red oak, from its local abundance. Red oak was largely clear of knots and easy to work when green. The construction techniques of riving, framing and pinning, joining by mortise and tenon, and turning were all traditional techniques

---

[41] This sample and the analysis of drawer construction that follows are based on Robert Trent, "Quantitative Analysis of Seventeenth-Century Pre-William and Mary American Drawer Construction" (seminar report for History 802, University of Delaware, 1972).

brought to New England by emigrating craftsmen. The greater reliance on mill-sawing was due to the limited labor supply, the presence of abundant water power and forests, and a tolerance for techno-logical advance. The use of small rectangular panels, which appear on the 1680 court cupboard, was particularly characteristic of East Anglian case construction. The joiner's use of the mortise and

Table 2: Correlation of Fifteen Seventeenth-Century New England Case Pieces in the Winterthur Collection with Nine Possible Types of Drawer Construction

	B		
rabbeted	4 examples	5 examples	2 examples
rabbeted front higher	1 example		1 example
1 dovetail	1 example		1 example
A	rabbeted	overlap	overlapped	C

Summary

rabbeted-rabbeted	26.66%
rabbeted-overlap	33.33%
rabbeted-overlapped	13.33%
rabbeted front higher-rabbeted	6.67%
rabbeted front higher-overlap	0
rabbeted front higher-overlapped	6.67%
1 dovetail-rabbeted	6.67%
1 dovetail-overlap	0
1 dovetail-overlapped	6.67%
	100.00%

Note: The axis AB indicates how the drawer is let into the front, while the AC axis indicates how the sides are joined to the rear.

tenon, which goes back to the later Middle Ages, had, by the late 1600s, been supplanted to a great extent in London by the cabinetmaker's technique of dovetailing, but mortise and tenon construction was still very much used in rural England. There were probably thirty joiners and one hundred carpenters working in Essex County who could use these rural techniques of construction. In design, the choice of the court cupboard form, its dimensions, its style and ornament were all imitative of English forms known by the yeoman class emigrating from England. Likewise the court cupboard continued to fulfill traditional English functions.

A content analysis of the 1680 court cupboard is a selection from the total number of statements we can make correlating what we know about its history with what we know about its material, construction, design, and function. Some statements tell us about the maker. In 1680 in Essex County there was at least one joiner capable of making this complex and expensive example of Jacobean case furniture. The high quality of workmanship indicates a well-trained craftsman with good tools and a thorough knowledge of joinery and either skill in turning or access to a turner. Other statements tell us about the owner. In 1680 in Essex County there was at least one man, Peter Woodbury, who wanted to own this sophisticated, expensive example of Jacobean case furniture designed in the latest fashion (for Essex County), a furniture form generally recognized as a status symbol. He was one of the wealthiest men in his community, and this furniture form was one of the costliest items in his inventory. The owner of an estate of £1,000 in Essex County in 1680 could own this court cupboard; in England he might not have been able to do so. Thus, the court cupboard reflects some of the aspects of social mobility usually attributed to the American experience.

Still other statements of content give evidence of the culture. The parallel saw marks on the sycamore indicate that it was mill-sawn, which predicates the existence of a sawmill in the region. The existence of an economically substantial patron ordering a piece of vanity furniture from a highly trained craftsman suggests a relatively high standard of living in late seventeenth-century Essex County. This piece of furniture (of which there are several other very similar examples from the same county) presents a combination of traditional and innovative features—traditional material and methods of construction, innovative features in the use

of sycamore, mill sawing, and the overhang. Judged in terms of other extant furniture forms of Essex County of this date, as far as current research has gone, the 1680 court cupboard is avant-garde. What was avant-garde for the tastemakers of Essex County in 1680 was a mixture of late medieval elements that did not yet reflect the baroque influences coming into popularity in contemporary England. Relative to what English yeoman farmers were buying and owning, this piece was up to date; relative to what was avant-garde in England and the continent, it was somewhat dated.

Interpretation: Interpretation of the significance of the 1680 cupboard will be as various as the interests and preoccupations of those who look at it. For persons who feel that statistics and money values are particularly revealing, the significance of this case piece might lie in the fact that it is the largest, heaviest, and most expensive item of furniture to be found in a seventeenth-century New England home. For persons interested in the image of New England Puritanism, the importance of this court cupboard could lie in its forceful revelation that, however plain the exterior of the yeoman house and the meetinghouse might have been, the interior of the home could be furnished with visually exciting and even sensuous forms that indicate a lively interest in what was fashionable in England. These Puritans of Essex County definitely did not reject the "vanities" and "conceits" of their homeland, but obviously enjoyed and emulated the heavy opulence and fancifulness of the Jacobean aesthetic. From the standpoint of style, the court cupboard represented more of a transition from medieval to renaissance usages than Puritan town planning, architecture, painting, education, or family organization of the same date. Persons interested in the "sea change" brought by the voyage across the Atlantic might find the meaning of this furniture form in the fact that the man who could afford it in Essex County would probably not have been able to afford it in East Anglia.

For students of seventeenth-century New England culture, the relevance of the cupboard might lie in the fact that, while it definitely includes some innovative features, its material, construction, design, and function are overwhelmingly conservative and represent an effort not so much to adapt to the novelties of the New World experience as to affirm familiar and prestigious Old World forms. It further suggests an ethos marked by transition from predominantly late medieval elements to Renaissance ones, a transition from a first- and second-generation preference for carved ornament to a third-generation preference for applied ornament, and an elite consumer's market for vanity furniture serving as status symbols. From the standpoint of frontier influence and colonial-provincial attitudes in the seventeenth century, this elaborate and finely wrought court cupboard vividly demonstrates how far its culture was from the subsistence level and what a distance the third generation, in Essex County, had moved itself psychologically from "the howling wilderness" that we are sometimes led to believe was its inescapable environment.

All or parts of the approach utilized above in analyzing a 1680 court cupboard should be applicable to other artifacts. Furthermore, it is hoped that the reasons advanced for the need of a model for artifact study, the model presented above, and its application to the cupboard will contribute to the development of a more systematic study of material culture. Interest in such study is extensive and growing, the related disciplines contributing to this study are numerous and substantial, the literature bearing on the field is extensive, and the rewards of such study are promising. Certainly the study of material culture deserves to take its place among other humanistic disciplines.

Furniture Craftsmen in Delaware Records

Harold B. Hancock

A WEALTH of information about Delaware turners, chairmakers, joiners, and cabinetmakers can be found in the Delaware estate inventories, tax assessment lists, deeds, orphans' court records, and indenture agreements, most of which are housed at the Hall of Records in Dover, Delaware. These records provide data to supplement the able accounts of Delaware furniture craftsmen by William MacPherson Hornor, Leon de Valinger, Charles Dorman, and Polly Scafidi.[1] The use of these records further illuminates the history of furniture making in Delaware during its golden age and indicates the many ways these craftsmen served the community before the decline of the art around 1850. Through these sources more than 200 previously unknown furniture craftsmen, who worked in the state before 1850, have been identified as well as more than 150 unknown apprentices, and new information has been found about previously known furniture craftsmen. The names of the cratfsmen working in Kent and Sussex counties are of special interest because these counties lacked local newspapers in the period before 1850.

The great majority of the eighteenth-century residents of the three lower counties on the Delaware, like those in the other colonies, were farmers. Isolated by bad roads, lacking ready cash, and unable to locate skilled labor, they became jacks-of-all-trades. Inventories of the goods and chattels of deceased persons frequently contain references to carpenter's tools, joiner's tools, cooper's tools, blacksmith's tools, shoemaker's tools, spinning wheels, bullet molds, candle molds, and spoon molds, demonstrating the versatility necessary for rural householders.

In order to practice their many skills, colonial craftsmen often bought tools manufactured in England. A general store such as the one operated by Joseph Peters in Wilmington prior to 1748 with a huge inventory amounting to £2,415.13.6 could provide most of the items needed by furniture craftsmen. In addition to cutlery, cloth, clothing, shoes, books, shoemaker's tools, and saddler's hammers, Peters's stock also included locks, H hinges, chisels, gouges, files, saws, planes, carpenter's tools, turner's tools, and joiner's bits. Items relating to the common crafts have been extracted from this unusual document and printed in Appendix 1.[2]

As the countryside became more settled and transportation and communication improved, and as more skilled labor was trained or emigrated from Europe, specialists in the manufacture of furniture appeared. The Delaware records provide many examples of the way specialties in furniture making developed. During most of the eighteenth century these craftsmen were called joiners, house joiners, or shop joiners. As early as 1704, Henry Bains was referred to in a Kent County deed as a joiner. The 1735 inventory of the goods and chattels of John Savage of New Castle County indicates the variety of tools, including several types of planes, saws,

[1] W. M. Hornor, Jr., "James McDowell, A Delaware Cabinetmaker," *Antiquarian* 15, no. 5 (Nov. 1930): 64; Leon de Valinger, "John Janvier, Delaware Cabinetmaker," *Antiques* 41, no. 1 (Jan. 1942): 37–42; Charles G. Dorman, "Delaware Cabinetmakers and Allied Artisans, 1655–1855," *Delaware History* 9, no. 2 (Oct. 1960): 1–107 (hereafter cited as Dorman); Polly Jose Scafidi, "Notes on Delaware Cabinetmakers," *Delaware History* 14, no. 4 (Oct. 1971): 262–78 (hereafter cited as Scafidi).

[2] New Castle County Inventories, Joseph Peters, Jan. 25, 1748, Division of Historical and Cultural Affairs, Hall of Records, Dover, Delaware. All inventories used in this study are located at the Hall of Records in Dover and will be cited according to county as NCC (New Castle County), KC (Kent County), or SC (Sussex County).

turning tools and planks, in a colonial joiner's shop.[3]

Occasionally eighteenth-century inventories mention turners and chairmakers. The 1777 inventory of Abraham Bryan, turner, of St. George's Hundred in New Castle County, is similar to John Savage's.[4] Timothy Hanson of Wilmington, previously known as a cabinetmaker, was manufacturing chairs exclusively at the time of his death in 1798. His extraordinary inventory (Appendix 2) lists such a large quantity of chairs that he must have employed a sizable staff and quantity production methods. His garret and third floor contained more than 100 Windsor and bamboo chairs. The contents of his shop included 34 chairs, 34 stools, 462 chair bottoms, 362 walnut arms, and 236½ feet of chair planks. Unfortunately the records do not indicate how he retailed his chairs.[5]

By 1790 Wilmington had become the center of furniture manufacturing in Delaware. The Wilmington collector of customs reported to Alexander Hamilton in 1791 that nine joiners and thirteen spinning-wheel and chairmakers lived in the vicinity. Benefiting from the enterprise of merchants, traders, and millers and located at the junction of the Brandywine and Christiana rivers, Wilmington was the largest town in the state and an important port. Sufficient wealth had developed. so that residents could afford to buy fine furniture.[6]

The term cabinetmaker appears only rarely in Delaware records prior to the American Revolution, but by 1800 it was widely used. *A Directory and Register for the Year 1814 . . . of the Borough of Wilmington and Brandywine* contained no joiners, one spinning-wheel maker, several turners and chairmakers, and numerous cabinetmakers. The shops of these craftsmen were concentrated on lower Market and Shipley streets.[7] Ziba Ferriss is a good example of a Wilmington cabinetmaker who, by his superior craftsmanship, had attracted a large clientele after the American Revolution. The 1794 inventory of his possessions (Appendix 3) lists such a number and variety of items—ranging from mahogany banisters and dough troughs to bureaus, bedsteads, and tables—that he must have employed several journeymen in addition to the two apprentices listed by the appraisers. His shop contained five workbenches.[8] In lower New Castle County the cabinetmaker John Janvier, Sr., of Odessa, established an enviable reputation for distinctive work. His inventory of 1801 (Appendix 4) is unusual in that it included such items as gold leaf, chair patterns, beeswax, a lockmaker's lathe, and seven kinds of wood.[9]

A study of the industrial census of 1850 revealed that furniture craftsmen in New Castle County were more likely to own larger shops with greater investment of capital and more apprentices than those in lower Delaware.[10] But the coming of the industrial revolution, the expansion of the railroad, and the use of steam power and mass production techniques in factories lessened the need for craftsmen, first in Wilmington and then in the southern part of the state. In 1847 Jesse Urmy of New Castle County accepted an apprentice to learn the art of a wood machinist—a skill looking more to the new age than to tradition. Twelve years later Urmy was listed in the state directory of 1859 as a Wilmington manufacturer of reapers and mowers. In the same year the well-known Wilmington cabinetmaker, William G. Jones, advertised his wares for sale at his "Cheap Furniture Warerooms" at the corner of Front and Shipley streets. The age of individual craftsmanship had departed, although the state directory of 1859 listed sixteen cabinetmakers in New Castle County.[11]

---

[3] NCC Inventories, John Savage, July 12, 1735.

[4] NCC Inventories, Andrew Bryan, Dec. 19, 1777.

[5] NCC Inventories, Timothy Hanson, Dec. 18, 1798.

[6] On the rise of Wilmington, see John A. Munroe, "The Philadelawareans: The Relations between Philadelphia and Delaware in the Late Eighteenth Century," *Pennsylvania Magazine of History and Biography* 69, no. 2 (Apr. 1945): 128–49; and Sara Guertler Farris, "Wilmington's Maritime Commerce, 1775–1807," *Delaware History* 14, no. 1 (Apr. 1970): 22–51.

[7] R. Porter, *A Directory and Register for the Year 1814 . . . of the Borough of Wilmington and Brandywine* (Wilmington: by the author, 1814), hereafter cited as *Wilmington Directory, 1814*. See [H. Clay Reed, comp.], *Readings in Delaware History: Economic Development* (Newark, Del.:

University of Delaware, Department of History and Political Science, 1939), p. 39. (Mimeographed.)

[8] NCC Inventories, Ziba Ferriss, May 15, 16, 1794.

[9] NCC Inventories, John Janvier, Jan. 31, 1801.

[10] Scafidi, pp. 262–66.

[11] NCC Indenture Book, 1847–53, p. 15, Division of Historical and Cultural Affairs, Hall of Records, Dover, Delaware; all indenture books used in this study are located in the Hall of Records and will be cited according to county as NCC Indenture Book, KC Indenture Book, or SC Indenture Book. See William H. Boyd and Andrew Boyd, eds., *Delaware State Directory, 1859–60* (Wilmington: by the authors, 1859), pp. 14, 173, 202–3 (hereafter *Delaware State Directory, 1859*).

The day of the individual craftsman who supplied the needs of the adjacent community lingered longest in Sussex County. Here spinning wheels were still being produced in the 1840s. Railroads did not reach the southern border of the state until 1859. The industrial revolution did not have the same impact on the southern part of the state as in northern New Castle County, with its close economic and social ties to Philadelphia. As late as 1859, fourteen cabinetmakers worked in Sussex County and nine in Kent County.[12]

The author's research has established that Delaware craftsmen frequently produced more than one type of furniture and followed more than one specific trade. In 1757 John Bell of Dover agreed to instruct an apprentice in "the Traid art and mystery of Shop Joiner or Cabinetmaker." Bell is referred to in a 1768 Kent County deed as a shop joiner; another deed in the same year calls him a cabinetmaker. Although the terms originally implied different techniques, they came to be used interchangeably with "cabinetmaker" finally succeeding the older term "joiner." Bell was the earliest Delaware craftsman to be called cabinetmaker. John Orr of Lewes is listed in Sussex County deeds at the turn of the century as a house carpenter, a shop joiner, and a house joiner. In a document dealing with the manumission of a slave in 1795, he is again called a house joiner, and in a similar manumission in 1798, he is referred to as a cabinetmaker.[13] Some clockmakers might also be called cabinetmakers. The inventory of George Crow of Wilmington (Appendix 5), distinguished clockmaker (see Fig. 1), reveals that at the time of his death in 1762 he had in his shop three unfinished clockcases and joiner's tools, besides a quantity of pine and mahogany boards.[14]

In the nineteenth century, labels became even

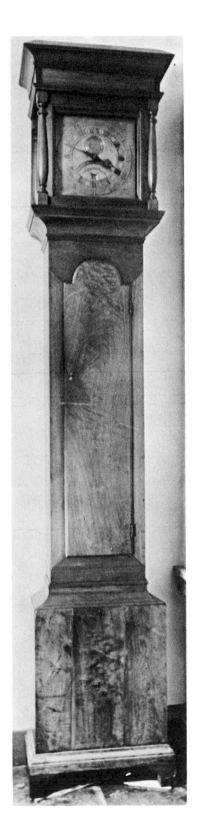

FIG. 1. George Crow, tall clock. Wilmington, Del., 1744. Walnut; H. 89", W. 18", D. 10". (Collection of Charles G. Dorman: Photo, Winterthur.)

---

[12] *Delaware State Directory,* 1859, pp. 202–3.

[13] KC loose indentures, Mar. 29, 1757, John Bell; Dorman, p. 52; Kent County Deed Book, S 1, pp. 249, 338, Kent County Courthouse, Dover, Delaware. All Kent County deed books are housed at the Kent County Courthouse in Dover. The deed books of New Castle and of Sussex counties used in this study are located in the Division of Historical and Cultural Affairs, Hall of Records, Dover, Delaware. Hereafter deed books will be cited as NCC Deed Book, KC Deed Book, and SC Deed Book. For John Orr, see SC Deed Book, P 15, pp. 259, 503; X 22, p. 468; Pennsylvania Abolition Society Manumissions, John Orr, May 27, 1795, June 7, 1798, Historical Society of Pennsylvania, Philadelphia, Pa.

[14] NCC Inventories, George Crow, Dec. 4, 1762.

FIG. 2. Purnel Hall, spinning wheel. Milford, Del., ca. 1850. Oak; H. 40½″, W. 21″, D. 7″. Stamped "P. Hall." on top of flat center section. (State of Delaware, courtesy Division of Historical and Cultural Affairs.)

more blurred. Elias James, for example, was indentured in 1829 to Perry Prettyman, chairmaker and spinning-wheel maker in Sussex County. The master never engaged in any other business, but by 1835 James accepted his first apprentice in cabinetmaking. Purnel Hall of Milford, mentioned as a cabinetmaker in indenture agreements, whose shop inventory is printed in Appendix 6, supplied the community with a variety of cabinets, chairs, cradles, bureaus, tables, and coffins prior to 1848. He also made a handsome spinning wheel stamped with his name (Fig. 2).[15] Samuel C. Walker was a cooper in Mill Creek Hundred in the first half of the nineteenth century, but he also made clockcases as evidenced by the clock bearing the name "S. C. Walker" in large letters on its face, which is owned by a descendant (Fig. 3). The walnut case is plain, but handsome, and the clock face is decorated with four gold shells in the corners.[16]

Hunting out new information about furniture makers in dusty records is as exciting as detective

work. But locating the names is only the beginning. The next step is to match the names with samples of furniture. Research concerning James G. Hendrickson (1801–1895), a Kent County cabinetmaker, resulted in the location of a signed Hendrickson bureau (Figs. 4, 5). The bureau, marked in chalk on the bottom of the lowest drawer, "october 11th 1819 / This was made and / James G Hendr[i]ckson / is the Builder," must have been one of the first pieces executed by Hendrickson, who was only eighteen in 1819. The dominant features of the bureau are Hepplewhite. The walnut chest has four graduated drawers trimmed with beading, and the straight front is decorated with inlay at the top and bottom.

Hendrickson spent most of his life in Frederica, Murderkill Hundred, Kent County. By 1830 he was married and the father of three children. The county indenture books show that in 1831 James G. Hendrixson concluded an apprenticeship agreement with Henry Hendrixson, age sixteen, probably a relative. Since misspellings are common in these records, there is no reason to doubt that James G. Hendrickson and James G. Hendrixson were the same person. Despite the merit of his early work-

[15] SC Indenture Book, A 1, p. 92; C, p. 104; G, p. 365; KC Inventories, Purnel Hall, Aug. 15, 1848.

[16] New Castle County deeds, Nov. 11, 1795, Jan. 21, 1803, in the possession of Mrs. Sara Pennington Evans.

FIG. 3. Samuel C. Walker, tall clock. Mill Creek Hundred, New Castle County, Del., ca. 1825. Walnut; H. 93⅝", W. 20⅛", D. 10¾". (Collection of James Henry Walker III: Photo, Winterthur.)

manship, Hendrickson did not prosper. He owned no real estate and little personal property and did not continue to work as a cabinetmaker, for he is not listed in any other indenture agreement or in the 1859 state directory list of cabinetmakers. He is probably the James G. "Henderson" of Frederica, born in Maryland, listed in both the census of 1850 and the state directory of 1874 as a carpenter. He died in the Kent County Almshouse in 1895, aged 94, and is buried in Potter's Field.[17]

The aim of this new listing of Delaware furniture craftsmen is to stimulate other students of the subject to search out still more information about furniture makers and their products.[18] In order to simplify the alphabetical listing of furniture craftsmen, each entry is headed by the name of the craftsman followed by his occupation as designated in the records of the period, his place of work, his birth and death dates or working dates shown in the documents, and the sources used in identifying the craftsman. In some cases additional comments are added after the sources. Appendix 7 contains a listing of all the Delaware apprentices mentioned in the records. An asterisk indicates apprentices who later worked in Delaware as master craftsmen.

[17] KC Indenture Book, C, p. 32; J. Thomas Scharf, *History of Delaware, 1609–1888*, 2 vols. (Philadelphia: L. J. Richards & Co., 1888), 2:1159. James G. Hendrickson was mentioned as a long-time resident of Frederica born November 4, 1801. Henry Hendrixson may have migrated to Indiana. See Betty Lawson Walters, *Furniture Makers of Indiana, 1793–1850* (Indianapolis: Indiana Historical Society, 1972), p. 110. "Henry Hendrickson, cabinetmaker. Born c. 1815, Delaware; w. 1850, Parke Co." U.S. Census of Population, Delaware, 1830, p. 288; U.S. Census of Population, Delaware, 1850, p. 220; Marriage Bonds, Elizabeth Hurlock to James G. Hendrickson, Dec. 29, 1824, vol. 21, p. 363; Burial Records, James G. Hendrickson, Kent County Almshouse, July 15, 1894, Division of Historical and Cultural Affairs, Hall of Records, Dover, Delaware. Also see Kent County tax assessment records for Mispillion Hundred for 1819 and for Murderkill Hundred for 1816–18, 1824–28, 1830–32, where his name is spelled variously Hendrixen, Hendrixson, and Hendrickson. All tax records cited in this study are located in the Division of Historical and Cultural Affairs, Hall of Records, Dover, Delaware. In William H. Boyd, ed., *The Delaware State Directory and Gazeteer* [for 1874–75] (Wilmington: Commercial Printing Company, 1874), p. 543, James Hendrickson is listed as a carpenter in Frederica.

[18] In connection with my research on Delaware furniture craftsmen, I would like to express appreciation for the assistance of Mrs. Margaret Chambers, Miss Elizabeth Moyne, and Mr. Mike Richards of the Delaware Division of Historical and Cultural Affairs. Mrs. D. Anthony Potter of Lewes and Miss Ruthanna Hindes of Hockessin graciously provided information about several cabinetmakers.

Fig. 4. James G. Hendrickson, bureau. Kent County, Del., 1819. Walnut; H. 37″, W. 38½″, D. 20¼″. (Privately owned: Photo, Thurston Studio.)

Fig. 5. Chalk inscription on bureau in figure 4: "october 11th 1819 / This was made and / James G Hendr[i]ckson / is the Builder." (Photo, Thurston Studio.)

Listing of Delaware Furniture Craftsmen

Eli Abbott
Carpenter and joiner
Sussex County, 1838
SC Indenture Book, D, p. 205

Elijah Adams
House carpenter and joiner
Northwest Fork Hundred, 1789
SC Deed Book, O 14, p. 320

Thomas Adams
House joiner and carpenter
Sussex County, 1834
SC Indenture Book, B 2, p. 310

Charles Allen
House carpenter and cabinetmaker
White Clay Creek Hundred, 1796
NCC Deed Book, O 2, p. 509

Eli Allen
Cabinetmaker
Wilmington, 1813
NCC Deed Book, N 3, p. 39

William H. Anderson
House carpenter and joiner
Sussex County, 1834–35
SC Indenture Book, C, pp. 45, 78

John Annit
Spinning-wheel maker
Sussex County, 1754
SC Deed Book, I 9, p. 40

William Arnell
House carpenter and joiner
Lewes, 1789
SC Deed Book, O 14, pp. 24, 93

Goved Atkinson
House carpenter and joiner
Kent County, 1835
KC Indenture Book, F, p. 32

Henry Bains
Joiner
Kent County, 1704
KC Deed Book, D 1, p. 31

Joshua Baker
Chairmaker
New Castle County, 1749
NCC Deed Book, Q 11, p. 303; New Castle County Orphans Court Book, C, p. 109, Hall of Records, Dover, Del. All Orphans Court records are located at the Hall of Records except those for Sussex County after 1770, which are housed in the Sussex County Courthouse, Georgetown, Del. All Orphans Court Books are hereafter cited by county, NCC, SC, and KC

John Baldwin
Cabinetmaker
Brandywine Hundred, 1825
NCC Brandywine Hundred Tax List, John Baldwin, 1825

William Baldwin
Cabinetmaker
Christiana Hundred, 1825–28
NCC Christiana Hundred Tax List, William Baldwin, 1825; NCC Indenture Book, 1826–29, p. 179

Abraham Barber
Joiner
Kent County, 1729
KC Deed Book, I 1, p. 186

John Bell
Shop joiner and cabinetmaker
Dover, 1757–68
KC loose indentures, Mar. 29, 1757; KC Deed Book, S 1, pp. 249, 338; Dorman, p. 13

James Bellach
Shop joiner
Dover, 1768–76
KC Deed Book, S 1, pp. 47, 70

Isaac Bewley
Carpenter and joiner
Christiana Hundred, 1806–12
NCC Deed Book, D 3, p. 89; L 3, p. 33

John Blackshair
Carpenter and joiner
Little Creek Hundred, 1804
KC Deed Book, I 2, p. 4

John Boggs
  Joiner
  Murderkill Hundred, 1763–64
  KC, Murderkill Hundred Tax List, John Boggs,
    1763, 1764; KC Inventories, John Boggs, Oct.
    23, 1765 .
  The 1765 inventory of Boggs's possessions in-
    cluded "a parcel of carpenter's tools."

Clement S. Bonsall
  Wood turner
  New Castle County, 1845
  NCC Indenture Book, 1836–54, pp. 464–65;
    Lewis Wilson, ed., *The Wilmington Directory
    for the Year 1845* (Wilmington: Lewis Wilson,
    1845) hereafter *Wilmington Directory, 1845*

Richard Bradley
  Joiner
  Sussex County, 1804
  SC Deed Book, 24, p. 253

Thomas O. Bradley
  Joiner
  Sussex County, 1779
  SC Deed Book, M 12, p. 275; SC Inventories,
    Thomas Bradley, Jan. 7, 1782

Jonathan Brady
  Joiner
  Mispillion Hundred, 1776
  KC Deed Book, R 1, p. 108

Joshua Brasure
  Cabinetmaker
  Tunnell's Store and Sussex County, 1849–52
  SC Indenture Book, F, p. 329; Scafidi, p. 275;
    Delaware State Directory, 1859
  Brasure was listed in the 1859 state directory as a
    furniture dealer

Henry Brereton
  Turner
  Sussex County, 1728–29
  SC Deed Book, F 6, p. 319

Andrew Brian
  Turner
  St. George's Hundred, 1727
  NCC Deed Book, H 1, p. 208

Andrew Bryan
  Joiner
  St. George's Hundred, 1762–77
  NCC Deed Book, U 1, p. 286; W 1, p. 467; NCC
    Inventories, Andrew Bryan, Dec. 19, 1777
  Andrew Bryan may be the "Andrew Brian" of
    1722 or his son. The inventory of Bryan's es-
    tate included a variety of saws, chisels, and
    planes as well as the book "Prices Carpenter."

James Buckingham
  Joiner
  Wilmington, 1793
  NCC Wills, J. Buckingham, Aug. 19, 1793 (all
    wills cited are in the Dover Hall of Records)

Richard Buckingham
  Joiner and cabinetmaker
  Wilmington, 1789–1802
  NCC Deed Book, S 2, p. 356; Z 2, p. 103

Benjamin Burleigh
  Turner
  Christiana Creek, 1728
  NCC Deed Book, I 1, p. 26

Isaac E. Burton
  Cabinetmaker
  Sussex County, 1838–50
  SC Indenture Book, D, pp. 207, 266; E, p. 430;
    F, p. 329; Scafidi, p. 266

Caleb Byrnes
  Cabinetmaker
  Wilmington and Stanton, 1732–94
  NCC Inventories, Caleb Byrnes, Apr. 23, 1794;
    Dorman, p. 17

John Caddy
  Chairmaker
  Sussex County, 1820
  U.S. Census of Population, Delaware, 1820, p.
    367

Andrew Caldwell, Jr.
  Turner and joiner
  Kent County, 1739
  KC Deed Book, M 1, pp. 43, 57

Campbell and Walls
  Turners and painters
  Duck Creek Hundred, 1850
  U.S. Census of Population, Delaware, 1850, p. 15
  The census lists this Kent County firm as en-
    gaged in the business of turning and painting.

Lemuel Carpenter
Chairmaker and spinning-wheel maker
Sussex County and Frederica, 1831
SC Indenture Book, B 2, pp. 107, 144

Thomas Cartmill
Turner
Brandywine Hundred, 1726–35
NCC Deed Book, H 1, p. 110; K 1, p. 406

Cornelius Carty
Joiner
St. George's Hundred, 1750
NCC Deed Book, Q 1, p. 424

Benjamin Chambers
Joiner
New Castle County, 1775
NCC Deed Book, B 2, pp. 353, 672

John Chambers
Joiner
Sussex County, 1722
SC Deed Book, F 6, p. 144

Gregg Chandler
Turner
Wilmington, 1845–50
NCC Indenture Book, 1847–53, pp. 139–40; 1849–54, p. 6; Dorman, p. 20

John Chapman
Joiner
Wilmington, 1749
NCC Deed Book, Q 1, p. 340

Jared Chesnut
Chairmaker
Wilmington, 1814–29
NCC Indenture Book, 1829–31, pp. 246–49; Dorman, pp. 20–21

John Clark
Joiner
Mispillion Hundred, 1756
KC, Mispillion Hundred Tax List, John Clark, 1756

Joshua Clark
Joiner
Mispillion Hundred, 1756
KC, Mispillion Hundred Tax List, Joshua Clark, 1756

Nehemiah Clark
Carpenter and joiner
Sussex County, 1754
SC Deed Book, I 9, p. 46

David Clayton
Chairmaker
Mill Creek Hundred, 1764
NCC Court of Quarter Sessions, May 1764, p. 14, Hall of Records, Dover
In 1764 the New Castle County Court of Quarter Sessions granted Peter Floyd's request that his indenture to Clayton be terminated since his master had left the area to avoid creditors.

James Cooper (Coupar)
House joiner and carpenter
White Clay Creek Hundred, 1771–79
NCC Deed Book, Z 1, p. 514; D 2, p. 233; NCC Orphans Court Book, F, p. 71

Samuel Corry
Joiner
Smyrna, 1758
KC Deed Book, S 1, p. 487

William Robinson Cotter
Cabinetmaker
New Castle County, 1829
NCC Indenture Book, 1829–31, pp. 138–39

Charles A. Cottingham
House joiner
Sussex County, 1850
U.S. Census of Population, Delaware, 1850, p. 197

John Cottingham
House joiner
Sussex County, 1850
U.S. Census of Population, Delaware, 1850, p. 197

Thomas B. Coursey
House carpenter and joiner
Kent County, 1831
KC loose indentures, 1831, Thomas B. Coursey

Isaac Cox
Chaise and chairmaker
Dover, 1771
Pennsylvania Gazette, June 13, 1771

Alexander Craig (Crage)
Joiner
Kent County, 1748–77
KC Deed Book, N 1, p. 218; KC Inventories, Alexander Craig, Dec. 21, 1777

Michael Crips
Joiner
Wilmington, 1797
NCC Deed Book, R 2, p. 211; T 2, p. 280

James Crosby
Spinning-wheel maker
Wilmington, 1814
Wilmington Directory, 1814, p. 15

George Crow
Clockmaker
Wilmington, 1740–62
NCC Inventories, George Crow, Dec. 4, 1762 (see Appendix 5)

Thomas Culbertson
Chairmaker
Mill Creek Hundred, 1786
NCC Deed Book, Z 2, p. 369

Joseph Cummins
Turner
New Castle County, 1850
U.S. Census of Population, Delaware, 1850, p. 225

William Danely
Turner
Sussex County, 1744
SC Wills, A 68, p. 11

John Davis
Turner
Pencader Hundred, 1743
NCC Deed Book, Q 1, p. 34

Isaac DeWees
Cabinetmaker
Kent County, 1775–1821
Pennsylvania Magazine of History and Biography 12 (1888), p. 35; KC, Murderkill Hundred Tax List, 1779; Leon de Valinger, ed., *Reconstruction 1790 Census of Delaware* (Washington: National Genealogical Society, 1954), p. 47; Ellen S. Rogers and Louise E. Easter, eds.,

1800 Census of Kent County, Delaware (Bladensburg, Md.: privately printed, 1959), p. 48; KC Administrations, Isaac DeWees, May 15, 1821.
DeWees served with Captain Craig's Marines in Philadelphia before he returned to live in Kent County, his birthplace.

Thomas Dickinson
House carpenter and joiner
Sussex County, 1747
SC Deed Book, H 8, p. 134

Edmund Dickoson
House carpenter and joiner
Sussex County, 1774
SC Deed Book, L 11, p. 393

Christopher Dingee
Joiner
Sussex County, 1730–50
Duck Creek Monthly Meeting, Marriage Records, C. Dingee to R. Elridge, p. 44, Pennsylvania Genealogical Society, Philadelphia; SC Deed Book G 7, p. 244; NCC Deed Book, Q 1, pp. 364–65

Obadiah Dingee
Joiner, house carpenter, and cabinetmaker
Wilmington, 1780–83
NCC Deed Book, F 2, p. 171; Z 2, pp. 274–75

Azael Dodd
Cabinetmaker
Indian River Hundred, 1836–50
SC Deed Book, C, p. 145; E, p. 348; Scafidi, p. 267

Isaac Dolby
Cabinetmaker
Camden, 1833–59
KC Deed Book, E, p. 32; G, p. 31; *Delaware State Directory,* 1859, p. 203; Scafidi, p. 267

Henry Downing
House carpenter and joiner
New Castle County, 1753–56
NCC Orphans Court Book, C, pp. 189, 255

John Eastwick
Chairmaker
Brandywine Hundred, 1809
NCC Deed Book, G 3, p. 207

Cornell Edgill
Joiner
Lewes, 1728–34
SC Deed Book, F 6, p. 315; G 7, p. 91

Solomon Edmonson
Shop joiner
Murderkill Hundred, 1779
KC Deed Book, W 1, p. 179

Jesse Eldridge
Joiner
Christiana Hundred, 1772–77
NCC Deed Book, C 2, p. 117; D 2, p. 272

Thomas B. Emory
Cabinetmaker
Dover, 1816
Delaware Gazette, June 20, 1816

Charles Empson
Joiner
New Castle County, 1728
NCC Deed Book, H 1, p. 257

James Erwin
Cabinetmaker
Wilmington, 1799
NCC Inventories, James Erwin, July 2, 1799;
   Dorman, p. 26

John Erwin
Joiner
Wilmington, 1762
NCC Deed Book, W 1, p. 89; Dorman, p. 26

Samuel Erwin
Joiner
Wilmington, 1797–98
NCC Deed Book, R 2, p. 148; NCC Inventories,
   Samuel Erwin, Dec. 26, 1798
Appraisers of Erwin's estate valued "all his car-
   penter Tools and Tool Cases" at $49.75; in
   addition his possessions included ten bamboo
   chairs, six Windsor chairs, six cherry chairs,
   and a frame shop worth $40.00.

John Evans
Cabinetmaker
White Clay Creek Hundred, 1806
NCC Deed Book, E 3, p. 358

Noel Evans
Joiner
Pencader Hundred, 1771
NCC Deed Book, Z 1, p. 426

James Ewing
Joiner
Kent County, 1739
KC Deed Book, M 1, p. 62

Alexander Farris
Cabinetmaker
Smyrna, 1831–59
KC Indenture Book, C, pp. 68, 87; E, pp. 109–10;
   I, p. 29; L, pp. 45, 56; Dorman, p. 25; Scafidi,
   p. 269

John Farris
Cabinetmaker
Kent County, 1842–50
KC Indenture Book, M, pp. 47–48; U.S. Census
   of Population, Delaware, 1850, p. 15

John Ferriss
Cabinetmaker
Wilmington, 1802
NCC Inventories, John Ferriss, Feb. 21, 1802;
   Dorman, pp. 28–30
Ferriss's inventory included unfinished cabinetwork, "three Pine Cupboards & Writing Desk
   in Shop," and walnut, gum, poplar, and mahogany boards. His "Joiner Shop (Frame)" was
   valued at $50.00, and the time of two appren-
   tices was worth $70.00.

Ziba Ferriss
Cabinetmaker
Wilmington, 1762–94
NCC Inventories, Ziba Ferriss, May 15, 16, 1794
   (see Appendix 3); Dorman, pp. 30–32

Samuel C. Finley
Cabinetmaker
Newark, 1836–59
NCC Indenture Book, 1836–40, pp. 147–50, 303–
   04; 1836–54, pp. 314–15, 431; 1839–42, p. 198;
   Scafidi, p. 267; *Delaware State Directory,* 1859,
   p. 202

Peter Brynberg Forman
Cabinetmaker
Wilmington, 1845–59
Wilmington Directory, 1845, p. 20; Dorman, p.

33; *Delaware State Directory*, 1859, p. 203
Forman was working in partnership with Milton
    Hartley (q.v.) in 1845

Andrew Franberg
    Joiner
    Wilmington, 1748
    NCC Deed Book, Q 1, p. 10

William French
    Cabinetmaker
    Wilmington, 1810–17
    NCC Deed Book, H 3, p. 287; T 3, p. 335

John Garretson
    Joiner
    New Castle Hundred, 1768
    NCC Deed Book, Y 1, p. 682

William Glenn
    Cabinetmaker
    Newark, 1837–59
    NCC Indenture Book, 1836–40, pp. 303–4; Sca-
    fidi, p. 267; *Delaware State Directory*, 1859, p.
    202

David Gordon
    House carpenter and joiner
    Duck Creek Hundred, 1779
    KC Deed Book, W 1, p. 187

James Gordon
    Joiner
    Sussex County, 1806
    SC Deed Book, 25, p. 428

John Gordon
    Cabinetmaker
    Dover Hundred, 1764–74
    KC Deed Book, U–V 1, p. 189; Dorman, p. 35

Isaac Gray
    House carpenter and joiner
    New Castle County, 1753
    NCC Orphans Court Book, C, p. 189

Joshua Greenberry
    Cabinetmaker
    Murderkill Hundred, 1850
    U.S. Census of Population, Delaware, 1850, p.
    228

Charles D. Groome
    Cabinetmaker
    Wilmington, 1845–59
    Wilmington Directory, 1845, p. 23; Dorman, p.
    36; *Delaware State Directory*, p. 203

Simon Guthrie
    Cabinetmaker
    Wilmington, 1836–59
    NCC Indenture Book, 1836–40, pp. 147–50; *Wil-
    mington Directory*, 1845; Dorman, p. 36

Jonathan and Samuel Hacket
    Cabinetmakers
    New Castle Hundred, 1806
    NCC New Castle Hundred Assessment List, 1806,
    Jonathan and Samuel Hacket

Simon Hadley
    Spinning-wheel maker and joiner
    Mill Creek Hundred, 1793–1821
    NCC Deed Book, S 2, p. 309; K 3, pp. 77, 326;
    X 3, p. 635

Purnel Hall
    Cabinetmaker and spinning-wheel maker
    Milford, 1831–48
    KC Indenture Book, B, pp. 92–96; E, pp. 96–97;
    Dorman, p. 36; KC Inventories, Purnel Hall,
    Aug. 29, 1848 (see Appendix 6)
    A spinning wheel with Hall's name is displayed
    in the summer kitchen of the John Dickinson
    mansion near Dover (Fig. 2).

John Handy
    Joiner
    Sussex County, 1786–1801
    SC Deed Book, N 13, p. 369; O 14, p. 656; X 22,
    p. 213

Timothy Hanson
    Cabinet- and chairmaker
    Wilmington, 1798
    NCC Wills, Timothy Hanson, Sept. 6, 1798;
    NCC Inventories, Timothy Hanson, Dec. 18,
    1798 (see Appendix 2); Dorman, p. 37

William Harbinson
    Windsor chairmaker
    Wilmington, 1814
    Wilmington Directory, 1814, p. 20

Ezekiel Harker
  Chairmaker and sign painter
  Wilmington, 1820
  Delaware Gazette, Aug. 29, 1820

Wallace Harmonson
  House carpenter and joiner
  Lewes and Rehoboth Hundred, 1791
  SC Deed Book, O 14, pp. 365, 412

George Harris
  House carpenter and joiner
  Broadkiln Hundred, 1832–50
  SC Indenture Book, B 2, pp. 200, 287; C, pp. 8,
    62, 208, 231; E, p. 41; F, pp. 15, 404

Peter Parker Harris
  House carpenter and joiner
  Broadkiln Hundred, 1794
  SC Deed Book, P 15, p. 301

William Harris
  House carpenter and joiner
  Lewes and Pilot Town, 1791–1803
  SC Deed Book, O 14, p. 564; Y 23, p. 413

Milton Hartley
  Cabinetmaker
  Wilmington, 1845–46
  NCC Indenture Book, 1836–54, p. 533; *Wilmington Directory,* 1845, p. 152
  Hartley was in partnership, briefly, with Peter Brynberg Forman (q.v.).

Job Harvey
  Joiner and shop joiner
  Wilmington, 1759–61
  NCC Deed Book; T 1, p. 582; NCC Orphans Court Book D, p. 28

Elijah Hatfield
  Carpenter and joiner
  Sussex County, 1776
  SC Deed Book, M 12, p. 56

Levi Hatfield
  Cabinetmaker
  Frederica, 1794
  KC Deed Book, E 2, pp. 23, 94

Thomas W. Hatfield
  Cabinetmaker, chairmaker, and turner
  Georgetown, 1830–49
  SC Indenture Book, B 2, pp. 35–36; F, p. 102; G, p. 365

Jonathan Hearn
  Chairmaker and spinning-wheel maker
  Laurel, 1830–45
  SC Indenture Book, C, p. 98; E, pp. 231, 519

Martin Hearn
  Spinning-wheel and cartwheel maker
  Laurel, 1835
  SC Indenture Book, C, p. 100

Jacob Hellings
  Turner
  Kent County, 1770
  KC Inventories, Jacob Hellings, Jan. 19, 1770

Thomas Henderson
  Cabinetmaker
  North West Fork Hundred, 1828–40
  SC Indenture Book, A 1, pp. 34–35; W. Wright Robinson, *A History of Seaford* (Seaford, Del.: Red Arrow Press, 1932), p. 12

James G. Hendrickson (Hendrixson)
  Cabinetmaker
  Kent County, 1831
  KC Indenture Book, C, p. 32; see also note 18 and figures 4 and 5

William Hickman
  Turner
  Sussex County, 1784
  SC Deed Book, N 13, p. 177

John Hill
  Joiner and house carpenter
  Wilmington, 1775–76
  NCC Deed Book, B 2, pp. 499, 680

Nehemiah P. Holland
  Cabinetmaker
  Sussex County, 1831–34
  SC Indenture Book, B 2, p. 97; C, pp. 20-21

Daniel Horsman
  House carpenter and joiner
  Sussex County, 1774
  SC Orphans Court Book, A, p. 207

William Hubbard
  House joiner
  Sussex County, 1831
  SC Indenture Book, B 2, pp. 78–79

John P. Hudson
  House carpenter and joiner
  Dagsborough Hundred, 1843
  SC Indenture Book, E, p. 321

Henry Hyland
  Joiner
  Christiana Hundred, 1739
  NCC Deed Book, B. v.2, p. 193

Irvine and Lea
  Joiners
  Wilmington, 1791
  Estate of Thomas May in account with J. Brook
    and R. May, p. 27, Winterthur Museum Li-
    braries, 72x161.4
  Transactions with the firm of Irvine and Lea in-
    cluded furniture hardware such as bedstead
    screws, drawer locks, escutcheons, and hinges.
    Presumably Samuel Lea, who was listed as a
    joiner in the account book, was a member of
    the firm.

Timothy Jackson
  Cabinetmaker
  New Castle and Newark, 1829–32
  NCC Indenture Book, 1826–29, pp. 123, 153;
    1829–31, pp. 27–28, 434–35; 1831–40, p. 211

William Jackson
  Joiner
  Murderkill Hundred, 1762–75
  KC, Murderkill Hundred Tax List, William
    Jackson, 1762; KC Inventories, William Jack-
    son, Aug. 11, 1775

Elias James
  Windsor and rush-bottom chair- and cabinet-
    maker
  Georgetown, 1829–43
  SC Indenture Book, A 1, pp. 92–93; C, p. 104;
    D, p. 176; E, p. 390
  One of James's apprentices, George Washington
    Draine, was guaranteed a complete outfit of
    clothing, including one fashionable hat, one
    broadcloth coat, one pair of cassimere pants,

one vest, one neck handkerchief or stock, one
fine shirt, one pair of yarn hose, and one pair
of fine boots, at the end of his apprenticeship.

Isaac Janvier
  Joiner
  New Castle, 1722–35
  NCC Deed Book, G 1, pp. 157, 467; K 1, p. 395

John Janvier, Sr.
  Cabinetmaker
  Odessa, 1749–1801
  NCC Inventories, John Janvier, Jan. 31, 1801
    (see Appendix 4); Dorman, pp. 42–43

Joseph Janvier
  Chairmaker
  White Clay Creek Hundred, 1786
  NCC Deed Book, G, v.2, p. 130

Joseph Jaquet
  House carpenter and shop joiner
  New Castle and St. George's Hundred, 1754–65
  NCC Orphans Court Book, C, p. 204; NCC Deed
    Book, Y 1, p. 25

Brazilla Jefferis
  Turner
  Wilmington, 1814–45
  Wilmington Directory, 1814, p. 46; Dorman, p.
    46

Thomas Jenkins
  Chairmaker
  Pencader Hundred, 1770
  NCC Deed Book, Z 1, p. 308

Burton Johnson
  Shop joiner
  Sussex County, 1795
  SC Deed Book, W 21, p. 312

John Johnson
  Cabinetmaker
  Wilmington, 1807
  NCC Deed Book, E 3, p. 384

John Johnson
  Joiner
  Kent County, 1752
  KC Deed Book, Q 1, p. 153

William Johnson
Joiner
Mill Creek Hundred, 1777–92
NCC Deed Book, L 2, p. 649; Dorman, p. 48

Amos Jones
Chairmaker
Wilmington, 1796–99
NCC Deed Book, P 2, p. 217; S 2, p. 456

Benjamin Jones
Cabinetmaker
Murderkill Hundred, 1799
KC Deed Book, F 2, p. 242

John Jones
House carpenter and joiner
Broadkiln Hundred, 1792
SC Deed Book, P 15, p. 113

William G. Jones
Cabinetmaker
Wilmington, 1807–59
NCC Indenture Book, 1829–31, pp. 215, 217–18,
320–21, 365–66; 1831–40, p. 371; Dorman, pp.
48–49; Scafidi, p. 276; *Delaware State Directory,* 1859, pp. 203, 265

Samuel Jump
Shop joiner
Sussex County, 1773
SC Deed Book, L 11, p. 343

Jasper Justis
Joiner
Wilmington, 1745–59
NCC Deed Book, N 1, p. 535; Q 1, p. 275; Dor-
man, p. 49

Justa Justis
Shop joiner
Wilmington, 1743–49
NCC Deed Book, U 1, p. 111; Q 1, p. 421

Peter Justis
Shop joiner and house carpenter
Wilmington, 1785–88
NCC Deed Book, F, v.2, p. 481; NCC Invento-
ries, Peter Justis, Jan. 19, 1788
A copy of "Swan's Architect" was included
among Justis's belongings in the inventory list-
ing.

George Kates, Jr.
Cabinetmaker
Wilmington, 1838–47
NCC Indenture Book, 1847–53, pp. 157–58; Dor-
man, p. 49

John Kersey
Joiner
Murderkill Hundred, 1765
KC, Murderkill Hundred Tax List, John Kersey,
1765

John Kettle
House carpenter and joiner
New Castle County, 1758–76
NCC Orphans Court Book, C, p. 301; NCC In-
ventories, John Kettle, July 29, 1776

Magnus Kettle
House carpenter and joiner
New Castle County, 1758–63
NCC Orphans Court Book, C, p. 301; NCC In-
ventories, Magnus Kettle, Apr. 14, 1763

Nicholas Kline
House carpenter and joiner
White Clay Creek Hundred, 1792
NCC Deed Book, O 2, p. 67

John Knowles
Joiner
Wilmington, 1750
NCC Deed Book, Q 1, p. 406

George Kollock
Shop joiner
Sussex County, 1769
SC Deed Book, L 11, p. 19

Andrew Lackey
Joiner
Little Creek Hundred, 1765
KC Deed Book, W 1, p. 22

Benjamin Laforge
Windsor chairmaker
Wilmington, 1789
NCC Deed Book, M 2, p. 16

Joseph Land
Joiner
New Castle County, 1737
NCC Deed Book, N 1, p. 30

Thomas Layton
House carpenter and joiner
  Sussex County, 1795
  SC Deed Book, W 21, p. 32

Joshua Littler
  Joiner
  Wilmington, 1747
  NCC Deed Book, H 3, p. 25

James Lofland
  Carpenter and joiner
  Sussex County, 1835
  SC Indenture Book, C, p. 74

George Rodney Luff
  Cabinetmaker
  Kent County, 1804
  KC Deed Book, I 2, p. 13

John Luff
  Cabinetmaker
  Wilmington, 1841–53
  NCC Indenture Book, 1826–29, p. 153; *Wilmington Directory*, 1845; Dorman, p. 51
  Luff formed a brief partnership with James Morrow (q.v.) in 1841.

Samuel McAnteir
  Chairmaker
  White Clay Creek Hundred, 1797
  NCC Deed Book, S 2, p. 51

Samuel and Thomas McClary
  Cabinetmakers
  Wilmington, 1841–59
  NCC Indenture Book, 1836–54, p. 550; 1839–42, pp. 362–63; 1847–53, pp. 55–56, 102; 1849–53, p. 54; Scafidi, p. 263; Dorman, p. 54; *Delaware State Directory*, 1859, p. 203

William McCoole
  Shop joiner
  New Castle County, pre-1779
  NCC Orphans Court loose papers, William McCoole, Apr. 20, 1779

John Macdonough
  Cabinetmaker
  Cantwell's Bridge, 1789–1807
  Rodney Macdonough, *The Macdonough Hack-*

staff Ancestry (Boston: Press of Samuel Usher, 1901), p. 76
  A Chippendale chest in a private collection is inscribed on a drawer, "Made by John Macdonough Cantwell's Bridge 1807." Probably the maker of the chest was John Macdonough (b. 1789), brother of Commodore Thomas Macdonough, the naval hero of the War of 1812. John Macdonough probably served an apprenticeship with John Janvier (q.v.) since later members of the two families intermarried.

Daniel McDowell
  Cabinetmaker
  Duck Creek Hundred, 1793–1830
  U.S. Census of Population, Delaware, 1820, p. 44; Dorman, p. 55
  The 1820 census taker valued McDowell's annual business at $2,000 and noted that his shop employed three journeymen.

James McDowell
  Cabinetmaker
  Duck Creek Hundred, 1820–60
  U.S. Census of Population, Delaware, 1820, p. 44; Dorman, p. 57; KC Indenture Book, E, p. 105; I, p. 130
  James McDowell's annual business was valued at $2,000 in 1820; his expenses were $1,200, and he employed three journeymen.

Robert McFarrin
  Cabinetmaker
  Milton, 1828–31
  SC Indenture Book, A 1, p. 50; B 2, pp. 107–8

Casperus McGinnis
  Windsor chairmaker
  New Castle County, 1784
  NCC Deed Book, F, v.2, p. 198; S 2, p. 316

John Maher
  Joiner
  Appoquinimink Hundred, 1750
  NCC Deed Book, Q 1, pt. 2, p. 328

John Martin
  House carpenter and joiner
  Kent County, 1796
  SC Deed Book, W 1, p. 539

Charles Mason
Joiner
Kent County, 1789
KC Deed Book, B 2, p. 41

George Massey
Cabinetmaker
Frederica, 1835
KC Indenture Book, F, p. 97

William Mecottor
Carpenter and turner
Sussex County, 1776
KC Wills, William Mecottor, Feb. 8, 1776, A 90,
p. 185

Joseph Mendenhall
Joiner
Wilmington, 1749
NCC Deed Book, Q 1, p. 254

Joseph Milby
Chairmaker and joiner
Sussex County, 1804–12
SC Deed Book, 24, p. 143; SC Inventories, Apr.
24, 1812
The inventory of Milby's goods lists 480 pieces of
chairmaker's timber in the rough, chairmaker's
tools, a workbench, and a lathe.

Nathaniel Milby
House joiner
Sussex County, 1775
SC Deed Book, L 11, p. 451

Robert Miller
Carpenter and joiner
Sussex County, 1786
SC Orphans Court Book, 1786–89, p. 82

James Milner, Sr.
Joiner
Wilmington, 1737–38
NCC Deed Book, N 1, p. 69

Moses Minor
Chairmaker
New Castle County, 1761–89
NCC Orphans Court Book, D, p. 14; NCC In-
ventories, Moses Minor, Apr. 23, 1789

Thomas Mobeny
Chairmaker
Duck Creek Hundred, 1820
U.S. Census of Population, Delaware, 1820, p. 44

James Moore
Turner
Duck Creek Hundred, 1770
KC Deed Book, T 1, p. 11

William Moore
Cabinetmaker
Christiana Hundred, 1820
NCC, Christiana Hundred Tax List, 1820, Wil-
liam Moore

Robert Morrison
Joiner and house carpenter
Wilmington, 1775
NCC Deed Book, B 2, p. 458

James Morrow
Cabinetmaker
Wilmington, 1837–43
NCC Indenture Book, 1836–40, pp. 266–67;
1836–54, p. 134; 1839–42, pp. 361–63, 508
In 1841 James Morrow was in partnership with
John Luff (q.v.).

Peter Morton
Joiner
New Castle Hundred, 1767
NCC Deed Book, W 1, p. 142

Jonathan Neall
House carpenter and joiner
Kent County, 1773
KC Deed Book, U–V 1, p. 108

Joseph William Neering
Chairmaker
Wilmington, 1784
NCC Deed Book, E 2, p. 194

Joseph Newlin
Cabinetmaker and carpenter
Wilmington, 1814
Wilmington Directory, 1814, p. 139
A labeled secretary at the Historical Society of
Delaware is marked Joseph Newlin, High
Street, Wilmington.

Richard Nicholas
  Turner
  Wilmington, 1742–43
  NCC Deed Book, N 1, p. 452

William H. Nichols (Nicholson)
  Cabinetmaker, chairmaker, and spinning-wheel
    maker
  Sussex County and Laurel, 1830–59
  SC Indenture Book, B 2, pp. 107–8; E, pp. 274,
    518; F, p. 296; Scafidi, p. 268; *Delaware State
    Directory*, 1859, p. 208

Samuel Niles
  Cabinetmaker, carpenter, and plane maker
  Wilmington, 1791–96
  NCC Inventories, Samuel Niles, Sept. 27, 1796;
    Dorman, pp. 62–63

Dell Noblett
  Cabinetmaker
  Wilmington, 1810–50
  NCC Indenture Book, 1836–40, pp. 85, 317–18;
    1839–42, p. 442; Dorman, pp. 63–64; Scafidi,
    p. 265

Hamilton Noblett
  Cabinetmaker
  Wilmington, 1838–46
  NCC Indenture Book, 1836–40, pp. 633–34;
    1839–42, pp. 37–38, 458; 1847–53, p. 25; Dor-
    man, p. 65

John Noblett
  Cabinetmaker
  Wilmington, 1840–48
  NCC Indenture Book, 1839–40, pp. 208–09, 298;
    1847–53, pp. 320–21; Dorman, p. 65

Adam Nutall
  House joiner
  Red Lion Hundred, 1783
  NCC Deed Book, G 2, p. 132

John Orr
  House carpenter and joiner, shop joiner, and
    cabinetmaker
  Lewes, 1794–1809
  SC Deed Book, P 15, pp. 259, 503; X 22, p. 468;
    Pennsylvania Abolition Society Manumissions,
    John Orr, May 27, 1795, June 7, 1798, Histori-
    cal Society of Pennsylvania; SC Inventories,
    John Orr, Mar. 7, 1809

Samuel Painter
  Rush-bottom chairmaker
  Wilmington, 1743–1829
  Wilmington Directory, 1814, p. 31; Dorman, p.
    66

Seth Pancoast
  Joiner
  Wilmington, 1746–59
  NCC Deed Book, Q 1, p. 99; T 1, p. 581

Anderson Parker
  Joiner
  Sussex County, 1750–82
  SC Orphans Court Book, 1744–51, p. 71; SC In-
    ventories, Anderson Parker, Mar. 26, 1782

Samuel Parker
  Cabinetmaker
  Sussex County, 1838
  SC Indenture Book, D, p. 162

Samuel Pasmore
  Cabinetmaker
  Sussex County, 1820
  U.S. Census of Population, Delaware, 1820, p.
    364

Rice Paynter
  Windsor chairmaker
  Sussex County, 1828
  SC Indenture Book, A 1, pp. 58–59

John Peterson
  Turner
  Wilmington, 1803–14
  Wilmington Directory, 1814, p. 31; Dorman, p.
    68

William Piles
  Joiner
  Sussex County, 1737
  SC Deed Book, G 7, p. 220

William Polk
  House joiner
  Sussex County, 1792
  SC Deed Book, O 14, p. 596

Thomas Short Porter
  Shop joiner
  Mispillion Hundred, 1771
  KC Deed Book, T, v.1, p. 152

Perry Prettyman
Windsor and rush-bottom chairmaker, spinning-wheel maker, and cabinetmaker
Sussex County, 1827–32
SC Indenture Book, A 1, pp. 64, 92; B 2, pp. 35–36, 77, 108–9, 146
Minos Phillips's 1831 indenture showed the wide range of Prettyman's skills. Phillips was to learn "windsor and rush bottom chair making together with ornamental painting and also the spinningwheel business in all its various branches of the several arts."

William Prettyman
Rush-bottom chairmaker
Laurel, 1831–33
SC Indenture Book, B 2, pp. 59–60, 315–16

Jesse Pyle
Cabinetmaker
New Castle County, 1803
NCC Deed Book, B 3, p. 118

Lewis Reece
Joiner and wheelwright
Mill Creek Hundred, 1770
NCC Deed Book, Z 1, p. 474

Thomas Reece
Carpenter and joiner
New Castle County, 1749
NCC Orphans Court Book, C, p. 122

Jesse Richard
Cabinetmaker
New Castle County (?), 1788
Unidentified account book, Wilmington, May 15, 1788, Jesse Richard, Historical Society of Delaware, Wilmington, Del.

George A. Richmond
Windsor chairmaker and painter
New Castle County, 1841
NCC Indenture Book, 1839–42, p. 398

Nelson Rickards
Chairmaker
Georgetown and Milford, 1837
Scharf, *History of Delaware*, 2:1191–92; Scafidi, p. 277

Elaias Riggs
House carpenter and joiner
Kent County, 1795
KC Deed Book, E 2, p. 196

Laurence Riley
House carpenter and joiner
Kent County, 1775–85
SC Deed Book, M 12, p. 37; KC Inventories, Laurence Riley, Sept. 19, 1785

Mary Riley
Chairmaker
Wilmington, 1832–59
NCC Indenture Book, 1847–53, p. 153; *Delaware State Directory*, 1859, pp. 151, 208; Dorman, p. 71; Scafidi, p. 272

Samuel Riley
Chairmaker
Wilmington, 1814–32
Wilmington Directory, 1814, p. 153; NCC Indenture Book, 1829–31, p. 33; NCC Administration Papers, Samuel Riley, Mar. 15, 1832; Dorman, p. 71

Levi Roach
House carpenter and joiner
Sussex County, 1784–91
SC Deed Book, N 13, p. 154; SC Inventories, Levi Roach, Mar. 18, 1791

John Roberts
Cabinetmaker
Murderkill Hundred, 1800
KC Deed Book, I 2, p. 154; F 2, p. 301

Robinson and Gwynn
Chair manufacturers
Wilmington, 1814
Wilmington Directory, 1814, p. 33; Dorman, p. 72
The chairmaker John Robinson, identified by Dorman, was probably a member of the firm.

George Robinson
Joiner
Christiana Hundred, 1759
NCC Deed Book, T 1, p. 162

James Robinson
  Cabinetmaker
  Christiana Hundred, 1816
  NCC, Christiana Hundred Tax List, 1816, James
    Robinson

John Robinson
  Chairmaker
  Christiana Hundred, 1821
  NCC Christiana Hundred Tax List, 1821, John
    Robinson

Thomas Robinson
  Cabinetmaker
  Christiana Hundred, 1825
  NCC Christiana Hundred Tax List, 1825,
    Thomas Robinson

John Rodney
  House joiner
  Lewes, 1802
  SC Deed Book, X 22, p. 366

Robert Rowen
  Chairmaker
  New Castle Hundred, 1798
  NCC, New Castle Hundred Tax List, 1798, Rob-
    ert Rowen

Philip Russel
  House carpenter and joiner
  Sussex County and Lewes, 1781–95
  SC Administration Papers, Philip Russel, A 97,
    p. 148, Sept. 24, 1795; SC Deed Book, M 12,
    p. 420; N 13, p. 449

Thomas Russell
  Joiner
  Murderkill Hundred, 1785
  KC Deed Book, E 2, p. 262

Ellis B. Sanders
  Cabinetmaker
  New Castle County, 1828
  NCC Indenture Book, p. 111

James Sanders
  Turner
  Duck Creek Hundred, 1788
  KC Deed Book, A 2, p. 132

Robert Sauy
  Shop joiner
  Sussex County, 1780
  SC Deed Book, M 12, p. 302

John Savage
  Joiner
  New Castle, pre-1735
  NCC Inventories, John Savage, July 12, 1735

James Schee
  Cabinetmaker
  Dover, 1796–1824
  NCC Deed Book, P 2, p. 219; KC Court of Gen-
    eral Sessions, Dec. 10, 1800, James Schee; KC
    Inventories, July 10, 1824, James Schee

John Seeds
  Joiner
  Christiana Hundred, 1750
  NCC Deed Book, Q 1, p. 387

Clifford Shanahan
  Cabinetmaker
  Milford, 1831–32
  KC Indenture Book, C, pp. 11–12, 141

Charles Shankland
  Cabinetmaker
  Mispillion Hundred, 1800
  KC Deed Book, G 2, p. 119

Thomas Shields
  Cabinetmaker
  St. George's Hundred, 1773
  NCC Deed Book, B, v.2, p. 253

Daniel Short
  House carpenter and joiner
  Nanticoke Hundred, 1844
  SC Indenture Book, E, p. 429

Joseph Singleton
  Joiner
  Mill Creek Hundred, 1782
  NCC Deed Book, D, v.2, p. 488

Thomas Skidmore
  Shop joiner
  Kent County, 1765
  KC Deed Book, R 1, p. 47

Hugh Smith
  Spinning-wheel maker
  Mill Creek Hundred, 1806
  NCC Deed Book, G 3, p. 162

James Smith
  Turner
  Sussex County, 1758
  SC Deed Book, I 9, p. 188

John Smith
  Joiner
  Murderkill Hundred, 1765
  KC Murderkill Hundred Tax List, 1813, John
    Smith; Dorman, p. 75

Samuel Spencer
  Cabinetmaker
  Mispillion Hundred, 1813
  KC Mispillion Hundred Tax List, 1813, Samuel
    Spencer

David H. Stayton
  Chairmaker, spinning-wheel maker, and cabinet-
    maker
  Camden, 1802–59
  KC Indenture Book, B, p. 105; C, pp. 117, 122;
    F, p. 58; I, p. 80; K, p. 62; Scafidi, p. 268; *Dela-
    ware State Directory*, 1859, p. 202

Joseph Stayton
  Chairmaker and painter
  Smyrna, 1835–42
  KC Indenture Book, F, p. 80; H, pp. 67, 126; M,
    p. 47

Thomas and James H. Stevenson
  Cabinetmakers
  Dover, 1808–65
  KC Indenture Book, F, p. 28; Dorman, pp. 77–79

David Stewart
  House carpenter and joiner
  Sussex County, 1773
  SC Deed Book, L 11, p. 387

Joshua Stockley
  Turner
  Sussex County, 1747
  SC Deed Book, H 8, p. 134

Felix Stout
  Turner
  New Castle County, 1850
  U.S. Census of Population, Delaware, 1850, p.
    225

Charles Stuart
  Spinning-wheel maker
  Pencader Hundred, 1789
  NCC Deed Book, I 2, p. 36

John Studdards
  Joiner
  Murderkill Hundred, 1738
  KC Deed Book, N 1, p. 208

John Taylor
  Cabinetmaker
  Frederica, 1816
  Mary B. D. McCurdy, "More on the History of
    Frederica," *Delaware History* 15, no. 2 (Oct.
    1972): 121

Samuel Taylor
  Cabinetmaker
  Brandywine Hundred, 1814
  NCC Brandywine Hundred Tax List, 1814, Sam-
    uel Taylor

Enoch Thomas
  Joiner
  New Castle County, pre-1815
  Enoch Thomas, Indenture, Feb. 4, 1815, Box 2,
    Group 6, Longwood MSS, Eleutherian Mills
    Historical Library
  Thomas's indenture with Duplanty, McCall and
    Company marked the end of work as a joiner,
    for Duplanty and McCall, a Brandywine cot-
    ton mill, agreed to teach him spinning, card-
    ing, and setting up cotton mill machinery.

Maurice Thomas
  Carpenter and joiner
  New Castle County, 1749
  NCC Orphans Court Book, C, p. 115

John Tomlin
  Cabinetmaker
  Murderkill Hundred, 1781–92
  KC Deed Book, Z 1, p. 56; KC Inventories, Jan.
    23, 1792, John Tomlin

Charles Townsend
  Cabinetmaker
  Dover, 1800
  KC Deed Book, F 2, p. 282

James Townsend
  Chairmaker
  Sussex County, 1760s
  SC Deed Book, I 9, p. 455

Henry Troth
  Joiner
  Wilmington, 1749–80
  NCC Deed Book, Q 1, p. 444; U 1, p. 494; G 2,
    p. 232; Dorman, pp. 79–80

Robert Turk
  Turner
  Sussex County, 1724
  SC Deed Book, F 6, p. 100

Lazruss Turner
  Shop joiner
  Laurel, 1828
  SC Indenture Book, A 1, pp. 47–48

John Twigg
  House carpenter and joiner
  Kent County, 1833
  KC loose indentures, 1833, John Twigg

Joseph Vance
  Shop joiner
  St. George's Hundred, 1780
  NCC Deed Book, B 2, p. 288

Samuel Vance
  Joiner
  New Castle County, 1736
  NCC Deed Book, L 1, p. 63

Henry Van Gaskin
  House carpenter and joiner
  Kent County, 1845
  KC Indenture Book, I, p. 65

William Vaughan
  Joiner
  Sussex County, 1755–75
  SC Deed Book, I 9, p. 95; SC Wills, A 105, p. 82

Henry Vining
  House carpenter and joiner
  New Castle County, 1752–57
  NCC Orphans Court Book, C, p. 274; Dorman,
    p. 82

Daniel Virdin
  Joiner
  Murderkill Hundred, 1771
  KC Deed Book, T, v.1, p. 176

James L. Voshall
  Cabinetmaker
  Little Creek Hundred, 1850
  U.S. Census of Population, Delaware, 1850, p. 57

James Wakeman
  Shop joiner
  Murderkill Hundred, 1788
  KC Deed Book, A 2, p. 18

David Walker
  Joiner
  Christiana Hundred, 1783
  NCC Deed Book, Y 2, p. 475

John Walker
  Joiner
  Duck Creek Hundred, 1779
  KC Deed Book, W 1, p. 139

Winder Waller
  Cabinetmaker and turner
  Sussex County, 1838
  SC Indenture Book, D, p. 35

Jonas Walraven
  Joiner and house carpenter
  Christiana Hundred, 1759–75
  NCC Deed Book, T 1, p. 372; B 2, p. 559

William Walton
  Cabinetmaker
  Murderkill Hundred, 1800
  KC Deed Book, F 2, p. 301

Jacob P. Ward
  Chairmaker
  Laurel, 1843–59
  SC Indenture Book, E, p. 274; *Delaware State
    Directory*, 1859, p. 202

John Ward
Cabinetmaker and chairmaker
Bridgeville, 1830–59
SC Indenture Book, C, p. 98; *Delaware State Directory,* 1859, p. 202

William C. Ward
Cabinetmaker
Sussex County, 1839
SC Indenture Book, D, pp. 105, 107

William Warrington
Shop joiner
Sussex County, 1814
SC Deed Book, A–H, p. 154

Joseph Watkins
Cabinetmaker
New Castle County, 1798
NCC Deed Book, U 2, p. 87

Thomas Watson
Turner
Kent County, 1729
KC Deed Book, I 1, p. 256

Joshua Way
Joiner
Wilmington, 1736–37
NCC Deed Book, L 1, p. 76

Benjamin Wharton
Turner
Sussex County, 1796
SC Deed Book, P 15, pt. 2, p. 630

George W. White
Cabinetmaker
South Milford and Cedar Creek Hundred, 1844–59
SC Indenture Book, E, p. 426; F, p. 73; *Delaware State Directory,* 1859, p. 202

James H. White
Cabinetmaker
Milford Hundred, 1830–31
KC Indenture Book, B, p. 96

Peter White
House carpenter and joiner
Sussex County, 1779
SC Deed Book, M 12, p. 277

Robert White
Cabinetmaker
Mispillion Hundred, 1809
KC Deed Book, L 2, p. 122

John Willey
Joiner
Sussex County, 1795
SC Deed Book, P 15, p. 507

Isaac Williams
House carpenter and joiner
Laurel, 1834
SC Indenture Book, C, p. 6

John Williams
Carpenter and joiner
New Castle, 1747
NCC Orphans Court Book, C, p. 91; Dorman, pp. 92–94

David Wolfe
Chairmaker and joiner
Lewes, 1804
SC Deed Book, Y 23, p. 389

John Wyatt
Cabinetmaker
Camden and Dover, 1836–59
KC Indenture Book, G, p. 31; *Delaware State Directory,* 1859, p. 202

George Young
Cabinetmaker and chairmaker
Wilmington, 1798–1803
Scharf, *History of Delaware,* 2:760; NCC Christiana Hundred Tax List, 1798, George Young; NCC Deed Book, Q 2, p. 323; T 2, p. 22; Dorman, p. 62. For an example of Young's craftsmanship, see figure 6.

FIG. 6. George Young, Windsor side chair. Wilmington, Del., ca. 1800. Painted and turned wood; H. 34½″, W. 19″, D. 14¾″. Stamped "G. Young" under seat. (Privately owned: Photo, Winterthur.)

Excerpts from the Inventory of the Goods and Chattels of Joseph Peters, Merchant

Wilmington, Delaware, January 25, 1748

	£		
2 doz & Gimlets 4/0 = 2 flat Iron & 1 Box ditto 10/ = 5 Sheep Sheers 5/ = 6 pairng Chisels & 6 Rub Sticks 4/	£ 1	3	0
5 padlocks & 5 In. Augors 17/ = 1 doz: Clasp pen knives & 1 doz: pocket ditto 9/	1	6	0
4 Chairs 1 Table & 1 pr. hand Iron 13/ = 1 window blind 8/ = 12 yds bare Skin 10/p £6.0 12½ yds plains 75/	10	16	0
parsel hob Nails & Sparrables 7/6 = 1 China Teapot & 6 Cups & Sassers 15/ = whip Saws 1 Cross Cut/do. £5	6	2	6
2 Swinging looking Glasses 40/ = 2 Small f[r]amd 20/ = 2 Smaller ditto 6/3 = 3 ps. Calico 54 Yds 3/ £8.2	11	8	0
5 pr. Corse wool Cards 15/ = 1 pr. fine ditto 3/6 = 2 best hand Saws 35/6 = 6 Tennat do. 60/ = 4 hand Saws 16/	6	9	6
6 padlocks 6/ = 29 lb Bees wax 29/ = 4 Box Irons 12/ = parsel Earthen ware 1/ = 6 mouse Traps & 4 hamers 5/	2	13	0
16 Carpenters Stock plains 16/ = 7 Tap bores & 3 drawing knives 10/ = 32 Gimletts 2/8 = 2 pr. Cotton Cards 4/	1	12	8
2 Scellits & parcel allam 6/ = old Iron kettle wth. some Chalk 2/ = 70 lb Hob & Sprig Nails 2/p £7.0	7	8	0
71 lb Shot 22/ = 11 Trowels 22/ = 6 Trunk locks & 4 small Bolts 6/ = 3 Sash Crews 2 bolts 2 pr. hings & 1 Padlock 2/6	2	12	6
12 Trunk locks 6/ = 2 Gunlocks 6/ = 2 Inside dorelocks 3/ = 11 Clasp Pen knives 4/ = 2 Spring latches 4/	1	3	0
4 Box locks 2/8 = 6 Horn Combs & a persl. Sleave buttens 3/ = 3 doz: boxlocks 24/5 = lancets 5/	1	14	8
31 Chest locks 31/ = 4 Cubbord locks 2/ = 5 drawlocks & box locks 9/ = 3 Inside dore locks 4/6	2	6	6
11 Cork drawers 1/6 = 2 pr. Hinges Some hooks & Eyes & drawing knives 4/ = 1 Coopers ax & Carprs. adge 9/	0	14	6
4 Sash lines & pulleys $ 5 pr. H hinges 15/ = 4 Padlocks & 2 Candle sticks 5/ = 10 large files 10/	1	10	0
2 Horselocks & 2 Trunk ditto 5/ = parsel desk mountg. 15/ = 1 pr. Tobaco Tong & 17 Steels 6/	1	6	0
1 Sadlers Hamers & 1 pr. Sheep Shears 2/ = 1 Sett Turners Tools 12/6 = 8 Chest of drawer locks 5/		19	6
14 bolts 7/ = 3 pr. Shoemaker nippers 1/6 = 4 large Inside dorelocks 8/ = 16 alle Hafts & 17 peging Alles 3/	0	19	6
1 rubing Stick 19 large files 3 doz & 8 Sadlers alles & Nedles & 1 markin Iron 28/ = 1 pr. Shomakers pinchers 2/	1	10	0
9 Shoemakers rubing Sticks & Bones 1/6 = 4 pr. Smal hinges & 16 Chisels & Gouges 10/ = 32 files 10/6	1	2	0
3 paper Shoemakers Tacks 3 punches & 3 papers alle blades 17/6 = 2 Small Hand Vices 6/ = 6 plain Bitts 12/	1	15	6

	£	s	d
10 Two foot Rules 15/ = 9 large Ditto 40/6 = 9 plain Bitts 5/6 = 6 rule yards 12/ = 4 hardnd horse locks 10/	4	3	0
9 pr. large Carptrs. Compasss & 10 pr. brass dividers 24/6 = 9 pr. Caprs. compasss 3/ = 33 small plain bitts 10/	1	17	6
15 pr. hallow & round Bitts 14/ = 2000 Tenter Hooks 7/ = 1 Inside dorelock & Stock Buckel 5/6	1	6	6
14½ doz: large sadlers Nails & 2 doz: Curten Rings 7/4 = 14 Sadle heads & 2 doz: Staple Nails 8/	0	15	4
3 doz: Sadlers Buckels 4 nedles & 9 Turf Nails 2/6 = 2 pr. mens. Stirups & 4 women do. 6/ = 4 horselocks 4/	0	12	6
5 half Cirb bridle bitts & 6 pr. Snaffel ditto & 4 doz: Black Buckels 10/ = 3 padlocks & sprigs 5 snuff boxes 5/	0	15	0
9 pr H hinges & 1 horse lock 20/ = 7 pr. T hinges 10/6 = 3 skilets 2 ship frying pans 7/6 = pr. hors Chains 13/4	2	11	4
13 3/4 Caliminco 17/2 = 3 doz: & 11 Stocklocks £5.17.6 = 3 Adges & 4 Trowels 20/ = 12 hatchetts 30/	9	4	8
2 parsell breed & Swish parsel laces & parl. Girdles 15/ = 3 Gunhamers 6 Comb Cases & 4 Nedle Cases 6/	1	1	0
5 doz: Joynter Bitts 15 = 10 pen knives wth. Sheathes 3/4 = 7 pen knives doubl. blades & 3 pr. sisers 4/6	1	2	10
10 papers Buckels 15 = 4 pr. fleems & Cases & 7 lock Spickets 8/ = 4 rasors 1/ = 6 fire Glass 2/6	1	2	10
4 Two foot rules & 8 one foot ditto & 5 Ivory ditto 13/ = 18 Clock pins & 1 pr horse fleems with Cases 4/6	0	17	6
1 ½ doz: large hard mettle [plates] ditto 40/ = 5 packets pins 32/ = 1 lb Green Tea 8/ = 1 doz bricklayer Trowels 24/	5	4	0
2 puter Teapots 9/ = 1 doz: Joynter plain Irons 10 = 1 Sett Turners Tools 13/ = 5 doz: Chisels & Googes 30/	3	2	0
2 doz: Sockett Chisels 22/ = 4 doz: large files 48/ = 3 Smith ruber files 7 = 7 doz: ditto 56/ = 6 doz Smal do. 20/	7	13	0
9 bottle four musterd 4/6 = 30 3/4 yd. white rufel 61/6 = 8 3/4 yd. white Buckram 17/6 = 4 doz Sml. Trunk locks 28/	5	11	6
3 doz: horse & Colt locks 45/ = 18 Small hand Vices 36/ = 14 lb Scuper Nails 7/ = 1 doz mouse Traps 4/	4	12	0
3 1/4 lb Nutmegs £6.10 = 4 Reems writing paper 30/ = 14 lb Chocolat 18/8 = 10 Augors 16/ = 2 box Irons 10/	10	4	8
500 Smal Brass Tacks 4/ = 3 bridle Bitts ½ hunters 4/6 = 2 ½ doz: Single Spring locks 30/ = 3 doz: buchr. knivs. 15/	2	13	6
1 doz: Split Bone Buchers knives 5/ = 1 doz: Cubbord locks 9/ = 3 doz: Chest ditto 36/ = 1 ½ doz Chest Locks 13/6	3	3	6
6 Ivory knives & forks 5/ = 6 Bone ditto 5/ = 1 doz: drawer locks = 3 doz ditto 24/ = 1 doz pen knives 3/	2	12	0
4 doz: dressing Box & Clock locks 24/ = 2 doz: Horse ditto 48 = 1 doz: Carpr. 2 foot rule 15/	4	7	0
6 pr. H hinges 3 pr. Chest do. 11/ = parcel Chest Straps 20/ = parsel H hinges 10/	2	1	0
parsel Butt & duftails do. 8/ = 2 doz: rule Joyntrs do. 20/ = 1 doz: & 11 Cubbor & 6 drawer locks 30/	2	18	0
6 Box Irons 18/ = 3 Pullback locks 7/ = 6 bolts & 16 brass padlocks 10/ = 4 Clockcase locks 6 Childr. Coffin handles 4/	1	19	0
4 Hones 8/ = 1 doz: mouse Traps 4/ = 5 Broad Axes 20/ = 3 pr. fire Shovels & Tongs 12/6 = 2 ½ doz: Splintr. locks 18/	3	2	6

8 doz: & 8 pulleys & Some Sash lines 10/ = 6 drawback locks & 18 pr. Snibills 7/6 = 2 doz: narw. hollan Tapes 18/ — 1 15 6

1 doz: Silk ferret Laces 3/ = 19 pr. Chisels & 2 doz: Gimblets 13/ = 5 pr. Sheep Shears 3/ = 9 pr. H Hinges 7/6 — 1 6 6

6 thumb latches 3/ = 4 pr. H hinges 4/ = 1 doz: whip saw files 10 = 1 doz: Smal ditto 3/ — 1 0 0

5 Ivory Table knives & forks 5/ = parsel Shoebuckels 20/ = 2 doz: & 1 raisors 6/ = 1 Sett locks for desk 5/6 — 1 16 6

1 doz: & 11 small sisers 5/ = 10 pr. Carpenrs. Cumpasss & 2 pr. H hinges 5/ = 11 Cork Srews 3/ — 0 13 0

18 Currey Combs 11/ = 6 doz: files 28/ = 2 doz: large Chest Locks 28/ = 1 doz: double spring Chest do. 20/ — 4 7 0

1 doz: plain Till do. 6/6 = 1½ doz pr. Coffin handles 7/6 = 6 Grose wood Screws 16/ — 1 10 0

2 doz: Carprs Squairs 36/ = 3 doz: Trowels 16/ = 1 doz: do. 14/ = 20 doz: plaster in Trowels 32/ — 4 18 0

5 Comp. Saws 6/ = 6 hand do. 20/ = 6 do. 18/ = 16 doz alle hafts 20/ = 5 doz: peging alle hafts 6/8 — 3 10 18

6 doz: H Gimlets 12/ = 4 doz: Smal do. 4/ = 10 Spike do. 5/ = 11 large do. 6/5 = 18 Joyntr bitts 10/ — 1 17 5

1 doz: plains do. 4/ = 1 doz half Ins. heading Chisels 8/ = 1 doz: Cribing do. 9/ = 8 broad do 6/ — 1 7 0

20 heading Chisels 10 = 18 Socket gouges 13/6 = 1 doz Turning Tools 10/ = 1 doz: do 10/ = 6 doz: furmers 18/ — 3 1 6

6 doz furmers Gouges 21/ = 4 doz: Carps Compass 10/ = 2 doz: ditto 10/ = 1 doz Sadle head 9/ — 2 10 0

1 doz: mortising Chisels 8/ = 2 doz black Nippers 9/ = 2 doz: brite do 18/ = 6 doz: moulding plains 18/ — 2 13 0

1 Grose peging blades 10 = 6 Grose Sole Tacks 10/ = 4 Grose alle blades 12/ = 1 lb niting pins 1/ — 1 13 0

2 doz & 4 plain Irons 9/ = 15 Carptrs Hamers 15/ = 9 Shomakers do. 10/ = 1 doz: Sadlers do. 18/ — 2 12 0

6 lb niting pins 9/ = 9 half In Augors 10/ = 6 Carprs hamers 6/ = 6 In Augors 10/ = 2 ½ Grose Sadr buckles 15/ — 2 10 0

1 doz: plain Gun locks 30/ = 6 fencd do. 18/ = 6 do. better 24/ = 6 ditto ½ brideld 27/ = 1 doz Swifeld Sturups 16/ — 5 15 0

2 ½ doz: plain do. 20/ = 2 ½ Grose Turf Nails 18/6 = 18 pr. Nippers 32/ = 6 Table knives & forks 7/ — 3 17 6

1 Grose Solid drops 26/ = 6 large Coopers Comps 12/ = 2 doz pr. Coffin handles 20/ — 2 18 0

1 doz Childrs. ditto 3/ = 12 Gun locks 28/ = 1 doz pr. pinchers 24/ = 10 Grose alle blades 25/ — 4 0 0

12 Grose Sole Tacks 20/ = 3 doz plain Irons 5/ = 1 doz: Sliding rules 40/ = 6 Gunter Scales 15/ — 4 0 0

6 size Sticks 12/ = 1 Grose Solid drops 26/ = 4 doz: plain Setts locks in sute 24/ = 4 doz: desk do. 24/ — 4 6 0

1 doz: hallow drops & 6 doz scuchions 27/ = 12 doz: brass handles wth. Iron wire & 4 doz: Scuchions 35/ — 3 2 0

6 doz: brass handles wth. brass wire 2 doz: Scuchions 25/ = 2 do: brass kit handles Joyntd 2 doz. Scuchions 37/ — 3 2 0

6 doz: plain polishd Joynted & 2 doz: Scuchions 52/ = 6 doz brass hands. wth. brass wire & 2 doz: Scuchins 25/ — 3 17 0

4 doz: & 2 polishd handls & 1 doz: & 2 Scuchions 35/ = 12 doz: handls wth. Screws & 6 doz: Scuchions 74/ — 5 9 0

parcel Hallow drops & Scuchions 7/6 = 11 doz: brass Screw Buttens 16/6 = 1 doz: brass Clock hinges 15/	1	19	0
1 doz: brass Side hinges 15/ = 1 doz: brass desk hinges 17 = 1 doz: brass prospect do. 6/ = 3/4 lb brass pins 6/	2	4	0
1 Grose In. wood Screws & 1 Gr ½ In do. = 13 paper Tacks & battens 50/ = 4 Coopers Adges 15/	3	12	0
3 Carprs. adges 10/ = 7 Cross Cutt Saws £ 7.0.0 = 2 Mills ditto 90/ = 1 old whip Saw 20/ = 1 Sledge 3/	13	3	0
1 frying pan 5/ = 3 Smith Vices 55/ = ½ faggot Steel 30/ = 5 doz: Swifeld Stureps Irons 75/	8	5	0
4 Cask nails 10.12.20 penney £34.0 = 2 p. Casks Nails 10 & 2 peny £12.0 = 1 p. Cask 3d Ditto £5.0	51	0	0
2 p. baggs Nails 30/ = 2 p baggs Clog Nails 10/ = 12 pr Chain nails 70/ = p Cask 4 Nails 90/	10	0	0
parsl 4d & 2d Nails £9.0 = 3 Chest Locks 12/ = 1 doz saw Setts 4/6 = parsl. Logwood £4.0	13	16	0

Excerpts from the Inventory of the Goods and Chattels of Timothy Hanson, Cabinet and Chairmaker

Wilmington, Delaware, December 18, 1798

Third Story & Garret	Dolls	Cents
17 frames of Sash 9 lights each at 45 Cents Pr frame	7	65
11 ditto 6 ditto 30 ditto	3	30
a lot of planes	2	—
1 Chopping Knife and box		45
11 Winsor Chairs at 60 Cents each	6	60
8 Bamboo ditto at 110	8	80
3 Armed ditto at 160	4	80
7 ditto not painted at 110 Cents	7	70
37 Bamboo Chairs not painted at 90 Cents each	33	30
83 Winsor Chairs not painted at 50 ditto	41	50
2 Stools not painted		75
3 Spinning Wheels, 1 reel & winding blades	1	50
1 Entry Cloth & bedstead Irons	3	50
4 Pillows, 1 old sacking bottom & 3 old blankets	5	25
a Remnant of Canvas	2	—
1 old Carpet & 4 Striped Coverlids	3	50
1 Pair of saddle bags	2	00
2 Trunks & 2 old flour Casks		25
Shop		
1 Grindstone	2	00
1 Glue Kettle		50
2 Iron Vises	10	00

	Dolls	Cents
a lot of boards and ceder posts	2	—
3 Sheets of brass wire for cellar Windows	3	—
1 Grind Stone & Work bench	1	—
34 Windsor Chairs at 60 Cents each	20	40
1 Fishing line & lead 25 Cents 1 Scratch bud & Taper 65 Cents		90
a large heap of Stone in the Street	20	—
5042 Rods at 60 Cents Pr 100	30	25
4267 feet at 150 Cents Pr 100	64	—
2330 Stretches at 112 Cents Pr 100	26	09
12 Top rails bent at 55 Cents Pr Dozen		55
45 Bamboo bows bent at 84 Cents Pr Doz	3	15
470 Ditto unbent 200 Pr. 100	9	40
462 Chair bottoms 110 Cents Pr Doz	42	35
236½ ft Windsor Chair plank at 300 Cents Pr 100	7	09
34 Stools @ 30 Cents each	10	20
1 Work bench	1	—
a lot of tools	15	—
1 work bench	1	—
1 Paint Stone & Muller	1	—
a lot of paintpots	1	—
a small quantity of dry paint		75
362 Walnut arms for Chairs at 50 Cents Pr Doz	15	—
a lath for Turning	1	—
a small heap of manure in yard	1	55

Appendix 3

Excerpts from the Inventory of the Goods and Chattels of Ziba Ferriss, Cabinetmaker

Wilmington, Delaware, May 15–16, 1794

New Furniture in the Store Room

1 Mahogany Bureau	6. –.–
1 Walnut Ditto	3.10.–
1 Ditto Desk	7.10.–
1 Low Post Bedstead	1. 2.6
1 Walnut Dining Table	2.12.6
1 High Post Bedstead	1.17.6
1 Pine Chest 12/6 1 Seamans Chest Do 15/	1. 7.6
1 Pine Table	12.6
1 Walnut Candle Stand	1. –.–
3 Ditto Tea Tables 21/8 each	3. 5.–
1 Ditto Breakfast Table	2. 5.–
1 Cherry Ditto	2. 7.6
1 Pine Dough Trough	10.–
1 Second hand Bedstead	7.6
16 Mahogany Bannisters @ 1/3 ea	1. –.–
20 lb of Hair to Curl for Upholdsters 8 p lb	.13.4
1 Poplar Candle Stand Painted Mahogany	
Colour	5.–
2 Boxes with Brass Furniture Hinges Coffin	
Plates &c	20. –.–

In the Work Shop

52 Joiners Moulding Planes @ 2/ each	5. 4.–
31 Carpenters Moulding Do large with Totes	
2/6	3.17.6
37 Ditto Do without Totes 2/	3.14.–
13 Smoothing Planes 1/	13.–
4 Jack Planes 1/10½	7.6
8 Fore Planes 2/6	1. –.–
4 Jointers Do 3/9	.15.–
3 Handsaws 2 @ 7/6 & 1 at 3/9	.18.9
3 Sash Saws & 1 Dove Tail @ 3/9 ea	.15.–
2 Iron Squares 1/3	2.6
A Lott of Sundries Chisels Gouges Brace	
Bitts &c	1. 2.6
3 Augers 4 Hatchets & 4 Candlesticks	13.4
1 Iron Clamp 11/3 1 Ditto stake 1/10½	13.1½
1 Turkey Oil Stone 22/6 4 Glue Kettles @	
2/ ea	1.10.6
2 Whip Saws for sawing Mahogany 15/ ea	1.10.–
2 Wooden Clamps 3/9 2 hold fasts 2/	
1 U for cutting screws 3/9	9.6
1 Frame Saw 5/ 1 Bench Vice 5/	
1 Grindstone comp. 15/	1. 5.–

30 Feet Mahogany Boards @ 1/			1.10.–
1 Walnut Close stool Chair			1.10.–
In the Shop Yard			
3377 Feet of Inch Walnut Boards @ 15 p 100		25. 6.6
1972 Do of Poplar Do 7/6		7. 7.10
150 Do Do 2 In Plank is 300 Ft. 9/	1. 7.–
712 Do Mahogany 1/6 foot		35.12.–
216 Do Oak scantlin 2¾ by 1¾ 7/6	.16.2½
611 Do Inch Pine Boards 7/6	2. 5.9¾
15 Sett of Bedstead Stuff 3/6 sett	2.12.6
2147 Feet of Inch Walnut Boards 17/6	19. 4.6
822 Do ½ Inch Do 15/	6. 3.3
360 Do of Wild Cherry tree Boards		
very good 18/	3. 4.9
250 Do Inferior 11/3	1. 8.11½
135 Do Do 11/3	15.2¼
84 Do Do 11/3	9.5
190 Table Gate Stuff 10/	19.–
630 Do Inch Walnut Boards 11/3	3.10.10½
466 Do Do 7/6	1.15.–
96 Do Do 5/	4.9½
225 Do Do 15/	1.13.9
22 Walnut Logs for Tea Table Pillars 6 ea	11.–
600 Feet of Lath 7/6	2. 5.–
380 Do Cedar Boards 12/6	2. 7.6
174 Do Oak Scantlin 8/4	14.6
275 Do White Pine Boards 18/9	2.11.6¾
1 Lott of Different Sorts of Offal Stuff	2. 5.–
1 Hearse for Carrying the Dead	3. –.–
1 Turning Lathe with the Appurtenances	3. –.–
1 Wheel Barrow	2.6
1 Cart & Geers	5. –.–
1 Sheet Iron Stove & Pipe much worn	18.9
5 Shop Benches @ 7/6 ea	1.17.6
2 Pitch Forks & 2 Hay Rakes	2.
2 Broad Shovels 5/ 2 Spades 5/	10.–
1 Iron Crow Barr 7/6 1 Wood saw 5/	12.6
3 Candle Stand Tops & Pillars @ 1/10½ ea	5.7½
1 Tea Table Pillar	6.–
1 Pr Chair Shaffts just saw'd out	2.6
6 Washing Machine Wheels 16/4	4.18.–

Excerpts from the Inventory of the Goods and Chattels of John Janvier, Cabinetmaker

Odessa, Delaware, January 31, 1801

Item	£	s	d
Shaving impliments 7/6, 1 Lot Odd Hinges & Locks 12/6	1	–	–
4 Small drawers containing small articles 10/		10	–
1 Lot plain Iron files & Gouges 11/3. 5 small Saws 6/		17	3
1 Lot Awles 2/6. 1 Diamond 17/6. 1 Lot Gimblets & Chalk Line 5/	1	5	–
1 Lot old Screws 6/ 2 patras. 18 pullies. 1 Spiket & Sosket 3/		9	–
1 Lot Sprigs 29/. 1 Lot Small Nailes 14/	2	3	–
12 Grose Small Screws. & 6 Gro. Larger ditto	3	5	6
40 pr Small Hinges 30/ 22 pr Small brass Hinges 20/	2	10	–
46 Drawer Locks 34/6. 8 Desk Locks 30/	3	4	6
12 prospect Locks 12/ 4 Chest Locks 8/	1	–	–
1 Lot Scuchings Knobs Rings &c	3	–	–
26 Brass Handles & Bolts 26/ 1 lb Brass pins 7/6	1	13	6
16 Small Chizles 12/ 1 ps parchment & Chair patterns 3/		15	–
3 Small boxes, some Soap Varnish & Sundry Small articles	1	–	6
1 2/3 Books Gold Leaf 7/4. 5 Sets Bed Screws 15/	1	2	4
27 lb Bees Wax 40/6. 11¾ lb Nailes 10/8. 6¾ lb Tallow 6/9	2	17	11
23¼ lb Glue 38/1. 9 Sheets Glass paper 1/6	1	19	–
1 Lot Hand saw files 22/2. 1 Lot flat files 11/	1	13	2
1 pr Sheep Sheres 1/ 1 furniture Cupboard 80/	4	1	–
7 Hand Screws 7/6 5 old Candlesticks & 4 pr. Snuffers 5/		12	6
1 Glue Kettle 7/6. 1 Vice & Bench 30/ 1 Lot Oylstone 10/	2	7	6
1 Grind Stone 15/ 1 Grindstone & Hanging 30/	2	5	–
1 Pitch Ladle 5/ 1 Iron Clamp 20/	1	5	–
1 Lot files 4/6 1 Lot flat files & Chizels 15/		19	6
1 Paint Stone Muller & Knives 15/ 1 Lot Old plaines 10/	1	5	–
2 Drawers Sundry Small articles 15/ 2 old framd Saws 5/	1	–	–
1 new framd Saw 5/ 1 Saw frame 3/9		8	9
1 Drawr Sundry articles 3/9 1 Work bench & Screw 22/6	1	6	3
4 Table plains 15/ 1 Moving plow 7/6	1	2	6
1 Set Inch plows & Groves 12/6. 3 hand Saws 15/	1	7	6
2 Sash Saws 15/ 2 Small Saws 5/ 7 Hammers 8/6	1	8	6
1 Lot Gages Mallets &c 5/ 7 Smoothing plains 26/3	1	11	3
5 Jack plains 18/9. 5 fore plains 18/9. 2 Jointers 15/	2	12	6
1 Vanier Saw 25/ 1 Work bench & Screw 22/6	2	7	6
3 hold fasts 15/ 3 old Saws 7/6 (2 Drawing Knives) (4 scrapers & 1 Steel 10/)	1	12	6
2 picture frame plains 11/3. 1 Lot Sundry articles 54/10	3	6	1
1 Lot old Chizels & Gouges 3/9. 1 Clamp 3/9		7	6
10 Iron Hand Screws 37/6. 1 Work bench 7/6	2	5	–
1 Work bench & Screw 22/6. 1 New Set brace & Bitts 45/	3	7	6
1 Old Set Brace & Bitts 15/ 1 Lot pollishing tools 5/	1	–	–
1 Horn Lock 1/6. 32 Hallow & Rounds 96/	4	17	6
2 Sets Groving plains 15/ 6 Rabbit plains 12/6	1	7	6
5 Beading plains 15/1 1Astrigal 1 Oy & 1 Cut & thrust 12/6	1	7	6
8 odd plains 15/ 1 Set Comb Makers tools 15/	1	10	–
Sundry Srew Drivers Sprig Awles Wire &c		12	6
Sundry patterns and Small articles through the Shop	4	10	–
1 Large 6 plait Stove (2 Side plates broken)	1	17	6
1 less 6 plait ditto 45/	2	5	–
1 New Sleigh Compleat	11	5	–
1 Wheel Lathe & turning tools	6	–	–
1 Clock Makers Lathe 7/6. 1 Screen 2/		9	6
6 old Chair frames 6/ 1 Cradle 12/6 Some Leather 3/9	1	2	3
1 old Brass kettle 10/ 1 paint Morter & pessels 3/9		13	9
Sundry paints & paint brushes 22/6	1	2	6
7 Oyl Jugs 14/ 32 Galls L Seed Oyl 24/6	1	18	6
5 Quarts Lamb Oyl 9/ 31 Brushes difft Sorts 38/9	2	7	9
1 Sign 10/ 29 lb Chalk 7/3 75 lb Whiting 18/9	1	16	–
1 Gun. 1 powder Horn & shot pouch 12/6		12	6
1 New Cord Bed Sted	1	5	–
1 New Mahogany Clock Case	16	–	–
1 " ditto	16	–	–
1 " " Desk	15	–	–
1 " " Circular Bureau	8	5	–
1 " " ditto Card Table inlayed	7	10	–
3 plain " ditto ditto " 6 of each	9	–	–
1 pr " ditto End Tables	5	–	–

1 New Wallnutt Desk	9	–	–
3 " do Square Cornered Bureaus			
75/ each	11	5	–
3 " do fluted do do			
90/	13	10	–
1 " do Breakfast Table	2	5	–
1 New Clock without a Case	14	–	–
1 foot Stove 20/ 1 Mahogany Corner board 10/	1	10	–
Sundry Old Iron 15/ 41 lb Curled Hair 66/	4	1	–
10 Set Bed pins 12/6 1 Screw tool 5/		17	6
2 Sets Bureau Brackets & 1 Set Stand feet		15	–
Sundry strips for Inlaying 5/ 3 pr old Scales			
Wts & 1 Hammer 15/		15	–
1 Stick purple wood 2/6 2 old Bags 3/9		6	3
2¼ Bus wheat 31/6. 5¾ Bus Rye 28/9	3	–	3
Sundry Wallnut Cuttings 15/ 1 half bushel &			
Sundry old Casks 15/	1	10	–

1 Mahogany Chair frame 10/ 1 Rope &				
Teakle 6/			16	–
1 Wood Saw & Horn 5/			5	–
613 feet Mahogany boards @ 1/6 p				
foot	45	19	6	
104 " half Inch ditto 1/3 p foot	6	10	0	
Some Holly plank 37/6	1	17	6	
640 feet Inch Wallnutt @ 25/ p. hund	8	0	0	
148 " half Inch ditto @ 20/	1	9	7	
131 " heart pine boards @ 18/	1	3	6	
248 " Sap ditto @ 10/	1	4	9	
104 " White pine @ 18/		18	8	
125 " Cedar Boards @ 18/	1	2	6	
927 " Poplar ditto " 12/6	5	15	10	
75 " Oak " @ 12/6	9	4	74.11.2	
1 3/4 Auger 3/ 3 Boxes 3/ 1 Iron Hair				
Twister 3/			9	–

Appendix 5

Excerpts from the Inventory of the Goods and Chattels of George Crow, Clockmaker

Wilmington, Delaware, December 4, 1762

In the parlour	£	S	D
Purse & apperal and Desk	9	–	–
three Beds & bed Cloths with 1 pair of bedsteads	24	–	–
1 Large looking Glass w glazed pictures & a tea chest	6	10	–
a Clock and case new 2 old India pictures & a bedstead	15	12	6
6 Rush Chairs china & Delph ware & a closet of pewter	6	10	–

In the Shop	£	S	D
a Clock & Case 3 unfinished Clocks and a gold watch	50	–	–
a bedstead & sacking bottom and a parcell of Books	6	10	–
a set of Clock and Watch makers Tooles bellows stake & melting pots	35	–	–
3 pair of Hand Irons shovels and tongs warming pan	2	15	–

In ye front and back rooms up stairs	£	S	D
a case of Drawers a Case with 6 bottles bed pan & box	2	19	–
a Case of Drawers bed bedsted and furniture	20	–	–
6 walnut chairs 1 oval 1 china and a tea table	5	18	–
a looking glass some pictures & sundry trifles	2	2	6

In ye Garret	£	S	D
a new clock and a quantity of brass & copper	10	10	–
a large brass Candlestick a bag of fethers & chaff bed	1	15	0
a gun a pair of pistols a bed tick & 2 baskets	1	7	6
an old bedsted a parcel of woolen yarn and some wool	1	–	–
2 old Chests and sundry other trifles	1	3	–

In the large Shop & kitchen	£	S	D
iron kettle & pots a bell mettal do. watering pots & gridle	1	10	–
5 brass kettles of divers values & 1 bellmetal do	4	12	6
Sundry trifles in the forge shop & kitchen	2	6	–
a pair of chair wheels & an unfinished box a bag of grass seed	5	5	–
3 unfinished Clock cases & joiner tooles & sundries in ye Loft	6	10	–
a quantity of leader rails & posts & pine boards	3	10	–
Hay in the Stable barn & on Cherry Island	21	10	–
a quantity of boards & rails 2 Cows & a hog	10	10	–
a pair of scales and Steelyards & a quantity of Mahoginy	8	5	–
2 riding chairs & harness &c and old horse watch Isinstas scales	32	5	–
a small Quantity of Barley	2	10	–

Appendix 6

Excerpts from the Inventory of the Goods and Chattels of Purnel Hall, Cabinetmaker and Spinning-wheel Maker

Milford, Delaware, August 29, 1848

Lott of new sash in granery		$2.00
1 work Bench do do		.50
Lott of Walnut Board do		6.00
do do cherry do do		2.00
do do gum do do		1.00
No. 1 Lott Gum board in Board yard		1.00
" 2 do do do		1.00
" 3 do do do		2.00
" 4 do White Oak do		2.00
" 5 do Poplar do do		4.00
" 6 do do do do		6.00
" 7 do Walnut do		3.00
" 8 do do do		1.00
" 9 do do do		1.00
" 10 do poplar scantling do		4.00
" 11 do poplar board do		3.00
" 12 do Gum do do		6.00
" 13 do poplar do do		4.00
" 14 do Gum do do		1.50
" 15 do scantling do do		1.50
" 16 do do do		1.00
" 17 do old scantling board &c		2.00
Old pump stocks & old lathe		.12½
3 Biers and cords	shop	2.00
Lott of Coffin boards	do	4.00
Lott of Mahony plank veneering &c	(shop)	10.00
Lott of walnut do	(shop)	1.50
do Table legs turned (cherry)	do	2.00
do poplar & oak board	do	.50
do scantling	do	.50
1 Table frame	do	.50
1 chairmakers Bench	do	.12½
1 Lott chair rounds & posts	do	.25
1 paint stone, muller and knife	do	1.00
4 work Benches	do	4.00
1 Turning Lathe	do	1.00
1 Lott Hand screws	do	2.50
1 stove and pipe	do	3.00
1 Tin Chest	do	.50
1 case paint cups oil varnish &c		1.00
All the tools in about the shop		5.00
1 Clamp		2.00
Walnut side board frame		.50
All the patterns, cuting boards &c		3.00

1 pr mahogany claw feet	.25
1 small case of drawers	.25
1 Lott Trussels	.25
1 Grindstone	1.00
Glue kettle & pot	.25
1 small grindstone and crank	.50
1 Iron vice	1.00
3 French post Bedsteads	6.00
2 Low post do	4.00
5 High post do	25.00
1 do do do	5.00
4 sett French posts	4.00
2 do high do	3.00
1 Mahogany Bureau	12.50
1 do do	12.50
1 do work stand	5.00
1 poplar cradle	1.00
1 cherry do	2.00
1 cherry dining Table	4.00
1 do Breakfast do	3.00
1 Large Walnut do	5.00
1 poplar wash stand	1.00
1 mahogany frame	.25
1 Desk and Case	1.50
1 Case on top of same	.25
1 do do do	.12½
1 Lott Bed screws	2.00
3 Braces and Lott of Bits	3.00
Lott Hardware, tin and sand paper in case	4.00
1 Lott Chair makers tools	1.00
1 apple peeler	.25
1 Lott packing pins	.25
1 old chest	.12½
1 screw clamp	.25
6 silver Table spoons (well worn)	9.00
6 do Tea do & 1 pr sugar tongs (well worn)	3.00
6 Brittania do do	.20
1 Cow Bell	.20
1 hand Bell	.25
Lott of glue	.50
1 Lott of corn growing	30.00
1 Doz. knives & forks	.75

Delaware Furniture Apprentices

Master	Apprentice	Location	Date
Abbott, Eli	James Hudson	Sussex County	1838
Adams, Thomas	William R. Ellis	Sussex County	1834
Anderson, William H.	Joseph Wharton	Sussex County	1834
	Jonathan Bacon	Sussex County	1835
Atkinson, Goved	William Norman	Kent County	1835
Baker, Joshua	William Patterson	New Castle County	1749
Baldwin, William	Jacob Stanhope	Christiana Hundred	1828
Bell, John	James Mannin	Dover	1757
Bonsall, Clement S.	William McCracken	New Castle County	1845
Burton, Isaac E.	Henry W. Long	Sussex County	1838
	Job J. Wingate	Sussex County	1839
	William Henry Draper	Sussex County	1844
	*Joshua Brasure	Sussex County	1849
Carpenter, Lemuel	John Hobbs	Frederica	1831
	Russel Hobbs	Sussex County	1831
Chandler, Gregg	William Mitchell	Wilmington	1846
	Jacob Blythe	Wilmington	1850
Chesnut, Jared	William D. Chesnut	Wilmington	1829
	Andrew Carnahan	Wilmington	1829
Clayton, David	Peter Floyd	Mill Creek Hundred	1764
Cooper, James	*Charles Allen	White Clay Creek Hundred	1779
Cotter, William Robinson	William Adams	New Castle County	1829
Coursey, Thomas B.	George Ralston	Kent County	1831
Cox, Isaac	William Marshall	Dover	1771
Dodd, Azael	Thomas Cooper	Indian River Hundred	1836
	Joseph E. Brown	Indian River Hundred	1843
Dolby, Isaac	Thomas Kimmey	Camden	1833
	*John Wyatt	Camden	1836
Downing, Henry	Samuel Bullock	New Castle County	1756
Farris, Alexander	Thomas T. Enos	Smyrna	1831
	Anderson Peters	Smyrna	1831
	John Butler	Smyrna	1834
	Jacob Beninghove	Smyrna	1840
	George W. Wilson	Smyrna	1845
	William J. Hurlock	Smyrna	1846
Farris, John	Frederic Cook	Kent County	1842
Finley, Samuel C.	*Simon Guthrie	Newark	1836
	James Stroud	Newark	1836
	*William Glenn	Newark	1837
	Robert Bayne	Newark	1840
	John Brian	Newark	1844

Master	Apprentice	Location	Date
	William Evans	Newark	1845
Gray, Isaac	Samuel Bullock	New Castle County	1753
Hall, Purnel	Lemuel Shockley	Milford	1830
	Isaac Gullett	Milford	1833
	James Wise	Milford	1833
Harris, George	John Collins	Broadkiln Hundred	1832
	Peter Martin	Broadkiln Hundred	1834
	Jacob Art	Broadkiln Hundred	1834
	George Torbert	Broadkiln Hundred	1835
	Alfred Walls	Broadkiln Hundred	1837
	Peter Pepper	Broadkiln Hundred	1837
	Henry Vinson	Broadkiln Hundred	1840
	Ishmael I. Steel	Broadkiln Hundred	1845
	Myers Fisher	Broadkiln Hundred	1850
Hartley, Milton	William McLane	Wilmington	1846
Harvey, Job	John Lewis	Wilmington	1761
Hatfield, Thomas W.	Wesley Oliver	Georgetown	1846
	Coard B. Torbert	Georgetown	1849
Hearn, Jonathan	*John Ward	Laurel	1830
	Philip Wainwright	Laurel	1842
	William T. Dawson	Laurel	1845
Hearn, Martin	William Green	Laurel	1835
Henderson, Thomas	Henry Gumby	North West Fork Hundred	1828
	George W. Adams	North West Fork Hundred	1828
Hendrickson, James G.	Henry D. Hendrixson	Sussex County	1831
Holland, Nehemiah P.	Levin Vincent	Sussex County	1831
	Henry Stockley	Sussex County	1834
Hubbard, William	Hooper Elliott	Sussex County	1831
Hudson, John P.	Benjamin B. Jones	Dagsborough Hundred	1843
Jackson, Timothy	Thomas Cunningham	Newark	1828
	Sylvester Welsh Williams	Newark	1828
	Edward Newland	New Castle	1829
	James Magee	New Castle	1829
	Gustavus Giles	Newark	1832
James, Elias	Edward G. Pepper	Georgetown	1835
	Isaac Wilson	Georgetown	1838
	George Washington Draine	Georgetown	1843
Jaquet, Joseph	*Magnus Kettle	New Castle	1754
Jones, William G.	Joseph Johnson	Wilmington	1829
	John Springer	Wilmington	1829
	David Crispen	Wilmington	1829
	Jacop Stanhope	Wilmington	1830
	William Charles Stuart	Wilmington	1832
Kates, George, Jr.	John Henry Manlove	Wilmington	1847
Kettle, Magnus	*John Kettle	New Castle County	1758
Lofland, James	Parker Booth	Sussex County	1835
McClary, Samuel, Jr.	Benjamin R. Wiley	Wilmington	1845
	Jacob S. Stiver	Wilmington	1847

Master	Apprentice	Location	Date
McClary, Thomas and	William H. Wilson	Wilmington	1849
Samuel, Jr.	Joniah Lawrence	Wilmington	1850
McDowell, James	William Smith	Duck Creek Hundred	1834
	James Hawkins	Duck Creek Hundred	1841
McFarrin, Robert	Jacob M. White	Milton	1828
	*William H. Nichols	Milton	1830
Massey, George	William Brown	Frederica	1835
Miller, Robert	Jeremiah Miller	Sussex County	1786
Minor, Moses	William Bradshaw	New Castle County	1761
Morrow, James and John Luff	William Spratt	Wilmington	1841
	*Samuel McClary, Jr.	Wilmington	1841
Morrow, James	Patrick Plunket	Wilmington	1842
	Gideon B. Guyer	Wilmington	1843
Nichols, William H.	*Jacob P. Ward	Sussex County	1843
	William Thomas King	Sussex County	1845
	Joseph Parson Ward	Sussex County	1848
Noblett, Dell	John Norris	Wilmington	1827
	*John Luff	Wilmington	1828
	Thomas Mitchell	Wilmington	1835
	*James Morrow	Wilmington	1837
	Henry Blackshare	Wilmington	1837
	John McGady	Wilmington	1842
Noblett, Hamilton	John Simons	Wilmington	1838
	Thomas B. Beeson	Wilmington	1839
	James Slack	Wilmington	1842
	John Bradford	Wilmington	1846
Noblett, John	George H. Calloway	Wilmington	1840
	Isaac Conyer	Wilmington	1841
	Edwin Cornell	Wilmington	1848
Parker, Anderson	Isaac Collins	Sussex County	1750
Parker, Samuel	James Gray	Sussex County	1838
Paynter, Rice	Robert Bromely	Sussex County	1828
Prettyman, Perry	John Hobbs	Sussex County	1827
	Thomas Hobbs	Sussex County	1827
	*Elias James	Sussex County	1829
	*Thomas Hatfield	Sussex County	1830
	Minos Phillips	Sussex County	1831
	Edward J. Pepper	Sussex County	1831
Prettyman, William	Hamilton Bell	Sussex County	1831
	James Nicholason	Sussex County	1833
Reece, Thomas	John Reece	New Castle County	1749
Richmond, George A.	James Anderson	New Castle County	1841
Riley, Mary	Charles Riley	Wilmington	1847
Riley, Samuel	David Matlock	Wilmington	1831
Sanders, Ellis B.	George W. Armstrong	New Castle County	1828
Schee, James	Thomas Mason	Dover	1800
Shanahan, Clifford	John Steward	Milford	1831
	Joshua Spencer	Milford	1832

Master	Apprentice	Location	Date
Short, Daniel	Barker Booth	Nanticoke Hundred	1844
Stayton, David H.	Henry Lockwood	Camden	1830
	Alexander Dill	Camden	1832
	James Mason	Camden	1832
	Joshua Adams	Camden	1835
	William Dulin	Camden	1841
	Abraham Hopkinson	Camden	1843
Stayton, Joseph	Absolom McElwee	Smyrna	1835
	Joshua R. Stevens	Smyrna	1838
	William Curry	Smyrna	1839
	Charles Edward Carroll	Smyrna	1842
Stevenson, Thomas and James H.	Silas C. Bush	Dover	1835
Turner, Lazruss	Charles Thompson	Laurel	1828
Twigg, John	George Spurry	Kent County	1833
Van Gaskin, Henry	Charles Hilyard	Kent County	1845
Vining, Henry	*Henry Hyland	New Castle County	1757
Walter, Winder	*John Martin	Sussex County	1838
Ward, William C.	Morgan Jones	Sussex County	1839
	Joseph Stephens	Sussex County	1839
White, George W.	Thomas I. Hilman	Kent County	1844
	Truston P. McWyatt	Kent County	1846
White, James H.	William Manlove	Milford Hundred	1830
Williams, Isaac	William Elliott	Laurel	1834
Williams, John	John King	New Castle	1747

The Genealogy of a Bookcase Desk

Nancy Goyne Evans

FEW PIECES of American furniture possess credentials as impressive as those belonging to a bookcase desk (Fig. 1) made in 1738 by Job Coit of Boston. This handsome walnut case piece claims the honor of being the earliest documented example of the block-front style in America and traces its ownership during the eighteenth century through one of the leading families of the Revolutionary Era. Because of the passage of time and the destruction of documents, the descent of the Coit bookcase desk can never be positively verified, but a combination of documentary and circumstantial evidence indicates that the case piece sold by Job Coit in 1738 to Daniel Henchman passed through the Thomas and John Hancock families to Moses Black and from Black through the Duncan, Wells, and Thorndike families (see chart) to Winterthur. Although the documentary chain of evidence identifying the desk (referred to in period documents as a desk and bookcase) is broken once, in the transition from the Hancock to the Black family, and although specific inventories identifying the desk are lacking in some cases, the close familial and business relationships between successive owners of the desk provide a strong supplement to specific mentions of inheritance. In addition, the likelihood of Job Coit's producing two desks of such advanced design, magnificent execution, and substantial cost during a single year is slim indeed.

The bookcase desk is signed twice in penciled script—once "Job Coit Jr/1738" on the outside bottom of the hooded drawer in the central compartment of the writing area (Fig. 2) and again "J Coit/1738" on an outer surface of one of the secret document drawers (Fig. 3). Since few such sophisticated pieces of cabinetry possess the pedigree and credentials of the Coit bookcase desk, it is worthwhile to sketch the pertinent details of Coit's life and business career.

Job Coit probably began his cabinetmaking career in 1713, the year he married Lydia Amie (or Amy) of Boston.[1] Coit was twenty-one years of age and undoubtedly had just completed his apprenticeship. Within three years he acquired, through several transactions, the property bounded on the east by Ann (North) Street that served as his shop and home until his death in 1741.[2] During the early years of his career Coit was appointed to several town offices in partial fulfillment of his civic responsibility as a member of the town meeting. He first served in the capacity of fence viewer in 1721 and then as an overseer of the poor in 1727. In the same year he became a member of the Artillery Company. When chosen on March 11, 1739, as one of the eight clerks of the market, he was permitted to decline the office.[3]

Although the name of the master with whom Coit served his apprenticeship is unknown, documentation exists indicating that Coit in turn took an apprentice. A receipt dated February 3, 1725/26, for work done by Coit for Joseph Baxter of Medfield, is signed by Joseph Davis, who indicated he had received the sum of eight pounds and

[1] Maude Roberts Cowan, *Members of the Ancient and Honorable Artillery Company in the Colonial Period* (n.p.: privately printed, 1958), p. 19. The marriage occurred on July 30. Coit's birth year is recorded here as 1692.

[2] Lydia Amy (mother of Coit's wife) to Job Coit and Lydia Amie Coit, George Peake and Tabitha Peake (a sister of Lydia Amy the elder) to Job Coit, Feb. 11, 1716, Registry of Deeds, 31:6, 7, Boston Court House.

[3] *A Report of the Record Commissioners of the City of Boston 1729–1742*, 28 vols. (Boston: Rockwell & Churchill, 1876–98), 12:247, 8:161, 202; Cowan, *Ancient and Honorable Artillery Company*, p. 19.

FIG. 1. Job Coit, bookcase desk. Boston, Mass., 1738. American black walnut (primary) and northeastern white pine (secondary); H. 99½″, W. 39⅝″, D. 24⅜″. (Winterthur 62.87.)

fifteen shillings "for my Master Mr. Job Coit."[4] It seems more than likely that Coit's sons also served apprenticeships with their father. Of the eight children born to Job and Lydia Coit, six lived to maturity. The younger three were daughters, the elder three, sons. Each of the young men is described in legal documents as a joiner or cabinetmaker. Nathaniel and Job, Jr., born in 1714 and 1717,[5] respectively, had completed their periods of apprenticeship by the time their father died in 1741, while

[4] Receipted bill from Job Coit to Joseph Baxter, Feb. 3, 1725/26, MS 63x69, Joseph Downs Manuscript and Microfilm Collection, Winterthur Museum Libraries (hereafter WM).

[5] *Report of the Record Commissioners*, 24:97, 126.

FIG. 2. Penciled signature on drawer bottom of Coit bookcase desk.

FIG. 3. Penciled signature on drawer side of Coit bookcase desk.

the youngest son, Joseph, was nineteen in 1741, old enough to have completed most of his training with his father. By the terms of the elder Coit's will drawn up on January 8, four days before his death, each of his two elder sons received a token legacy of five shillings in consideration of what they "heretofore had of me."[6] No doubt Coit was referring to the training he had given them and, perhaps, tools and/or cash he had furnished to start them in business.

Although no other signed Coit pieces are known, the Coit bookcase desk represents a high point in Boston cabinetmaking in the first half of the eighteenth century. Few patrons were in a financial position to order such a large and elaborate piece, although a number of craftsmen working in Boston in this period possessed sufficient skill to execute a commission of this quality. The blocked facade of the desk drawers, worked from solid two-and-one-half-inch black walnut plank, represents the earliest documented use of this surface treatment, predating the first known appearance of the block-front style in Newport, Rhode Island, the center of its greatest development, by more than twenty years.[7] The blocking continues down into the frame supporting the double case, which possibly has been cut down slightly over the years.

Within the writing area (Fig. 4) additional blocking follows a sweeping course across the front of five sets of small double drawers. Above, six open compartments are crowned by small, ogee-arched hoods and divided by thin walnut partitions, each shaped in an ogee curve on the front edge. The small drawer with its double ogee-curved apron in the central compartment is flanked by fluted, sham-front document drawers. These drawers are actually accessible from the back by releasing and sliding forward the entire central section. Removal of the central section also reveals four small, roughly finished, stacked drawers against the backboard, or rear wall, of the lower case.

The plate-glass mirrors facing the two single-arch doors of the bookcase are modern, but internal evidence in the framing indicates that this was the original treatment prior to clear glazing of the doors in the late nineteenth century to display a Chinese export porcelain tea service, which is shown by photographs of the desk when it was in

Fig. 4. Interior of Coit bookcase desk.

---

[6] Will of Job Coit, 1741, Probate Court, Boston Court House.

[7] R. Peter Mooz, "The Origins of Newport Block-Front Furniture Design," *Antiques* 99, no. 6 (June 1971): 882–86.

private hands. The interior has been entirely fitted with new shelves, compartments, and drawers in recent years, but the handsome shells inlaid in light wood in the pediment are original. The curves of the double scrolls above the shells are outlined by simple moldings and a narrow bead. Two of the three finials appear to be replacements. It is unfortunate that the original brasses were removed in recent years and replaced by others of an earlier style. The outlines of the former hardware can still be seen on the drawer fronts.

In comparing the two penciled signatures, "J Coit" and "Job Coit Jr," which appear within the writing area of the desk, it can be seen that the calligraphy is very similar. Whether it represents the hand of one person or two is difficult to say; the only real discrepancy appears to be in the formation of the letter "J." What is more important is that nowhere in documents is the elder Coit referred to as "Junior." He apparently was the first Job in the family in two generations; his father, a husbandman of Gloucester, bore the name Nathaniel.[8] But Job Coit's son, Job, could very well have used the term "Junior" from time to time. By May 1738, young Job just passed his twenty-first birthday, and it seems more than likely he would have had a hand in so important a commission. It is possible that the "Jr" following one of the signatures was an afterthought added by the younger Job, as it is noticeably smaller in size and is written close to the edge of the drawer bottom.

The bookcase desk may have been the last substantial order executed by either craftsman. On January 12, 1741, Job, Senior, passed away at the early age of forty-eight, and the younger Job died in 1745.[9] On April 16, 1745, Rebeckah, wife of Job Coit (Junior) filed an estate inventory valued at £82.8.0. Almost half that sum represented "Joyners Work not finisht and Joyners Tools" valued at £31.4.0. Within eighteen months Rebeckah married Jeremiah Townsend.[10] It is interesting to speculate on possible family connections with the cabinetmaking Townsends of Rhode Island.

On September 23, 1742, an inventory was made of the possessions of Job Coit, Senior; his real and personal property were evaluated at £1747.9.8 old tenor. This figure represents a substantial estate for a craftsman with a family of six children, four of whom were still living at home. A few of the items listed in his personal estate are noteworthy: "a Jappan Desk in the Great Room" £3.0.0 and "a Looking Glass" £2.10.0; "A Feather Bed 43 lb Bolster pillows" valued at £6.9.0 and "one Do. 55 lb bolster pillows £8.5/ 2 Do. Bolster pillows 64 lb £9.12/" totaling £17.17.0, all expensive items possibly representing an exchange of services with an upholsterer in the city. And then there was "a Negro Woman" valued at £50.0.0, an unusual addition to the household of a craftsman. The entries for shop fixtures, tools, materials, and new furniture in Coit's estate are interesting and important to record for this early period.

To 3 frame Saws & 4 Do. £10. Sundry small Tools in the Shop £5	£15.0.0
To 2 holdfasts & Glew Pott 22/ Grindstone Lath & 4 Benches 60/	4.2.0
To 2 large Desks 3 small Do.	16.10.0
To one old Table To Black walnott 50 feet @9d	4.17.6
To Mehogony 50 foot @9d Cherry Tree 400 foot @8d	15.4.2
To 30 lb Lead To Lamblack	2.0.0[11]

Few accounts of cabinetwork from the shop of Job Coit have come to light. The most extensive of these is the bill documenting the original ownership of the bookcase desk (Fig. 5).[12] Drawn up by Joseph Coit on behalf of his mother, it was sent to Daniel Henchman on February 28, 1742, a year after Job Coit's death. The document includes work done for Henchman between the years 1734 and 1740. Except for the listing of the case piece, dated May 10 (1738), all references are to work on two bedsteads including construction, fitting out, repairs, and "setting up." Compared to the com-

---

[8] Guardianships of Nanny, Elizabeth, and Lydia Coit, 1743, microfilm 122, Suffolk Co., Mass., Probate Records, WM.

[9] Cowan, *Ancient and Honorable Artillery Company*, p. 19; Job, Jr., is mentioned as serving as a city constable in 1742/43. *Report of the Record Commissioners*, 14:2, 17:49–50.

[10] Inventory of Estate of Job Coit [Junior], 1745, Probate Court, Boston Court House; *Report of the Record Commissioners*, 28:265.

[11] *Boston News-Letter*, Dec. 16, 1742; *Boston Gazette*, Oct. 22, 1751; Administration Appointment, 1751, microfilm 125, Suffolk Co., Mass., Probate Records; Division of Estate of Job Coit, 1752, microfilm 126, Suffolk Co., Mass., Probate Records. By this time Job's son Nathaniel had also passed away. Guardianships of Elizabeth, Lydia, and Joseph Ricks Coit, 1752, microfilm 126, Suffolk Co., Mass., Probate Records, WM. Inventory of Job Coit, 1742, Probate Court, Boston Court House.

[12] Bill from the Estate of Job Coit to Daniel Henchman, Feb. 28, 1742, Hancock Collection, Box 15, Baker Library, Manuscripts and Archives Division, Harvard University (hereafter BL).

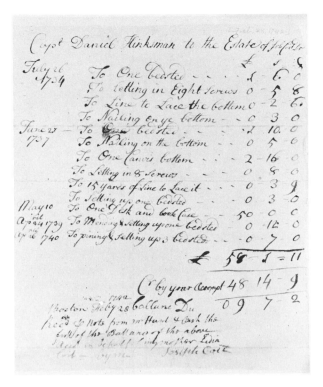

FIG. 5. Bill from the estate of Job Coit to Daniel Henchman. Boston, Mass., Feb. 28, 1742. Paper; H. 7³⁄₁₆″, W. 6⁵⁄₁₆″. (Baker Library, Harvard University: Photo, Fogg Museum, Harvard University.)

plete charges of £1.17.2 and £5.2.9 for the bedsteads, the cost of the bookcase desk at £50 was substantial. By way of further comparison with then current market values, a barrel of pork purchased by Coit in Henchman's store, where he was a steady customer, cost £13 only one month following delivery of the bookcase desk.[13] These prices are expressed in the "old tenor" of the province, which in 1737 could be equated at five to one with English sterling.[14]

Biographical information about Daniel Henchman indicates that he was well able to afford such a prestigious piece of furniture. By 1738 when he was forty-nine years of age, Henchman had built a prosperous business and was enjoying the bountiful fruits of financial success. As a noteworthy citizen of the town, he served at times as justice of the peace, church deacon, overseer of the poor, and lieutenant colonel of the Boston militia; eventually he became a benefactor of Harvard University. Henchman has been described as "the most eminent and enterprising bookseller that appeared in Boston, or indeed in all British North America, before 1775."[15] Starting in business in a small way as a stationer and bookseller sometime prior to 1712, his early trade was carried on in the immediate Boston area. In 1713 Daniel married Elizabeth Gerrish, and with the business and financial assistance provided by his father-in-law, John Gerrish, a trader, Henchman's trade expanded rapidly. In time he branched out into both bookbinding and publishing, printing such materials as sermons, almanacs, and treatises on popular or controversial subjects of the day. By 1724 he employed an agent in London to provide him with merchandise at wholesale prices.

Like most colonial merchants, Henchman engaged in diversified occupations as well as his more specialized book business. He traded in agricultural produce, logwood, molasses, rum, indigo, and the products of the New England fisheries. He likewise stocked manufactured items from England. As his business grew and his capital increased, he invested in real estate and in shares in foreign ventures, particularly to London, the West Indies, and the southern colonies. In 1728 Henchman along with four other partners devised a scheme to establish the first paper mill in New England at Milton. The venture enjoyed only limited success, but the manufacture was able to hold its own for at least the first ten years.[16] By the 1730s when he built his new residence on Queen (Court) Street, Henchman had begun patronizing the cabinet shop of Job Coit as well as that of David Mason, while at the same time he made substantial purchases from Jacob Hurd, "Goldsmith," to whom he supplied sizable lots of both silver and gold for working.[17]

One of Henchman's younger partners in the paper mill was Thomas Hancock, who had completed an apprenticeship to the book trade in the shop of Samuel Gerrish only four years earlier at the age

[13] Ledger "B" of Daniel Henchman, 1729–45, Hancock Collection, BL.

[14] J. M. Davis, *Currency and Banking in the Province of Massachusetts Bay* (New York, 1901), p. 367, as quoted in W. T. Baxter, *The House of Hancock* (1945; reprint ed., New York: Russell & Russell, 1965), p. 13.

[15] From Isaiah Thomas, *History of Printing* (Worcester, Mass.: Isaiah Thomas, 1810), 2:422, as quoted in W. T. Baxter, "Daniel Henchman, A Colonial Bookseller," *Essex Institute Historical Collections* 70 (1930): 1.

[16] Baxter, "Daniel Henchman," pp. 2–5, 17–27.

[17] Bill from David Mason to Daniel Henchman, 1731, Hancock Collection, Box 14; Ledger "B" of Daniel Henchman, 1729–45, Hancock Collection, BL.

of twenty-one. By the end of 1724, Hancock set up in business in Ann Street, probably with some parental help, and immediately embarked upon an energetic career in bookselling, bookbinding, and publishing. With the same enthusiasm he began to cultivate social contacts with leading businessmen and branched out into general merchandising. Gradually he became involved in overseas trade, exchanging products of the Atlantic fisheries for manufactured goods in London and New England staples for likely cargoes in the West Indies. So successful was Hancock in these ventures that by 1736, at the age of thirty-three, he had amassed a considerable fortune. He purchased a piece of land on the southern slope of Beacon Hill where he began laying out elaborate gardens and making plans for a splendid and stylish house of Massachusetts granite with quoins and other ornamental work of Connecticut freestone. From England he imported large numbers of seeds, shrubs, and trees, along with marble hearths, flocked wall hangings, blue and white Dutch tiles, and several costly articles of furniture. During the years that followed, Hancock's fortunes continued to rise as he took his place among the leaders of the community.[18]

During his early years in the bookselling business Hancock developed a fast friendship with Daniel Henchman that led in 1730 to marriage between Hancock and Henchman's only child, Lydia. This marriage provides the basis of the descent of the Coit bookcase desk in the notable Hancock family. The marriage of Thomas and Lydia Hancock proved to be childless. When Thomas's older brother John died in Braintree leaving three young children, the Hancocks adopted his young son John and brought him to Boston to live with them. The boy was provided with the best education then available in Massachusetts, graduating from Harvard in 1754, and was groomed for a place in the family business. John proved a less able merchant than his uncle, but his political acumen carried him far along the road to personal success aided, of course, by a series of well-timed events, influential friends, and his own popular image among the people. On August 28, 1775, John, then a bachelor of thirty-eight, married Dorothy Quincy II, daughter of Edmund Quincy IV. The two children born of this marriage died young, leaving no direct heir

to carry on this branch of the family and to inherit the vast estate left by John Hancock upon his death on October 8, 1793.

Each of these families, in turn, came into possession of the bookcase desk constructed in the shop of Job Coit and delivered on May 10, 1738, to the new residence of Daniel Henchman in Queen Street. The tall case piece stood in the Henchman home for thirty odd years before its removal to the Hancock home on Beacon Hill. Because Henchman stipulated that no inventory of his property be taken at his death, which occurred in 1761, the location of the bookcase desk in the house cannot be pinpointed. Henchman bequeathed his estate to his daughter and son-in-law with his wife Elizabeth receiving an annual income of £200 and retaining use of the house and its furnishings during her lifetime.

Sometime between 1765 and the early years of the seventies, Elizabeth Henchman died, and, according to the terms of Daniel Henchman's will, the bookcase desk was presumably transferred to the Hancock mansion. Lydia Hancock, her daughter, enjoyed some use of it before the siege of Boston caused her to flee the city in 1775. She died in Connecticut in the following year without returning to her residence. By the terms of her will, her nephew John received the residue of her estates from both her husband, who had died in 1764, and her father after minor bequests were made to relatives, friends, and charities.[19] Although Coit's masterpiece was not mentioned specifically in Henchman's or Lydia Hancock's will, it is reasonable to assume that the desk was inherited by John Hancock and stood in his Boston home throughout the exciting events of the Revolution.

John Hancock died in 1793 without having prepared a will, an oversight that caused his wife Dolly, or Dorothy, considerable hardship. But for the first time in three generations, an inventory was made of the property of this wealthy and influential family. That Hancock as governor of Massachusetts enjoyed the luxury of a well-appointed household cannot be doubted from the description of the furnishings in the mansion. The value of his personal estate alone was estimated by the appraisers at approximately £10,000. For the purposes of

---

[18] Discussion of Thomas Hancock and his house from Baxter, *House of Hancock;* and Walter Kendall Watkins, "The Hancock House and Its Builder," *Old-Time New England* 17, no. 1 (July 1926): 3–19.

[19] Will of Daniel Henchman, 1761, Probate Court, Boston Court House; Will of Thomas Hancock, n.d., Hancock Family Papers, MS H.5.11, Boston Public Library; Will of Lydia Henchman Hancock, 1777, Probate Court, Boston Court House.

this study two items in the inventory are of particular interest: "1 Dest and Book case" £2.0.0 in the "Back Parlour"; and "1 Desk and Book Case Walnut" £1.4.0 in the "S. West Garret."[20] More than likely the Coit case piece was the one that had been relegated to the attic, since the appraisers specifically noted it was constructed of walnut. The bookcase desk was too fine a family piece to dispose of and yet after half a century it was no longer fashionable and would hardly have been suitable for use in the living quarters of a socially prominent family or in the rooms where important guests were lodged.

The court appointed Dorothy Hancock administratrix. As the widow, she received a portion of the estate, including the mansion house, barn, and gardens, along with Hancock's Wharf and the buildings situated there. Unfortunately, she was allotted no income from the estate for living expenses and maintenance. Consequently, she had to seek revenue from other sources. She sold the pasture land behind the house to the city of Boston in 1795 for £4,000.[21] One of the other ways in which she raised funds was through the sale of some of the household furnishings of the mansion. Although an inventory of the estate was not filed until January 28, 1794, and Dolly did not officially receive her widow's dower until more than a year later, it is possible that the first sale took place as early as October 23, 1793, only a few weeks after Hancock's death. Listed in the *Columbian Centinel* on October 19 under "Sales at Auction" is this notice placed by Lewis Hayt: "A Variety of genteel Household Furniture, consisting of elegant Mahogany Chairs, nail over seats stuffed and covered with satin hair, 2 Arm do to match, mahogany 4 post Bedsteads, fluted feet pillars, 2 Easy Chairs covered with Silk Damask, pier & other Looking Glasses, desk & Bookcase, mahogany sideboard, 4 capital Blue Silk Damask window Curtains, complete, 1 suit yellow do. bed curtains with Squabs to answer, plated Candlesticks, with a general assemblage of useful articles, &c."[22]

It is important here to note the mention of a bookcase desk. Since the furniture in the garret was apparently little used, it seems logical to assume that the walnut piece could more easily be given up than the bookcase desk housed in the "Back Parlour," one of the rooms on the entrance floor. In any event there were several other sales of household furnishings prior to Dorothy Hancock's second marriage in 1796 to Captain James Scott. The second sale followed the first by only two weeks; another took place in 1795.[23] There are no formal records and only a few scattered references documenting subsequent ownership of furnishings from the Hancock mansion. The Coit bookcase desk can be traced back through a single family to within a generation of its sale at one of the early auctions, and circumstantial evidence provides the rest of the documentation linking the history of the desk now at Winterthur to the desk sold by Dorothy Hancock.

Moses Black, a well-to-do merchant of Boston and Braintree (Quincy), through whose wife's family the Coit desk descended until it reached Winterthur, acquired the bookcase desk sometime before his death in 1810[24] and very likely before the turn of the century. Despite his apparent affluence, information about Moses Black is very limited. Evidently no business or family papers have survived, and so most of the facts concerning his life are found only in public records. Black arrived in Boston as a boy of fifteen in 1764 on board the sloop *Deborah* from Philadelphia. On the passenger list he is described as "a Youth for Education."[25] Under the guidance of his uncle, Andrew Black, he trained for a career as a merchant. Some small insight into Black's mercantile affairs can be gleaned from the receipt book of Caleb Davis,[26] who made substantial purchases of flour for his bakery from the Black warehouse. The Blacks also sold tea in Boston, and the elder Black had some business transactions with the mercantile house headed by John Hancock.[27] In addition to his trad-

---

[20] Inventory of Estate of John Hancock, 1795, Probate Court, Boston Court House.

[21] Herbert S. Allan, *John Hancock, Patriot in Purple* (New York: Macmillan Co., 1948), p. 362.

[22] Also quoted in Mabel M. Swan, "The Furniture of His Excellency, John Hancock," *Antiques* 31, no. 3 (Mar. 1937): 120.

[23] Swan, "Furniture of . . . John Hancock," p. 120.

[24] *Columbian Centinal* (Boston), Oct. 10, 1810.

[25] *Report of the Record Commissioners*, 29:262.

[26] Receipt Book of Caleb Davis, 1768–69, Papers of Caleb Davis, Massachusetts Historical Society. Davis was described in his estate papers as a "Shugar Baker." Granting of Executorship of Estate of Caleb Davis, 1797, microfilm 148, Suffolk Co., Mass., Probate Records, WM.

[27] *Report of the Record Commissioners*, 25:177; Abraham English Brown, *John Hancock, His Book* (Boston: Lee & Shepard Publishers, 1898), app. 7, "Hancock's Business Associates not Mentioned Elsewhere in This Volume." Listing for Andrew Black.

ing and wholesale interests Moses had petitioned and was granted approval in 1778, by the selectmen "to Retail at his Shop" in King Street. When Andrew Black passed away in 1785, his nephew Moses seems to have taken over his business as well.[28]

In 1778, the year he was granted permission to retail on his own account, Moses Black married Rosanna Duncan Maxwell, a widow who was eighteen years his senior and a close relative by marriage of his Uncle Andrew. Following Rosanna's death in 1784 and that of his uncle the next year, Moses married Esther Duncan, a niece of his first wife and a woman some years his junior.[29]

Black's business must have prospered. By 1788 he was in a financial position to purchase the Quincy homestead in Braintree, the former seat of Edmund Quincy IV, father of John Hancock's wife, Dorothy, an estate that included a mansion house, farmhouses, stables, outhouses, a garden, orchards, and considerable land (Fig. 6). Black maintained a complement of agricultural and domestic help on the Braintree estate, and in 1792 he was one of a small number of persons in the community who paid the highest amount in taxes on their real estate.[30] The "United States Direct Tax

FIG. 6. Eliza Susan Quincy, *Seat of Edmund Quincy II and His Descendants*. Braintree (Quincy), Mass., 1822. Black and white wash; H. 5¾", W. 7½". (Massachusetts Historical Society.)

of 1798" sheds further light on Black's holdings. At that time he owned in partnership with Joseph Black, Jr. (possibly Blake) two rental stores on the Long Wharf in Boston valued at two thousand dollars and twenty-eight hundred dollars, respectively. As a leader in community affairs, Moses Black served as a representative to the General Court on several occasions.[31] He was a member of the First Congregational Society, and in 1799 he and President John Adams had been "voted . . . the thanks of the town . . . for the present to the town of a clock in the meeting house."[32]

Moses Black died at the age of sixty-one on October 10, 1810. In an administration *de bonis non* dated February 9, 1813, the court appointed his wife Esther to administer the estate. Under her direction appraisers made an inventory of the Braintree property the following May. The "homestead consisting of 225 acres of land and the buildings thereon" was valued at fifteen thousand dollars. Among the household furnishings an interesting item is the one hundred forty-four ounces of wrought silver valued at $158.40; but of prime

[28] *Report of the Record Commissioners*, 25:75; Will of Andrew Black, 1785, microfilm 142, Suffolk Co., Mass., Probate Records, WM.

[29] *Report of the Record Commissioners*, 30:331, 455. It is highly unlikely that the Coit desk came to Moses Black through either the Maxwell or the Duncan families, since Rosanna Duncan Maxwell Black's first husband was listed at his death as a shopkeeper and the parents of both Rosanna and Esther Duncan lived in New Hampshire. William Maxwell, Will, 1774, Probate Records. Boston Court House; James Duncan Phillips, "George Duncan, Emigrant to Londonderry, New Hampshire, and Founder of the Duncan Families of New England," *Essex Institute Historical Collections* 86, no. 3 (July 1950): 253–55.

[30] Because of financial reverses Edmund Quincy IV was forced to sell his Braintree property to his brother-in-law, the merchant Edward Jackson of Boston, in 1755. In 1765 Jackson's executors sold the estate to Robert Williams, identified as a baker of Boston. No record was found of a land transaction between Williams and Black, but in 1788 Moses Black received all rights to the property from the Jackson heirs for the consideration of five shillings. Registry of Deeds, Boston Court House, 86:211, 105:207, 162:153. Today the house is frequently referred to as the "Dorothy Q" house after the first Dorothy Quincy, sister of Edward IV and wife of Edward Jackson. Bureau of the Census, *Heads of Families at the First Census of the United States in the Year 1790, Massachusetts* (Washington, D.C.: Government Printing Office, 1908), p. 196; William S. Pattee, *A History of Old Braintree and Quincy* (Quincy, Mass.: Green & Prescott, 1878), p. 623.

[31] *Report of the Record Commissioners*, 22:61. The name Blake is used in the will of Moses Black; Pattee, *History of Old Braintree*, p. 55.

[32] *The New England Historical and Genealogical Register*, 72 vols. to date (Albany, N.Y.: J. Munsell, 1864–), 18:121, 123, 127.

DESCENT OF THE COIT BOOKCASE DESK

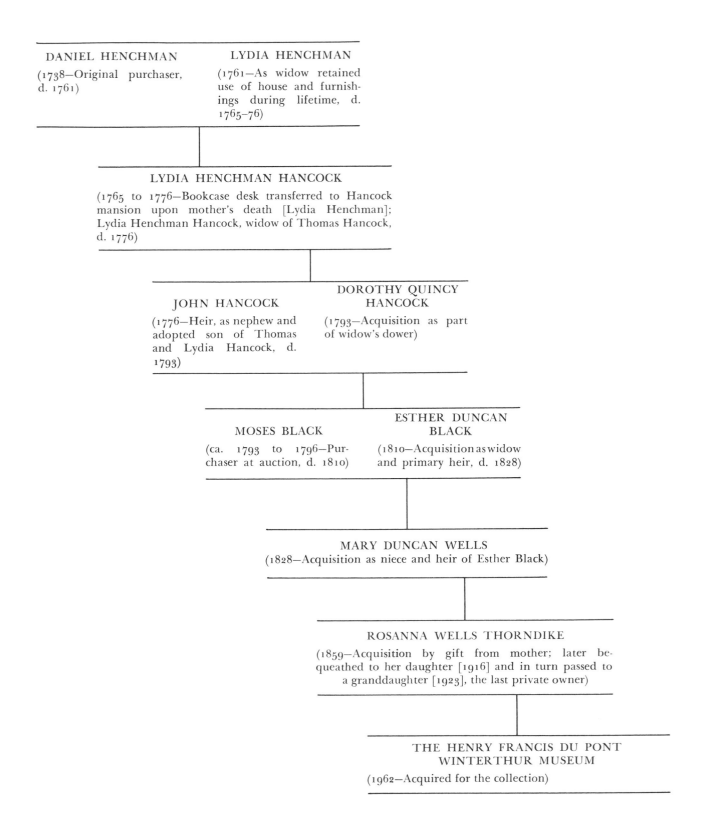

DANIEL HENCHMAN
(1738—Original purchaser, d. 1761)

LYDIA HENCHMAN
(1761—As widow retained use of house and furnishings during lifetime, d. 1765–76)

LYDIA HENCHMAN HANCOCK
(1765 to 1776—Bookcase desk transferred to Hancock mansion upon mother's death [Lydia Henchman]; Lydia Henchman Hancock, widow of Thomas Hancock, d. 1776)

JOHN HANCOCK
(1776—Heir, as nephew and adopted son of Thomas and Lydia Hancock, d. 1793)

DOROTHY QUINCY HANCOCK
(1793—Acquisition as part of widow's dower)

MOSES BLACK
(ca. 1793 to 1796—Purchaser at auction, d. 1810)

ESTHER DUNCAN BLACK
(1810—Acquisition as widow and primary heir, d. 1828)

MARY DUNCAN WELLS
(1828—Acquisition as niece and heir of Esther Black)

ROSANNA WELLS THORNDIKE
(1859—Acquisition by gift from mother; later bequeathed to her daughter [1916] and in turn passed to a granddaughter [1923], the last private owner)

THE HENRY FRANCIS DU PONT WINTERTHUR MUSEUM
(1962—Acquired for the collection)

importance here is the entry for "1 Desk & book case 25.00."[33]

Esther Black survived her husband by an indeterminate number of years. Because the Blacks had been childless, Esther apparently chose as her primary heir her niece Mary Duncan Wells, daughter of her brother George. When as a small child Mary was left motherless, she lived for some years with her Aunt Esther Black. Documentation for the descent of the desk has been provided by Mary's daughter Rosanna Lamb Wells Thorndike. In her will of 1916 Rosanna instructed her two sons to distribute selected articles of her furniture "to the person whose name I have marked thereon."[34] In the bottom of the upper long drawer of the bookcase desk, she pasted a label bearing the name of her daughter. Below this name Rosanna Thorndike provided the following information: "Belonged to great-great-great Aunt Black (Rosanna Duncan). From her came to great great Aunt Esther Duncan (Black) in 1786. From her to grandmother [her mother] Mary Duncan Wells in 1828. From her to Rosanna Wells Thorndike 1859."

Although Rosanna Thorndike was mistaken in believing that Rosanna Duncan Black, Moses's first wife, had once owned the bookcase desk, she provided the link in the chain of descent confirming that her own mother received the desk from Esther Black. The case piece descended from the daughter of Rosanna Thorndike to a granddaughter, who was the last private owner. Finally, in 1962 the Job Coit bookcase desk entered the collection of The Henry Francis du Pont Winterthur Museum.

---

[33] Inventory of Estate of Moses Black, 1813, Probate Court, Norfolk County Court House, Dedham, Mass.

[34] A check of probate indexes in six counties in Massachusetts and two in New York has failed to turn up any probate information regarding the death date or estate of Esther Duncan Black; James Duncan Phillips, "The Duncans of Londonderry, N.H.: The Children of George the Emigrant," *Essex Institute Historical Collections* 87, no. 3 (July 1951): 6; Will of Anna L. Thorndike, 1916, Probate Court, Middlesex County Court House, Cambridge, Mass.

Index

Notes on Contributors

Kenneth Ames is assistant professor, Department of Art, Franklin and Marshall College.

Betty-Bright P. Low is research and reference librarian, Eleutherian Mills Historical Library.

Nancy E. Richards is associate curator, Winterthur Museum.

E. McSherry Fowble is assistant curator and in charge of graphics, Winterthur Museum.

Philipp Fehl is professor, Department of Art and Design, University of Illinois at Urbana-Champaign.

E. McClung Fleming is head, education division, Winterthur Museum.

Harold B. Hancock is professor, Department of History, Otterbein College.

Nancy Goyne Evans is registrar, Winterthur Museum.

Portfolio 9

was composed and printed by Connecticut Printers, Inc., Hartford, Connecticut and bound by Complete Books Company, Philadelphia, Pennsylvania. The types are Baskerville and Bulmer, and the paper is Mohawk Superfine. Design is by Edward G. Foss.